Counselling and
Communication in
Health Care

Counselling and Communication in Health Care

Edited by
HILTON DAVIS and LESLEY FALLOWFIELD
Academic Unit of Psychology, The London Hospital Medical College, London, UK

JOHN WILEY & SONS

Chichester · New York · Brisbane · Toronto · Singapore

Other Wiley Editorial Offices

John Wiley & Sons, Inc., 605 Third Avenue,
New York, NY 10158–0012, USA

Jacaranda Wiley Ltd, G.P.O. Box 859, Brisbane,
Queensland 4001, Australia

John Wiley & Sons (Canada) Ltd, 22 Worcester Road,
Rexdale, Ontario M9W 1LI, Canada

John Wiley & Sons (SEA) Pte Ltd, 37 Jalan Pemimpin #05–04,
Block B, Union Industrial Building, Singapore 2057

Library of Congress Cataloging-in-Publication Data:
Counselling and communication in health care / edited by Hilton
    Davis and Lesley Fallowfield.
        p.   cm.
    Includes bibliographical references and index.
    ISBN 0-471-92818-6 (ppc)
    ISBN 0-471-92965-4 (paper)
    1. Health counseling.   2. Medical personnel and patient.
I. Davis, Hilton.   II. Fallowfield, Lesley.
R727.4.C68   1991
610.69'6—dc20   90–13078
                                                        CIP

British Library Cataloguing in Publication Data:
Counselling and communication in health care.
    1. Counselling and communication in health care.
    1. Counselling
    I. Davis, Hilton   II. Fallowfield, Lesley, *1949–*
361.323

    ISBN 0-471-92818-6 (ppc)
    ISBN 0-471-92965-4 (paper)

Typeset by Inforum Typesetting, Portsmouth
Printed and bound by Redwood Books, Trowbridge, Wiltshire,
England

For
Liz, Owen, Cara and Rachel
and
Jonathan, Caroline and Andrew

Contents

List of Contributors

Helen Bender
District Principal Child Psychotherapist, Department of Child Psychiatry, The London Hospital. London, E1 1BB.

Paul Bennett
Lecturer in Health Psychology, School of Psychology, University of Wales College of Cardiff, P.O. Box 901, Cardiff, CF1 3YG.

Jack Cadranel
Principal Clinical Psychologist in Child Health, Department of Clinical Psychology, St. James University Hospital, Beckett Street, Leeds, LS9 7TF.

Hilton Davis
Reader in Health Psychology, Academic Unit of Psychology, The London Hospital Medical College. Turner Street, London, E1 2AD.

Aleda Erskine
Principal Clinical Psychologist (Specialist in Health Psychology), Department of Psychology, Royal Northern Hospital, Holloway Road, London, N7 6LD.

Lesley Fallowfield
Senior Lecturer in Health Psychology, Academic Unit of Psychology, The London Hospital Medical College. Turner Street, London, E1 2AD.

Roy Goulston
General Practitioner, Department of General Practice, The Medical School, Guy's Hospital, London, SE1 9RT.

Tony Hobbs
Principal Clinical Psychologist, Dudley Clinical Psychology Services, Cross Street Health Centre, Dudley, West Midlands, DY1 1RN.

Paul Kennedy
Principal Clinical Psychologist, National Spinal Injuries Centre, Stoke Mandeville Hospital, Aylesbury, Buckinghamshire, HP21 8AL.

Keith Nichols
Senior Lecturer, Department of Psychology, University of Exeter, Exeter, EX4 4QG.

Shirley Pearce
Senior Lecturer, Department of Psychology, University College London, Gower Street, London, WC1E 6BT.

Nichola Rumsey
Senior Lecturer in Psychology, Department of Nursing, Health & Applied Social Studies, Bristol Polytechnic, Coldharbour Lane, Bristol.

Julia Segal
Research Counsellor, ARMS Research Unit, Central Middlesex Hospital, Acton Lane, London, NW10 7NS.

Paula Shaw
Infertility Counsellor, Ashburton Cottage, 43 North Road, Highgate Village, London, N6 4BE.

Richard Shillitoe
Clinical Psychologist, Department of Clinical Psychology, Scalebor Park Hospital, Moor Lane, Burley in Wharfdale, West Yorkshire, LS9 7AJ.

Fiona Stewart
Postgraduate Research Fellow, Department of Mental Health, University Medical Buildings, Foresterhill, Aberdeen, AB9 2ZD.

Andy Tyerman
Consultant Clinical Psychologist (Physical Health and Rehabilitation), Aylesbury Vale Health Authority, Rayners Hedge, Croft Road, Aylesbury, Buckinghamshire, HP21 7RD.

John Weinman
Professor of Psychology, Unit of Psychology, The Medical School, Guy's Hospital, London, SE1 9RT.

Preface

If you really want to help somebody, first of all you must find him where he is and start there. This is the secret of caring. If you cannot do that, it is only an illusion, if you think you can help another human being. Helping somebody implies your understanding more than he does, but first of all you must understand what he understands. If you cannot do that, your understanding will be of no avail. All true caring starts with humiliation. The helper must be humble in his attitude towards the person he wants to help. He must understand that helping is not dominating, but serving. Caring implies patience as well as acceptance of not being right and of not understanding what the other person understands.

Kierkegaard 1859

Countless impressive advances have been made in medicine over the past century. The development of a wide variety of drugs, innovative surgical techniques, and diagnostic technology means that we can cure people of many previously fatal disorders. We can preserve and extend the lives of the seriously ill and can even create life in the laboratory. Despite all these benefits and breakthroughs, people are manifestly unhappy about many of their interactions with professional health carers. Though grateful for cure or relief of their ailments, sick people and their relatives often claim that modern medical treatment, with its emphasis on high technology, is an unpleasantly dehumanising experience. It could be argued that medical scientists know more about bacteria, viruses and abnormal cells than they do about the unfortunate people who harbour them. Perversely, as our ability to treat disease and disability increases, many more individuals face a lifetime of chronic handicap or ill-health. Providing them with the sorts of psychological support and encouraging coping strategies likely to maximise and enhance their quality of life is a vital part of care. Counselling is a means of assisting people to understand and to cope more effectively with their problems and to facilitate the changes that may be necessary to bring this about. Patients are people first and foremost; the sick and disabled do not inhabit a social vacuum, thus the failure to acknowledge their psychosocial needs is neither good science nor good medicine.

We believe that communication and counselling form the basis of both physical and psychological care for all patients and their families, and that these should be urgently incorporated into health care practices in a systematic and informed way. We therefore begin the book with a critique of the present health care system. By doing this we do not intend personal criticism of professionals working in the health service. We are aware of the

dedication and competence of the majority of people in the caring professions. We are also aware of the constraints imposed upon them by the
present system; high caseloads and limited time. It is important, however, to
be conscious of the deficiencies indicated by the research in this area, and for
us all to attempt to instigate change both in personal terms and in matters of
policy.

The book then continues in Chapter 2 with a definition of counselling and
descriptions of theoretical frameworks that underpin counselling. Chapters
3 to 17 are written by specialists to indicate how counselling and good
communication are relevant to a range of specific areas within medicine.
Each author has been asked to illustrate the kinds of patients that might
benefit from counselling and the type of problems and concerns they have.
They also discuss specific ways of helping people with the identified problems, before considering the implications of what they have to say for the
health care system in their area. In particular we were concerned to know
something about the care as it exists currently and the changes to the system
that the authors thought were required. We have selected these chapters to
illustrate most major areas of health care. It is not an exhaustive review, as
we have deliberately omitted areas in which there has been considerable
previous coverage. This includes the treatment of AIDS, as well as various
subjects more closely related to psychiatry than medicine (e.g. addictions).
We begin with general practice, before considering diabetes, renal disease
and disfigurement as examples of chronic conditions. Brain injury, spinal
injury and multiple sclerosis are included to illustrate disabling conditions.
We have tried to demonstrate issues for the field of obstetrics and gynaecology by considering pain and infertility. We then move on to children's
services with chapters on genetic counselling, neonatal intensive care, disability and serious childhood illness, before finishing with examples of life-
threatening disease in adults, including cancer and heart disease. Following
these specialist chapters, Section III of the book indicates how and to what
extent improved communication can be beneficial by surveying relevant
evaluation studies, before considering the organizational and training implications of the practices we are advocating in Chapter 19.

Various conventions that we have adopted (and sometimes enforced on
reluctant contributors) require some explanations. Although 'client' appears
to be the most commonly used word in the counselling literature, we prefer
the descriptor patient. This word does have unfortunate connotations of
passivity or of being patient; qualities which we do not necessarily encourage in people who present for counselling. However, we do not use the
word in this sense, rather we see the patient as a person who, in a health care
setting, is suffering in some way. Client in a health care setting, especially in
the current political climate, has an inappropriate consumerist flavour about
it. In the Concise Oxford Dictionary, client is defined in various ways including 'employer of any professional man, customer' and derives from the

word 'cliens' meaning 'dependent, client, adherent, retainer, follower or vassal'!

We also attempt to avoid sexist language and do not assume the sex of either patient or counsellor unless specified. We have chosen neutral terms wherever possible, but where necessary we have chosen to use the admittedly clumsy but accurate strategy of he or she, him or her, etc.

Throughout the book we hope to provide the reader with a better understanding of what counselling in a wide variety of different medical settings is all about. We feel that all health care professionals would gain more from their work and that their patients would benefit if the maxim of Kierkegaard quoted earlier were to be a standard part of modern medicine.

Hilton Davis and Lesley Fallowfield 1990

Section I

CONTEXT AND THEORY

1 Counselling and Communication in Health Care: The Current Situation

Isolation is the most prominent image in my head in recalling the five years before my wife died. The loneliness of coping with rapidly deteriorating abilities and not understanding why or how it happened or what we could do about it. Trying to be personally strong for her and the family, but doubting myself all the time. The doctors never saw us, not even the GP, except at our request, usually at a crisis. No one else came; not the health visitor, nurse or social worker. Perhaps they thought we could manage: they never said! Our friends never came. Were they frightened, embarrassed, lazy, critical or just apathetic? The only time I dared to talk was to the psychiatrist who gave me half an hour and some drugs. I didn't want to be told, I wanted someone, someone to listen. We managed and I think it was largely because of my wife. She couldn't walk, hold, speak or wash, but she smiled and she loved. This put life into perspective, even if lonely, and gave us something to treasure, something not diminished by her death . . . but still no one came.

These are the words of a man whose wife had multiple sclerosis complicated by uncontrolled diabetes. It presents a side of illness that is rarely seen in full by those who provide health care. The family were not poor, nor chaotic. They were intelligent people who coped well, yet struggled with intense feelings for long periods in ways invisible to the outsider. Neither the husband nor wife were psychiatrically disturbed, and to a large extent hid their feelings, not wanting to be seen as weak by each other or by people outside, the family. If such feelings were shown on rare occasions, the recipients, whether friends or professionals, were disconcerted, seemingly because they did not know what to do or say; they had a deeply ingrained problem-solving approach, which can be inappropriate in such circumstances. What this *family* required was psychological care.

THE ADEQUACY OF PRESENT HEALTH CARE

Few people would doubt the inadequacies of the present health care system, given long waiting lists, queues in surgeries and enforced closure of wards. These deficiencies are commonly viewed as resource problems. They are, however, partly due to a conceptual problem. The present model of care is

Counselling and Communication in Health Care. Edited by H. Davis and L. Fallowfield
© 1991 John Wiley & Sons Ltd

biomedical, and therefore omits systematic concern and provision for the psychosocial aspects of disease (Engel, 1990), and loses sight of the notion expressed by Paracelsus that 'The most fundamental principle in medicine is love'. We will explore this by focusing upon studies of patient satisfaction, and professional communication before looking at the provision of psychosocial care.

Satisfaction

Fitzpatrick (1984) has argued that the study of patient satisfaction has serious weaknesses both in the definition of the concept and in the ways it has been measured. To a large extent this relates to a failure to use a systematic model of psychological functioning in preference to ad hoc, lay conceptions. Nevertheless, consistent evidence suggests that there are very high levels of dissatisfaction with aspects of health care, and that it is the interpersonal behaviour of professionals that attracts the most criticism.

Cartwright and Anderson (1981) found that although 90% of patients were satisfied overall with their family doctor, 30% criticised the comfort of the waiting room and 23% the doctor's failure to explain fully. Dickson, Hargie and Morrow (1989) note that most complaints to the National Health Service Ombudsman involve communication problems as an underlying consideration. The Royal Commission on the National Health Service (1978) found that 31% of in-patients and 25% of out-patients were dissatisfied with the information they were given about their progress. Cunningham, Morgan and McGucken (1984) found in two studies 58% and 80% dissatisfaction with the way in which the diagnosis of Down's Syndrome was communicated to parents. Fallowfield, Baum and Maquire (1986) found that over 50% of the women in their study of breast cancer thought that the information they had received was inadequate, despite them being in a clinical trial that required the surgeons to obtain informed consent. More recently a consumer survey of 915 people revealed that between 80 and 90% wanted their GP to listen to them more, and give more explanation of the illness and treatment (Which?, 1989). Hughes and Lieberman (1990) found a 50% dissatisfaction rate with out-patient services for parents of children with cancer. They complained of the long waiting times, the inadequacy of the information and the embarrassment felt in taking up too much time and asking stupid questions. Korsch, Gozzi and Francis (1968) found that 24% of mothers who attended a paediatric out-patient clinic were dissatisfied.

Ley (1982) concluded that there was an average rate of dissatisfaction with medical communication of about 37% ranging from 11% to 65%. The dissatisfaction rate for hospital samples was 38%, for general practice and community samples 26%, and for psychiatric patients 39% (Ley, 1988). He also concluded that such dissatisfaction reflects upon other aspects of the clinician-patient interaction, is not reduced by untutored attempts to improve the situation, and has not decreased in the last twenty years. He suggests that it is not whether patients are given information that determines satisfaction, but whether they are informed in ways that are understood and remembered. These results may also underestimate the real situation because of the tendency to give socially desirable responses to questionnaires, the anxiety involved in directly criticising the doctor (since their treatment may be adversely affected) and because patients' expectations of professional behaviour might be rather low.

Professional communication skills

Deficiencies in the abilities or motivation of some health care personnel to communicate appropriately is endorsed in studies of their actual behaviour. Maguire and Rutter (1976) found that senior medical students failed to obtain 67% of the information readily available to them from willing patients. Eighty % of the students were rated as poor in coverage of personal issues. They showed premature focus in accepting the first problem presented as the only issue of concern, although 24% even failed to discover the patient's main problem. Most accepted imprecise information, failed to deal with many of the patients' comments relevant to their problem, or to explain the reason for the interview.

Weiner and Nathanson (1976) found that postgraduate trainees asked too many questions without allowing the patient to lead spontaneously, did not clarify vague information and did not give adequate answers to the patients' questions. Maguire *et al.* (1986) found that although a group of young doctors had improved since they were previously assessed towards the end of their undergraduate training, they did not reach what the authors considered an acceptable standard. They were poor at beginning and ending interviews, including explaining its purpose, introducing themselves, summarising the information obtained, checking accuracy and making concluding statements. They were also poor in clarifying patient statements, using open questions and inquiring about psychosocial problems.

Platt and McMath (1979) were dismayed at the level of incompetence observed in physicians at all levels, and described the various defects. These included: failure to greet the patient, to introduce oneself properly or explain and justify what was to happen; failing to listen to, understand, or support the patient's story; failing to take account of the patient's feelings and personality, or the process of interviewing and the difficulties in it; and a high control style as opposed to a partnership.

Waitzkin (1984) summarised several studies and suggested that doctors dominate in questioning, interrupting and not allowing enough time for the patient to speak. He showed that physicians failed to personalise the situation by not discussing the patient's feelings, life-style and daily situation. The failure to take a social history, solicit the patient's views or look at the personal or family impact of disease has been frequently noted. Byrne and Long (1976) found a narrow organic focus, and suggested an active prevention of either a close relationship or the patient's expression of feelings. Seventy-five % of consultations were 'doctor-centred' and unresponsive to patient needs. Closed questions predominated with the tendency to assume no other problem but the first. Little attempt was made to clarify whether the problem had been identified or understood properly, and little opportunity was afforded the patient to ask questions. Inappropriate and premature reassurance was also a frequent feature.

Although it is difficult to help someone without knowing what is worrying them and what they expect, this appears to occur frequently in practice. Korsch et al. (1968) found that 65% of parents' expectations in a paediatric clinic were not mentioned to the physicians, and only 24% of their main worries were elicited. Maguire (1976) similarly found little attempt by surgeons to elicit the worries of women suffering from breast disease. Lazare et al. (1978) found that although 99% of the patients in their study had treatment preferences, only 37% voiced these spontaneously to the doctor, and only 63% with prompting.

In contrast to the difficulty of eliciting information, it may appear relatively easy to provide information once the diagnosis has been formulated. However, Maguire, Fairburn and Fletcher (1986) found that the ability of doctors to communicate information about test results, diagnosis, aetiology, treatment and prognosis was very poor, even in doctors who had previously had training in interviewing skills, where the focus was on eliciting rather than providing information. They were particularly unlikely to elicit the patient's views, negotiate, repeat or reinforce advice, encourage questions or check the patient's understanding. Waitzkin (1984) estimated that only about one minute per 20 minute consultation was allocated to information giving. Boreham and Gibson (1978) found that the majority of patients in their study were not given what the authors judged to be basic and important information about their problem and its treatment.

Ley (1988) concluded that clinicians frequently present information in ways patients do not understand. They tend to overestimate the patient's understanding (Samora, Saunders and Larson, 1961) whereas most have a poorer, or different, understanding of terminology, anatomy and disease than the clinician (Boyle, 1970), and may not interpret what is said in the ways intended, even when the clinician's words are well chosen. These problems are compounded by the patient's tendency not to ask questions. Ley (1988) found that 42% of patients failed to ask questions about the diagnosis, 41% about the treatment, and 75% about other advice, even though they wanted to do so. This means that the clinician is not given feedback on the patient's understanding, and cannot identify and remedy ignorance or misconceptions unless he or she takes responsibility for encouraging questions or otherwise checks upon understanding.

Such findings are by no means only related to the medical profession, but apply equally to other groups such as nurses. Maguire (1985) and Macleod Clark (1985) indicate not only a high degree of dissatisfaction with nurse communication, but also limited actual communication, both in quality and quantity.

In summary, therefore, it would appear that there is a long list of deficiencies in professional communication skills. These include:

1. Failure to greet the patient appropriately, to introduce themselves, and to explain their own actions.
2. Failure to elicit easily available information, especially major worries and expectations.
3. Acceptance of imprecise information and the failure to seek clarification.
4. Failure to check the doctor's understanding of the situation against the patient's.
5. Failure to encourage questions or to answer them appropriately.
6. Neglect of covert and overt cues provided verbally or otherwise by the patient.
7. Avoidance of information about the personal, family and social situation, including problems in these areas.
8. Failure to elicit information about the patient's feelings and perceptions of the illness.
9. Directive style with closed questions predominating, frequent interruptions and failure to let the patient talk spontaneously.
10. Focusing too quickly without hypothesis testing.
11. Failure to provide information adequately about diagnosis, treatment, side-effects, or prognosis, or to check subsequent understanding.
12. Failure to understand from the patient's viewpoint and hence to be supportive.
13. Poor reassurance.

It is important to note that this list is not intended to imply that all professionals have inadequate communication abilities all the time; there are many who are amazingly gifted in this respect. However, the evidence discussed here suggests that there are sufficiently large numbers of people with poor communication to be of enormous concern. This is illustrated by Krebs (1976) who considered the concept of respect, a central notion in counselling, in interactions in a hospital setting. Although he found that only 6% were disrespectful, this amounted to an estimated 100 000 disrespectful exchanges per week. At any time such events are likely to have a negative impact in being emotionally significant and remembered for longer, but they may be particularly hurtful when people are ill and therefore more vulnerable.

Psychosocial care

The biomedical orientation to health care means that psychosocial problems are neglected, as seen in the last section. This neglect has extensive consequences, because of the very high frequency of such problems. It is estimated that as many as 25 to 33% of patients in general practice have emotional, psychological, social or familial rather than physical problems (Abel Smith, Irving and Brown, 1989). Many people with physical disease also have psychosocial problems as a result. For example, Hughes and Lieberman (1990) found evidence of abnormal anxiety levels in 72% of parents of children with cancer, even though many were in remission, with 33% showing moderate or severe symptoms, and another 33% showing marked communication difficulties.

All such problems tend to fall under the medical umbrella, yet are not catered for appropriately. By default it is the GP who provides care, even though the inappropriateness of this can be argued on the grounds that these problems are not medical and may not be helped by the medical model. Rowland and Irving (1984) point out the extent of this medicalisation of life problems by noting that in 1980 39 million prescriptions for psychotropic drugs were issued at a cost of £58 million. Many GPs have had little training in this area, and consequently may not have the skills and will rarely have sufficient time to deal with these problems, even if they have the personal emotional strength and the inclination.

An obvious alternative is to employ people who are appropriately trained to deal with these problems, but this has not happened generally. Only 50 general practice counselling schemes existed in the UK in 1977 (Abel Smith *et al.*, 1989) and many were unpaid (Waydenfeld and Waydenfeld, 1980). Although the numbers have grown, this has been slow, because of the reluctance of family practitioner committees to fund such work. Brown and Abel Smith (1985), for example, note that there were only 120 marriage guidance counsellors working in general practice in England and Wales in 1983. A growing number of psychologists now also work in this setting, but there are very few of them.

The situation is the same in hospitals, where there is also a high incidence of distress in patients and their relatives. According to Breakwell and Alexander-Dann (1989) there is a mean of only 7.41 psychologists per district health authority. Although 9.2% of other clinical staff had counselling in their job description, none except psychologists, who were the smallest profession apart from dieticians and health education officers, were expected to have a relevant qualification. In a recent survey (Fallowfield and Roberts, 1990) only 268 people were identified in the UK as having cancer counselling as a significant component of their job. Most of these were part-time, and 44.2% saw less than 11 patients each. Only about 25% had a counselling qualification, only 42.9% used a theoretical framework in their work and

36.4% were completely unsupervised. Even though there is clear evidence for the benefits of psychological preparation for surgery, little has been done to include this in routine care (Johnston, 1990).

This situation is changing slowly, particularly with the statutory requirement in the UK for abortion counselling, for example, and government encouragement in relation to HIV and infertility. However, this leaves many other serious disorders neglected. One solution is to use the psychiatric services. However, there are both theoretical and practical reasons why this may not be appropriate. Theoretically, most people with such problems are not ill. It is therefore reasonable to question, like Szasz (1960), the rationale of referral to psychiatrists trained largely in medicine, generally retaining an illness model and treating predominantly with drugs. In practice there are delays inherent in referral to a specialist, who is also usually less conveniently situated. However, even if psychiatry is the most appropriate referral, this still requires expertise in the identification of psychosocial problems, and there is considerable doubt about the GP's skills in doing so. It is also unlikely that psychiatric services could cope with what would amount to a twenty-fold increase in referrals according to Cooper *et al.* (1975) who found that only one in 20 people with minor psychological disturbance were referred from primary care for psychiatric advice.

A major paradigm shift is required to conceptualise such problems outside the medical framework. There should be many more people who are psychologically trained to work alongside and have the same status as the medical professional. The fact that GPs in the Waydenfeld and Waydenfeld (1980) study suggested classifying counsellors as receptionists or secretaries so as to enable some remuneration for their skills is indicative of the priority given to this currently.

THE CONSEQUENCES OF POOR COMMUNICATION

Since low priority is given to communication and counselling, and relevant skills are lacking in a significant proportion of professionals, the consequences affect both the process of health care and outcome in economic, physical and psychosocial terms.

Dissatisfaction

As discussed earlier, a major effect of poor communication is dissatisfaction. Such feelings detract from the value of the consultation by interfering with its real concerns, and in turn prevent effective communication. It is likely that the patient will speak less freely, be less relaxed and less able to concentrate upon the matter in hand. Dissatisfaction may also stop the patient from visiting the same professional again, or even other professionals.

Professionals themselves will find their work unsatisfactory. Health care is a highly stressful occupation, and interpersonal factors and communication with both patients and colleagues account for much of the difficulty (Gerrard, Boniface and Love, 1980).

Inaccurate diagnosis/understanding

As a result of poor communication, the accurate exchange of information between the professional and patient is likely to be severely limited. Patients may not be given the opportunity to talk openly, may not be listened to carefully, may not be invited to clarify what has been said, and may not be given the opportunity to comment upon the professional's understanding of the situation. The information acquired by the professional will therefore be limited both in quantity and quality, with the likelihood of the diagnosis becoming inaccurate and unreliable. This means that the probability of treating or advising the patient appropriately will be diminished.

Important physical problems are frequently missed (Weiner and Nathanson, 1976) especially in people with previous psychiatric diagnoses (Maguire and Granville-Grossman, 1968). The rate at which psychosocial and psychiatric problems are missed is somewhere between 50 to 80% in GPs, hospital physicians and surgeons. For example, Maguire et al. (1980) found that only 22% of women with psychiatric problems following mastectomy were identified by routine services. The identification rate is only 33% when the patient is reasonably well known to the physician (Brody, 1980). Johnston (1976 and 1982) found little concordance between patients' actual worries and those attributed to them by nurses, a strong tendency for nurses to overestimate the extent of patients' worries and to be less accurate than fellow patients.

Poor communication is also associated with poorer follow-up monitoring of their progress if patients cannot provide appropriate information or are not heeded when they do. For example, doctors appear to underestimate the side-effects of treatment (Maguire et al., 1980) and pain and discomfort (Maguire, 1976). They also overestimate how satisfied people are, how well they manage their treatment (Devlin, Plant and Griffen, 1971), their compliance (Brody, 1980) and their quality of life (Palmer et al., 1980; Fallowfield, 1990).

Compliance

Compliance refers to the act of the patient adhering to the treatment or advice given by the professional. Reasons for non-compliance are multidimensional and vary between individuals, but there is a strong relationship between non-compliance and the patient's dissatisfaction with communication (Korsch et al., 1968). Becker and Rosenstock (1984) found that compliance related to the doctor's sincerity, respect, concern, attention, provision of information in response to the patient's request, and the patient's feeling that their expectations were met. Waitzkin (1984) summarised research suggesting that doctors who were more perceptive of the non-verbal cues of emotion and expressed their own tension and anxiety non-verbally were more likely to satisfy their patients and possibly to obtain better compliance. It is, therefore, not surprising, in view of the evidence already presented about dissatisfaction and professional communication, that the rate of non-compliance is extremely high and averages at almost 50% (Ley, 1982) for taking prescribed medicine or following other advice.

Although dissatisfaction with the consultation seems an important determinant of non-compliance, the relationship is not simple, but again it is professional–patient communication that mediates many of the other factors involved. These include: the duration and complexity of treatment and the costs to the patient in terms of required behaviour change and restrictions; the patient's understanding and retention of the treatment and its perceived credibility and efficacy; vulnerability and severity of the illness as perceived by the patient; the support and encouragement given; and the problems caused by the treatment itself. Thompson (1984a) also identified factors such as the standard of service (e.g. waiting times), and the professional's lack of awareness and hence failure to question on the matter of compliance or to persuade the patient of the need to comply.

Outcome

Logically it follows from what has been said so far that poor communication must affect treatment outcome both physically and psychologically. Failure to elicit relevant information about symptoms and worries can result in inaccurate diagnosis, inappropriate treatment advice and therefore poorer outcomes. Since poor communication is associated with noncompliance, there will be obvious effects upon outcome. For example, underestimation of toxicity in chemotherapy and therefore the failure to ameliorate side-effects is associated with patients withdrawing from therapy and failing to gain potential benefits (Maguire et al., 1980).

Poor communication may also increase patient stress/distress and therefore complicate and slow down physical recovery with unnecessary anxiety and depression that hinders psychosocial adaptation. Fallowfield et al. (1986) found that 46% of women who thought they had been given inadequate information about their breast disease were significantly anxious or depressed in comparison with 23% of those given adequate information. The relationship found between pre-operative anxiety and post-operative outcome (Newman, 1984) also suggests that unnecessary stress and anxiety should be avoided, and improved communication before surgery does improve outcome (see Chapter 18).

If the role of the professional is, at least in part, to reassure people appropriately, then poor communication will interfere with this and therefore increase distress and complicate psychosocial adaptation. Given the failure to elicit expectations and major concerns (Korsch *et al.*, 1968) and nurses' relative ignorance of patients' worries (Johnston, 1982), it is not surprising that reassurance fails. Maguire (1976) found that surgeons' attempts at reassurance tended to fail leaving unnecessary anxiety because they used fixed reassurance strategies unrelated to the patient's specific worries.

Knowledge, memory and understanding

Adaptation to disease is to some extent a function of knowledge and understanding. Only through adequate understanding will the person be able to carry out treatment schedules in an appropriate way without error, or be able to make predictions about future consequences. Poor communication, however, will impede the acquisition of such knowledge. For example, Muss *et al.* (1979) found that patients undergoing cancer treatment did not know about life-threatening side-effects (e.g. bleeding and infections), thus limiting their ability to react appropriately and avoid adverse outcome. In summarising such studies Ley (1982) found that between 7 and 53% of patients claimed not to have understood what they had been told, with the estimate rising considerably to between 53 and 89%, when their understanding was actually tested. In considering only the understanding of medication, which is perhaps the most important of all, Ley (1988) concluded that from 5–53% of patients do not have adequate knowledge of drug dosage and schedule, and from 19–55% are unclear about the purpose of their drugs.

To some extent the problem is one of the physicians communicating less than they intend. For example, Hulka *et al.* (1975) found that around 65% of the physicians in their study communicated less than 75% of the information they intended. On the other hand, the problem is enhanced by the fact that patients forget what they have been told. Dickson *et al.* (1989) estimated that 30 to 50% of information in a consultation is forgotten quickly by most people. Ley (1982) found an average loss of 45% (range 28–71%) in 13 reviewed studies. In a more extensive review Ley (1988) found similar figures for both hospital and general practice consultations, and studies of situations requiring informed consent were no better.

Although one could argue that multiple contacts with the physician would improve recall, because of repetition, this does not appear to be the case. For example, Pozen *et al.* (1977) found low knowledge of their condition (myocardial infarction) and treatment in patients six months after discharge. Ley (1988) concluded that recall is particularly poor in those with low levels of medical knowledge, low anxiety, low intelligence and poorer education. However, this natural tendency to forget is not helped by the professional's tendency to provide information in ways that the patient does not understand, because of difficult vocabulary and confusing terminology. Although these problems do not help adaptation to disease or eventual outcome, they are also potentially dangerous in that patients are more likely to carry out treatment instructions wrongly.

Self-reliance

A final point to be made relates to patients taking some responsibility for their own health care. Self-responsibility is important, as it may enhance prevention of disease, increase treatment efficiency, and relieve the pressure on overworked professionals. Although it is possible that poor communication may aid self-reliance by forcing the patient to take control and seek alternative solutions, it has the disadvantage of alienating the patient from potential help, and preventing an effective partnership, even if the patient has the necessary knowledge, resources, determination, time and skills. A more likely possibility, given the need for support when one is ill and emotionally vulnerable, is that unnecessary dependence upon the professional is fostered. Patients who are given and retain relatively little information about their illness may passively abdicate responsibility to the professional no matter how competent. Such a course may not facilitate realistic appraisal, and is therefore not conducive to the best possible adaptation, particularly if the problem is not medical, but psychological and social (Oldfield, 1983).

REASONS FOR INADEQUATE COMMUNICATION AND COUNSELLING

Medical ethos

In contrast to the 19th century, current medicine is characterised by high technology, what Maguire (1984) calls the 'bio-engineering ideology'. Previously the limited range of effective treatments meant that the medical role was more one of providing comfort. This included diagnosing and monitoring, doing the little that was possible, but then encouraging people and supporting them in their suffering. Since then, enormous strides have been made, both in curing and alleviating symptoms. Investigative tools are now extremely powerful, and drug and surgical techniques continue to develop rapidly.

With the advent of antibiotic treatments and immunisation, many of the major acute causes of death have been virtually eradicated. Such success has resulted in major changes in the pattern of disease, without corresponding changes in orientation. What remains are the more chronic conditions for which there are no easy cures and for which adaptation is a more realistic goal than cure. As Dickson *et al.* (1989) remark, care has to be oriented much more to the person, and the concept of health has to be defined more broadly, to consider the intellectual, emotional, social and spiritual, yet this has lagged behind. That changes are occurring, albeit slowly, is evident from the interest being shown in the notion of quality of life (Fallowfield, 1990). The problem is, however, that the frameworks and skills to cope with people with chronic disease, to aid their adaptation, may have to be relearnt. The pattern of short-term treatment by many different specialists must revert to longer term, individual doctor–patient relationships (Korsch et al., 1968).

Underwood, Owen and Winkler (1986) fearing a widening gap between medical expertise and the primary needs in society, argue strongly for the re-examination and redefinition of the medical task. The dominant biomedical approach, which they call the 'clockwork model' with its mechanistic concepts and removal of the person, appears to provide heroic solutions for the 'fortunate few, rather than the needy many'. Instead they propose a social approach to medicine, suggesting that social reform in the past has had the greatest effects upon mortality and that this holds true today. Within this conception, medicine becomes only one of several social responses to improved health and is based upon a biopsychosocial model as proposed by Engel (1990).

Power and its defence

Medicine is one of the most powerful professions in our society, and such power may contribute to the failure to adopt adequate communication and counselling strategies. This imbalance in power between the doctor and patient is evident from medical directiveness in interaction (Waitzkin, 1984). This in itself, as Thomspon (1984b) describes, inhibits communication, because the doctor's style does not foster free expression of the patient's feelings and ideas. Their inferior role constrains patients from taking a more active part in the consultation (Stiles et al., 1979). It produces reticence, which, as Ley (1988) suggests, will in itself contribute to difficulties, because of the absence of the beneficial effects of patient feedback upon the clinician's performance. Such imbalance is likely to be even greater, with further effects upon communication, as soon as the differences and distance between doctor and patient are increased by socio-economic and cultural disparity.

Failure to communicate appropriately may also be a way of the professional retaining power. Providing the patient with information demystifies and dilutes this power. Waitzkin and Stockle (1972) have also argued that patient feedback is actually discouraged as a way of maintaining medical power. Whatever the arguments, open communication is threatening in the sense that professionals' failings become more evident both to themselves, with effects upon self-esteem, and to the patient. For example, in a study in which patients were rehearsed in the questions they wanted to ask, thus becoming more assertive, the doctors were disconcerted and tended to construe the patient negatively as more angry and anxious (Roter, 1979). The threat is of course all the more powerful in that open communication may also be personally dangerous, given the danger of litigation and professional censure.

There is, however, a strong argument that the retention of power is for the benefit of patients. This 'encourages doctors to maintain a distance from their patients, so as to strengthen their image as authority figures and increase their power to reassure patients' (Maguire, 1984). However, as Thompson (1984a) suggests, other factors besides credibility are involved in making someone a persuasive communicator, including likability, enthusiasm, negotiation and trustworthiness. Such a view also neglects the need to encourage self-reliance in the patient.

The expert model

Many of the failings described earlier in the chapter are predictable from an assumption that many professionals implicitly adopt a framework to make sense of their relationship with the patient that is inappropriate. Cunningham and Davis (1985) have termed this the Expert model, which is akin to the guidance-cooperation model described by Szasz and Hollender (1956). It is a model that may well be shared by the patient, according to Boreham and Gibson (1978), and to some extent derives from the attempt to meet patient expectations of the omnipotent doctor. It is also partly a function of the impossibility of the job of the professional, who is supposed to have appropriate information and quick solutions readily available for every possible problem.

Using an Expert model, clinicians construe themselves as experts in relation to diagnosis and treatment. This is perhaps valid, and is certainly important for the clinicians' self-confidence and therefore the ability to perform their duties. However, this tends to over-generalise to all aspects of the patient and their relationship. The assumption implicit in the model is that the expert knows what he or she is doing and that the patient has little to offer to the debate. In essence this predicts that the professional leads the conversation, asks the questions he or she thinks appropriate, does not listen to the 'inappropriate' or 'silly' comments of the patient, interrupts frequently, and neglects the patient's perspectives. On the basis of the information extracted the expert can then proceed to make a decision about the nature of the problem, its aetiology and course, and then prescribe the appropriate treatment, irrespective of the values, resources, strengths, opinions, abilities and circumstances of the patient.

Whatever the origins of the model, it has the consequences of neglecting the patient as a person, underestimating the importance of communication, and not according the respect to patients that they merit and must be given for their long-term benefit. It is interesting to see how sometimes even the most caring people may patronise and be disrespectful to the disabled, the poor and to those from cultural minority groups.

While the model may work well with comatose or anaesthetised patients, in most other circumstances the fallacy of the model becomes obvious, in that, for example, the patient may not comply. For the expert, this may serve only to emphasise the patient's lack of expertise and, of course, the disrespect within which they are held. It widens the gap between the two and reduces even more the opportunity for adequate communication to occur.

Such a model may caricature the real situation, but it does have implications for how to begin the process of change. One may, for example, begin to train the professional by exploring alternative models of the professional–patient relationship such as that of a partnership (Cunningham and Davis, 1985) in which the doctor and patient are each assumed to have relevant expertise that complements the knowledge and skills of the other. This is similar to the model of mutual participation discussed by Szasz and Hollender (1956).

Frameworks and policies

The professional's failure to make explicit his or her model of the professional–patient relationship mirrors the lack of attention professions as a whole give to establishing clear frameworks and policies in relation to whole person medicine. Health care policies are largely disease oriented and do not appear to emphasise the integrity of individuals, their quality of life, social context and psychological well-being. Unless these are emphasised in policy, it is unlikely that resources will be directed accordingly.

The naive frameworks used by some professionals to conceptualise the behaviour, motivation, and feeling of their patients is worrying. The notion that information should be withheld from patients for fear of increasing hopelessness, anxiety and depression can be disputed both theoretically and empirically. For example, Ley (1982) cites evidence that:

1. Between 66 and 93% of patients approved of being told they had cancer or were terminally ill.
2. There is no increase in distress as a result of extra information about test results or access to case-notes.
3. There is no reduction in compliance or increased side-effects with fuller information about drugs. On the contrary, as predictable from psychological theories (e.g. Kelly, 1955), there is evidence of increased emotional disturbance where information is inadequate (Fallowfield et al., 1986).

Maguire (1984) cites the lack of frameworks and naivety in explaining the reluctance of doctors to cover psychosocial matters with patients. They believe, for example, that people will automatically tell the doctor of any important issues, although we know that they are rarely given the opportunity to do so. Insufficient time is given as a reason, but this implies that psychosocial matters lack importance. Another reason is the fear of opening Pandora's box. If the doctor is exposed to the real human impact of disease, he or she may feel ill-equipped to cope with the problems. It should not be forgotten that closeness to the patient's problems may compromise the doctor's emotional stability unless he or she has been well trained and is well supported. There is also a belief that anxiety and depression are inevitable consequences of serious disease and that little can be done about it except to jolly people along. Maguire also mentions the erroneous belief that focusing upon the negative might make things worse by causing more worry.

Professions drive services

A further reason for the lack of attention to psychological care is the fact that services are not responsive to consumer opinion. Policy and resources are directed by politicians, without systematic channels for consumer feedback, other than through the ballot-box. Clinicians do have some responsibility for the ordering of priorities within the health service and many seem unwilling to make opportunities for more patient involvement. Individuals cannot comment directly, for example, upon the professional's rudeness or other communicative deficiencies for fear their treatment will be affected. Other channels are complex and require determination, organization and articulation. One rarely sees a suggestion box in any health care setting.

Without such feedback, it is impossible for service providers to know the views of patients and to respond appropriately. It is not surprising, therefore, to find professionals holding views quite contrary to those of their patients. Surveys in the USA until recently showed relatively few physicians routinely informing their patients that they had cancer while the vast majority of the public wanted to know (Ley 1988). Gerle, Lunden and Sandblom (1960) have discussed the conflict in the medical profession on this point, indicating the diversity of rigidly held views, despite evidence such as that of Kelly and Freisen (1950) that 89% of patients who knew they had cancer appreciated being told. Eighty-two % of patients without cancer also said that they would prefer to be told if they did develop this disease. Nevertheless, as Waitzkin (1984) indicates, in studies of dying patients in the 1960s and 1970s, 69% to 90% of doctors tended to withhold information from them.

Although a complete reversal of the attitudes of medical staff has occurred (Novack et al., 1979) in respect to information about death, there remain deficiencies in relation to more routine matters. Waitzkin (1984) for example, found that in 65% of 336 consultations, doctors underestimated the patient's desire for information, and would continue to be unclear about patient views until direct and effective feedback methods are available.

Professional selection and training

A final reason for the failure to consider the psychological and social care of the person relates to the selection and training of professionals. It is most certainly true that in general very limited attention is given to teaching the principles and skills of communication and counselling in all professions. Although this is an important issue, we will not discuss it further here, but will return to it in Chapter 19.

SUMMARY

Although there are many professionals in the health services who are very caring and many who are highly skilled in interacting with their patients, the general situation appears to be unsatisfactory. There is considerable patient dissatisfaction which relates above all to criticisms of professional communication skills. Such complaints are supported by observations of widespread deficiencies in consultation behaviour. These include: failing to provide the opportunity for patients to express their views and to listen when they do; a focus on the organic; a highly directive style in which on-going guidance/explanation and negotiation are omitted; deficiencies in information giving; and inadequacies in giving effective reassurance.

The direct consequences of these inadequacies are worrying, since they are contrary to the benefits to be expected from effective health care. The effects are interrelated, and include patient dissatisfaction, non-compliance, inaccurate diagnosis and monitoring, and inappropriate treatment advice. In physical terms it is highly likely that the outcomes of such a situation will be relatively poor, which is criticism enough given the narrow focus of modern medicine upon the organic. However, from a broader perspective of holistic medicine the outcomes are much worse.

The present situation not only works against effective physical cure, it does little to address the psychological and social factors which play a part in the aetiology of disease. Furthermore, there is little concern or help for the psychosocial impact of disease processes upon the individual, family and wider community. In fact, the stresses inherent in ill-health are exaggerated by present day care with increased distress caused by inept communication practices. Additionally, the lack of respect accorded to patients, and limitations imposed upon their knowledge and understanding all combine to reduce the patient's self-confidence and efficacy, with consequent increase in dependence and reduction in self-reliance.

The reasons for this situation include the narrow biomedical model of disease, the power of the profession of medicine, vested interest in the maintenance of power, and lack of consumer participation and feedback. This is further enhanced by the failure to select and train students appropriately in more general psychological skills including those of communication.

Underlying this, however, is the presence of inadequate frameworks for making sense of the behaviour of patients and the process of communicating with them.

Our argument is that to produce whole patient care, a narrow understanding of physical medicine is inadequate, and that a biopsychosocial model is much more appropriate (Engel, 1990). This must include a usable model of human psychological functioning, an understanding of the relationship between the professional and patient, an awareness of the nature and process of face-to-face communication and the skills to engage in the process. Although there are many aspects of the psychological sciences that may contribute to this understanding, counselling has a great deal to offer, and it is this that we intend to explore in detail in the remainder of the book.

Many of the deficiencies in communication would be removed if all professionals had basic counselling skills. This in itself would be beneficial, but would not be a panacea. Just as there is a need for specialists in all areas of medicine, so there is a need for more advanced and specialist counsellors to work with people on more complex and longer term difficulties. Rowland, Irving and Maguard (1989) examined the role of counselling in general practice and concluded that specialist counsellor attachments were necessary. That such people exist already in most areas of medicine is certainly true, but their numbers are extremely small and they are generally considered a luxury and secondary to physical treatment. As Abel Smith *et al.* (1989) comment, although the assumed benefits of counselling are being increasingly recognised in medicine generally, with impetus given particularly by the AIDS fear, there remains very little importance attached to it, as indicated by the poor allocation of resources in personnel terms or training.

We sincerely hope that this will alter and that this book plays some part in the changes that are necessary. Returning to where we began, we hope that both the basic skills of communication and the provision of more advanced counselling would go some way to meeting the needs of the family described in the husband's words at the beginning of this chapter. Such provision would have given them the psychological care they required. It would have enabled them to feel a part of the wider community, and to maintain the dignity and respect that they certainly deserved.

REFERENCES

Abel Smith, A., Irving, J., and Brown, P. (1989). Counselling in the medical context. In W. Dryden, D. Charles-Edwards and R. Woolff (Eds), *Handbook of counselling in Britain*. London: Tavistock/Routledge.

Becker, M. and Rosenstock, I. (1984). Compliance with medical advice. In A. Steptoe and A. Mathews (Eds), *Health care and human behaviour*. London: Academic Press.

Boreham, P. and Gibson, D. (1978). The informative process in private medical consultations: a preliminary investigation. *Social Science and Medicine*, **12**, 409–416.

Boyle, C. (1970). Differences between patients' and doctors' interpretation of some common medical terms. *British Medical Journal*, **2**, 286–289.

Breakwell, G. and Alexander-Dann, C. (1989). Counselling in the non-primary sector of the NHS: A survey of DHAs. *Counselling*, **70**, 17–25.

Brody, D. (1980). An analysis of patient recall of their therapeutic regimens. *Journal of Chronic Diseases*, **33**, 57–63.

Brown, P. and Abel Smith, A. (1985). Counselling in medical settings. *British Journal of Guidance and Counselling*, **13**, 75–88.

Byrne, P. and Long, B. (1976). *Doctors talking to patients*. London: HMSO.

Cartwright, A. and Anderson, R. (1981). *General practice revisited: a second study of patients and their doctors*. London: Tavistock Publications.

Cooper, B., Harwin, B., Depla, C., and Shepherd, M. (1975). Mental health care in the community: an evaluative study. *Psychological Medicine*, **5**, 372–380.

Cunningham, C. and Davis, H. (1985). *Working with parents: frameworks for collaboration*. Milton Keynes: Open University press.

Cunningham, C., Morgan, P., and McGucken, R. (1984). Down's syndrome: is dissatisfaction with disclosure of diagnosis inevitable? *Developmental Medicine & Child Neurology*, **26**, 33–39.

Devlin, H., Plant, J., and Griffen, M. (1971). Aftermath of surgery for anorectal cancer. *British Medical Journal*, **3**, 413–418.

Dickson, D., Hargie, O., and Morrow, N. (1989). *Communication skills training for health professionals*. London: Chapman & Hall.

Engel, G. (1990). The essence of the biopsychosocial model: from 17th to 20th century science. In H. Balner (Ed.), *A new medical model: a challenge for biomedicine?* Amsterdam: Swets & Zeitlinger.

Fallowfield, L. (1990). *Quality of life: the missing measurement in health care*. London: Souvenir Press.

Fallowfield, L., Baum, M., and Maguire, P. (1986). Effects of breast conservation on psychological morbidity associated with diagnosis and treatment of early breast cancer. *British Medical Journal*, **293**, 1331–1334.

Fallowfield, L. and Roberts, R. (1990). Cancer counselling in the U.K. *Psychology and Health*. (In press).

Fitzpatrick, R. (1984). Satisfaction with health care. In R. Fitzpatrick, J. Hinton, S. Newman, G. Scambler, and J. Thompson (Eds), *The experience of illness*. London: Tavistock.

Gerle, B., Lunden, G., and Sandblom, P. (1960). The patient with inoperable cancer from the psychiatric and social standpoints. *Cancer*, **13**, 1206–1217.

Gerrard, B., Boniface, W., and Love, B. (1980). *Interpersonal Skills for health professionals*. Reston, Virginia: Reston Publishing Company.

Hughes, P. and Lieberman, S. (1990). Troubled parents: vulnerability and stress in childhood cancer. *British Journal of Medical Psychology*, **63**, 53–64.

Hulka, B., Kupper, L., Cassel, J., and Babineau, R. (1975). Practice characteristics and quality of primary medical care: the doctor-patient relationship. *Medical Care*, **13**, 808–820.

Johnston, M. (1976). Communication of patients' feelings in hospital. In A. Bennett (Ed.), *Communication between doctors and patients*. London: Oxford University Press.

Johnston, M. (1982). Recognition of patients' worries by nurses and by other patients. *British Journal of Clinical Psychology*, **21**, 255–261.

Johnston, M. (1990). Counselling and psychological methods with postoperative pain: a brief review. *British Psychological Society Health Psychology Update*. Issue 5.

Kelly, G. (1955). *The psychology of personal constructs*. New York: Norton.

Kelly, W. and Freisen, S. (1950). Do cancer patients want to be told? *Surgery*, **27**, 822–826.

Korsch, B., Gozzi, E., and Francis, V. (1968). Gaps in doctor-patient communication: doctor-patient interaction and patient satisfaction. *Pediatrics*, **42**, 855–871.

Krebs, R. (1976). Disrespect: a study in hospital relationships. *Hospital and Health Services Administration*, **21**, 67–72.

Lazare, A., Eisenthal, S., Frank, A., and Stoeckle, J. (1978). Studies on the negotiated approach to patienthood. In E. Gallagher (Ed.), *The doctor : patient relation in the changing health scene*. Washington, DC.: DHEW Publishers.

Ley, P. (1982). Satisfaction, compliance and communication. *British Journal of Clinical Psychology*, **21**, 241–254.

Ley, P. (1988). *Communicating with patients: improving communication, satisfaction and compliance*. London: Croom Helm.

Macleod Clark, J. (1985). The development of research in interpersonal skills in nursing. In C. Kagan (Ed.), *Interpersonal skills in nursing*. London: Croom Helm.

Maguire, P. (1976). The psychological and social sequelae of mastectomy. In J. Howells (Ed.), *Modern perspectives in the psychiatric aspects of surgery*. New York: Brunner Mazel.

Maguire, P. (1984). Communication skills and patient care. In A. Steptoe and A. Mathews (Eds), *Health care and human behaviour*. London: Academic Press.

Maguire, P. (1985). Deficiencies in key interpersonal skills. In C. Kagan (Ed.), *Interpersonal skills in nursing*. London: Croom Helm.

Maguire, P., Fairburn, S., and Fletcher, C. (1986). Consultation skills of young doctors. *British Medical Journal*, **292**, 1573–1578.

Maguire, P. and Granville-Grossman, K. (1968). Physical illness in psychiatric patients. *British Journal of Psychiatry*, **115**, 1365.

Maguire, P. and Rutter, D. (1976). History-taking for medical students: 1. Deficiencies in performance. *Lancet*, September 11, 556–558.

Maguire, P., Tait, A., Brooke, M., Thomas, C., and Sellwood, R. (1980). Effects of counselling on the psychiatric morbidity associated with mastectomy. *British Medical Journal*, **281**, 1454–1456.

Muss, H., White, D., Michielutte, R. *et al.* (1979). Written informed consent in patients with breast cancer. *Cancer*, **43**, 1549–1556.

Newman, S. (1984). Anxiety, hospitalization and surgery. In R. Fitzpatrick, J. Hinton, S. Newman, G. Scambler, and J. Thompson (Eds), *The experience of illness*. London: Tavistock.

Novack, D., Plumer, R., Smith, R., Ochitill, H., Morrow, G., and Bennett, J. (1979). Changes in physicians' attitudes toward telling the cancer patient. *Journal of the American Medical Association*, **241**, 897–900.

Oldfield, S. (1983). *The counselling relationship: a study of the client's experience*. London: Routledge & Kegan Paul.

Palmer, B., Walsh, G., McKinna, J., and Greening, W. (1980). Adjuvant chemotherapy for breast cancer: side effects and quality of life. *British Medical Journal*, **281**, 1594–1597.

Platt, F. and McMath, J. (1979). Clinical hypocompetence: the interview. *Annals of Internal Medicine*, **91**, 898–902.

Pozen, M., Stechmiller, J., Harris, W., Smith, S., Donna, F., and Voigt, G. (1977). The nurse rehabilitator's impact on patients with myocardial infarction. *Medical Care*, **15**, 830–837.

Roter, D. (1979). Altering patient behaviour in interaction with providers. In D. Oborne, M. Gruneberg, and J. Eiser (Eds), *Research in psychology and medicine*, Volume 2. London: Academic Press.

Rowland, N. and Irving, J. (1984). Towards a rationalization of counselling in general practice. *Journal of the Royal College of General Practitioners*, **34**, 685–687.

Rowland, N., Irving, J., and Maguard, A. (1989). Can general practitioners counsel? *Journal of the Royal College of General Practitioners*, **39**, 118–120.

Samora, J., Saunders, L., and Larson, M. (1961). Medical vocabulary knowledge among hospital patients. *Journal of Health & Human Behaviour*, **2**, 83–89.

Stiles, W., Putnam, S., Wolf, M., and James, S. (1979). Interaction exchange structure and patient satisfaction with medical interviews. *Medical Care*, **17**, 667–679.

Szasz, T. (1960). The myth of mental illness. *American Psychologist*, **15**, 113–118.

Szasz, T. and Hollender, M. (1956). A contribution to the philosophy of medicine: The basic models of the doctor-patient relationship. *Archives of Internal Medicine*, **97**, 585–592.

Thompson, J. (1984a). Compliance. In R. Fitzpatrick, J. Hinton, S. Newman, G. Scambler, and J. Thompson (Eds), *The experience of illness*. London: Tavistock.

Thompson, J. (1984b). Communicating with patients. In R. Fitzpatrick, J. Hinton, S. Newman, G. Scambler, and J. Thompson (Eds), *The experience of illness*. London: Tavistock.

Underwood, P., Owen, A., and Winkler, R. (1986). Replacing the clockwork model of medicine. *Community Health Studies*, **10**, 275–283.

Waitzkin, H. (1984). Doctor-patient communication: Implications of social scientific research. *Journal of the American Medical Association*, **252**, 2441–2446.

Waitzkin, H. and Stoeckle J. (1972). The communication of information about illness: clinical, sociological and methodological considerations. *Advances in Psychosomatic Medicine*, **8**, 180–215.

Waydenfeld, D. and Waydenfeld, S. (1980). Counselling in general practice. *Journal of the Royal College of General Practitioners*, **30**, 671–677.

Weiner, S. and Nathanson, M. (1976). Physical examination: frequently observed errors. *Journal of the American Medical Association*, **236**, 852–855.

Which? (1989). *You and your GP*. October. London: Consumers' Association.

2 Counselling Theory

DEFINITION

Counselling is a word used in many ways. Abel Smith, Irving and Brown (1989) give a number of meanings in the medical setting ranging from listening attentively to disciplinary censure. It is therefore important to define what we mean as precisely as possible, even though the complexity of the activity makes simplicity difficult. The activities covered by the term vary on a number of dimensions including the people involved, their relationship, their behaviour, the problem and content of their interaction, their goals, the duration of the interaction and the outcomes. In consequence we take a very broad view and use counselling to refer to a range of situations, encompassing specialist psychological help on one hand, and a set of qualities and skills for communicating effectively on the other. We will relate the latter to all situations in which health care professionals interact with patients, and equate the term counselling, like Egan (1982), to *helping*.

Counselling/communication skills

We will use counselling or counselling skills to refer to the qualities and abilities necessary for any health care professional to help people, whatever their problem, whatever the speciality. These are the skills of enabling communication in the consultation situation. In effect we begin from the Oxford Dictionary, which defines counselling as to 'advise (a person to do)'. This highlights three elements of the activity we assume to be covered: it involves at least two people: the aim is for one of these people to help the other (one seeking advice, the other attempting to give it); and there must be at least minimal or tacit agreement about the nature of their interaction. This means that counselling does not occur when one person tries to help another who does not want such help; it is a cooperative endeavour. Our only objection to the dictionary definition is that it is a little narrow. Apart from advice giving, other possibilities include giving information, decision making, helping the patient to clarify their own problem or even facilitating the development of their own solutions.

We will use the notion of counselling skills to refer as much to the GP consulted about a simple bacterial infection, or the physiotherapist seen as

Counselling and Communication in Health Care. Edited by H. Davis and L. Fallowfield
© 1991 John Wiley & Sons Ltd

the result of damage to a limb, as to the psychologist consulted about stresses in an individual's life and his or her perceived inability to cope with them. However, not all professionals consulted in the health care context are necessarily good helpers/counsellors and, as we saw in the previous chapter, many lack very basic communication skills. Nevertheless, they are in a counselling situation; a situation where their help is solicited and where they may or may not have the appropriate skills to provide the help required.

The importance of advice in any context, to return to the dictionary definition, is that people are free to reject it. This is true in the medical situation, including, for example, the relatively simple interaction in which drugs are prescribed. People can always reject what is said to them, indicating their autonomy. The high degree of non-compliance illustrates this. Therefore, an interaction must always be regarded as one of cooperation or partnership, if it is to be successful at more than a chance level.

Counselling, therefore, at a basic level equates to good communication. It refers to a process of enabling individuals to describe their problem, and listening sufficiently well that the helper can grasp the meaning and offer appropriate advice. This has to be given in ways understandable and acceptable to the people seeking help. One might give information or prescribe dictatorially, but cooperative negotiation with full involvement of the patient is much more likely to be effective. We are proposing, therefore, that although doctors may regard themselves as consulting and not counselling, if they are to be maximally effective, they should be using basic counselling skills.

Some situations may appear to differ from counselling, as when the patient knows what he or she wants (e.g. specific information) and simply demands it from the professional. However, even here basic negotiation must occur to check why the person needs the information and its appropriateness. It must then be provided in terms that are intelligible to and tailored for the patient, and this requires a good knowledge of the person. Subsequently there has to be some enquiry to ensure the patient's grasp of the material. Again this has to assume a cooperative relationship and the use of basic skills.

The process we have described is that of education in the sense of information giving, and a distinction may or may not be drawn between this and counselling. It is, however, a rather arbitrary division, because the same processes are involved in both. Counselling may involve giving information, sometimes called advisory counselling, and may not be effective if attention is not given to the characteristics of the person potentially acquiring the information. As Gibran (1980) said about the teacher, 'If he is indeed wise he does not bid you enter the house of his wisdom, but rather leads you to the threshold of your own mind' (p. 67). That information on its own may not help is illustrated by the fact that diabetic education programmes do not appear to be particularly effective in improving glycaemic control (see

Shillitoe, Chapter 4). Similarly, some health promotion may not have the expected effects, probably because the information is not tailored to the individual (Bennett and Hobbs, Chapter 17).

Specialist counselling

Counselling will also be used to refer to the specialist, highly skilled psychological endeavour of helping people with complex psychological and relationship problems. Here the terms counselling, psychological therapy or psychotherapy become synonymous. We prefer the word counselling, however, because it avoids the implication of an illness model with an expert curing a passive recipient. The point made by Smith, Glass and Miller (1980) is well taken when they said, 'The possibility ought to be considered more seriously that the locus of those forces that restore and ameliorate the client of psychotherapy resides more within the client himself and less within the therapist and his actions' (p.188).

Patterson (1986) described a number of distinctions drawn between counselling and psychotherapy. Objectives may be said to differ, with counselling more concerned with personal growth and optimal development, and psychotherapy more to do with removing handicaps and repairing structures. Counselling has been said to occur with essentially normal people as opposed to the deficient, or the more severely disturbed. The setting may also differ; the medical/psychiatric versus the non-medical. Another distinction is the content of the problem, with personality issues relating to psychotherapy, and educational, vocational, and questions of choice relating to counselling. In all cases, however, Patterson shows the differences to be arbitrary and not universally accepted by those involved in this area. Although Smith *et al.* (1980) add the further dimensions of the psychological depth of the interaction and the amount of training needed, they also conclude that it is difficult to draw reliable distinctions without using arbitrary judgements.

At this specialist level, counselling has additional elements to those already discussed in relation to basic counselling skills. These include: a more formal relationship concerned with psychological and social issues both directly and indirectly; a broader range of skills and techniques; and a broader and explicit theory relating to individual psychological functioning, the relationship between the counsellor and counsellee and the processes of change. Counselling at this level also implies a much more extensive training in the psychological realm, more formal qualification, and an appropriate support system to back up the counsellors in their work.

The British Association for Counselling (1989) says: 'Counselling is the skilled and principled use of relationship to facilitate self-knowledge, emotional acceptance and growth, and the optimal development of personal resources. The overall aim is to provide an opportunity to work towards living more satisfyingly and resourcefully. Counselling relationships will vary according to need but may be concerned with developmental issues, addressing and resolving specific problems, making decisions, coping with crisis, developing personal insights and knowledge, working through feelings of inner conflict or improving relationships with others'. They add that, 'The counsellor's role is to facilitate the client's work in ways that respect the client's values, personal resources and capacity for self determination'.

The definition stresses the importance of a partnership, which at all levels is one of cooperation and assumes respect for the person being helped, who has an important, if not the most important, contribution to make to the helping process. More strongly, however, we suggest that nothing can occur except in the context of the individual's understanding, values, desires, expertise and environment. This intimately relates to the aims of counselling, in that the fundamental aim is to help people to help themselves, to feel effective. This means respecting their strengths and abilities or assuming their potential, not taking over from them.

Other dimensions

Our distinction between skills and specialism is like that drawn by Nelson-Jones (1983) who talks of counselling relationships, in which counselling is the primary activity, and helping relationships, in which counselling skills are only one part of the helper's relationship with the other person. These differ, but also have commonalities, both in skills (e.g. listening) and in underlying frameworks. We are using the term counselling to relate to any situation in which there is a mutually agreed attempt by one person to help the other. The reason for seeking help is not a defining characteristic. The criteria in common are: the relationship between helper and helped; the qualities of the counsellor; the respect accorded to the individual; the person's freedom of choice; the emphasis upon self-help; and finally the awareness of the processes involved.

Although counselling can be a direct source of help in enabling people to explore and understand their world more fully and therefore adapt more effectively, it is also a vehicle for making choices about other sources of direct help and treatment options, encompassing the many specific medical/ surgical and psychological techniques described throughout this book. These include the various drug and surgical options for different conditions, and dietary and exercise regimes. They include the many and varied psychological methods, such as relaxation, desensitisation, stress innoculation, rehearsal, fixed role therapy, sensate focus and pain coping strategies. These are strategies adopted as a result of counselling, which involves explicit exploration of problems, appropriate goal-setting, negotiation and planning.

A frequent distinction encountered in various guises in health care relates to the explicit aims of the activity of counselling, contrasting education or information giving with emotional adaptation. Terms such as advisory versus personal counselling (Nichols, Chapter 5), or educational psychosocial versus psychotherapeutic psychosocial intervention (Massie, Holland and Straker, 1989) relate to this. In reality it may be impossible to separate the two except as a matter of emphasis in particular cases. Both involve helping people to change, on the one hand by the acquisition of information, and on the other by dealing with emotion that accompanies information such as the disclosure of a serious diagnosis.

Nelson-Jones (1983) classified counselling interviews into five types, which included developmental, problem-focused, decision-making, crisis and supportive counselling, none of which are necessarily mutually exclusive. These categories relate to the content of counselling, and involve differences in the type of problem, which we will explore later in the book by considering the differences that arise within a variety of medical specialities.

There are also differences in terms of the number of people with whom counsellors work at any one time. Individual work can be contrasted with working in groups, varying in size from a couple with sexual or relationship problems, or a whole family, to a group of individuals who share a common problem, such as a chronic disease or disability (e.g. heart disease, eczema or alcoholism). The choice of format depends upon a variety of factors, such as the preferences of the counsellor and the people involved, and the nature of the problem. Although there are overlaps in the qualities demanded of the counsellor and the theoretical models applied, there are differences and each format has its own advantages. Individual work enables the needs of the individual to be given full attention, but it does not allow direct consideration of other people, such as a partner, or a child, who might be part of the problem. An obvious advantage of a group derives from the support that each member can gain from the others. Some people may receive help more readily in the context of potentially helping others, as in a group situation. As Spiegel, Bloom and Yalom (1981) have commented, 'Seeing themselves contribute to others' well-being enhances a sense of worth and value and reduces feelings of powerlessness and uselessness' (p. 528).

In this chapter we are concerned with distinctions which relate to the theoretical frameworks underlying and guiding the work of counsellors from different orientations. We will describe a selection of these. A fundamental assumption of counselling is that if you understand what you are doing, you will be more effective. Similarly here, we propose that it is important to try to make explicit the frameworks underlying counselling itself, so that greater expertise can be encouraged.

COUNSELLING THEORIES

A wide range of theories can be adopted to guide counsellors (e.g. Patterson, 1986). Nevertheless, there are broad categories albeit with many variants.

We cannot present a comprehensive overview of all the theories, but have selected five, which represent the broader categories, and which are amongst the more influential and common frameworks to be found in use. Each derives from the specialist situation of helping people with psycho-social problems, although they all have application to more general helping as defined earlier.

Each of these models is an invention that is potentially useful; they are alternative ways of looking at situations as a means of making them more meaningful and easier. Although Yalom (1989) said that, 'the capacity to tolerate uncertainty is a prerequisite for the profession (of psychotherapy)', adopting a framework of any sort is one way of helping to deal with uncertainty. However, he cautions that the 'temptation to achieve certainty through embracing an ideological school and tight therapeutic system is treacherous: such belief may block the uncertain and spontaneous encounter necessary for effective therapy' (p. 13).

In practice, some people find a particular model usable and stick with it. Others use concepts from several or use different models on different occasions. As Patterson (1986) says, there are criteria by which theories can be formally evaluated, including applicability, clarity and precision, parsimony, comprehensiveness, operationality, empirical validity and fruitfulness. However, it is the individual's perception of usefulness of the theory that currently decides adoption. There is no absolute truth and many questions remain to be answered in this area. Whatever the model adopted by the individual, it is important that it contributes to the counsellor's confidence. As Bandura (1989) suggests, a person's motivation, direction and capacity relate to his or her beliefs about self-efficacy, and this applies as much to the counsellor as to anyone else. Whether different models are more or less likely to produce effective counsellor behaviour remains to be demonstrated, but it is possible that counsellors of different persuasions act similarly in some fundamental way, which is why we begin with the approach of Rogers.

Carl Rogers

Rogers has arguably had the foremost impact upon the field of counselling both directly and in his influence upon other theorists. Like many therapists in the USA in the early part of this century, Rogers was exposed to both behavioural and Freudian thinking in his early work in the field of child guidance. His extensive experience of diverse methods led eventually to his own remarkably creative formulations, which were presented in ways attempting to facilitate scientific evaluation and development. His ideas were well organised, relatively clear, tested to a refreshing degree and tentative, always available to further refinement.

Perhaps the most attractive aspect of his work is the respect accorded to individuals, and indeed this is a central concept of his theory. He moved from the 'external frame of reference' of the psychodynamic and behavioural schools, and made the views of the person the focus of both theory and therapy. The unit of concern was not the stimulus, response or past unconscious conflict, but the individual's own perceptions. His work has, therefore, attracted such descriptions as humanistic and phenomenological.

Rogers wrote extensively, but one of the most important publications in terms of clarity and conciseness appeared in an impressive volume edited by Koch (Rogers, 1959). Central to his work is the theory of therapy. However, this implies a theory of human functioning, or personality, as well as a theory of interpersonal relationships, both of which he elaborated to an extent. These frameworks were also explored in relation to what could be considered ideal adjustment in Rogers' theory of the fully functioning individual or the theoretical aim of therapy. He also began to explore the theoretical implications of his work for a variety of human areas which involved interpersonal activity and behaviour change, including family life, education, group leadership and group conflict.

The person

Roger's view of the person is respectful and positive. He assumed that people are essentially constructive, trustworthy and cooperative. The capacity for self-control and adaptation is assumed no matter how disturbed people are or how desperate their situation.

The focus of the framework is the experience of the individual. Rogers used the term 'organismic experience' to refer to the totality of experiences impinging upon the person from birth, and it is this experience as perceived by the individual that constitutes reality. In motivational terms, it is assumed that every organism has a natural tendency not only to maintain itself (e.g. to survive) but also to develop, differentiate and grow. 'Actualisation' or 'actualising tendency' are used to refer to this, which implies a valuing process, where experiences perceived as maintaining and enhancing are valued positively.

As the person develops, the total experience of the organism is seen as differentiating into that which relates to the self, and all other experience. Self-experiences form a perceptual whole referred to variously as the *self* or *self-concept*. This is defined as 'the organized, consistent conceptual gestalt composed of perceptions of the characteristics of the "I" or "me" and the perceptions of the relationships of the "I" or "me" to others and to various aspects of life, together with the values attached to these perceptions' (Rogers, 1959, p. 200). Rogers further assumed the development of a universal need for *positive regard* in transactions with others, and that from such experiences developed the need for *self-regard* (i.e. the need to experience oneself positively).

Maladjustment

It is the differentiation between organismic and self-experience that becomes the major vehicle for the explanation of maladjustment and hence the need for counselling. It is assumed that while organismic and self-experiences are *congruent*, the individual is optimally adjusted psychologically. However, *incongruence* between these is predictive of lesser degrees of adaptation and arises because of the development of what Rogers has variously termed *conditions of worth* or *introjected values.*

It is assumed that while the individual experiences *unconditional positive regard* from significant others, organismic and self-experience remain congruent. However, conditional positive regard leads to the situation where self-regard becomes similarly conditional or selective, with the result that certain self-experience will be avoided, signifying values imposed from outside (i.e. introjected) regardless of their appropriateness to the individual. These are *conditions of worth*, or the situation in which the individual perceives himself or herself to be worthy only under certain conditions and not others.

This implies a situation in which organismic valuing and self-valuing processes become divergent. Because of the need for self-regard, the person becomes selective in perception, with experiences contrary to the introjected values being distorted or denied to awareness. This means that certain organismic experiences are not perceived accurately or not perceived at all as part of self-awareness or the self-concept, and Rogers saw this as potentially reflected in discrepancies in the individual's behaviour. Any experience that is incongruent with the self-concept is essentially a threat to the self through the need for self-regard. If experienced in awareness, such incongruence produces anxiety, and it is assumed, therefore, that the threat is met with the defences of denial and distortion of experiences to maintain compatibility with the self.

This defensive reaction has various consequences but includes rigidity of perception and lack of openness to experience. This in turn has consequences for the actualisation tendency with organismic and self-actualisation becoming divergent. It is assumed that adaptation is hindered and that the possibility of change is reduced. This process was also applied by Rogers to the extreme situation of psychotic breakdown, where extreme incongruence is hypothesised to result in the disorganisation of the self-concept, if the defenses of distortion and denial are not maintained and the incongruence comes to accurate awareness.

Therapy

On the grounds that incongruence is the basic problem in people seeking help psychologically, Rogers' theory of therapy consists of a series of statements postulating a set of necessary conditions that put in motion a process enabling the individual to change and become congruent. He proposed six conditions:

1. That two people are 'in contact'.
2. That one is incongruent as defined earlier.
3. That the other, the counsellor, is congruent at least in relation to the first person, if not in all situations.
4. That the counsellor gives unconditional positive regard.
5. That the counsellor has empathy for the other.
6. That the person is minimally aware of the counsellor's unconditional positive regard and empathy.

The theory states, therefore, that if the counsellor is *congruent, empathic* and gives *unconditional positive regard*, and that the person being helped is at least partly aware of this, then the process of change will occur. Rogers, therefore, placed emphasis not upon the techniques of counselling, but upon these three fundamental qualities or attitudes of the counsellor and upon the consequent relationship with the person counselled. Congruence refers to the counsellor being genuine and not playing a role. He or she is assumed to be consistent, well adjusted in the relationship with the person, not defensive, open to his or her own feelings and those of the other person, and able to express these freely and willingly. Empathy is the attempt to understand the other's viewpoint accurately, as though the counsellor were having the experiences, yet at the same time being aware that they are the experiences of the other person. Unconditional positive regard is where the counsellor accepts, values or 'prizes' the person, and respects him or her without evaluating.

The process of change, once started, is assumed to have a number of related themes or directions, which are not necessarily directly related causally. Rogers was careful not to be too specific in the absence of appropriate observation, and chose to leave the mechanisms vague. The directions include: increasing freedom for the person to express his or her feelings; gradual increment in reference to the self; increasing discrimination of such experiences; and greater accuracy in the awareness of them. These allow an increasing awareness of incongruity, with greater consequent awareness of the associated threat, leading to experiencing more fully feelings previously denied or distorted. These experiences in turn produce changes in the self-concept, and this reduces incongruence between organismic and self-experience, and therefore enables the person to be more open to experience, including a greater awareness of the counsellor's unconditional positive regard. This is assumed to be associated with increases in unconditional self-regard, acceptance of self as the locus of evaluation, and therefore reducing conditions of worth or evaluation via the views of others.

Again in his 'if . . . then . . .' style, Rogers posited that if these processes occurred, then the following outcomes would be seen. The person would become more congruent, open to experience, less defensive, more realistic and objective and more effective in solving problems. The person would become better adjusted psychologically, less vulnerable to threat, more realistic in self-ideal, more congruent in self and ideal self, and less tense and anxious. He or she would become more positive in self-regard, more accepting of self-evaluation and self-directing. In turn, he or she would perceive others more realistically and accurately, and would be more accepting. Behaviour changes would occur, and these would be experienced as more in his or her control. The person would be perceived as more mature by others, and would be more creative, adaptable and able to express his or her own aims and values.

Developments and comments

Rogers has had a vast influence upon the whole area of counselling. His non-directive or client-centred therapy is still practised, and many of the basic ideas about counsellor characteristics have been incorporated into other models (e.g. Egan, 1982). Some medical colleges have implemented core curricula for the teaching of medical interviewing based on a patient-centred approach incorporating many of Roger's ideas (Lipkin *et al.*, 1984). A considerable amount of research has also been stimulated, much of it related to the characteristics of empathy, warmth and genuineness and their relationship to the process and outcome of counselling (e.g. Truax and Carkhuff, 1967).

There have also been developments in theoretical terms. The major change has been the greater emphasis placed on cognitive processes and the ways the individual analyses information as he or she explores experiences and generates alternative meaning and organization. Examples of these developments are demonstrated by a number of authors in the book by Wexler and Rice (1974). Therapy has changed somewhat, therefore, in giving more emphasis to techniques of facilitating these cognitive processes and the reorganization of experiences. For example, empathic responding is not just seen as a demonstration of the counsellor's attitude, but also serves as a way of helping the person to overcome deficiencies in information processing. Wexler (1974) refers to the role of the counsellor as a 'surrogate information processor'. Empathy is, therefore, given greater priority than previously as a technique for therapeutic change, because it is the only condition that translates directly into overt behaviour and can influence the immediate experience of the person counselled. Wexler also argues that empathy by its nature implies the other two conditions of congruence and unconditional positive regard.

Rogers presented his theories as a basis for development, and not as complete and absolute frameworks. He was at pains to express his ideas tentatively and clearly, pointing out what was unknown or less than certain. He was well aware of attempting to facilitate the scientific process in this way. A clear exposition of the theory and definition of its concepts enables the process of hypothesis testing to occur and hence the further development of the theory. He was careful to relate his propositions to research findings. As a result he actually pre-empted much of the subsequent criticism directed at his work by suggesting, in a footnote to his chapter in 1959, that counsellor characteristics may not be both necessary and sufficient for change to occur and that patient characteristics may be seen as important determinants of therapeutic outcome.

Much of the criticism directed at the theory has been to question whether the counsellor characteristics, or rather the six conditions as a whole, are either necessary or sufficient for the process of change, even though they may be desirable and beneficial. Ellis (1959) for example, suggested that change can occur without contact with another; that incongruence need not be present for change to occur; that counsellors may not be congruent, show unconditional positive regard or empathy and still be beneficial; and that change can occur without the patient perceiving such characteristics in the counsellor.

Undoubtedly Ellis is correct in suggesting that change can occur in the absence of any or all of the conditions. However, people are more likely to change under the conditions posited than without them, and research has shown the benefits (Truax and Carkhuff, 1967). Nevertheless, it is important not only to consider the counsellor, but also the person requiring help. It is not unreasonable, given that people differ so much, that they may respond differently to the same therapeutic conditions. In illustration Patterson (1986) suggested that the person's motivation to change, or actualising tendency, is the only necessary condition for behaviour change, and that this varies greatly and is likely to interact with therapeutic conditions in determining not only the process, but also the outcome of counselling.

Essentially this requires an exploration of individual differences as they relate to process and outcome, and this has been neglected by Rogers and other researchers in this area. In fact, compared to other models, Rogers' theory of personality remains relatively unelaborated. Rachman (1971) actually extended this in saying that an appropriate model, like an analysis of variance, needed to consider not only counsellor and patient characteristics, but also therapeutic techniques, and, perhaps most important for effective understanding, a knowledge of the interaction between these three factors.

In conclusion, although Roger's theory is not the whole story in explaining the helping process, the points made about counsellor characteristics and the relationship with the person seeking help are nevertheless important at all levels. Unconditional positive regard, genuineness and empathy, whatever the nature of the help required, are unlikely to harm and will predictably foster improvements in the professional–patient relationship, thereby enabling better communication and the prospect of more effective help. As Truax and Carkhuff (1967) have said in summarising the research on therapist variables, 'the person (whether a counsellor, therapist or teacher) who is better able to communicate warmth, genuineness and accurate empathy is more effective in interpersonal relationships no matter what the goal of the interaction' (p. 116).

Sigmund Freud

There are many variants of psychoanalysis, but since all derive from the work of Freud, it is his theory that we will describe. His ideas have been elaborated and developed in many different ways, but the foundations of Freud's way of thinking about people are still evident in many specific theories, in many of the assumptions of abnormal psychology and psychiatry, and in Western lay assumptions about human functioning. Such influences can, for example, be seen in the work of Rogers in similarities relating to defence mechanisms and the importance of the therapeutic relationship, albeit used in different ways.

Freud wrote prolifically over a 40-year period beginning at the end of the last century. He was an amazingly creative thinker with enormous courage indicated by his persistence in spite of the antagonism generated towards his ideas. The theory is not simple, and was never systematically written down in one place as a coherent framework, largely because it was ever developing throughout Freud's life. It probably remains, however, the most comprehensive theory ever formulated, potentially giving insights into all areas of psychosocial functioning. His observations on the psychotherapeutic situation are remarkable and he developed important techniques that remain valuable today.

The person

By being biological and deterministic, Freud's view of the person is very different to that of Rogers' or the other models to be presented. His ideas presumably derived from his medical training and the general scientific influences of his day (e.g. notions of energy and steam). Many have argued that his view of the person is belittling and disrespectful, since the individual is passively at the mercy of instinctual drives and irrational and unconscious processes. This is further emphasised in therapy, where the individual is seen as in the hands of the more rational and expert professional. In contrast, some have argued that Freud was very respectful in having a strong belief in the ability of the person to be rational and to triumph over the irrational. As Kline (1984) has said, the individual may be seen as 'an heroic figure who, struggling against a primarily vicious nature, has done surprisingly well' (p. 36).

The person as seen by Freud is a closed energy system fuelled by psychic energy transformed from physical energy. The system is comprised of three parts which are intimately interrelated and ultimately connected to the reality of the outside world. Developmentally the *Id* is the first of these subsystems. It is the inherited part of our behaviour and includes the biological drives or instincts. These energise and direct all actions, the aim of which is the satisfaction of these needs or impulses. The Id is seen as 'a cauldron full of seething emotions' that operate according to the *pleasure principle*. Needs result in excitation or tension that is unpleasant; this sets in motion processes by which tension is reduced and such reduction is perceived as pleasurable. These processes are the *primary processes*, they are inborn and directed towards the immediate satisfaction of needs. They are also seen as completely divorced from the outside world, amoral, and illogical.

The instincts were classified by Freud into two major and opposed groups, *Eros* and *Thanatos*. The former involved the maintenance and preservation of life in general, although a major focus for Freud was the sexual drive, the energy of which was referred to as the *libido*. Thanatos, in contrast, included the urges to restore the person to the inanimate state before life, and therefore involved aggressive self-impulses directed towards the death and destruction of the individual.

The processes of the Id were assumed not to be under conscious control and, in fact, the notion of the unconscious became central to the whole theory. Freud assumed most mental functioning to be unavailable to conscious awareness, either because the processes had never been conscious or because experiences were repressed, or pushed into the unconscious.

The *Ego* is the second subsystem. It was assumed to develop from the Id, and to function as an interface between the Id and reality, constraining or controlling the instinctual impulses. It functions according to the *reality principle*, not the pleasure principle, imposing delays upon need gratification as the result of environmental necessity, although the aim of drive gratification remains the same. The methods by which the Ego operates are called the *secondary processes*, which involve reason and logic, and equate to information processing systems for the evaluation of internal and external experiences. In addition, however, they involve largely unconscious processes by which the person defends against anxiety.

The third subsystem is the *Superego*, which develops from the Ego. It is again assumed to be unconscious and represents the influences of society upon the individual. It incorporates the standards of society, and acts as an overall controller of the amoral Id impulses. It has two components, which may be termed the *Conscience* and the *Ego-ideal*, relating respectively to what one should not do and what is perfection. Freud postulated that the Superego was derived early in life from the parents, with whom the child identified and whose external authority was introjected to form an internal authority or morality.

All adult behaviour is the result of the interaction of these three sub-systems. The Ego mediates between the demands of the outside world and the dictates of the Superego, whilst attempting to gratify the instinctual needs of the Id. However, the whole system is not fully formed at birth. Freud postulated five developmental stages, with the three in the first five years of life given particular significance for the whole of the person's subsequent psychological development. In the absence of strong Ego functioning at this early stage, these stages involved the immediate gratification of components of libidinal impulses, centred at first around the mouth (*Oral stage*), then the anus (*Anal stage*) and then the penis or clitoris (*Phallic stage*). Relative frustration or overindulgence of particular needs (e.g. feeding) were assumed to result in fixations which led to characteristic behaviour thereafter and accounted for personality differences. The *Latency* and *Genital* stages take the child up to adulthood. The former is assumed to be a period in which the libidinal impulses are relatively inactive to surface again in the latter, during adolescence, when sexual and social functioning come together and mature.

The Phallic stage assumed particular importance, because of its relation to the therapy devised by Freud, and the development of the Superego in this period. Essentially this involved the variable resolution of the child's love-hate relationships with the parents (i.e. Oedipus and Electra complexes) by identification with one parent in particular. This identification with, or introjection of, the parent into the psyche formed the basis of the Superego.

This brief overview is not complete without consideration of the concept of anxiety and associated defences. Anxiety was construed as an unpleasant Ego experience, which signalled danger, and which required action to reduce the state of tension by rational or irrational means. Freud identified three types of anxiety: *realistic anxiety* related to environmental dangers; *moral anxiety* involved conflict with the Superego; and *neurotic anxiety* was the fear of Id impulses being sufficiently strong to overwhelm the Ego, thereby finding immediate expression.

A variety of defence mechanisms are postulated as the ways in which the Ego normally deals with much of this anxiety, by unconsciously denying, falsifying or distorting experience. People are assumed to vary in their use of these, depending upon their own developmental fixation points. The most common is *repression*, in which experiences are either made unconscious or prevented from reaching consciousness. *Fixation* is another defence mechanism in which the person remains fixed at a particular point in development and does not move on. *Regression* involves the return to an earlier stage as a way of dealing with current difficulties. *Reaction-formation* is the tendency to defend against anxiety by being or doing the opposite of the impulses provoking the threat, whereas *projection* defends by attributing one's anxiety provoking impulses to external sources such as other people.

Maladjustment

Normal adjustment involves developmental processes in which the individual comes to sexual maturity without major fixations. It is represented by a balance between the three subsystems with an appropriate distribution and redistribution of energy between them. The Ego copes with reality, developing defences to enable the use of Id energy, and to control and juggle the demands of the Id and the Superego, which gives a constructive moral framework.

Maladjusted behaviour or *neurosis* derives from the same processes as described above, and can be understood as an imbalance between the three subsystems of the mind, arising from a number of possible sources. Essentially this implies that adaptation to and enjoyment of life is prevented by a combination of: a) insufficient libidinal energy being made available to the Ego to enable reality based adjustment; b) inhibition of healthy Id pulses; and/or c) over-punitive Superego functioning. For example, the Ego can function inappropriately by having insufficient energy to cope with the demands upon it. This may occur where the individual is blocking energy from the Id by setting up and maintaining strong defences that in themselves require plentiful energy to work. This may be because of the need to repress anxiety provoking impulses and conflicts from the past. As a result, the defences may not be sufficiently strong to block the impulses of the Id, which may overflow into substitute ways of obtaining gratification, producing overtly meaningless behaviour identified as neurotic symptoms.

Therapy

Freud's methods of psychotherapy or *psychoanalysis* are aimed at removing the causes of the neuroses, thereby restoring a balance between the Id, Ego and Superego. This involves removing strong Ego defences, thus freeing more energy for the functioning of the Ego and reducing the power or punitiveness of the Superego. A prerequisite for this is therefore an anslysis of the conflicts that provoked the defence measures in the first place. These are assumed to be unconsciously repressed conflicts that arose from difficulties early in life, and were inappropriately resolved because of the immaturity of the Ego at that time.

The central concern of therapy is therefore to discover these conflicts, bring them to awareness, explore them, and resolve them more effectively than had been the case previously. To do this Freud specified the need for intensive analysis ideally in daily sessions over several years. The patient reclines on a couch in an undistracting room without sight of the analyst, who endeavours to train the person to free associate. This is the technique evolved by Freud to trace the chains of associated meanings from the present back to childhood and the repressed unconscious material. Essentially the patient is required to voice all that comes into his or her head without omission, regardless of its perceived triviality, indecency, hostility, social acceptability or logic. The aim is a gradual reduction of all conscious censorship of the content of the mind.

Another important technique is the analysis of dreams, which are also used as material for free association. Freud believed that dream material was the 'royal road' to the unconscious, because defences were assumed to be more relaxed during sleep than at any other time. As they are assumed to be wish-fulfilling and relatively undisguised, it follows that dream images are close to the latent content of the mind, and therefore evidence of the nature of the conflicts for which the analysis searches.

A major part of therapy is the process of overcoming the patient's resistances. This is not just a matter of reducing the patient's defence mechanisms, and therefore the unwillingness to reproduce repressed material. It also involves overcoming resistance to giving up the gains for the person inherent in the maladaptive behaviour, and his or her resistance to the therapeutic relationship.

The attempt to uncover the unconscious conflicts enmeshes the analyst in the important process of interpretation. The analyst tries to discover the reasons for the person's behaviour. He or she tries to find consistency of meaning and to share this with the patient, with the intention of enabling him or her to develop insight into the problems. Insight is assumed to be the crucial element in making conscious what was previously unconscious, and therefore resolving the conflict. Insight into the *transference relationship* was regarded as particularly important by Freud, as the key to conflict disclosure.

The transference relationship refers to the intense feelings that the patient develops for the therapist out of all proportion to what the situation merits. Freud interpreted his observation of this pattern as a re-creation of the original conflicts which he came to see as related to the way in which the Oedipal complex was resolved in early life. He inferred that the patient transferred feelings from the earlier relationship with the parent onto the therapist. This mirroring, therefore, of the previous and crucial relationship became the focus of therapy. The analysis of the transference was intended to enable insight into the original problem, such that the repressed conflicts could be resolved much more effectively given the relative maturity of adult reasoning compared to that of the child.

Developments and comments

The general framework and many of the concepts have been explored, elaborated and developed by many writers, and not without generating heated controversy (Kline, 1984). Perhaps the most notable variation is the work of Jung, who, like Freud, was also a prolific writer and wide-ranging in his thinking. For example, he put much less emphasis upon the libido. He elaborated a typology of people, contrasting the *introvert* (looking inward) with the *extrovert* (looking outward) and relating these to four styles of thought, including *sensing, feeling, intuiting* and *thinking*. He also conceptualised the mind as having threelayers: the 'persona' (the appearance presented to the outside world), the 'personal unconscious' and the 'collective unconscious'. The latter refers to common human wisdom, partly in the form of archetypes, or basic models.

Another disciple of Freud who went on to develop his own theory was Adler. He rejected the emphasis upon the sexual drive and instead conceptualised basic motivation in the form of an inborn 'inferiority complex', and the consequent drive for superiority. Another influential figure in the USA is Hartmann, who focused more on the Ego, elaborating and exploring Ego functions and proposing the autonomy of the Ego from the Id. The work of Erik Erikson, also classed as an Ego psychologist, is similarly important, since he emphasised the social influences upon the development of the Ego, and outlined a much more detailed set of stages spanning the whole of life. As Kline (1984) argues, a particularly important influence in the UK has been the work of the object relations theorist, Melanie Klein, who emphasised the first months of life and was concerned with the mother-infant relationship. These and other important contributions are well described by Hall and Lindzey (1978).

Freud has had a remarkable influence upon western psychological thinking and the counselling field in particular. The comprehensiveness of his work has been important. The importance given to childhood, the structure of the mind and the elaboration of the concept of the unconscious are a few of the many important theoretical contributions he made. His discovery of the transference relationship and the development of free association have made major contributions to the understanding of ways of helping people change psychologically.

His work generated enormous criticism throughout his life and subsequently. Many of the criticisms, such as the overemphasis upon biological factors, the pessimistic and deterministic nature of the theory, and the neglect of the social and interpersonal aspects of living, have been addressed to a large extent by the theorists mentioned briefly above. Perhaps the most important criticism, however, has been the question of the scientific validity of the theory. Many of the concepts have been criticised on the grounds of clarity of definition and the ability to measure them objectively. Indeed, there are doubts about the internal consistency of the theory as a whole, and the difficulty in testing the theory at all scientifically has been of major concern to modern psychology (Kline, 1984). Nevertheless, the creativity of the theory has to be admired, and it has had enormous heuristic importance to all those concerned with the processes of helping and psychological change.

George Kelly

We have chosen Kelly's theory of personal constructs as our third example because again it has had an important impact in its own right in the USA, the UK, Europe and Australasia, as well as major effects upon many theorists within the field of cognitive-behavioural counselling (Neimeyer, 1986). At the time it was formulated in the 1950s, it represented a novel approach and was an extraordinary example of original creative thinking; a true alternative to the other major approaches. That Patterson (1986) should pay it the compliment of calling both the theory and the therapy unorthodox suggests that this is still the case.

The theory was presented eloquently, formally and systematically in two volumes (Kelly, 1955), and has been discussed extensively since then (e.g. Adams-Webber and Mancuso, 1983; Button, 1985). As Bannister and Fransella (1986) say, it is stated at a very abstract level so as not to limit its application to particular human circumstances. Kelly attempted to define his concepts very clearly and to relate them together systematically, explicitly and consistently. He elaborated the implications of his ideas in ways that are explicit and testable, and provided methods (e.g. the Repertory Grid) for doing so. He also contributed greatly to the practice of counselling by devising valuable and flexible techniques for enabling people to explore and change their lives.

The model is extremely respectful, by being reflexive. It accords similar character to both the person being studied and the psychologist studying him or her, and is applicable to both individually and to the relationship between them. Kelly presented a much more rational view of people than we have seen so far, and the theory has been frequently classified as a cognitive approach. However, Kelly himself denied this by stressing his non-acceptance of the cognitive-emotional dichotomy implicit in the notion of cognition. 'The classic distinction which separates these two constructs has, in the manner of most classic distinctions that once were useful, become a barrier to sensitive, psychological inquiry' (Kelly, 1969, p. 140).

The person

Kelly proposed that the person be construed as a scientist, and the whole of his theory is then an elaboration of this analogy. This includes the notions that the individual in everyday life builds a theory or model of the world, derives hypotheses from the theory, applies them to specific situations, tests them and evaluates the results. Although the individual's theory is unique and personal, and does not necessarily mirror 'reality', it is nevertheless not random or arbitrary, but is constantly subjected to predictive validation and potentially changed. Central to this is the assumption that there are many different ways of conceptualising events and that any particular view can be subjected to change at any time (i.e. *constructive alternativism*).

The basis of the theory is expressed by what Kelly called the Fundamental Postulate, which stated that, 'A person's processes are psychologically channelised by the ways in which he anticipates events' (Kelly, 1955, p. 46). This has a series of implications, the first of which is that the theory is about the person as a whole being, and not about specific aspects such as learning or emotion. The word 'processes' implies that by nature the person is in motion, and does not need to be pulled or pushed by postulating other internal and external forces. Motivation is therefore assumed and it is the direction only that needs to be explained, and this is dealt with by stating that people are directed by their anticipations.

Essentially then the theory is about people striving to obtain a personally meaningful understanding which enables prediction and hence adaptation. This basic notion was further elaborated by a set of corollaries, which we will describe very briefly. Kelly proposed that the basis of the person's ancitipations of future events were the themes or regularities observed in the past (*construction corollary*). He called these 'constructs', since they represented replications of previous events. They were also assumed to be bipolar (*dichotomy corollary*) thereby attributing meaning directly to something, and by reference to its contrast. The patient who uses the construct 'warm' to describe or anticipate the surgeon is also denying whatever is the contrast pole of this construct for that individual. It could, for example, be 'aloof' in the construct 'warm-aloof.'

People may be seen as 'honest–dishonest', 'aggressive–gentle', or 'wears fashionable clothes–shabby'. This is not to say that constructs are conscious verbal labels. They are the meanings attributed to events by the individual, and may include those that cannot be put into words. Since they are bipolar, the person has to make choices about which poles to use in anticipating events, and these are determined by the implications of the choices in defining or elaborating the construct system (*choice corollary*). By 'construct system' we mean the total set of constructs that the person has for the anticipation of all aspects of their world. Each is assumed to be unique, both in quality, content and organization (*individuality corollary*), although there may be similarities between people (*commonality corollary*).

The construct system is organised as a hierarchy (*organisation corollary*) with some constructs more important (*superordinate*) than others by virtue of their power to anticipate those that are *subordinate*. Construing the doctor as 'good' as opposed to 'bad', for example, is superordinate, in that it implies a number of other constructs including 'respectful', 'talks to me', 'is friendly' and 'competent'. However, each construct applies only to certain events/ objects and therefore has a specific *range of convenience* in what it can anticipate (*range corollary*). Some may apply to people, but not fruit, for example; others may apply to children but not adults. It is also possible that individual constructs or subsystems can be applied in isolation, and may not necessarily be compatible in the anticipations derived from them (*fragmentation corollary*).

People gradually change their constructs and the organization of them as a result of the experience of their anticipations being validated or otherwise (*experience corollary*). To some extent this in itself is regulated by the person's construct system, as implied by the choice corollary, in that people will change in ways that make most sense to them personally. Change is also limited, however, by the rigidity or permeability of existing constructs (*modulation corollary*), which refers to the extent to which a construct is able to include in its range of convenience new events, objects or experience.

The final corollary (*sociality*) specifies a major focus of the whole theory and relates to the interaction between people. It states that people can interact only to the extent that they are able to construe the construction processes of the other person. As the starting point for thinking about interaction, it is particularly important for understanding the process of counselling. The implication here is that we cannot interact effectively by simply fitting people into our own ways of seeing things, but we have to try to understand the ways they view the world.

Kelly elaborated these basic statements extensively. He discussed, for example, the ways in which constructs differ. This included the rigidity of their implications, as in propositional constructs which are tentative or hypothetical, as opposed to pre-emptive or constellatory constructs, which specify a more rigid relationship, as in stereotypical thinking. He also elaborated the notion of tight construing, in which anticipations are unvarying, and loose construing, in which predictions vary much more. Another particularly important aspect of the theory is the way in which the concept of emotion is handled (McCoy, 1977). For Kelly emotion is a construct like any other in so far as it is an anticipation of an event. The event in this case, however, is the person's own construing and in particular the anticipation of change. He defined *anxiety*, for example, as the awareness that an event with which one is confronted lies outside the range of convenience of one's construct system. Awareness, therefore, is a construct or discrimination the person is making to note that 'they cannot make sense' as opposed to 'can make sense' of the event in question. Similarly *threat* is defined as the awareness of an imminent comprehensive change in the constructs that are central to our understanding of ourselves (*core role constructs*).

Maladjustment

Psychological distress or disorder is conceptualised in terms of the construction processes outlined above. As Neimeyer (1986) said, at a general level disorder is characterized by the failure of the construct system to accommodate appropriately to changing events in the person's world, even though aspects of the system may have been constantly invalidated. The construct system constrains the person to view the world in a fixed way that does not allow movement or flexibility.

More specifically, many aspects of the construct system and the processes involved in it may be related to problematic behaviour. For example, the individual may deal with anxiety, as defined above by avoiding all instances in which such anxiety might arise, thus preventing the development of an adequate system by decreasing the possibility of validatory or invalidatory experiences. Another possibility is that the process of change is prevented by hostility, which Kelly defined as the effort to extort validational evidence for anticipations that have already failed. This may occur, for instance, when the person acts in ways that make others behave as the individual predicted they would.

It may also be that the structure and content of the system relates to the disorder directly. For example, stutterers may have a well articulated system about themselves as a stutterer, but a much less coherent and meaningful system about themselves as a fluent speaker (Fransella, 1972). People diagnosed as neurotic tend to have a more tightly organised construct system than other people, are polarised in their thinking and intolerant of incompatible constructions. They are also more likely to construe themselves negatively, and opposite to their notion of the ideal or their view of other people, who are seen in a much more favourable light (Winter, 1985).

Therapy

It follows from what has been said that counselling is a process by which the individual's construct system is explored, and an attempt made to produce change in content, use and organization of the construct system. This is done within the counselling relationship using whatever techniques may be useful, selected as theoretically compatible with the aims for the particular person.

Kelly viewed the therapeutic relationship as a partnership akin to that between a research student and academic supervisor. The counsellor has general expertise in defining, exploring and testing hypotheses, and uses this to apply to the specific problem, about which the individual has the greater knowledge and expertise. Like the research student, the person who needs help is seen as in the business of carrying out experiments. In general the approach is non-directive, and 'more invitational and exploratory' (Neimeyer, 1986).

The first task of the counsellor is to find out how the individual construes the world. This involves an *acceptance* of the individual, a willingness to see the world as he or she does and the adoption of what Kelly called 'the credulous approach'. This is a fundamental attitude of assuming the importance of the individual's views and accepting, at least temporarily, the intrinsic truth of these regardless of the reality or, more accurately, the views of others, including the counsellor.

Along with assessment, the second general role of the counsellor is to help the individual to set up hypotheses (based upon present constructs), to design and conduct tests of these and to evaluate the results. Neimeyer (1986) used the term 'collaborative empiricism' to describe this role relationship, within which the counsellor also has a direct validational function. Like Freud, Kelly refers to the transference relationship, but uses the term more simply to signify the individual's use of previously developed constructs to anticipate the counsellor's behaviour. Therefore, by acting in a variety of different ways the counsellor can serve to validate or invalidate these views, as is thought necessary, with the possibility of the person changing these constructs, which will then have implications for anticipating other significant people in their lives.

Experiments are set up to enable a variety of changes, including 'slot changes' at the simplest level. The aim here is not to change construct content, but to change their use. For example, the chronically ill person may be helped to view himself or herself as 'of some value to the family' as opposed to 'of no value' on the construct 'valuable–not valuable'. Alternatively, the counsellor may help the person to change a construct entirely, not just the pole that is chosen. This involves a process of reinterpretation, as in the case of a mother observing her son closely, and as a result changing her construction of him from 'deliberately disobedient' to 'does not understand what she requires of him'.

Other strategies include developing constructs to anticipate events not previously understood properly by the individual, or attempting to make implicit, pre-verbal constructs explicit. Inconsistent constructs may be integrated. The predictive validity of a construct or system of constructs may be systematically tested. The range of applicability of constructs may be altered and their meanings changed by alterations in the relationships between constructs.

The techniques used depend upon the constructions of the individual, the requirements for change and the stage in the process. In theory there is an infinite range, with possibilities limited only by the knowledge and ingenuity of the counsellor and individual. Methods may be derived from all other types of counselling or invented for the particular circumstances at the time. The choice is not a random matter, but, like the design of an experiment, is a question of theoretical consistency with the requirements of the hypothesis being tested.

One frequently used technique is *enactment*. This is basically role-playing, and varies from spontaneous short role-plays between the individual and counsellor, to longer term enactments in daily life. This is called *fixed role therapy*, and involves the person in playing a role carefully formulated by the counsellor from a self-characterization written by the individual. This is a short sketch, written in the third person, where the individual describes himself or herself from the point of view of a sympathetic and intimate friend. The characterization sketch is analysed to determine the major constructs used by the person. A new sketch is then written to change the constructs, not to the opposite of those used, but to represent a related but different viewpoint, at 45 degrees, as it were, to the original.

This new character is negotiated and changed as necessary to be plausible and acceptable to the individual. With support and help, the person then takes on the role, and acts as though he or she were this new person for two to three weeks, at the end of which the role is put aside. Essentially, the aim is to enable the person to see that there are alternative ways of viewing themselves and all other aspects of their world and that they can change if they wish. It is also an experiment, or perhaps a concentrated set of experiments in which the person can explore different viewpoints and their implications.

Developments and comments

At its birth Kelly's theory was highly elaborated and perhaps, as Patterson (1986) notes, the most systematic of all available theories. Although stated relatively simply at one level, at another its complexity is enormous, requiring very careful study. Its originality and uniqueness make it somewhat difficult to grasp, not to mention the redefinition of commonly used concepts to be consistent with the theory. Nevertheless, it is worthy of careful study, and will be of enormous value heuristically for many years to come.

To date there has been considerable theoretical discussion (e.g. Bannister, 1977; Adams-Webber and Mancuso, 1983). However, although aspects of the theory have been elaborated (e.g. Hinckle, 1965; McCoy, 1977) there have been no fundamental changes to the theory as originally proposed. A wealth of empirical publications have appeared, some applying the theory directly, but many more using the assessment methods devised by Kelly and elaborated by others subsequently. In particular, the use of repertory grid technique has proliferated (e.g. Fransella and Bannister, 1977; Beail, 1985) in a variety of settings, with extensive developments in multivariate analyses of the resulting data (Slater, 1976).

Perhaps because of the complexity of the theory, as Patterson (1986) has argued, there are relatively few people practising personal construct counselling. Nevertheless, there is a growing movement and the theory is used therapeutically in innovative and beneficial ways (e.g. Epting, 1984), and has had a very wide influence upon counselling generally, and especially upon the cognitive approaches to be illustrated next. However, the approach has not been without its critics. Wessler (1986) for example, has questioned Kelly's notion of the person as a scientist on the grounds that scientists do not have to act on their theories and do not necessarily apply what they know and do to the real world. He has suggested an alternative model of the person as a manager, since the manager not only requires knowledge, but must act upon it to plan and make decisions.

Albert Ellis

The cognitive-behavioural theories can be seen as a welcome synthesis of many diverse frameworks and are arguably the most dominant force in current counselling (Smith, 1982). These theories differ considerably, as described in Dryden and Golden (1986), but they share many common assumptions and are sufficiently similar to be grouped together. The major assumption is that all behaviour, adaptive or otherwise, is the result of underlying schemata. These are more or less conscious, enduring cognitive structures, mental activity or information processing systems. The term cognition is somewhat vaguely defined but refers variously to conceptions, ideas, meanings, beliefs, thoughts, inferences, expectations, predictions, or attributions. These are assumed to mediate all behaviour directly, including emotional expression, and are the major focus for change in counselling.

Cognitions are assumed to vary from individual to individual and are acquired throughout the course of life. This includes the possibility of there being cognitions derived from early childhood experiences that nevertheless exert strong influences upon the person as an adult. In general the assumption is that disordered behaviour results from inadequacies in cognitive processes, and counselling is therefore concerned with identifying, exposing and changing these. This includes changing false assumptions, irrational conclusions, absolutest thinking, inaccuracies and misconceptions, so that the person thinks, feels and behaves on a more rational basis.

The theory chosen to represent this general approach and described here is that of Ellis. He was one of the very early contributors to cognitive-behaviour therapy. Although trained as a psychoanalyst, he is another therapist who came to reject this approach and went on to develop what has become known as rational-emotional therapy (RET).

The person

Ellis views people as fundamentally goal-directed, 'happiest when they establish important life-goals and purposes and actively strive to attain these' (Dryden and Ellis, 1986, p. 132). Although cognition is accorded particular importance in human functioning, it is seen as interacting with emotion, behaviour, and events that activate the person's reactions. He also views the person as somewhat irrational in thinking and believes this to be a biologically determined tendency. However, this is contrasted with a second biological tendency, which involves the ability of people to choose how to think and behave, in the sense of being able to see that they may be irrational, to know they can change such thinking, and to strive to do something about it.

Ellis's concept of cognition is largely concerned with evaluative thought expressed as *rational* and *irrational beliefs*. These are both evaluative, but the former are considered helpful and do not interfere in people's achievement of their goals. They are also preferential or relative, and not absolute. In contrast, irrational beliefs are defined as interfering with the pursuit and attainment of goals and they tend to be absolute and obligatory.

Maladjustment

Disturbed behaviour is largely underpinned by irrational beliefs. Although there may be many behavioural variants of disturbance, Ellis postulates two major categories. The first is *ego disturbance*, in which the person comes to have a global negative self-image, which is irrational, and therefore absolute and unhelpful to goal attainment. This contrasts with the more adaptive alternative of self-acceptance, involving more differentiated self-perceptions (including the negative) and a more relative stance that does not interfere with the individual's aims in life. The second category of disorder is called *discomfort disturbance*. Here the individual is unable to tolerate the frustration of immediate gratification, even though such discomfort might enable goal attainment in the long term.

Each individual problem is conceptualised in terms of what is called an 'expanded ABC framework.' In this model, the A refers to activating or antecedent events. Although these can be actual events in the environment relevant to the attainment of goals, they may also be present or past thoughts, emotions or behaviours. Bs are defined as beliefs about the activating events, and mediate between these events and their consequences, Cs. These beliefs may be simple or single, but are more likely to exist in a chain of related beliefs. They are all rational, irrational or irrelevant, depending upon their relativeness. They include direct *observations* and *inferences*, both of which may be evaluative or not, depending upon their relevance to the individual's goals. They also include *preferential* and what Ellis called *musturbatory evaluations*, both of which can be positive or negative. The former are rational (i.e. relative and helpful in goal attainment) whereas the latter are irrational, and therefore absolute and unhelpful. The latter are also likely to be associated with inferences that are erroneous, including over-generalisations, delusions of certainty, non-sequiturs and focusing upon the negative.

In its simplest form, it is assumed in the model that Cs follow from activating events and the individual's beliefs about them. These consequences can be cognitive, emotional, behavioural or combinations of these. It is again assumed that there can be chains of consequences, such that states like depression or anxiety can arise. Anger may be included here as an important feature, as well as drug and alcohol abuse, for example, and many other problems. The actual relationships, however, between As, Bs and Cs is much more complex and interactive than stated here, but the model serves to clarify what might otherwise be impossible to untangle.

Therapy

The aim of counselling is to help people to identify irrational beliefs, to challenge them and to replace them with rational beliefs, so that they can be more accepting of themselves and successfully follow long-term goals while tolerating unchangeable life conditions. Additionally the counsellor aims to facilitate the individual's acquisition of the necessary skills to help prevent the occurrence of future problems.

The role of the counsellor is not dissimilar to that of 'an authoritative (but not authoritarian!) and encouraging teacher' (Dryden and Ellis, 1986). Although the counsellor takes a very active and directive role, Ellis nevertheless assumes the importance of therapeutic conditions similar to those of Rogers. He believes that the counsellor should attempt to accept the person unconditionally, to be open and genuine in the counselling session, and to be empathic both with respect to the person's feelings and, of course, their cognitive functioning.

He also suggests the need for appropriate humour and informality. This follows from the belief that people who are disturbed tend to take themselves too seriously, and the counsellor attempts, therefore, to provide a model that is lighter and counters this. On the other hand, he argues for not showing excessive warmth for most people, on the grounds that this may make people feel better, without enabling their irrational beliefs to be challenged appropriately and changed. It is also believed to reinforce low frustration tolerance which is related to comfort disturbance mentioned earlier.

A major vehicle for enabling change is the technique of disputing irrational beliefs. This includes: *detecting* or looking for beliefs that are self-defeating; *debating*, in which the counsellor asks questions designed to dispute the evidence for and validity of irrational beliefs; *discriminating* or helping the person to see the difference between absolute and relative preferential beliefs; and *defining*, where the person is helped to specify beliefs more accurately. Counsellors may also use methods to make the person repeat or generally think about rational self-statements at regular intervals during their daily lives, and may use bibliotherapy, in which people are encouraged to read potentially useful books. Role-playing is common, especially where the counsellor adopts the person's irrational beliefs and the person then tries to dispute them (*rational role reversal*). *Shame-attacking exercises* are used, where people behave in ways they believe to be silly, while still thinking well of themselves, and a wide variety of behavioural techniques, including in vivo desensitization, methods to facilitate discomfort tolerance, skill training and rewards to maintain the various programmes.

Developments and comments

There is no doubt that the work of Ellis and other cognitive theorists has made an extremely valuable contribution to the understanding and practice of counselling, and these approaches have been widely adopted. Their popularity relates to the fact that they are applicable to a wide range of problems. The approach is based upon relatively parsimonious and simple theory, and it generates a wide range of very practical methods, because of its technical eclecticism. Its appeal may also be related to the feeling of potency given to the practitioner. The counsellor is potentially able to feel confident in knowing how to help a large number of people with many different problems, given the variety of specific techniques to be tried.

In its emphasis upon techniques, the approach is very different to that of Rogers, for example. It is similar to Kelly's approach in its technical eclecticism, although it is much simpler in explaining disturbance. Unlike these theories, however, there is more of a tendency to impose a model of disturbance upon the person who needs help, and less emphasis is given to the expertise of the individual in contributing to their own development. The individual's own explanation of the problem is given less significance, and the counsellor's expertise is implied to be somewhat superior, in, for example, his or her logical reasoning. It could be predicted, therefore, that to an extent the cognitive approach may be more likely to undermine the individual's self-efficacy, unless careful attention is given to this. Indeed, considerable attention is given by Ellis and others to the notion of *resistance*, which may arise from the fact that the counsellor is more actively in the business of selling a viewpoint to the person.

These theories warrant considerable study. They are of particular interest in their clarity and diversity of concepts, and are expressed in ways that foster the possibilities of useful research to test and hopefully aid in the development of counselling theory generally. The valuable generation of practical techniques to enable people to change is a major asset of the cognitive approach, and will no doubt be important in creating further hypotheses about change processes, and hence in the future development of our understanding of counselling.

Gerard Egan

The final approach to be described is that of Gerard Egan (1982). Its importance relates to the fact that it has synthesized many of the ideas originally expressed in the counselling literature with those from more diverse areas of psychology, and it is therefore often described as eclectic. Egan,

nevertheless, owns to a strong acceptance of behavioural principles as developed by Skinner and modified by the more cognitive orientations we
have just described.

His model is abstract, yet extremely practical, encompassing a description
and justification of both the qualities of good counsellors and the processes
by which change occurs within counselling. An extremely attractive feature
of the theory is that Egan expressed the framework succinctly, clearly and
systematically in one place, and then elaborated it in detail subsequently. Its
clarity and simplicity not only provide direct guidance for counsellors, it
also gives a very useful framework upon which counsellor training can be
based.

Egan describes his approach as a problem-management model, applicable
to any context in which people need help. It is, therefore, not limited to the
psychological realm, but can easily encompass the situation of general
health care. The approach is essentially a very general framework for helping, or more accurately for helping people to *help themselves*.

The person

Egan has not elaborated a systematic model of the person. The focus of the
theory is upon the process of helping. He does, however, make some explicit
assumptions that are not unlike Wessler's (1986) model, mentioned earlier,
of the person as *manager*. A very respectful stance is taken in that people are
assumed to be responsible for their own behaviour and situation. The implication is that you cannot solve people's problems, but only help them to
do so. It is also assumed that people are essentially capable, even if they
appear otherwise. Their capacity is seen as hindered by a lack of *working
knowledge* in dealing with their problems, together with experiences that
have taught them that they are relatively helpless and their self-defeating
beliefs about themselves. Bandura's (1989) notion of *self-efficacy* is influential
in that individuals are assumed to seek help when they believe themselves
incapable of solving current problems.

Helping

Since the aim of counselling is to help people to manage their problems
more effectively, at a fundamental level, this must involve strengthening
their beliefs in themselves and their expectations of success. This may be
achieved by helping them gain some success, modelling potential strategies,
encouraging and supporting their efforts and reducing their anxieties.
However, another important aim is to help people achieve clear models by
which they can pursue specific courses of action with prerequisite information and skills and then evaluate the outcomes.

Following the image of the individual as a manager, the counsellor is seen as a consultant, whose attributes include being fit, intelligent, socially skilled, pragmatic, hard-working, respectful, genuine and flexible, with a thorough working knowledge of the processes of helping. The relationship between the counsellor and individual is one of participation as opposed to direction. The consultant may adopt a variety of roles, including listening, teaching, challenging, supporting and advising, but never takes over re-sponsibility. Egan does, however, acknowledge the social influence of the counsellor upon the individual, but emphasises the need for this to be to-wards independence and self-responsibility. He also emphasises the need for clarity in the relationship from the beginning, arguing for an explicit contract, with implications for negotiation and agreement, commitment on both sides, and the regular review and potential revision of the contract.

Egan describes the process of helping as three stages, each of which makes specific requirements upon the participants. The model is hierarchical in that each stage builds upon what has been established at the previous level.

Stage one: problem clarification: The aim of this stage is to explore the present-ing problem from the individual's viewpoint. It is crucial to begin with a knowledge of the sense that people make of their own situation. The helper's understanding is not so important at this stage. Allowing the person to outline these feelings takes time, because the problems may be complex, the person may not have a clear view of the problem, and the initial problem may not be the central concern of the individual. People frequently present relatively minor problems or only part of the difficulty as a way of testing to see whether the helper can be trusted. As this implies, the relationship between the person and helper is of central importance, and the aims of this and all subsequent stages are only likely to be achieved to the extent that a good working relationship is initially built and subsequently strengthened.

To realise the aims of problem exploration and relationship building, particular helper skills and qualities are required. These include what Egan described as foundational qualities of respect, genuineness, spontaneity, and openness to the experiences of the person wanting help. Like all the other characteristics to be described, these must be demonstrated not just as-sumed. They are attitudes in the sense used by Rogers, of a general stance taken towards the person to be helped, and manifest in all that the helper says and does. Therefore, respect, for example, may be shown by valuing people, accepting and not judging them, working hard on their behalf, not manipulating them, and acting in a completely confidential way. Such re-spect is endorsed by the failure of outcome research to find differences as a function of therapy type, format, and duration, which prompted Smith *et al.* (1980) to say, 'The possibility ought to be considered more seriously that the locus of those forces that restore and ameliorate the client of psychotherapy reside more within the client himself and less within the therapist and his actions' (p. 188).

These fundamental qualities will also be shown by the other important helper skills, including *attending*, or being completely with the person during the session, *active listening*, and *empathy*. There is also a need for the skills of *probing* and appropriate *responding*, to enable the person to talk freely, and to explore problems in ways that enable them to be made relatively specific and concrete.

Stage two: setting goals: The aim of this stage is to achieve a clear overview of the individual's problems, so as to set goals. In some cases it will be easy to gain a clear picture by simply listening. However, in other instances this may not happen. The person may have taken too narrow a view of the situation, or have a distorted or inaccurate picture. Some people generate several different and alternative explanations for their situation; some have no explanation at all: and others have models that have no implications whatsoever for how to begin to tackle the problem. In all these instances the task of the helper is to enable the individual to develop a more useful understanding of their situation, involving greater accuracy and objectivity.

Once this has been done, it serves as the basis for the next step, which is to help the person to decide what he or she would like to achieve by way of management. This may involve setting a single goal or a series of sub-goals leading to a final desired outcome. In either case the role of the counsellor is to help the person formulate goals that are clear, specific, measurable, realistic, adequate, owned by the person and time-limited.

At this stage of the process, Egan specifies the need for all the skills and qualities of the previous stage, as well as some that are more specific to Stage Two. Firstly the counsellor must have the ability to take in and put together the model of the situation that has been entrusted to him or her by the individual. This is the whole picture involving the individual, his or her behaviour, feelings, thoughts, other people, and the context. Secondly, there is a need for what Egan calls *challenging skills*, whose aim is to help the person to change their current views. They are meant to challenge the model presented by the individual in a way that enables alternatives to develop. *Information-giving* is one of these skills that has obvious implications for change. *Summarising* is another in which the helper puts together the main features of what the person has said as a precis for the person's comment. Other skills include *accurate advanced empathy*, the ability to express what the person implies but does not say; *confrontation*, where the counsellor directly changes discrepancies in the person's views; *self-disclosure*, where the counsellor presents his or her own experiences for the person to consider; and *immediacy*, where the counsellor directly discusses the relationship between himself or herself and the individual. The final group of skills described in relation to this stage are those to do with *goal-setting*.

Stage three: facilitating action: The aims of this stage are to help the person to plan ways of achieving the goals set in the previous stage, to help him or her to carry out these plans and to evaluate the outcomes. There are always a variety of ways of reaching specific goals, and the task is, therefore, to think of them all, to make a careful selection, to foresee the difficulties, to prepare the person appropriately, and provide support and encouragement while they are carried out. Evaluation is not necessarily the end of the process, but the point at which stock is taken of achievements. It may be, for example, the beginning of a loop back to any of the previous stages, in that both success and failure have implications for a better understanding of the problem, a change of goal, or a change in the means by which the goal is to be achieved.

Again this stage requires all the helper skills of the previous stages, plus those specific to Stage Three. The first set Egan calls *programme-development skills.* These involve the skills of helping the individual to think of all the possible means of reaching the goals, and requires creativity, thinking broadly and brainstorming. The counsellor must also be able to help the individual to evaluate all the possibilities and select the best option or combination. The second set are *facilitating-action skills*, which involve helping the person to make whatever preparations are necessary to carry out the plans. This includes trying to consider the likely difficulties to be encountered and helping the individual to acquire the necessary information or skills to do what they have decided. Supporting individuals in their subsequent efforts involves various abilities, but particularly encouragement, valuing them, and challenging them to look at what is happening. The last skills are to do with *evaluation.* These operate throughout this stage in helping the individual monitor progress. They include helping people to consider the quality of their participation, the adequacy of their decided course of action and the adequacy of the goals so far as they relate to changing the initiating problem.

Comments

Unlike the models previously described, Egan does not make assumptions about psychological disorder, the reasons for problems or the ways of dealing with them. Nor does he propose an explicit model of personality. It is a framework for making sense of the process of helping people regardless of the content of their problem, be it psychosocial or physical, present or future, pleasant or unpleasant. The criteria for helping are simply the acknowledgement by the individual of a problem and the desire for help.

Although it can be seen as a failing, not to make such things explicit, it can also be an attribute in that it allows the incorporation of other models. One can, for example, within the framework see the individual through the eyes of Rogers, Freud or Kelly, if it is thought useful. One might employ any or all of these models at various times as a way of developing different perspectives that might benefit the individual seeking help.

In the same way, the framework does not specify the techniques by which problems may be either assessed or resolved. By the abstract nature of the model, methods for assessing and dealing with specific problems will be generated according to the problem, the resources, values and characteristics of the individual, and the goals selected. A huge variety of possible ways of helping the person explore their situation may be relevant, from observation to specific tests. Any or all of the therapeutic techniques of other models may be used, if the problems are specifically social and psychological, although the possible range of actions for solving problems is infinite.

Egan regards his ideas as a tool or framework to help people to consider counselling, which is undoubtedly complex. As is clear from the different theories available, counselling can be approached from many viewpoints and can lead to many different types of helping activity. What the present framework does is, not to provide an alternative to other approaches, but to offer a structure for considering them all. It provides a guide for critical thinking, a way of organising other approaches, and a means of using any one or all of them as may be felt necessary to accomplish the basic aim of helping.

As Egan himself comments, his framework is not to be used rigidly. It is intended as a means of helping and guiding counsellors, and not as a structure for constraining and dominating them. He cautions against the mechanical use of the model, since in specific instances the real situation may not be as differentiated as the model suggests and the sequences may not be as straightforward. It does not include a timetable, nor tell one when to move from stage to stage. The stages may also not be as orderly as described. This can be true, for example, when the person has multiple problems, each of which may be at a different stage at any one time. Nevertheless, to judge by the growing popularity of the framework, it would seem to be meaningful and useful to many people in a variety of settings.

CONCLUSIONS

We began this chapter by discussing the definition of counselling, and concluded that it related to a range of activities in which one person agreed to provide help for one or more other people. At one end of this range are specialists whose role is to help people with psychosocial adaptation. At the other end are all health care professionals, such as physicians, health visitors or physiotherapists, whose role is primarily to provide specialist technical physical help, but who also need appropriate basic counselling skills to do their job effectively. Although their aim might be to treat cancer, there is still the need to relate to the patient effectively, to explore and clarify the problem from the patient's viewpoint, negotiate and set aims, support the person through the appropriate treatment and evaluate the outcome: all while helping him or her to retain dignity.

The chapter continued by considering different theoretical models. Four of these, by Rogers, Freud, Kelly and Ellis, are psychological in the sense that they were created to understand and help people with psychological and social problems. Each remains in current use and has added enormously to the general understanding of the provision of psychological help. Rogers has told us a great deal about the importance of counsellor characteristics in the establishment of an effective relationship and in enabling change to occur. Freud has not only demonstrated the importance of the relationship, but has made us focus upon the significance of events in terms of the unconscious meanings underlying behaviour. The possibility that people may do things for reasons other than those of which they are aware is stressed by this approach.

Kelly has given us a picture of the complexity of individuals and the importance of understanding the ways in which people make sense of themselves and all other aspects of their psychological, social and physical world. He has also given us a view of the creativeness of change and the helping process. Ellis and other cognitive theorists have elaborated the extent to which irrational cognition occurs and the relationship between such information processing and psychological disturbance.

All these approaches and many others have contributed in a general way to theory, and in the suggestion and formulation of specific techniques related both to assessment and to the treatment of psychosocial problems. The question remains, however, about the extent to which these frameworks contribute to the more general concern of this book, which is overall health care, encompassing physical, as well as the psychological well-being.

This is the concern of the rest of the book, and therefore we will restrict ourselves to only a few general remarks at this point. Our view is that each of these models informs us about the helping process no matter what the specific concern of the patient. It can be argued that much illness has causal elements that are psychological, as in behaviour that is dangerous in itself (e.g. smoking, careless driving) or in living under stressful conditions. As we have seen, health care personnel, such as GPs, are faced with many people who have predominantly psychosocial problems and are not physically ill. Even when there is physical illness, however, there are always psychological and social consequences requiring attention from those providing help. Since all physical illness occurs in people who are functioning psychologically, all the models described are relevant in a very general and basic way to all professionals in health care. The endeavour of relating to patients, communicating with them and treating them is inherently psychological. Roger's therapeutic characteristics, for example, may be sensibly heeded by all workers, who would also gain by understanding the conceptual frameworks patients use for making sense of what is happening to them (see Kelly).

We think that Egan's framework is particularly important to the general health care setting because of its pragmatism. His model is clear and systematic, and integrates many of the ideas of the other models, or allows the use of such models as necessary. One of its most attractive features is that it does not focus upon problems that are exclusively psychological. Its concern is with helping people no matter what the problem, be it psychological, social, spiritual or physical, in the present or in the future. Therefore Egan's eclectic approach is applicable to the endeavours of the physician as much as the nurse, or the psychologist. It provides a model for enabling all to understand the skills and processes operating in the situation where one person requires help, of any kind, from another, who agrees to try. It relates as much to the GP prescribing antibiotics for an infection as to the preventive situation of helping people to change their behaviour or diet in order to avoid future disease.

This model acknowledges naturally enough the need for specialist and technical information in relation to the aetiology, pathology, natural history, assessment and treatment of disease. Needless to say, such information will vary to some extent depending upon the type of patient and type of disease being treated. The model does not limit technique. It allows for the use of techniques from chemotherapy and surgery, to dietary control and exercise. It allows for physical techniques to control pain just as much as relaxation training and reinforcement schedules, or the plethora of other psychological methods for relationship problems, sexual difficulties, anxiety or depression.

However, the model does propose that the application of all such information and technique is dependent upon the professional understanding the process of helping and having the appropriate helping or counselling skills available. The implication is that if these are missing, then specialists will be seriously limited in the extent to which their expertise is of benefit. It can certainly be argued that even if specialists are able to dispense their wares, the help provided will still be narrow. 'Unfortunately, professionals may be effective in delivering the technical services of their own profession and still be deficient in terms of the human encounters involved. If they are helpers in the sense in which this term is being used in this book and not just good technicians, they deal with their clients from a holistic perspective, helping them to face crisis situations resourcefully as full human beings' (Egan, 1982, p. 4).

The model proposes the need for respect, empathy, and listening skills, not only to establish a relationship, but also to enable the problem, whatever it is, to be explored adequately and clarified appropriately. If there is to be an effective exchange of information, there needs to be a mutually respectful relationship between the professional and the individual, who must work together as partners. This is necessary to enable the negotiation of aims, creation of action, encouragement and support of what the patient must do, and evaluation of outcome, all of which also requires the skills and qualities described in this chapter.

Given the inadequacies in medical communication behaviour, it is reasonable to conclude that many of Egan's qualities and knowledge of the helping process are absent from a large proportion of those currently working in health care. It follows, therefore, that the systematic application of such a counselling model would be expected to change professional behaviour appropriately and improve many of the problems identified earlier. We will explore these propositions and their implications in the remainder of the book, beginning with a look at a number of specialist areas in the next section.

REFERENCES

Abel Smith, A., Irving, J., and Brown, P. (1989). Counselling in the medical context. In W. Dryden, D. Charles-Edwards, and R. Woolff (Eds), *Handbook of counselling in Britain*. London: Tavistock/Routledge.

Adams-Webber, J. and Mancuso, J. (1983). *Applications of personal construct theory.* Toronto: Academic Press.

Bandura, A. (1989). Perceived self-efficacy in the exercise of personal agency. *The Psychologist*, **12**, 411–424.

Bannister, D. (1977). *New perspectives in personal construct theory.* London: Academic Press.

Bannister, D. and Fransella, F. (1986). *Inquiring man.* London: Croom Helm.

Beail, N. (1985). *Repertory grid technique and personal constructs: Applications in clinical and educational settings.* London: Croom Helm.

British Association for Counselling (1989). *Invitation to membership.* Rugby: BAC.

Button, E. (1985). *Personal construct theory and mental health.* London: Croom Helm.

Dryden, W. and Ellis, A. (1986). Rational-Emotive Therapy (RET). In W. Dryden and W. Golden (Eds), *Cognitive-behavioural approaches to psychotherapy.* London: Harper & Row.

Dryden, W. and Golden, W. (1986). *Cognitive-behavioural approaches to psychotherapy.* London: Harper & Row.

Egan, G. (1982). *The skilled helper.* Monterey: Brooks/Cole.

Ellis, A. (1959). Requisite conditions for basic personality change. *Journal of Consulting Psychology*, **23**, 538–549.

Epting, F. (1984). *Personal construct counseling and psychotherapy.* Chichester: Wiley.

Fransella, F. (1972). *Personal change and reconstruction.* London: Academic Press.

Fransella, F. and Bannister, D. (1977). *A manual of repertory grid technique.* London: Academic Press.

Gibran, K. (1980). *The prophet.* London: Heinemann.

Hall, C. and Lindzey, G. (1978). *Theories of personality.* Chichester: Wiley.

Hinckle, D. (1965). *The change of personal constructs from the viewpoint of a theory of implications.* Unpublished PhD thesis, Ohio State University.

Kelly, G. (1955). *The psychology of personal constructs.* New York: Norton.

Kelly, G. (1969). Humanistic methodology in psychological research. In B. Maher (Ed.), *Clinical psychology and personality: Selected papers of George Kelly.* London: Wiley.

Kline, P. (1984). *Psychology and freudian theory.* London: Methuen.

Lipkin, M., Quill, T., Napodano, J., *et al.* (1984). The medical interview; a core curriculum for residencies in internal medicine. *Annals of Internal Medicine*, **100**, 277–284.

Massie, M., Holland, J., and Straker, N. (1989). Psychotherapeutic interventions. In J. Holland and J. Rowland (Eds), *Handbook of psychooncology*. New York: Oxford University Press.

McCoy, M. (1977). A reconstruction of emotion. In D. Bannister (Ed.), *New perspectives in personal construct theory*. London: Academic Press.

Neimeyer, R.A. (1986). Personal construct therapy. In W. Dryden and W. Golden (Eds), *Cognitive-behavioural approaches to psychotherapy*. London: Harper & Row.

Nelson-Jones, R. (1983). *Practical counselling skills*. New York: Holt, Rinehart & Winston.

Patterson, C. (1986). *Theories of counselling and psychotherapy*. New York: Harper & Row.

Rachman, S. (1971). *The effects of psychotherapy*. Oxford: Pergamon Press.

Rogers, C. (1959). A theory of therapy, personality, and interpersonal relationships, as developed in the client-centered framework. In S. Koch (Ed.), *Psychology: A study of a science*. New York: McGraw-Hill.

Slater, P. (1976). *The measurement of intrapersonal space by grid technique*. London: Wiley.

Smith, D. (1982). Trends in counselling and psychotherapy. *American Psychologist*, **37**, 802–809.

Smith, M., Glass, G., and Miller, T. (1980). *The benefits of psychotherapy*. Baltimore: Johns Hopkins University Press.

Spiegel, D., Bloom, J., and Yalom, I. (1981). Group support for patients with metastatic cancer: a randomised prospective study. *Archives of General Psychiatry*, **38**, 527–533.

Truax, C. and Carkhuff, R. (1967). *Toward effective training in counseling and psychotherapy*. Chicago: Aldine.

Wessler, R.L. (1986). Conceptualizing cognitions in the cognitive-behavioural therapies. In W. Dryden and W. Golden (Eds), *Cognitive-behavioural approaches to psychotherapy*. London: Harper & Row.

Wexler, D. (1974). A cognitive theory of experiencing self-actualization and therapeutic process. In D. Wexler and L. Rice (Eds), *Innovations in client-centered therapy*. New York: Wiley.

Wexler, D. and Rice, L. (1974). *Innovations in client-centered therapy*. New York: Wiley.

Winter, D. (1985). Neurotic disorders: The Curse of certainty. In E. Button (Ed.), *Personal construct theory and mental health*. London: Croom Helm.

Yalom, I. (1989). *Loves executioner and other tales of psychotherapy*. London: Bloomsbury.

Section II

SPECIALIST AREAS

3 The Role and Development of Counselling Skills in General Practice

JOHN WEINMAN AND ROY GOULSTON
Unit of Psychology, The Medical School,
Guy's Hospital, London SE1 9RT

INTRODUCTION

For many GPs, the recent emergence and popularity of counselling has been timely and welcome. Modern general practice is evolving in its approaches to patients and to postgraduate training, and counselling methods have become an integral part of this process. Driven by a dissatisfaction with the older doctor-centred model of patient care, many GPs have been positively influenced by social and psychological approaches to the understanding of health and illness and have sought to develop different ways of working with patients. Counselling, with its emphasis on active listening, empathy and shared decision-making has influenced and facilitated these recent developments.

This chapter consists of three related sections. The first sets the scene by discussing the context of general practice and its suitability for different types of counselling work. The second section provides examples of different applications of counselling approaches by GPs and other health professionals in primary care. In the final section there is a consideration of the involvement and training of GPs in counselling, followed by a discussion of the role of different health professionals and of the efficacy of counselling in general practice.

THE GENERAL PRACTICE CONTEXT

The most obvious aspect of a GP's work is the very wide range of problems seen, which means that the GP must use listening skills in order to be open to all possibilities with each new consultation. Thus, in current approaches to training in general practice, an increasing importance is attached to identifying patients' own views of their problems as an essential component of a successful consultation (Pendleton *et al.*, 1984).

Counselling and Communication in Health Care. Edited by H. Davis and L. Fallowfield
© 1991 John Wiley & Sons Ltd

A second important characteristic of general practice is that a very signifi-cant proportion of patients present with psychological problems or with physical complaints which have clear psychological facets (e.g. Williams and Clare, 1979; Gray, 1988). However, many GPs are still not very skilled at either detecting or managing these problems (Goldberg *et al.*, 1982). There is also recent evidence that patients do not necessarily see their GP as the best person to manage these sorts of problems (Salmon and Quine, 1989; Wein-man and Hough, 1986). Despite this, the GP is ideally placed to pick up psychological problems when patients first present and current training in general practice emphasises the development of listening and counselling skills as a critical part of the GP's role.

A third important characteristic of the GP's work stems from the fact that most people seek their help on a few occasions each year. This means that many GPs will know a great deal about their patients, their families and the circumstances in which they live, including any current crises. Thus the GP is well placed not only to sense whether a particular patient might need extended counselling, but also whether they would be likely to benefit. It may also be possible to identify individuals who are at risk of psychological distress because of their difficult circumstances (e.g. caring for a dependent relative) or because of a distressing event (e.g. bereavement) and to use counselling preventively.

APPLICATIONS OF COUNSELLING IN GENERAL PRACTICE

It should be clear from the preceding section that GPs have an opportunity to use counselling skills in every consultation. However, since it is beyond the scope of this paper to overview all the many problems and different applications of counselling in general practice, four contrasting areas will be outlined.

Managing patients with social and emotional problems

Many patients present to GPs with clear psychological problems or with physical symptoms which may reflect difficulties in coping with current life stresses. If they see the GP at a relatively early stage, appropriate help may enable them to avoid more serious and long-term difficulties. With these patients a range of counselling approaches may be used effectively to sup-port them through a difficult time or to help them make sense of and cope with an ongoing difficulty. To illustrate these points, examples are presented of patients seen by one of us (RG).

With many patients living in difficult circumstances, often with quite insoluble health or social problems, the most appropriate and useful coun-selling skills are those of listening, taking the individual seriously and giving space to express emotions. Such support and the knowledge of its availability from their health centre may enable patients to cope with their difficulties and possibly avoid more long-term psychological distress.

In other patients, the same range of skills may work by helping them to share a 'dark secret' with someone. Typically this will be an incident or set of experiences in the person's past and which still hurts but has never been shared or divulged. A rather sad woman in her fifties telephoned and attended the surgery frequently, complaining of many different physical symptoms, none of which had been found to be 'abnormal'. One particular day, after seeing her many times, the GP sensed that she really wanted to talk about something and encouraged her to do so. After some hesitations, she began to discuss her regrets about not having children and suddenly became quite upset. On being given time to reflect on this, she slowly and painfully described how she became pregnant as a young woman, as the result of an illicit encounter with her older sister's husband. Despite a great deal of vilification from her family, she never revealed the identity of the baby's father and went on to have the baby. Tragically the baby died two years later as the result of an accident. She had harboured these painful experiences for over 30 years and often pondered them during her unrewarding life. She said that it had taken so long to be able to discuss these experiences because she needed to be absolutely sure that she would be taken seriously. Having shared her dark secret, she did not dramatically change, but felt considerably relieved to have done so and attended much less frequently.

With other patients, listening and attending is not sufficient since it is necessary for them to be able to make sense of what is happening or has happened in their lives in order to feel relief or to be able to make helpful changes. For example, a university lecturer in a homosexual relationship attended one day with a sore throat and appeared quite distressed. After the GP had commented on his apparent distress, the man described in great detail how his lover had recently left him after a long relationship. This had resulted in aggressive encounters with his former lover and his new partner, with physical violence and injury occurring on a number of occasions. Although he found it helpful to describe these experiences, he still felt bad, particularly about his repeated aggressiveness. At this point the GP helped him to piece together and make sense of a number of violent encounters which he had described and, in doing so, he began to understand something about the origins of his aggression with people he loved. He talked in great detail about his father who had been very pushy and ambitious for him but who had also been extremely intolerant of any failure or set-back. As a result he had been beaten frequently by his father, supposedly in his best interests. From these conversations with the GP, this man was able to make sense of what had been happening to him by being able to see the connections between his parental role model in childhood and his present behaviour, particularly in times of frustration or rejection.

Despite many counselling sessions, some patients may never resolve their crises and the primary care counsellor's role may be essentially supportive. However there are also patients for whom a counselling approach can be used to bring about positive changes in cognition or behaviour. An example here is of a 70-year-old woman with hypertension who attended for a routine blood pressure check-up. The GP noticed that she seemed upset and tentatively commented on this. She then told him that some months ago she had taken over care of her two grandchildren after her daughter's marriage had broken down. She had found this enormously rewarding but just recently her son-in-law had remarried a woman with two children and had taken his children to live with him. Her son-in-law then prevented her from sending her grandchildren presents and reported that the children were very happy and had no great desire to see her, a fact which had been verified by the children's social worker. As a result she had felt hopeless, rejected and very low. The counsellor spent a great deal of time in looking at the recent events, helping her to develop a different interpretation of what had happened. As the children were close to their father and got on very well with their new step-siblings, she came to see how the children might prefer to be in that environment, and no longer saw the events in terms of her being rejected. This new construction was made possible by being given time to discuss and explore what had happened and by being provided with other ways of looking at what had happened.

Patients with physical and/or terminal illnesses

In addition to the routine use of listening and facilitation skills, there are many other ways in which counselling skills can be used to help patients cope with different aspects of physical illness. Here a selection of situations is presented to demonstrate the breadth of relevance.

There are many occasions in general practice where patients are faced with difficult decisions (e.g. whether to attend for screening; whether to discontinue treatment or try a new one). Part of the GP's task is to be able to provide useful information to facilitate patients' decision-making. For example, in the case of an older person with a hernia, the first task will be to explain the different treatment options (e.g. wearing a truss; undergoing surgery) as well as a clear indication of the associated outcomes and potential risks. After this, the patient may still need to explore his or her own fears and concerns and then to make the best decision for the particular situation.

A similar approach can be adopted with patients who are about to undergo a specific treatment or stressful investigation, particularly if it involves hospitalisation. For example, with impending surgery patients will express very different fears and concerns. Some may be particularly worried about the possible pain or subsequent disfigurement, whereas others may be very frightened of general anaesthesia. Here again the GP's task will be to explain, identify specific concerns and then to help the patient to find ways of coping or coming to terms with them. Not only is this important in helping the patient to prepare for a treatment or investigation, but there is also evidence that this type of preparation can facilitate recovery (Weinman and Johnston, 1988).

After a patient has been diagnosed as having a serious physical illness, there are many opportunities for counselling both the patient and their relatives. For example, in the case of a patient recovering from a myocradial infarction, the GP may need to explore many issues when the episode is over and the patient has returned home. There are likely to be many fears and concerns, as well as a need for information and support. If there are certain aspects of the patient's lifestyle which need to be changed in order to reduce the likelihood of a re-occurrence, then these need to be dealt with by using a range of counselling skills to enable the patient to see the need for change and to identify and try out strategies for effecting this. Many of the issues discussed in the next section on promoting healthy behaviour are especially relevant in this context. Moreover, the GP should recognise that patients' spouses may also want to discuss their own concerns, as well as their own role in facilitating any necessary life-style changes.

Finally, GPs also spend time with patients who are facing death as well as with their bereaved relatives after the death has occurred. Here GPs need to use listening skills to understand what it is that each patient knows, feels and needs to know about their condition. They need to be flexible in their approach and to recognise that, as patients change in their own perceptions of their illness, their way of coping may change together with their need for information and support. Thus the task of the GP will be to create an ambience in which dying patients can feel free to discuss anything they want and to be helped to deal with the emotional and the practical issues which confront them.

Promoting healthy behaviour

General practice lends itself to health promotion approaches and GPs are being strongly encouraged to develop this area of their work (e.g. Calnan and Johnson, 1983). Also in the World Health Organization's (1981) proposal of Health for All by the Year 2000, there is a major emphasis on primary health care as the optimal context for health promotion (Diekstra, 1990).

In contrast to the conventional mass media approaches to health promotion, many experts now feel that this work should take a much greater account of individual behaviour patterns, beliefs and barriers to behaviour change. It is in this latter situation that counselling skills can be used to explore the individual's views of the nature and causes of a particular health risk or unhealthy behaviour in order to plan and promote appropriate behaviour change. Egan's (1982) approach is particularly relevant since the model involves shared planning of behavioural goals and action plans. Also when the patient meets a problem in his or her attempt to bring about health-related behaviour change, a counselling approach demands that the counsellor and patient explore the problem in order to identify a new and more viable course of action.

Similar points can be made about the problems reported by health professionals in the low adherence of patients to medical treatment or advice. This is partly due to communication failures (e.g. Ley, 1977) and partly reflects the difficulties in taking the appropriate action. Recent work on psychological interventions to improve adherence incorporate many of the component skills involved in counselling, particularly active listening and shared involvement in setting goals and in promoting action (Meichenbaum and Turk, 1987).

Using a counselling model as a framework for one to one training in general practice

In our training programme for general practitioners who wish to become trainers, we use a counselling model as a basis for the skills which need to be learned for the successful facilitation of the trainee's learning. Starting from the premise that trainees are 'adult learners' (Cross, 1982) whose learning will be strongly problem-based, our programme for would-be trainers develops skills in active listening, challenging and the facilitation of problem-solving. This use of a counselling approach to training has been described elsewhere (Woolfe, Murgatroyd and Rhys, 1987). It takes account of the individuality of each learner as well as the importance of the trainer/trainee relationship as an essential part of the learning process.

DEVELOPING AND EVALUATING COUNSELLING WITHIN GENERAL PRACTICE

So far this paper has explored the relevance and applicability of counselling within the general practice setting. This final section will deal with more practical issues.

To what extent do GPs undertake counselling?

Although there are a number of studies evaluating the efficacy of counselling in general practice, there appears to be relatively little systematic data on its popularity and use by GPs. Some data is available from a recent postal survey (Grimwade, 1989) of all the 197 GPs in our health district. Only 97 returned the questionnaire casting some doubt on the generalisability of the findings. However there was a much higher return rate from GPs in Group Practices (73%) and Health Centres (88%) than from single-handed practitioners (22%), perhaps indicating the greater opportunities and commitment from GPs in the larger set-ups.

Without specifying what they actually did, a significant majority (n=73) reported that they counselled patients, but, since only a relatively small number (n=22) set aside special appointments for this, their general definition of counselling must be fairly loose. A majority (n=66) wanted to undertake more counselling, if they had time, and nearly all saw it as an important part of general practice, giving it a high or medium priority as an area for development of services. Only about a third had received any training and much of this was fairly unsystematic. An even smaller number of practices employed a counsellor and a very large number of patients were still being referred to other services for counselling.

How can counselling skills be developed by GPs?

The results from the above survey clearly need to be replicated and extended. Nevertheless the relatively small number of GPs with training in counselling is a potential source of concern and raises important questions about training. As far as we know, there have been no systematic attempts to describe or compare different approaches to counselling training for GPs. In view of this we will provide a brief description of the framework which we have developed for training GPs in the South East Thames Region (Weinman and Medlik, 1985).

Our course consists of three phases which build on each other. The first consists of eight weekly half-day sessions designed to enable GPs to master the basic counselling skills set out in the Egan (1982) approach. The next phase builds on this by developing the skills for dealing with different problems (e.g. bereavement; working with adolescents; alcohol dependence; relationship problems). There are 12 sessions which alternate between those in which a new area is explored and those in which the participants feedback and discuss their own attempts at counselling in that area. The final phase of the course comprises eight sessions which provide an opportunity for detailed supervision of participants' current counselling work together with an exploration of interpersonal processes which take place during counselling.

The three phase training model described above falls far short of the very intensive training courses offered by some counselling organizations. Nevertheless it does appear to have been very successful in allowing GPs to develop and apply basic skills, as well as making them more aware of their own approach and of the processes involved in counselling.

To what extent is GP counselling effective?

Any treatment evaluation study needs to include appropriate outcome measures and, in the case of counselling in general practice, it is not clear what the best measures should be. Although counselling is used to help people cope more effectively, this is rarely measured as an outcome. Since it is inferred that better coping will bring about an improved psychological state or less pill-taking, these endpoint measures are typically used. However, one recent study of psychological treatments in general practice provides very clear evidence of improved coping following treatment (Milne and Souter, 1988) and this would seem to be a useful direction for future evaluative work.

Using the more conventional outcome measures, there is evidence indicating that counselling within a GP practice can lead to reduced levels of prescription of psychotropic medication. For example, in a two-year study of counselling in nine GP practices, Waydenfeld and Waydenfeld (1980) found a 30% reduction in psychotropic prescribing and a 48% reduction in the prescribing of other drugs. Other studies have also reported significant reductions in psychotropic medication use following counselling (Cohen and Halpern, 1978; Anderson and Hasler, 1979).

There have also been evaluations of counselling offered to more specific client groups. These have varied greatly in their quality and in the type of intervention which was included under the heading of 'counselling'. However, one of the better studies by Holden, Sagovsky and Cox (1989) evaluated a course of eight half-hour general practice-based counselling sessions, provided by health visitors for women with postnatal depression. The evaluation showed a clear positive effect of counselling since 69% of the women in the treatment group recovered, as compared with 38% in a control group. Unfortunately the design of the study does not allow one to determine whether counselling had a specific effect or whether the therapeutic effect was due to the extra time and attention given. However, the follow-up interviews indicated that the important ingredients included the supportive component of the counselling as well as the opportunity to divulge and discuss emotions, particularly guilt. A third of the counselled women did not show any therapeutic improvement, providing a further indication that brief counselling will not be effective with all patients and that some may need more intensive psychological or psychiatric help.

Which health professionals should be offering counselling in general practice?

This paper has been mainly concerned with the development and application of counselling skills by GPs. However, other health professionals are beginning to offer counselling to general practice patients. Eventually this will result in a situation where different health professionals (i.e. GPs; counsellors; social workers; community psychiatric nurses, etc.) will appear to be offering the same sort of help. This may generate concerns about whether this overlap of skills is appropriate and whether the practice of counselling should be restricted to those with a specified level of training. For example, Rowland, Irving and Maynard (1989) argue strongly that counselling should be offered only by fully trained counsellors since they believe that the GP's task is concerned more with the exercise of clinical skills (i.e. diagnosis and treatement). Although these authors make a good case for the contribution of counsellors in general practice, they seem to have failed to understand that there have been important recent changes in the approaches and models used by GPs. Following influential publications such as those by Pendleton *et al.* (1984) and Tuckett *et al.* (1985), there has been an increasing acceptance by GPs that an understanding of the patient's view is vital to the process of the consultation and that its outcomes should be based on shared involvement in decision-making. Thus counselling integrates well with this emerging framework for general practice both in the context of routine consultations and for work with patients with social and emotional problems.

The potential demand for counselling in general practice is enormous and cannot be met by current resources. The recent influx of other health professionals with counselling skills is a welcome development, as are the recent moves by GPs to acquire and use counselling skills themselves. What is needed now are good studies to evaluate the efficacy of different models of counselling for different aspects of general practice work. Until we have this information, we cannot be certain of the extent to which counselling approaches will be of lasting value in general practice. Nor will we know about the cost effectiveness of counselling in the different areas of general practice work which we have described. For the present, all the indications are that counselling is becoming an essential component of many aspects of the GP's work in treatment, prevention and training.

REFERENCES

Anderson, S. and Hasler, J. (1979). Counselling in General Practice. *Journal of the Royal College of General Practitioners*, **29**, 352–356.

Calnan, M.W. and Johnson, B.M. (1983). Influencing health behaviour: How significant is the general practitioner? *Health Education Journal*, **42**, (2), 39–45.

Cohen, J. and Halpern, A. (1978). A Practice Counsellor. *Journal of the Royal College of General Practitioners*, **26**, 86–94.

Cross, P. (1982). *Adults as learners: Increasing participation and facilitating learning*. San Francisco: Jossey Bass.

Diekstra, R. (1990). Psychology, health and health care: a view from the World Health Organization. *Psychology and Health*, **4**, 51–63.

Egan, G. (1982). *The skilled helper*, (2nd ed) Monterey: Brooks/Cole.

Goldberg, D., Steele, J.J., Johnson, A., and Smith, C. (1982). Ability of primary care physicians to make accurate ratings of psychiatric symptoms. *Archives of General Psychiatry*, **39**, 829–833.

Gray, D.P. (1988). Counsellors in general practice. *Journal of the Royal College of General Practitioners*, **38**, 50–5.

Grimwade, K. (1989). *Counselling within Primary Care*. Report for Lewisham & North Southwark Community Health Council.

Holden, J.M., Sagovsky, R., and Cox, J.L. (1989). Counselling in a general practice setting: controlled study of health visitor intervention in treatment of postnatal depression. *British Medical Journal*, **298**, 223–226.

Ley, P. (1977). Psychological studies in doctor-patient communication. In S. Rachman (Ed.), *Contributions to medical psychology* (Vol. 1), Oxford: Pergamon.

Meichenbaum, D. and Turk, D.C. (1987). *Facilitating treatment adherence*. New York: Plenum Press.

Milne, D. and Souter, K. (1988). A re-evaluation of the clinical psychologist in general practice. *Journal of the Royal College of General Practitioners*, **38**, 457–460.

Pendleton, D., Schofield, T., Tate, P., and Havelock, P. (1984). *The consultation: An approach to learning and teaching*. Oxford: Oxford University Press.

Rowland, N., Irving, J., and Maynard, A. (1989). Can general practitioners counsel? *Journal of the Royal College of General Practitioners*, **39**, 118–120.

Salmon, P. and Quine, J. (1989). Patients' intentions in primary care: measurement and preliminary investigation. *Psychology and Health*, **3**, 103–110.

Tuckett, D., Boulton, M., Olson, C., and Williams, A. (1985). *Meetings between experts*. London: Tavistock Press.

Waydenfeld, D. and Waydenfeld, S. (1980). Counselling in General Practice. *Journal of the Royal College of General Practitioners*, **30**, 671–677.

Weinman, J. and Medlik, L. (1985). Sharing psychological skills in the general practice setting. *British Journal of Medical Psychology*, **58**, 223–230.

Weinman, J. and Hough, S.C. (1986). *Discrepant role perceptions in doctors and patients*. Paper presented at the 21st International Congress of Applied Psychology, Jerusalem.

Weinman, J. and Johnston, M. (1988). Stressful medical procedures: an analysis of the effects of psychological interventions and of the stressfulness of the procedures. In S. Maes, C. Spielberger, P. Defares, and I. Sarason (Eds), *Topics in health psychology*. Chichester: Wiley.

Williams, P. and Clare, A. (Eds) (1979). *Psychosocial disorders in general practice*. London: Academic Press.

Woolfe, R., Murgatroyd, S., and Rhys, S. (1987). *Guidance and counselling in adult and continuing education*. Milton Keynes: Open University Press.

World Health Organization (1981). *Global strategy for health for all by the year 2000*. Geneva: WHO.

4 Counselling in Health Care: Diabetes Mellitus

RICHARD W. SHILLITOE
Department of Clinical Psychology, Scalebor Park Hospital,
Moor Lane, Burley in Wharfedale, West Yorkshire, LS29 7AJ

Sensitive clinicians are well aware of the psychosocial impact of diabetes mellitus. As they watch patients develop and change through many years, even a lifetime, of contact, they gain an appreciation of the complexities of living with the disorder, how one person copes and another struggles, and how management advice must be tempered with an understanding of the patient's perception of the disease and their home circumstances. It is often difficult to incorporate such observations into effective management strategies, increasingly so as technological medicine makes greater and greater demands on both staff and patient. Yet, because the main burdens of the disease are psychosocial rather than medical, they must be incorporated if a productive treatment alliance is to be formed and maintained. The relevance of counselling in the treatment of diabetes mellitus forms the subject matter of this chapter, which begins with some general information on the disease and its management.

DIABETES MELLITUS: THE DISEASE

There are two main types of diabetes mellitus: type I or insulin-dependent diabetes mellitus (roughly synonymous with the old term 'juvenile onset' diabetes mellitus) and type II or non-insulin-dependent diabetes mellitus (once called 'maturity onset' diabetes mellitus). Both are disorders of the metabolic systems responsible for the storage and utilisation of glucose, the main energy source derived from food. The regulation of glucose levels is largely under the control of the hormone insulin, which facilitates the uptake of glucose by body cells. Its absence leads to excessive levels of glucose in the blood, but an impairment of the body's ability to use it. Insulin also stimulates protein synthesis and is involved in fat storage: clinical manifestations of its shortage include weight loss and wasting, dehydration, excessive urination and thirst. If untreated, there is the threat of coma and

Counselling and Communication in Health Care. Edited by H. Davis and L. Fallowfield
© 1991 John Wiley & Sons Ltd

death. Hyperglycaemia, and its opposite hypoglycaemia, are constant threats to the patient with insulin-dependent diabetes mellitus, whereas those with the non-insulin-dependent disease generally retain sufficient insulin to make rapid swings of blood glucose unlikely. This is not to say that this type of diabetes is innocuous; the disease may be present but undetected for several years, during which time the degenerative changes associated with diabetes may proceed silently and unchecked.

THE MANAGEMENT OF DIABETES MELLITUS

Degenerative changes, such as neuropathy, vascular disease, renal failure and visual impairment are observable in many patients after several years. To a certain extent they are preventable, because a major determinant of complications is poor blood glucose control, although genetic susceptibility also plays a part.

The main aim of management is to keep blood glucose within the normal range, in order to maintain feelings of wellbeing and to minimize the risk of complications. Management is, primarily, by behavioural self-management: regulating blood glucose by deliberate actions in the absence of the body's natural control mechanisms. This includes strict diet, daily medication (tablets or insulin), exercise and regular self-monitoring of blood glucose.

As the importance of tight blood glucose control in the prevention of complications becomes increasingly recognised, so treatment regimens become more complicated in order to achieve normal blood glucose levels whenever possible. This is especially true for the patient requiring insulin. The behavioural and emotional demands made by such regimens are great. One patient summed up her feelings like this:

They say that, if you have to have a chronic disease, diabetes is the one to go for. I was told that I should be able to continue with my normal life-style, and that the treatment would be designed around that.

Nowadays, I have to give myself four injections each day. I prick my finger and test my blood sugar before each meal and at other times if I feel peculiar. Whenever I go out I carry an identification card in my purse, and sugar lumps, syringe, bloodletting device and blood-testing strips in my bag.

I have to re-apply for my driving licence every three years, and I have my insurance loaded. I daren't skip a meal. I eat a high-carbohydrate low-fat diet, and try to persuade my family to do the same. I can't get cross and snap at my husband without him accusing me of being hypoglycaemic, and forcing food upon me. If the children are ill or just come home feeling thirsty, my heart races and I worry that I've passed diabetes on to them. I worry about their future, and about mine as well.

When my husband is away on business I still have my diabetes to keep me company. When we go on holiday, my diabetes comes too.

Now, what was that about leading a normal life-style?

PSYCHOLOGICAL DIFFICULTIES AND DIABETES MELLITUS

There is increased psychological disturbance associated with diabetes, and some evidence that mortality is related to the psychosocial impact of the disease (Davis, Hess and Hiss, 1988). Patients in poorer metabolic control have greater difficulties in daily life, including anxiety and depression, than those in good control. Much of this remains undetected by health professionals unless they look for it specifically. It is, however, well known to patients and their families. The underlying mechanisms are partly psychological and partly physiological. For example, hormones which increase during stress oppose the action of insulin. This produces glycaemic changes which the diabetic individual cannot regulate by normal homeostasis. Further, stress, depressed mood or high levels of anxiety can result in less accurate self-care, with subsequent glycaemic disturbance.

COUNSELLING IN DIABETES MELLITUS

Because diabetes mellitus is life-long, the psychological needs and concerns of patients are likely to differ at various times in their diabetic 'career'. Some of these can be linked to crises or major changes in life-style or circumstances, during which metabolic control may be compromised. Hamburg and Inoff (1983) drew a distinction between developmental crises, which involve transition between stages of the life span, such as entering adolescence or becoming married, and life crises resulting from unexpected events that put cherished life values and goals in jeopardy (e.g. learning of the diagnosis of diabetes, or the onset of complications). Specific circumstances in which psychological difficulties may be present and where counselling might be of value will now be described.

Impact of diagnosis: children and adolescents

Most newly diagnosed children and adolescents show symptoms of depressed mood, irritability, feelings of friendlessness, social withdrawal and anxiety. In about one-third, greater adjustment problems occur, usually in the form of more severe affective disturbance. However, at one year post-diagnosis, nearly all youngsters rate their mood and self-esteem as good (Kovacs *et al.*, 1986). Longer lasting problems indicate significant adaptational difficulties, which may require intervention. Although most children and their families learn to cope, it is likely that the sensitivity of care staff helps determine the pace and ease with which this is achieved. The need to learn self-care skills has to be balanced with the emotional needs of the child and family. Although it is easy to concentrate on the former at the expense of the latter, the acknowledgement and expression of feelings are important steps in gaining mastery over them and staff should know how to facilitate this.

There is little evidence to support the commonly expressed views of earlier writers that anxiety, low self-esteem, hostility and poor peer relationships are common and lasting characteristics of children with diabetes. Some youngsters may be more vulnerable to adaptational difficulties than others, however, and these may be both age and sex related. Early-onset diabetes may interfere with the development of a satisfactory body image in girls (Ryan and Morrow, 1986). This may be related to the tendency for adolescent girls with diabetes to be relatively shorter, heavier, and less mature sexually than their healthy peers. There is some evidence that, for boys, the onset of diabetes when entering puberty has a particular impact upon social and peer group identity (Ahlfield, Soler and Marcus, 1983).

Impact of diagnosis: parents

Initial parental reactions, often involving anxiety, shock, disbelief and insomnia, bear a strong similarity to grief and mourning. They are seen more often in mothers than fathers. These reactions fade progressively, although 11% of mothers remain 'slightly depressed' after one year (Kovacs *et al.*, 1985). Some of the common worries and concerns expressed by parents are shown in Table 4.1.

The everyday management tasks are worrisome, particularly for mothers of newly diagnosed and younger children. Many feel considerable guilt about inflicting pain when giving injections. Others complain of lack of help and support from husbands. As with most diseases, the reactions of fathers have been under-researched and little is known about their experiences. In this respect, the autobiographical account of Thomas (1985) is valuable. Practical concerns tend to fade, as experience teaches parents that they can cope with problems which initially seemed mountainous, such as giving injections and dealing with hypoglycaemic reactions. Dietary restrictions remain an ever-present source of concern, as do more global worries about

Table 4.1. Common worries of parents

Uncertainty concerning child's future:
   Possible threat of child's death
   Difficult to make plans for child
   Worries about stigma
Restrictions on parents' own life
Handling well-meaning relatives
Fears of having 'caused' the child's ill-health:
   Feelings of guilt and anger
   Feelings of shame
Altered relationship with child
Altered relationship with other children
Feeling helpless and incompetent
Uncertainties about responsibilities for management

overall control and the future. These may be hidden from the professional unless their expression is specifically facilitated.

Effects of diabetes on family life

Family difficulties assume added significance when diabetes is present. Diabetes may, in itself, cause problems, but generally it exaggerates difficulties which already exist or brings to the surface ones that are dormant. Good control is more likely to be found in a stable cohesive family where members are supportive but not overprotective, where independence is not stifled, where parental relationships are sound and where channels of communication are clear and effective. The direction of causality is unclear, but the relationship is probably reciprocal, and care givers need to be aware of the feelings and reactions of all family members.

Effects of diabetes on adolescence

The transition from parental to self-management, which occurs during adolescence, is a time of particular difficulty for youngsters and their parents. The balance between over-protectiveness and under-involvement is difficult for many parents. For the maturing youngster, management tasks may be at odds with the developmental tasks of adolescence. Risk-taking, personal independence and freedom may conflict with the treatment requirements of a planned and predictable routine. At an age when peer conformity is important, the adolescent with diabetes may be distanced from peers by delayed physical maturation and the need for regularity in behaviour. Youngsters become depressingly aware of handicaps, limitations and potential problems, and these commonly find expression in rejection of the regimen. It can be an unhappy time for all, care staff included: they might feel that the youngster is particularly vulnerable and in need of support, yet offers of help are likely to be rejected.

Diabetes and eating disorders

Given that diabetes management focuses attention upon food and that insulin causes weight gain, it is not surprising to find an increased prevalence of eating disorders in adolescents and young adults with diabetes. This can cause problems with metabolic control through, for example, binge eating or self-enforced vomiting. The relationship between the diabetes and the eating disorder may be complex. In some patients diabetes appears to be just a handy tool in the attainment of the primary goal, which is weight loss, whilst in others weight loss is not so much an end in itself, but a step on the path to the manipulation of those around the patient (Brooks, 1984).

Brittle diabetes

A small number of insulin-dependent patients have enormous problems in maintaining an acceptable standard of glycaemic control, leading to numerous hospital admissions. Such 'brittle' patients are nearly always female, overweight, and in their teens or early twenties. They often display a cheerful unconcern about their situation. Substantial emotional and family problems generally feature in their personal lives. They appear to engage in potentially dangerous behaviour 'partly because they are ignorant of its consequences, but more often because it "pays" in the sense of fulfilling other needs, whether for love, approval or escape from an otherwise insoluble conflict' (Tattersall and Walford, 1985 p. 76).

DIABETES MELLITUS IN ADULTS

Adults are frequently concerned with the effects of the illness upon personal relationships, but feel unable to verbalise these anxieties in everyday life. Some find it difficult even to admit to having diabetes. A major fear is of hypoglycaemia in public places and the feelings of personal weakness and loss of self-esteem that would ensue. Difficult aspects of the regimen include embarrassment or inconvenience at having to eat at predetermined times, and the requirements of blood-testing, especially when away from home or travelling. The largest single problem for most patients is dietary adherence.

Emotional responses may be powerful; feelings of guilt, anger and injustice are common. So too are ambivalent feelings about care staff; patients recognise the importance of their expertise and experience, yet feel that they do not comprehend the enormity of the task of living with diabetes. They resent their own continual dependence upon medical services. These feelings emerge during discussion groups. Health professionals may be surprised at the vehemence with which they are expressed, as they are seldom heard in the hustle and bustle of the out-patient clinic.

Diabetes places extra burdens upon marital relationships. The partner, more so than the patient, is likely to report the existence of problems. Lassitude and irritability are frequently cited. They are particularly evident during the evening and at week-ends and are disruptive socially and interpersonally (Surridge et al., 1984). Common concerns of young married patients include the possibility of passing the disease on to any children, the increased risk of infant mortality, and impotence (Campbell and McCulloch, 1979).

Priorities change with age. Holvey (1986) has discussed the special concerns of the elderly with diabetes. He emphasised the discrepancy that often exists between expectations of the 'golden years' or retirement and the altogether different reality of living with diabetes, declining health and a reduced income.

THE DEVELOPMENT OF COMPLICATIONS

Patients who develop complications are likely to have not one but a number of degenerative changes. For a patient who developed diabetes in childhood, complications may be evident as early as young adulthood. These may signal many years of reduced or deteriorating levels of personal functioning. Some specific complications which are unpleasant and distressing in their own right or which require unpleasant and distressing management, are outlined below.

Visual impairment

Patients often express fears of blindness (Wulsin, Jacobson and Rand, 1987), even from an early age. Partial loss of sight may be just as disturbing as complete loss of vision. The onset of visual impairment, fluctuations in visual acuity, and the adaptation required are all potential causes of distress. Photocoagulation by means of laser therapy is an effective treatment for proliferative retinopathy, but many treatments are often necessary over long periods of time, during which patients may require support.

Sexual dysfunction

Disturbance of sexual functioning may affect up to half of all patients at some point after diagnosis. Male impotence is widely recognised, but problems for women are also common, albeit less well publicised (Newman and Bertelson, 1986). Although neurological damage is a common cause, psychological factors may be just as important. Open communication between sexual partners and care givers is necessary if emotional and relationship difficulties secondary to sexual problems are to be prevented.

Renal disease

Renal failure develops in about 30% of patients. Continuous peritoneal dialysis and kidney transplantation are being made available to this group of patients with increasing frequency, and with good results. However, nephrologists and diabetologists often comment on the difficulty of maintaining the confidence of patients in the face of long-term, unpleasant therapy, with attendant additional dietary restrictions, side effects, and curtailment of life-style.

DIFFICULT AND DEMANDING REGIMENS

As a general principle, the more complex, flexible and demanding a regimen becomes, the less reliably the required self-care behaviours will be performed. This has, for example, been documented (Shillitoe, 1988) in the extent to which patients fail to self-monitor their blood glucose (or falsify the results, fabricate them altogether or fail to act upon them). Another example is the frequency (at least one-third) with which patients who commence intensive insulin therapy by means of continuous subcutaneous infusion choose to revert to a less demanding regimen even though the quality of metabolic control may be poorer (Jornsay, Duckles and Hankinson, 1988).

Individuals who are unable to meet treatment demands may feel a sense of failure or helplessness. They may feel guilty about letting the care team, themselves or their family down, and may have difficulty in admitting the extent of their difficulties. Their need for support and encouragement may be high, but their problems may be attributed by staff to personality or motivational problems, which imply that no further action is necessary. Staff have to balance their need to have patients in good metabolic control with the patient's own need for good psychological adjustment. At times, the two may not be compatible or easily achieved. In fact, the wholehearted pursuit of normal blood glucose levels may itself be associated with psychological penalties, such as higher scores on depression inventories (Rovet and Ehrlich, 1988).

METHODS OF COUNSELLING

Counselling and education

The term 'counselling' appears frequently in the literature where it usually means education and information giving. 'Nutritional counselling' is perhaps the most frequent usage. There is, indeed, a great deal to be learned by patients before they can be said to be proficient in self-management. Most education programmes, however, whilst successful in teaching patients the facts of diabetes management, fail miserably in having any lasting effect upon metabolic control (Shillitoe, 1988). The failure of knowledge-based courses has been taken to indicate that programmes should pay greater attention to the personal meaning of diabetes to the individual patient: 'If patient educators want to facilitate change in attitudes and behaviours, they should . . . place emphasis on adapting patient education programmes to encourage exploration and change in the personal meaning of having diabetes' (Anderson, 1986 p. 87). This could be achieved by incorporating counselling skills such as open and reflective listening into educational encounters. Anderson, Nowacek and Richards (1988) went on to suggest a number of further strategies for uncovering and modifying personal meaning. These include clarification exercises such as sentence completion taks (e.g. 'When I think about having diabetes I feel . . .'; 'What I wish my friends and family would understand about my diabetes is . . .'), role playing and acting as resource persons for other patients with diabetes. The task of teaching, however, generally falls to health professionals who are neither trained counsellors nor trained educators. Without specialist training they may have difficulty in implementing such suggestions.

Family counselling

Some families, showing particular maladaptive patterns of communication and interpersonal conflicts, have been described as 'psychosomatic' families (Minuchin, Rosman and Baker, 1978). Minuchin and colleagues have presented some experiemental, but uncontrolled, evidence that children with diabetes who become caught up in these family disputes experience metabolic changes which disrupt blood glucose control. If this is true, then family therapy may well improve relationships in such families, with consequent improvements in control.

Although formal family therapy requires specialist training which makes it available to only a few, Sargent and Baker (1983) pointed out that there is a lot that health professionals can do even without such training. They stressed, first, that the focus of consultations and treatments should be placed firmly upon the family unit rather than upon the diabetic member alone, and second, that the health professional's role is *not* to suggest solutions, but rather to assist the family in arriving at strategies and plans based on the family's developing understanding of diabetes and its treatment. In this way, the family becomes actively involved in care: solutions to problems are generated by the family, rather than being imposed from outside, and are therefore more likely to be implemented.

Group counselling

Many different types of group have been described for people with diabetes (Shillitoe, 1988). Most combine discussions of feelings and reactions to diabetes with topics of a more overtly educational nature. One of the most interesting applications of group methods is that reported by Oehler-Giarratana and Fitzgerald (1980) who ran a group composed of young patients already showing serious complications. All were either blind or partially sighted, many had deteriorating renal function and many were hypertensive. Discussions concentrated upon the practical difficulties of adjusting to limited function, as well as trying to find a 'meaning' behind the symptoms. The opportunity to express these feelings was particularly welcomed by participants.

Patients as counsellors

Many countries have national diabetes associations. These almost certainly perform important supportive functions for members who actively participate in branch meetings. One activity of particular relevance to the present discussion is the organization of summer holidays for children or adolescents with diabetes. In addition to their recreational and educational value, they have a cathartic function and allow participants to express, often with considerable venom, fears and feelings about the disease, the future, and about care givers. Weekend workshops for parents and whole families are a more recent extension of this approach.

The exploration of alternative models of regular care delivery in the light of such experiences is gaining ground, especially for youngsters. These include peer-support of the newly-diagnosed, and the arrangement of semi-formal or informal meetings away from hospital settings. They also involve the transition from staff-dominated towards patient-dominated discussions in an attempt to 'de-professionalise' support.

This may not be appropriate for all. Concern has been expressed in relation to other illness populations about the imposition of burdens with which patients may be ill-equipped to cope, and the suitability of some patients to take on supportive roles. Further, Pelser *et al.* (1978), found that of 40 patients who attended group therapy sessions, 20 decided to undertake specialist training with a view to starting their own groups. Yet, if the goal of management is to help patients to lead a reasonably normal life with diabetes in the background, then this figure seems very high.

Counselling and complications

Holmes (1986) has provided a valuable discussion of the psychosocial effects of functional deterioration as a result of complications. One of the main tasks of the health professional is to help the patient through the adaptation process. Guidelines for this are summarised in Table 4.2. A rehabilitation programme with many of these features has been designed for the visually

Table 4.2. Coping with complications: guidelines for care staff

---

Maintain open communication; elicit patient's fears, anticipate and discuss predictable crises

Help patient and key family members understand likely psychological reactions and stages that each will experience

Help the patient and family plan for activities and responsibilities which can be continued despite functional loss

Help mobilize any necessary support from outside the family

Tailor rehabilitation goals so that progress is achievable

Maintain positive attitude and expect progress to be possible and worthwhile

Help family maintain positive attitude and abstain from explicit or implied criticism

Help family cope with changing psychological reactions

Help maintain cohesion in family while helping the patient function as independently as possible

---

Based on Holmes (1986)

impaired (Bernbaum, Albert and Duckro, 1988), combining individual coun-selling with a self-care support group.

ORGANIZATIONAL ISSUES

Effective diabetes management, thanks to its complexity and combination of acute demands and chronic effects, requires a team of carers. The usual 'core' team of physician, nurse, dietician and patient is augmented as re-quired by an outer circle which may include, for example, a chiropodist, ophthalmologist, and nephrologist. All of these individuals should possess some counselling skills.

It is also desirable for a psychologist (or other individual with particular expertise in counselling and knowledge of the psychosocial effects of chronic disease) to have a close affiliation with the regular team of carers. Team membership is desirable because splitting care into separate physical and emotional components creates confusion over roles and responsibilities, and also disrupts communication, offering opportunities for the so-minded patient or family to play one care giver against another. This is especially likely if the counsellor is unfamiliar with current management practices, and such a person may lack credibility with patients and colleagues. Close team membership may signal to the patient that periods of emotional turmoil or adjustment difficulty are the norm, whereas referral to a distant figure may result in the patient feeling threatened or resentful at the perceived implica-tion of mental disturbance.

An additional and important role for counsellors lies in providing support for the core team. Josse and Challener (1987) described the main contribu-tions as uncovering and helping to resolve boundary and hierarchical diffi-culties between team members, pinpointing clinic practices likely to be confusing to patients, and in helping with difficult cases. The education of team members in communication skills and in providing theoretical frame-works of how patients and families cope with chronic disease were also seen as important tasks.

Tattersall and Walford (1985) pointed out that physicians are particularly vulnerable when dealing with patients whose emotional and adjustment problems affect their medical management. By virtue of their training and responsibilities, they have an overwhelming fear of missing organic disease, and feel more at ease exploring physical symptoms than psychological states. They may have stereotyped views of the sorts of patient who are likely to have personal problems, to show poor compliance or to deceive their physicians, and these may bear little relation to reality. A counsellor can illuminate these dark areas and help carers understand such prejudices and beliefs.

Team membership is feasible when care is based at a diabetes unit in a hospital, or at a diabetes day centre. It presents problems when care is devolved to small locally based clinics, as may be the case in rural districts, or is the responsibility of primary care staff. Under these circumstances, enhancing the role of nurse specialists could be explored. These people are an increasingly valued resource, but they often work in isolation, and in a style not anticipated by traditional nurse training. Although training in counselling forms a growing part of the nurse's postgraduate education, there is also a need for an appropriate support system in order to ensure that they work effectively.

CONCLUSION

Diabetes is a chronic disorder which carries with it increased morbidity and mortality. Modern management methods can reduce these and enable most patients to live full lives. However, the effects of living with diabetes and the demands of the regimen may cause difficulties in coping, which can often be anticipated by the care system. All carers should be educated in the ways that people cope with chronic disease and should be taught some counselling skills. The ready availability of an individual well versed in such skills is an asset to the regular team of carers.

USEFUL ADDRESS

British Diabetic Association
10 Queen Anne Street,
London.
W1M 0BD
Tel: 071-323 1531

REFERENCES

Ahlfield, J.E., Soler, N.G., and Marcus, S.D. (1983). Adolescent diabetes mellitus: parent/child perspectives on the effect of the disease on family and social interactions. *Diabetes Care*, 6, 393–398.

Anderson, R.M. (1986). The personal meaning of having diabetes: Implications for patient behaviour and education. *Diabetic Medicine*, 3, 85–89.

Anderson, R.M., Nowacek, G., and Richards, F. (1988). Influencing the personal meaning of diabetes: research and practice. *Diabetes Educator*, 14, 297–302.

Bernbaum, M., Albert, S.G., and Duckro, P.N. (1988). Psychosocial profiles in patients with visual impairment due to diabetic retinopathy. *Diabetes Care*, 11, 551–557.

Brooks, S.A. (1984). Diabetes mellitus and anorexia nervosa: another view. *British Journal of Psychiatry*, 144, 640–642.

Campbell, I.W. and McCulloch, D.K. (1979). Marital problems in diabetics. *Practitioner*, 223, 343–347.

Davis, W.K., Hess, G.E., and Hiss, R.G. (1988). Psychosocial correlates of survival in diabetes, *Diabetes Care*, 11, 538–545.

Hamburg, B.A., and Inoff, G.E. (1983). Coping with predictable crises of diabetes. *Diabetes Care*, 6, 409–416.

Holmes, D.M. (1986). The person and diabetes in psychosocial context. *Diabetes Care*, **9**, 194–206.

Holvey, S.M. (1986). Psychosocial aspects in the care of elderly diabetic patients. *American Journal of Medicine*, **80** (suppl 5a), 61–63.

Jornsay, D.L., Duckles, A.E., and Hankinson, J.P. (1988). Psychological considerations for patient selection and adjustment to insulin pump therapy. *Diabetes Educator*, **14**, 291–96.

Josse, J.D. and Challener, J. (1987). Liaison psychotherapy in a hospital paediatric diabetic clinic. *Archives of Disease in Children*, **62**, 518–522.

Kovacs, M., Brent, D., Steinberg, T.F., Paulauskas, S., and Reid, J. (1986). Children's self-reports of psychologic adjustment and coping strategies during first year of insulin-dependent diabetes mellitus. *Diabetes Care*, **9**, 472–479.

Kovacs, M., Finkelstein, R., Feinberg, T.L., Crouse-Novak, M., Paulauskas, S., and Pollock, M. (1985). Initial psychologic responses of parents to the diagnosis of insulin-dependent diabetes mellitus in their children. *Diabetes Care*, **8**, 568–575.

Minuchin, S., Rosman, B.L., and Baker, L. (1978). *Psychosomatic families: Anorexia nervosa in context*. Cambridge, Mass: Harvard University Press.

Newman, A.S. and Bertelson, A.D. (1986). Sexual dysfunction in diabetic women. *Journal of Behavioral Medicine*, **9**, 261–270.

Oehler-Giarratana, J. and Fitzgerald, R.G. (1980). Group therapy with blind diabetics. *Archives of General Psychiatry*, **37**, 463–467.

Pelser, H.E., Groen, J.J., Stuyling de Lange, M.J., and Dix, P.C. (1978). Experiences in group discussions with diabetic patients. *Psychotherapy and Psychosomatics*, **32**, 257–269.

Rovet, J.F. and Ehrlich, R.M. (1988). Effect of temperament on metabolic control in children with diabetes mellitus. *Diabetes Care*, **11**, 77–82.

Ryan, C.M. and Morrow, L.A. (1986). Self-esteem in diabetic adolescents: relationship between age at onset and gender. *Journal of Consulting and Clinical Psychology*, **54**, 730–731.

Sargent, J. and Baker, L. (1983). Behavior and diabetes care. *Primary Care*, **10**, 583–594.

Shillitoe, R.W. (1988). *Psychology and diabetes: Psychosocial factors in management and control*, London: Chapman and Hall.

Surridge, D.H.C., Williams-Erdahl, D.L., Lawson, J.S., Donald, M.W., Monga, T.N., Bird, C.E., and Letemendia, F.J.J. (1984). Psychiatric aspects of diabetes mellitus. *British Journal of Psychiatry*, **145**, 269–276.

Tattersall, R.B. and Walford, S. (1985). Brittle diabetes in response to life stress: cheating and manipulation. In J.C. Pickup (Ed.) *Brittle diabetes*. Oxford: Blackwell Scientific Publications.

Thomas, D. (1985). Living with a diabetic child. In J.D. Baum and A.-L. Kinmonth (Eds), *Care of the child with diabetes*, Edinburgh: Churchill Livingstone.

Wulsin, L.R., Jacobson, A.M., and Rand, L.I. (1987). Psychosocial aspects of diabetic retinopathy. *Diabetes Care*, **10**, 367–371.

5 Counselling and Renal Failure

KEITH A. NICHOLS
Department of Psychology
University of Exeter, Exeter, EX4 4QG

I will use this chapter as an opportunity to review what I have learned about counselling in a renal unit since 1978, the year in which my service to the local renal unit began. At that time, the basic notion held at the unit was that 'psychological input' in the form of counselling and psychological therapy was something which was administered when a person surviving by dialysis deviated from the norm and stopped being 'a happy patient'. The psychological service was used rather like a fire brigade, to subdue emotional hot-spots and contain troubled behaviour. Things are quite different now. Most importantly, my work has changed from the pattern of receiving people who had been referred by the staff for counselling, to an approach which results in *all* those attending the unit (including partners) having an automatic provision of preventive counselling which is usually provided by the nursing staff rather than myself.

The disadvantage of the earlier, characteristically medical approach was that people were often 'sent' for counselling rather than being invited to request to see a counsellor whenever they felt in need of support or found themselves struggling badly with their situation. Being 'sent' to the counsellor was often a cause for embarrassment and shame, however, since those involved often tended to regard the event as suggesting failure and weakness on their part. This meant that motivation was not always high, or was replaced by resentment. Furthermore, it meant that the 'ticket' of obvious distress was necessary in order to be noticed by the staff as needing help; the thought of heading off the difficulties at an earlier stage was, to all intents and purposes, absent. In other words, it was a very selective scheme of referral which operated on a casualty rather than preventive basis. This was not effective nor efficient and a search was begun for an alternative based on preventive principles.

Renal units have the major advantage of having a high staff/patient ratio combined with long term contact with patients. Sometimes this contact lasts well beyond ten years, thus allowing for the development of stable relationships between the staff and the patients. The nurses in particular have a high

Counselling and Communication in Health Care. Edited by H. Davis and L. Fallowfield
© 1991 John Wiley & Sons Ltd

degree of contact through dialysis and dialysis training, home dialysis supervision and transplant aftercare. It became apparent to me that the objective of providing the unit with a counselling resource which would operate on a preventive basis could be achieved by exploiting this advantage. If much of the work of basic, preventive counselling was undertaken by nurses then their numbers would be sufficient to provide all those receiving treatment and their partners with counselling support.

THE APPROACH TO COUNSELLING

Earlier chapters have dealt in detail with the nature of counselling and there is no need to rework this material. However, it is relevant, as part of this historical narrative, to mention the basic concept of counselling which influenced the developments to be described. I have always regarded counselling as having two modes, advisory counselling and personal counselling.

Advisory counselling

The key characteristic of this style of counselling is that the main traffic of communication flows from the counsellor, although the communication is modified according to the needs of the person with whom he or she is working. The work includes giving information and advice, shaping attitudes, supplying objectives for behaviour change and rehabilitation plans, and clarifying present and future medical intentions. The basic content of advisory counselling is, therefore, to do with what the counsellor needs to say. Such work must be conducted in a counselling style though with close attention to the reactions of the person or people involved. It is of critical importance that these reactions are expressed and explored, and thus advisory counselling is essentially interactive.

Some might doubt the suitability of using the term 'counselling' for such work. However, as the vast literature on medical communication demonstrates, the asymmetric doctor/nurse centred style of communication not only fails to achieve effective information exchange but is often a source of stress (Hauser, 1981; Ley, 1982; Maguire, 1984). If staff approach the task of information exchange in the role of counsellor with a conscious intent to remain patient centred despite delivering information, experience suggests that this counters some of the usual shortcomings (see Chapter 5 in Nichols, 1984). To summarise, the counsellor meets the individual knowing what has to be said, yet he or she stays aware of the critical importance of an interactive style and the need to make it a two-way exchange.

Personal counselling

By contrast the key characteristic of this mode of counselling is that the counsellor arrives at a session knowing only that he or she has to provide a safe, interpersonal environment and an opportunity for the person involved to express and explore feelings and experience. The objective is to allow the recognition and expression of the profound reactions which the struggle with renal failure usually provokes. The counsellor seeks to give 'permission' for these normal but distressing emotional processes and, importantly, a sense of them being valued by the staff. As in all effective counselling, this emotional care clears the way for reappraisal, problem solving and target setting.

THE CONTEXT AND THE COUNSELLING TASK

Renal failure is not highly prevalent, there being about 40 000 people in complete renal failure in the UK at the present time. The common causes include chronic glomerulonephritis (tissue damage resulting from abnormal antibodies), infections and a failure of the small blood vessels in the kidneys resulting from diabetes or high blood pressure.

The onset of renal failure may be progressive, with many months or years of predialysis monitoring and treatment. For some, though, events take another course and, without prior warning, they find themselves precipitated into total renal failure. In the past, such an occurrence was inevitably fatal, with death following within a matter of days. Now, as is well known, life can be continued by means of the techniques of dialysis and renal transplantation.

In haemodialysis, blood is diverted from a major blood vessel, and passed through an artificial kidney which simulates kidney function. Direct access to major blood vessels is essential since high blood flow rates are necessary. The standard technique involves surgery to create a junction between an artery and vein in the forearm. This is called a fistula. Cannulae (large needles) are then inserted into the fistula to draw and return blood for the duration of a dialysis session. Dialysis sessions usually take about 4–5 hours, at a frequency of three times per week. The assistance of a partner or nurse is necessary. Training for home dialysis takes six months on average, and requires the acquisition of significant skills and acceptance of considerable responsibility. Fistulas may fail and, for some, this initiates a difficult struggle for 'access'.

In peritoneal dialysis, a permanent catheter is inserted into the abdominal cavity. A fluid, termed 'dialysate', is fed into the body cavity through the catheter. This fluid attracts water, ions and certain breakdown products of general metabolism which accumulate in the blood. After an appropriate time the dialysate is drained, thus carrying these substances away. The operation is then recycled with fresh dialysate. A machine system can be used, with dialysis sessions on alternating nights. Usually, though, CAPD (continuous ambulatory peritoneal dialysis), a bag change system with four bag changes per day, each day, is favoured. CAPD offers the advantage of 'steady-state' as opposed to 'tidal' blood chemistry, better control of hypertension, reduced cardiovascular stress, fewer problems with anaemia and fewer dietary restrictions. It is marginally cheaper, does not need a partner's assistance and requires less training time. However, peritonitis is often a major problem with this technique.

Both these techniques are successful in sustaining life in the event of kidney failure but they do not offer a perfect or problem free substitute for normal kidney function. The overall mortality rate for those surviving by dialysis is approximately 10% per year.

Life with these techniques cannot be described as a return to full and free normality. In the space of this short chapter it will be impossible to represent the real character of survival by dialysis and the profound impact which it can have upon a family. However, I hope that by use of an extended case outline, some hints at what is involved and the task which nurse counsellors must take on can be conveyed to you.

Case study: haemodialysis and a failed transplant attempt

This case study compresses a great number of events which befell a young mother and her family during a period of five years. The subject of the study, Marion, went into unexpected renal failure following a viral infection. She was 31, married, and had two children of 3 and 5 years. Her husband, Ian, worked as an engineer earning a modest income on which they totally depended. After a few days of an influenza-like infection, Marion appeared to deteriorate. Initially her GP did not diagnose renal failure and she spent several very frightening days as she became nauseous with violent headaches, found her joints and muscles stiffening and aching and generally became alarmingly weak. She was admitted to the general hospital and quickly transferred to the renal unit. Her condition was stabilised with emergency haemodialysis. Within a few days the position was clear and both Marion and her husband were told of this and given an indication of what would now happen. Her kidneys were both in irreversible total failure. She was to receive long-term haemodialysis. This meant attending the renal unit three times a week for a period of about six hours (the approximate time between arrival and departure) for a dialysis session. Initially she would be dialysed by the nurses. However, over the following months both she and her husband were required to train to self-sufficiency in the technique, and this meant that her husband had to attend many of the sessions too. After this, a machine was to be installed in her home and she would conduct her own treatment there with the help of her husband. This was indeed exactly the pattern of events which took place.

The psychological burden upon Marion and Ian at this point was enormous. Marion had changed from a normal healthy mother and wife to a person who was very much weakened and who needed constant medical and nursing intervention. Both of them felt anger towards the GP for failing to identify the renal failure although, in fact, early diagnosis would have made little difference to the outcome. Nevertheless, there was no real way to discharge this anger. The event of the renal failure and the slowly emerging implications of the situation were extremely frightening to them both. Almost immediately it became clear that the logistical demands alone were a nightmare. They depended on Ian's income yet he was required to be at the unit on many of the dialysis sessions for training. Marion needed to be with her children and, in particular, to cope with starting her oldest child at school. She, though, had to be away at the unit three times a week. With travel this took up at least eight hours. She thus felt the very great discomfort of being a mother too far away to be of any help to her children should a crisis arise. Ian had to absorb the fact that his wife was now the victim of a life-threatening illness which was not reversible. At the same time he had to maintain the basics of family life for the children, keep his job secured, and learn the wholly new skills of haemodialysis (including venepuncture, setting up a dialysis machine, monitoring and running a dialysis session).

The staff at the unit clearly realised that this young couple were under extreme stress and did their best to offer maximum flexibility and support. Using the backup of local family and friends, care for the children was managed for the six-month training period. Ian successfully juggled work and dialysis shifts so that he obtained sufficient training sessions to become proficient. Dialysis transferred to the home with the assistance of a home-care sister from the unit.

Haemodialysis is a close enough simulation of kidney function to avert death. It does not, however, bring about a restoration of normal health and vitality. Patients tend to suffer from the effects of uraemia, a condition caused by the accumulation of toxins such as urea between dialysis sessions. Anaemia and high blood pressure are also significant problems. Although the control of anaemia has improved with the recent advent of a new drug called erythropoietin, unfortunately Marion had to go without its benefits and suffered quite severe anaemia. The combined effect of these problems, together with the severe constraints of dialysis on time and mobility often has a very erosive effect on morale. Yet further demands are imposed by the host of irksome minor ills associated with uraemia. Figure 5.1 lists the range of effects which can impinge on those surviving by haemodialysis and thus influence their psychological state.

In these terms, Marion returned home a weakened and distracted woman. Early hopes of re-establishing normality were abandoned. She did not have the physical power and energy to run the home properly, cope with the children, walk into town for shopping, or offer a sexual relationship. Ian and the nearby members of the family devised a pattern for substituting her in her domestic and maternal roles.

loss of physical energy and muscle power (can eventually be considerable, e.g. climbing stairs or even turning taps can become difficult).

minor physical ills—itching skin, nausea, giddyness, constant fatigue, restless legs, cramps, headache.

the constraints of dialysis (unavoidable routines which take time, interrupt activity, inhibit travel).

the discomfort, tensions and risks of dialysis (needling, the enforced immobility during sessions, blood leaks or clots, air bubbles).

dietary constraints and liquid intake limits.

threats for the future (failure of vascular access, infections, long-term deterioration of health and reduced life expectancy).

major losses in occupational, social, recreational, sexual and family roles.

losses to the sense of personal worth and power, the experience of being a long-term burden.

Figure 5.1. Renal failure and haemodialysis: physical impact and stressors

Likewise it fell to Ian to run the dialysis sessions three nights a week once he had returned home from work. Usually it would be midnight before the sessions were finished.

Marion hated haemodialysis because she felt trapped in a small room with a machine for five hours. She also found it physically uncomfortable, verging on painful at times. Much more seriously, she began to hate herself. In such a short space it is impossible to catch the full range and depth of her feelings but basically they were to do with being in the way, being a burden on her family and especially her partner. Her inability to be an effective mother (in her eyes) and wife pressed down on her very heavily. As the years passed, one thought in particular became familiar, 'They truly would be better off without me, he could find a proper wife and the children could have a proper mother'. I do not need to elaborate upon the extraordinary sadness and isolation that life takes on when a person wakes to this thought each day.

Initially, however, she did not give way to the situation because there was some hope. After running into increasing problems with haemodialysis she was converted onto CAPD (continuous ambulatory peritoneal dialysis) and life took on an improved tone. Although her strength did not return, she found benefits in this alternative system of dialysis and gained a little in morale. This also coincided with increasing hope that she might soon receive a transplant. Towards the end of her fourth year there were problems with recurrent peritonitis and the efficiency of her dialysis began to fade as a result. This created great tension since the possibility of a return to haemodialysis increased. She began to be obsessive about being near her telephone in case a call came through offering a transplant. She found going out of the house increasingly bothersome. Relationships with her husband and the children came under greater strain as a result.

The last significant event in this history came with a transplant attempt. This took place after about five years of dialysis. When successful, renal transplants offer a restoration of normal kidney function and thus the very real prospect of a return to near normal health and energy. Regrettably, there is a large shortfall in the supply of healthy kidneys for transplantation and there is no certainty that the operation will prove successful. Surgical problems or, more likely, rejection of the transplanted kidney by a massive immune reaction cause a steady flow of failed transplants. Both the wait for a transplant (which can go on for many years) and the uncertain outcome mean that there is much emotion associated with the whole issue. Marion's spirits lifted enormously the first few days after her operation. However, consistent with the pattern of events that had befallen her during the preceding five years, things did not go well. Her new kidney appeared to begin working and then faltered. She produced a massive rejection reaction and although the staff made every effort possible, after several weeks it had to be faced that the attempt was a failure and the kidney was removed. Worse, because of her general condition, there was no alternative to the resumption of haemodialysis.

Almost everybody involved with Marion harboured doubts about her ability to carry on with home haemodialysis. These doubts proved accurate and there followed a period of dialysis at the unit, combined with considerable support. It was clear, though, that she had completely lost heart and was fading. She was very sad and tearful and lost weight rapidly. Once a pretty woman, she became sallow, drawn and painfully thin. I spoke to her a few days before she died and it was clear that death was the thing she now longed for. No longer bitter but bitterly sad that she was soon to part with her children and Ian, her thoughts were again centred on the notion of being an obstacle to the happiness of her family. Her death saddened the unit since bonds grow and people in treatment link with staff as if in an extended family.

Marion had been a part of the unit life for several years and much effort and care had been devoted to her and her family. Many of the staff were distressed by the nature of her death. Ian, who had throughout the entire time maintained a hope of cure and thus had persevered with much courage was numbed. He could see that Marion longed for escape but he did not want to be left on his own with the children. He felt cheated. The children, though, were so used to 'mum being away in hospital' that for the first few weeks at least little seemed to change.

A proportion of people with renal failure suffer a pattern of events similar to this story. Fortunately a significant number have an easier time with a period of relatively trouble free dialysis followed by a successful transplant. Overall, it is a complicated picture with little by way of reliable figures on which to assess the size of these proportions and the total experience of the population. Quality of life can be influenced by so many factors; the staff, the unit as a whole, the different types and styles of treatment, other medical complications such as neuropathy and cardio-vascular problems, levels of support, marital factors and family issues.

With the time span of treatment frequently exceeding ten years, people may have phases in their history which swing from one extreme to the other. Those involved in counselling work in a renal unit must, therefore, be prepared for great variation in circumstance amongst patients. Virtually none will be problem free, but there will be a great range in the severity and frequency of the various difficulties. It will also be clear from Figure 1 that counselling sessions often have to take place with a person who feels lethargic and unwell. Again, this is very variable, but the counsellor should never lose sight of it and needs a degree of flexibility in modifying sessions accordingly. At times, it will be best to discuss whether a full session should be left until another day, in which case a few minutes supportive contact will have to suffice.

Needless to say the psychological reaction to renal failure does not bear a predictable relationship with the medical circumstances of a specific individual. It has been instructive for me to meet people who have suffered extreme difficulties yet seem resilient psychologically. I think particularly of a man in his early forties who was in renal failure as a late life complication of diabetes. Despite a dialysis history in which he encountered just about every known problem and despite increasing retinopathy with visual impairment combined with the loss of a foot, both a result of microvascular failure from the diabetes, he remained psychologically robust. In contrast, other people who have actually lacked the feature of recurring difficulties have had periods of tremendous emotional upheaval, sometimes even after a successful transplant.

It is a familiar experience for me in this type of counselling work to discover that those who react to renal failure with a prolonged depressive or anger based pattern are often those whose sense of personal worth has been heavily dependent on 'doing'. That is, 'I am worthwhile because of my business success' or 'I am worthwhile because of my work as a nurse'. When the renal failure obstructs the 'doing', the person is left stripped of the mainstay to his or her sense of personal worth. The depressive collapse or the angry lashing out at the family, the staff and the unit express the tremendous psychological wound that the renal failure has created. A typical example of this pattern is that of a middle-aged business man who, prior to the onset of renal failure, had been noted for his tremendous energy and his committed involvement. This was not only with his business, but also in local community activities. Above all he was a great organiser and problem-solver. His kidneys failed and he was established with comparative ease on peritoneal dialysis. However, he rapidly became a polar opposite in character. His wife despaired because he did nothing all day and depended on her entirely. If she did not give him his drugs they went untaken. If she did not organise him, he simply sat motionless and morose for hours. The key feature which emerged in counselling was that in his eyes he was now valueless because he had been forced to abandon his work and activities. Not only was there grief but also very powerful self-condemnation.

SURVEY FINDINGS

There is, of course, a substantial literature reporting the general psychological disposition of people with renal failure. These findings have been summarised elsewhere (Nichols 1989), but it is relevant to give a brief indication of the trends to be found in this literature. Most surveys report a substantial proportion of people (up to 75%) who cannot comply with the dietary and fluid restrictions associated with dialysis. They are inevitably prone to depressed episodes, anxieties and persistent worries, with assessment of prevalence ranging between 35% and 69%. Indications are that approximately 25% experience unequivocal 'clinical' depression. The suicide rate is substantially higher than the normal population (at least 100 times more frequent). Partners are often equally badly affected psychologically, with up to 75% experiencing anxieties and depression. Full return to work is achieved by as little as 25% of those on dialysis. Useful collections of research material from which these findings are drawn include Levy (1981 and 1983), especially the papers by Kaplan De-Nour (1981 and 1983). Other relevant papers include Abram, Moore and Westvelt (1971), Farmer, Snowdon and Parsons (1979), Kutner, Fair and Kutner (1985), Livesley (1982) and Nichols and Springford (1984). A further general finding, which those likely to be involved with counselling in a renal unit should note, is that the sense of personal worth and general morale may be further undermined as a result of sexual dysfunction. This is a very common problem for those on dialysis, affecting both men and women (Degan, Strain and Zumoff, 1983).

Although renal transplantation is a possible escape route from dialysis it too may bring many stresses. These may be greatly amplified if the transplant involves a live donor as opposed to a cadaveric donor. The failure of a transplant attempt is usually a tremendous disappointment, at times equivalent in emotional effect to a death in the family. If, however, the transplant from a live donor fails then the psychological impact will usually be that much greater. Not infrequently guilt on the part of the recipient becomes a significant psychological complication. Approximately 20–30% of grafted kidneys will fail before 12 months. Simmons (1983), in a long term follow-up study, recorded 71% and 47% survival rates respectively for live and cadaver-doned grafts within a five to nine year timespan. Those with surviving grafts were generally in a fairly good state physically and only a few had serious psychological problems. Some people do find problems with the transition from the invalid role back to near normality, others become oppressed by the ever present risk of the kidney failing and thus an enforced return to dialysis. Obsessive patterns may result and Muthny (1984) gives a useful review of such psychological problems.

The position of children who are in renal failure is a concern which, regrettably, cannot be covered in this chapter. Levy (1981 and 1983) and Fielding *et al.* (1985) serve as useful sources. Mention should be made though, that much damage can result to the relationships between adults in renal failure and their children. Children can tire of the constant atmosphere of illness, particularly when there is no visible cure to the problem. The near inevitable fatigue and irritability on the part of the parent can create resentments and negative comparisons with other parents. In contrast, other children will sense the risks and impact of the illness and worry greatly over the issue of handicap and death.

THE STRATEGY FOR COUNSELLING INTERVENTION

Earlier, I presented the view that because renal failure is inevitably associated with a high level of stress and psychological demand all the patients of a renal unit and their partners should be offered a supportive counselling facility on a preventive basis. The only obvious way to cope with the numbers involved and also provide frequent contact is to engage the nurses in this counselling endeavour. Having now also presented a case and thus a brief glimpse of the extent and nature of the problems which people in renal failure may face, it will be obvious that there is a drawback in this scheme. People like Marion and her family are in great psychological difficulty. For the counsellor and psychotherapist alike, work with them is not for the beginner; experience and skill will be needed. Furthermore, involvement with such people places a heavy personal load on a counsellor, and this, again, is unsuitable for a novice in counselling. It is quite easy to provide nurses with instruction in basic counselling skills in order that they may undertake routine, supportive counselling duties. However, a proportion of people demand very much more than basic counselling skills and the provision of cover for these requires additional resources.

A strategy outlined in Nichols (1984) emphasises a two-tier approach as a means of dealing with this problem. Nurses are accepted in post at our renal unit on the assumption that they will attend training in, and then implement, a set of practices called psychological care. This takes place in the context of a primary nursing scheme. Each fully qualified nurse has overall responsibility for the whole range of nursing duties with up to five patients and their partners. In psychological terms there are several key roles. Perhaps the most fundamental is that of the nurse as a supportive, professional companion. In other words, she is entrusted with the task of building a relationship with the people under her care in which they feel there is permission to express and explore personal feelings and problems associated with the situation. It is important that this behaviour should be valued by the staff, with time being set aside for it.

Holding preventive objectives in mind, the nurses are schooled in the two modes of counselling described earlier. Great value is placed on advisory counselling (we used to call it informational care, or caring by informing), wherein each nurse seeks to maintain the information retained by her patients at a level which generates realistic expectations of the immediate future. At the same time they are encouraged to use their primary nurse as a companion/personal counsellor on a regular basis. This notion of 'companion' may seem unusual, yet it is central within this scheme. People often report how valuable it is to have a link with someone on the staff who can truly comprehend the psychological experience of dialysis and transplantation. Furthermore, it is of tremendous value that this member of staff does not have a brief to 'treat and discharge' when psychological problems arise, rather there is an alternative brief to make an enduring, supportive relationship which is free of a time limit and functions on a reliable, on-demand basis. The nurse counsellor is thus available to listen, to encourage a full and honest expression of feeling, to assist with a review of problems and help formulate plans to deal with these. She will also function as the patient's advocate within the unit generally. It is a very person-centred approach and, with the preventive emphasis, carries the advantages listed in Figure 5.2. As the scheme has evolved the 'home sisters', that is nurse-counsellors who

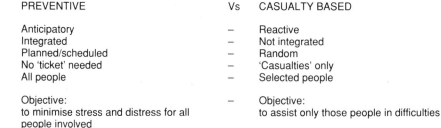

PREVENTIVE	Vs	CASUALTY BASED
Anticipatory	–	Reactive
Integrated	–	Not integrated
Planned/scheduled	–	Random
No 'ticket' needed	–	'Casualties' only
All people	–	Selected people
Objective: to minimise stress and distress for all people involved	–	Objective: to assist only those people in difficulties

Figure 5.2. Style of counselling in medicine

visit and monitor all patients on home-dialysis, have an extended relationship with those people under their care which may last for years. The unit-based, primary nurses rotate to a new set of patients every two months.

Training and supervision opportunities for nurses in counselling vary greatly from region to region but in general they are modest. In addition the work demands which renal nurses face are very large, despite being units with a high staff-patient ratio. Thus, a reality to be dealt with in this type of scheme is that there are definite limits to what the nurses can take on and achieve in terms of counselling. Hence, there is a need for a second tier of more 'advanced' counselling support.

At Exeter the nurses have a very clear message, 'if your counselling work with a person feels like it is getting too demanding of expertise or time, then involve the unit psychologist to function either as an advisor or to assist with direct work on the case'. In other units such a back-up role can equally well be maintained by a more senior nurse with advanced counselling training, a medical social worker, or psychiatrist. In general, the greater proportion of the work is at a level which our nurses can deal with and, fortunately, they seem to be in full accord with the notion that basic supportive and counselling duties are a legitimate extension of the nurse's role. Clearly, with a limited time budget, there are times when the staff are virtually overwhelmed by the duties of physical nursing and dialysis. It is not a permanent state, though, and even in such periods they always have capacity for monitoring their patients' psychological state and making some provision for care.

Overall, whether counselling is undertaken as an element of a scheme such as this or as an individual venture, the case work will prove much the same. There is nothing unique about counselling related to renal failure; the basic skills, objectives and evaluation are similar to those dealt with elsewhere in this book. I would certainly recommend most strongly that a style of work is adopted which allows close and regular contact with the other staff at a unit. Firstly, treatments can change dramatically and up-to-date information always helps. Secondly, most of the people involved face unavoidable threats, restrictions, discomforts and losses. Transplantation may delay these considerably, yet it it still appropriate to regard renal failure as a condition bringing about slow physical decline and, eventually, death. The problems encountered may range from the trivial to that, literally, of terminal care. Counselling in this setting can be a demanding role. Thus, those taking it on should always place a high priority on seeking an enduring source of support for themselves. Isolation in the role is hazardous. Membership in the team as a whole will help to provide this.

Naturally, I am often asked, 'Does it work?' In one sense the scheme has never fulfilled its potential. We have never actually had a full complement of nurses who are properly experienced in this work and confidently settled into the role. The tendency amongst nurses to move specialities after a year or so together with changes within the Health Service which have pushed Exeter (and most other units) into crisis survival tactics rather than service development, create real difficulties. In reality, we are constantly introducing nurses to the work only to lose them as they are beginning to become effective. Fortunately though, the higher grade nurses (sister and above) are much more settled. Even so, my assessment of the psychological work currently undertaken by our nurses is that it represents a dramatic improvement in the quality of care compared with that observed at the unit some years ago. Furthermore, there are signs of some other units following a similar path, which means that there may be some impressive developments during the coming decade.

REFERENCES

Abram, H.S., Moore, G., and Westvelt, F. (1971). Suicidal behaviour in chronic dialysis patients. *American Journal of Psychiatry*, **127**, 1199–1204.

Degan, K., Strain, J.J., and Zumoff, B. (1983). Biosocial evaluation of sexual function in end-stage renal disease. In N.B. Levy (Ed.), *Psychonephrology 2*. New York: Plenum.

Farmer, C.J., Snowdon, S.A., and Parsons, V. (1979). The prevalence of psychiatric disorder among patients on home dialysis. *Psychological Medicine*, **9**, 509–514.

Fielding, D., Moore, B., Dewey, M., Ashley, P., McKendrick, T., and Pinkerton, P. (1985). Children with end-stage renal failure: psychological effects on patients, siblings and parents. *Journal of Psychosomatic Research*, **29**, 457–465.

Hauser, S.T. (1981). Physician-patient relationships. In E.G. Mishler, L.R. AmaraSingham, S.T. Hauser, R. Liem, S.D. Osherson, and N.E. Waxler (Eds), *Social contexts of health, illness, and patient care*. Cambridge: Cambridge University Press.

Kaplan De-Nour, A. (1981). Prediction of adjustment to chronic haemodialysis. In N.B. Levy (Ed.), *Psychonephrology*. New York: Plenum.

Kaplan De-Nour, A. (1983). An overview of psychological problems in haemodialysis. In N.B. Levy (Ed.), *Psychonephrology 2*. New York: Plenum.

Kutner, N.G., Fair, P.L., and Kutner, M.H. (1985). Assessing depression and anxiety in chronic dialysis patients. *Journal of Psychosomatic Research*, **29**, 23–31.

Levy, N.B. (1981). *Psychonephrology*. New York: Plenum.

Levy, N.B. (1983). *Psychonephrology 2*. New York: Plenum.

Ley, P. (1982). Giving information to patients. In R.J. Eiser (Ed.), *Social psychology and behavioural science*. Chichester: Wiley.

Livesley, W.J. (1982). Symptoms of anxiety and depression in patients undergoing chronic haemodialysis. *Journal of Psychosomatic Research*, **26**, 581–584.

Maguire, P. (1984). Communication skills and patient care. In A. Steptoe and A. Mathews (Eds), *Health care and human behaviour*. London: Academic Press.

Muthny, F. (1984). Postoperative course of patients during hospitalisation following renal transplantation. *Psychotherapy and Psychosomatics*, **42**, 133–142.

Nichols, K.A. (1984). *Psychological care in physical illness*. Beckenham, Kent: Croom Helm.

Nichols, K.A. (1989). Renal Failure. In H.J. Lacey and T. Burns (Eds), *Psychological management of the physically ill*. London: Churchill Livingstone.

Nichols, K.A. and Springford, V. (1984). The psychosocial stressors associated with survival by dialysis. *Behaviour Research and Therapy*, **22**, 563–574.

Simmons, R. (1983). Long-term reactions of renal recipients and donors. In N.B. Levy (Ed.), *Psychonephrology 2*. New York: Plenum.

6 Counselling and Disfigurement

NICHOLA RUMSEY
Department of Nursing, Health & Applied Social Studies, Bristol Polytechnic, Coldharbour Lane, Bristol, UK.

INTRODUCTION

This chapter is concerned with the relevance of counselling for people who are disfigured. The World Health Organization and the American Medical Association have described disfigurement as 'an altered or abnormal appearance. It may be alteration of colour, shape or structure or a combination of these. Disfigurement may be a residual of an injury or disease or it may accompany a recurrent or chronic disorder or function or disease . . . with disfigurement there is usually no loss of body function and little or no effect on activities of daily living.' (from Bernstein, 1988). This description reflects the medical approach which currently dominates the provision of care for the disfigured in the UK, and which focuses primarily on the presence or absence of functional deficits associated with the disfigurement. In this chapter it will be suggested that as disfigurement can have far reaching effects on people's everyday lives, the medical approach is inadequate and in some cases may even be inappropriate. It is also suggested that counselling, ideally as part of a multidisciplinary approach, could go a long way to redressing the current inadequacies in the provision of care for these people.

Why do people with disfigurements experience problems in our society? The importance of physical appearance is apparent in many ways, for example, consumers in both the USA and the UK spend large sums of money on cosmetic products (Cash and Cash, 1982). The cosmetic industry constantly exerts pressure through advertising and through the media about how we should look, dress and act. These endorse the view that beautiful people have happy professional and social lives. Those people with an abnormal physical appearance have to cope with these pressures and with the stigma associated in our society with people who look 'different'.

The importance of physical appearance in many aspects of social functioning is also widely recognised. A person's physical appearance is usually the first information that is available to the perceiver, and it remains continuously available during social interaction. Research has shown that the

Counselling and Communication in Health Care. Edited by H. Davis and L. Fallowfield
© 1991 John Wiley & Sons Ltd

way we look forms a potent and immediately evident basis for an initial evaluation, and that although the impact of physical appearance lessens as we get to know people better, our first impressions may intrude into and affect any subsequent evaluation of the person.

During the 1970s and 1980s there has been a large increase in the amount of research directed towards the potential benefits of having an attractive physical appearance, (for a review see Bull and Rumsey, 1988). However, research into the related topic of the social disadvantages which may be associated with disfigurement remains a neglected area. Scant attention has been paid to the psychological and social problems experienced by people considered to be ugly, disfigured or deformed. Despite indications that an aesthetically unattractive appearance may impair social functioning, there has been little recognition either by society or psychologists of the problems encountered by people who deviate from society's norms primarily in terms of appearance, and not necessarily in body functioning.

This neglect both in research and in service provision is particularly re-grettable as in addition to those born with disfiguring congenital conditions and those in whom disfiguring diseases develop in later life, there have recently been increases in the numbers of disfigurements resulting from muggings, terrorist attacks and other acts of violence. Improved surgical and medical techniques have meant that an increasing number of people are surviving with horrific, very visible injuries as a consequence, for example, of the Falklands war, road traffic accidents, industrial injuries, and terrorist bombings. Improved care of cancer patients has also meant that more pa-tients survive after the removal of tumours.

Considerable advancements have been made in the anatomical and func-tional rehabilitation of malocclusion, cleft lip, craniofacial anomalies, and traumatic disfigurement. Yet despite these advances and despite the fact that there are numerous indications that disfigurements can cause extensive problems in many aspects of everyday life, counselling and other interven-tions designed to cater for patients' psychological and social needs are still rarely available.

COMMON PROBLEMS ASSOCIATED WITH DISFIGUREMENT

The lack of research in this area makes it difficult to provide a definitive overview of the issues for those interested in counselling and disfigurement. However, there are indications that problems for the disfigured occur with greater frequency at particular times and in particular situations (Bull and Rumsey, 1988), and that individual factors will vary the way they react. Although the lack of research makes it impossible to provide general an-swers as to how these problems should be tackled in a counselling situation, the issues discussed in this section are likely to be important and should be considered when counselling interventions are being planned.

The type and location of the disfigurement

Several factors relating to the type of disfigurement should be considered, as these may affect the problems experienced by the person. In general, those disfigurements affecting the face are particularly problematical, due to the heavy involvement of the face in communication and the difficulties posed in concealing facial disfigurements effectively. Whether or not people subscribe to the view espoused by Cicero that 'The countenance is the reflection of the soul', people with facial abnormalities are likely to be at a disadvantage in the process of impression formation. Disfiguration of the hands can also pose difficulties as once again they are widely used in communication, and cannot always be hidden.

Some researchers have tried to equate the level of disfiguration (for example, mild, moderate or severe) to the experience of social and psychological problems. However, the findings from this research are far from clearcut, with no apparent relationship existing between the level of disfigurement and long-term adjustment.

Another important aspect to take into account is the aetiology of the disfigurement. Once again there are many factors which may play a part in the problems experienced. Is the disfigurement the result of a congenital problem present from birth, or was there a later onset? Some research has suggested that congenital disfigurements tend to produce a more negative reaction from others than those which result from traumatic injury (Bull and Rumsey, 1988). In the case of traumatic injury or of disfigurements with an onset after birth, the prior levels of physical attractiveness, self-esteem and social skill should be considered. Is the person able to accept the differing reactions to their new physical appearance, able to rely more on other aspects of their personality, or mourning 'the way things used to be'? Is the disfiguration likely to be temporary (for example adolescent acne), recurring (for example, eczema), or permanent (for example, a port wine stain). If the origin of the disfigurement is the result of some sort of trauma, is there any guilt or blame attached to it? Is the patient a 'hero' or a 'victim?' Are there any compensation claims still to be resolved (if so, the person may have a vested interest in experiencing problems). Is the disfigurement associated with a life threatening disease such as cancer?

The birth and early development of disfigured children

Parents have expectations and hopes for their children even before birth and many prospective parents worry about whether their child will be 'whole'. At birth, the two most common questions are 'Is it a boy or girl?', and 'Is it all right?'. Adverse reactions to having produced a child that is in some way congenitally disfigured begin at this point. Several authors have observed the concerns and responses of parents of children born with a cleft lip and/

or palate. Parents initially worry about the survival of their child, most commonly because of feeding or respiratory difficulties. These worries give way to others concerning the child's speech, dentition and social development. Lansdown (1981) suggested that the birth of a congenitally disfigured child is a shock to the family system, akin to a bereavement reaction, in which parents experience a variety of emotions including grief, anxiety, frustration, guilt, hurt, inadequacy, rejection, resentment, shock, stigmatisation and withdrawal. Other researchers have concentrated on how the news is broken to parents, their prior means of coping with stress, the nature of the marital relationship, the infant's capacity to interact normally, and the role of environmental supports, all of which should be considered within the context of a counselling relationship.

One common dilemma facing the family with a disfigured child is the issue of hospitalisation, as operations may frequently be necessary for cosmetic or functional repair. Parents must strike a balance between the likelihood of increasing the child's chances of physical and social adaptation (by having the operation and hopefully reducing the level of disfiguration) and the physical and social reactions the child may experience as a result of lengthy treatment and hence separation from family and friends.

A current and relevant debate concerns the ethical issues associated with plastic surgery for Down's Syndrome. Major issues here include society's acceptance or otherwise of the facial abnormalities associated with Down's Syndrome and indeed, with other disfigurements; whether plastic surgery might lead to parental denial of the child's limitations; the infliction on the child of avoidable pain and trauma; the impact on the decision-making process of the opinions of the surgeons, the parents and other interested parties; and the cost of surgery. Both with this and with other related problems facing those with young disfigured children, the potential benefits of understanding and informed advice and support, preferably offered as part of a counselling relationship are clear and are discussed more fully below.

The family environment

The family environment is of crucial importance to the development and well-being of disfigured people. The attitudes, expectations and degree of support shown by the people closest to the person are likely to have an enormous influence on the way they perceive their own disfigurement. A disfigured person will have good prospects in a family that shows little concern for the role of physical appearance in a successful and fulfilling life. If the family is supportive and positive, the disfigured member will be able to develop a self-image that is essentially positive. In long-term relations, others will therefore be able to react more to the person's personality than to the disfigurement.

Communication difficulties may frequently occur in families. For example, children may not want to hurt their parents by talking about their problems openly, and their parents may feel that a cheerful exterior should be preserved at all costs.

The later development of disfigured children

In later life, disfigured children may encounter a variety of problems at school. For example, anxieties concerning appearance (experienced by the child and/or the parents) are likely to be at their height during the first year at a new school, and between the ages of 10 and 16 years. The onset of a disfiguring condition caused by a traumatic injury or by a very visible condition such as vitiligo (which affects the pigmentation of the skin) or psoriasis, at the prepubertal or pubertal stage is likely to be particularly upsetting. Stereotyping by other children on the basis of physical appearance has been demonstrated from the age of 5 years (Bull and Rumsey, 1988). This stereotyping usually manifests itself in nicknames and teasing, and frequently works to the disadvantage of the disfigured child.

Anecdotal evidence together with a limited amount of research suggests that disfigured people may have more difficulty than nondisfigured people in obtaining jobs, in settling down in new work environments and in meeting new people, than their nondisfigured counterparts. There is also some limited evidence that they tend to marry at a lower rate, and have fewer children. Access to counselling for children and their parents at later stages of development can once again be seen to be crucial.

Disfigurement and society

What of the influence exerted on disfigured people and their families by the society in which they live? Human societies have always had in their midst the physically deformed or ugly. Reactions to such people have varied, but have in general been that of abhorrence. From the first cave paintings to the present, all cultures have been involved in representing and interpreting the human form, with the majority endorsing the value of youth and beauty, and many associating distortions of the human form with evil and terror (Macgregor, 1974). Facial deformity in particular has been associated with mental retardation. Hogarth's 18th century paintings of depravity and in-mates of mental institutions are notorious for portraying ugly or deformed faces.

Most people have a desire to conform to the standards of the society in which they live, and a failure to do so (whether temporary or permanent) sets people apart both in their own estimation and in the opinions of others. The powerful pressure that society exerts on disfigured people can be illus-trated by the enormous increase in the demand for cosmetic surgery in recent years.

Patients seeking surgery

Prior to the advent of plastic surgery in Western culture, the band of those considered to be in the realms of normality was broader. Now, with surgeons able to offer 'improvements' in the appearance of many, our perceptions of the acceptability of physical deviations has become narrower (Kalick, 1982). Concerns have been reawakened in many people who had formerly accepted their disfigurements. The availability of 'corrective' surgery, whilst offering hope for many, also exacerbates the problems posed to the disfigured by society's emphasis on the body beautiful.

In the case of those seeking aesthetic plastic surgery, the motivation behind the desire to change appearance should be considered. Does the drive come from the patient, the family and or the surgeon? Has a particular event precipitated the request, or is it the result of a long-standing desire? Are the patients' expectations of the outcome realistic. For example, do they expect the disfigurement to be removed, or (more realistically in the majority of cases) made less noticeable? In what ways do they expect life to be different without the disfigurement? Is there a particular problem they believe an altered appearance will solve, or do they (again, probably more realistically) feel that a change in their appearance will give them more confidence in their everyday dealings with other people?

How will they cope if the outcome of the operation is disappointing? Assuming it is successful, how much more or less attention do they expect to receive from others? Do they have the social skill to cope with the increase in positive attention? Will they mind if no-one notices the difference, or if they are paid *less* attention, as they are no longer considered abnormal and their new appearance affords them the anonymity in the crowd that has previously been lacking.

Self-esteem

Some researchers have specifically considered the relationship between disfigurement and self-esteem. As children get older, they meet others outside the family, and encounter images from books, radio, and television concerning their peers. Many of these experiences are potentially negative for the self-esteem of those children who are visibly different from the norm. Regardless of what people do actually think about them (the evidence is mixed) there seems little doubt in the minds of many disfigured people that members of the general public do hold negative attitudes towards them. Systematic research on this topic is meagre. The bulk of information comes from classical and modern literature, religious writings, folklore, popular humour, and from the personal accounts of the visibly stigmatised. In a host of written and oral accounts, the theme of being pitied, subordinated, stared at, or ignored appears. People with enlarged red noses caused by angioma, for example, may complain that people frequently mistake them for a drunk. Those with facial paralysis may state that others take them for 'a wise guy' because they talk out of the side of their mouths. It is therefore small wonder that many suffer from a lack of self-esteem, a problem that good counselling could do much to redress.

Social interaction

The most common problems associated with disfigurement seem to be encountered in social interaction, especially in initial encounters. Disfigured people report that they experience staring, feelings of pity and revulsion in others, and that people frequently go to lengths to avoid them. Research has shown that in many cases, avoidance does occur. People may increase their pace, avert their gaze or pretend not to notice that the disfigured person is attempting to engage them in an interaction. Although this behaviour is frequently the result of the desire of the general public to avoid a situation in which they are not quite sure how to behave, the avoidance is frequently interpreted by the disfigured person as 'rejection'. The interaction style of many disfigured people may become hampered by a fear of this rejection and consequent problems relating to a lowering of self-esteem may pervade many aspects of social functioning.

The expectation of negative reactions may become a self-fulfilling prophecy, with the disfigured person behaving in a way which elicits reciprocal negative behaviour from others. Many become preoccupied with the effect their appearance has on other people, and tend to monitor the reactions of others very closely. Some adopt a technique of hostile bravado, whilst other appear to be very shy, or very aggressive. Whatever the interaction style, there is frequently dissatisfaction with the quality and quantity of the social interaction achieved, and widespread reports of loneliness from disfigured people (Bull and Rumsey, 1988). However, research has also suggested that if a disfigured person does manage to strike up a conversation, members of the public may well be more pleasant and helpful than they would to a nondisfigured person (Rumsey, 1983).

In sum it can be seen that some consensus exists as to the events and situations frequently associated with problems for disfigured people. However, it should be borne in mind that the situations mentioned above are not by any means problems for all disfigured people, and that individual factors must always be taken into account when considering counselling.

RECOMMENDATIONS FOR THE COUNSELLING OF DISFIGURED PEOPLE

Although there is little scientific evidence that counselling is beneficial for disfigured people, those with experience of caring for the disfigured are in agreement that counselling represents an extremely relevant intervention for many. This view is endorsed by the organisations set up specifically to deal with matters of concern to disfigured people ('Let's Face It' and 'The Disfigurement Guidance Centre'), although there is as yet no consensus as to how this counselling should best be provided.

In addition to the skills and attributes characteristic of good counselling, which have been outlined earlier in the book, those wishing to work in the field of disfigurement should have a good knowledge of the treatment and problems commonly associated with disfigurement, and a working knowledge of the health care system. Counsellors need to be somewhat eclectic in approach, able to adopt various styles and techniques according to the differing and changing needs of those they seek to help. For example, as many problems experienced by disfigured people are associated with social interaction, counsellors may find it useful to consider the potential benefits of social skills training for some people.

Individual differences in the levels of social skill of disfigured people are enormous. However, for many, it may be helpful to teach patterns of social behaviour that enable the nondisfigured to appear at ease in social interaction, thus making a relaxed and favourable response more likely. The social skill variable has been shown to have a significantly greater impact on the behaviour and impressions formed by other people than the presence or absence of a disfigurement (Rumsey, Bull and Gahagen, 1986). As mentioned above, those who deliberately counter the problems they experience in social interactions by being particularly charming and active in taking the initiative in opening and sustaining the interaction tend to fare better than others who rely on the nondisfigured to take the lead (Rumsey, 1983). It would, of course, be grandiose to assume that just by changing some aspects of social behaviour all the problems experienced by the disfigured person would vanish, but the technique can be very useful as part of a wider counselling approach.

A good knowledge of camouflage makeup would also be useful, together with an awareness of when the use of this can be an advantage, and when overuse can be a problem. Counsellors also need to be aware of the potential benefits of self help groups. These (with or without the presence of a counsellor) may be helpful for particular subgroups of disfigured clients such as adolescents, who may prefer to discuss their concerns with peers rather than adults, or for parents of disfigured children. In addition, it may be useful for those undergoing surgical procedures to meet with others for whom treatment is complete. Skilful management of these groups by a counsellor, or someone experienced with group work, may be necessary to ensure that the experience is positive for participants.

Some believe that counselling of the disfigured should be undertaken only by those who have first hand experience of the problems, either from being disfigured themselves or from being closely associated with a disfigured person. However, it is the belief of the author that effective counselling can be provided by others beyond this circle, although the latter should be ready to revise their understanding of a problem in favour of those with first hand experience when necessary.

From the common problems associated with disfigurement outlined in the section above, it can be seen that counselling interventions would be appropriate at many stages of a disfigured person's life. It is also evident that counselling should in an ideal world, be offered in a variety of settings including the home, the GP surgery, and the hospital for both in- and out-patients. (The desirability of counselling in the hospital setting is discussed in more detail below). Counselling is also needed for a variety of different people. Although disfigured people themselves may need help, so too may those involved with them, their families, friends and colleagues, and also, in some cases, the staff involved in their care.

Counselling for the disfigured

There is a need for the provision of counselling for disfigured people who experience problems as a result of particular life events, for example moving to a new school, a new job, moving to a new neighbourhood and the beginning or ending of a relationship.

This link between life events and problems associated with disfigurement can be illustrated by the case of Jane, aged 24 years, who on beginning a new job as a personal assistant had a sudden crisis of confidence and felt that others would judge her unfavourably because of a facial port wine stain. Her preoccupation with what her colleagues thought of her began to interfere with her work. A short course of individual counselling was sufficient to help her to concentrate on promoting her excellent secretarial and organisational skills. Her confidence soon returned as she came to realise that others were evaluating her favourably as a result of her work performance, and that only transitory attention was being paid to her facial appearance by the other people at work.

For those with a disfigurement of sudden onset, counselling is needed in the acute stages of care to deal with emotional issues such as guilt, fear or grief associated with the injury, and subsequently to help the person come to terms with their disfigurement. For those who are left with disfiguring scars or an abnormal appearance after an operation the issues may be different.

Edith was 47 years old when the removal of a malignant facial tumour left her with a badly misshapen face. Initially she needed counselling in order to address her fears of the possibility of the cancer remaining after surgery. Subsequently she needed help to deal with the shock she experienced over her markedly changed appearance and the numerous problems she felt stemmed from this. She continued to need counselling support for three years after her initial operation as subsequent plastic surgery procedures were carried out to improve her facial appearance and function. In this time she was helped to come to terms with the fact that although her cancer was probably cured, the changes to her appearance were permanent and there was a limit to the amount the surgeons could offer in the way of improvements to her altered appearance.

Patients who seek surgery to improve their appearance should ideally receive counselling before their operation to ensure that their motivation is appropriate and their expectations of the outcome are realistic. If this is not available, some patients may need counselling after their operation as their expectations of their new appearance may not have been met. Some patients may be disappointed with the lack of reaction to their new appearance. John, for example, requested surgery to reshape his broken nose and reduce scarring which had occurred as a result of a road traffic accident. The surgical result was good, but John found it very difficult to cope with having an appearance which was considered 'normal' as this led to a marked decrease in the amount of attention he received from members of the general public.

The families of disfigured people

There is a glaring lack of provision of counselling help for the families of disfigured people, especially those who have little contact with the health service. While there is a recognition that parents of children born with congenital disfigurements need help to cope with the variety of emotions they experience as the result of this, there is little or no provision for the problems which occur for the families of disfigured people in later life. This is true despite evidence that the issues and dynamics of adaptation by the family may become more intricate and demanding as time goes on (Bernstein, 1988).

Counselling could be enormously useful in offering support and advice with issues such as how to help the child develop a high level of self-esteem. Trust (1986) suggested a strategy that works well. She recommended that parental harmony can be fostered by a joint agreement on how to deal with the disfigurement, for example, by establishing standard responses to public interest and enquiry, avoiding constant camouflage of the disfigurement and encouraging the child to participate in as much group activity as possible. In addition, Trust felt that parents should encourage the disfigured child to develop skill in the 'performing arts' (in order to facilitate confidence in communication and interactive skills) and to find some form of activity at which the child can excel (in order to promote self-esteem).

Other common issues include how to deal with staring, teasing and enquiries. In the case of Tina, a nine-year-old with a badly repaired cleft lip and palate, role play and social skills training techniques were useful as these gave the child, her parents and her older sister the chance to rehearse ways of dealing effectively with questions and unwanted attention. In addition to increasing Tina's confidence in public, the provision of an agreed strategy had the added benefit of reducing the strain experienced by the parents as a result of constant disagreements about the most appropriate way of dealing with the general public.

For those families with a member who becomes disfigured as the result of an accidental injury, counselling is relevant (and very necessary) at many stages.

In the case of Julie, a 14-year-old severely burned as the result of a camping gas explosion whilst on holiday with her parents, counselling was initially required to help the parents come to terms with their worries about Julie's survival and their guilt over the accident. Subsequently, their concerns shifted more towards Julie's well-being and how she would cope with the disfiguring burns. Counselling was also useful at this stage in helping the parents address practical issues such as how to cope with the other siblings while Julie was in hospital, how to plan future operations, and so on. Counselling was then used as a technique to prepare the family for Julie's return home. They were helped to accept that although she was pleased to be going home, Julie still tired easily, and might avoid physical contact as she found it painful when the skin graft areas were touched. Ways were suggested to the family of how Julie's apprehension concerning the reactions of family and friends to her appearance could be minimized.

Counselling techniques in the school and work place

In the United States, group counselling techniques have successfully been used to prepare peers and colleagues for the return of a disfigured person into the school or work place (Cahners, 1983). This provides a useful forum for imparting practical information, such as what the person is and is not capable of doing, and the purpose of various dressings and prostheses. Group sessions can also be used to work through the worries and concerns of the colleagues and friends. They can address issues such as what they should say, how they should react and how much they should encourage the disfigured person to do. Although these sorts of programmes have been shown to be beneficial for the disfigured and their colleagues (Bernstein, 1976), the possibilities of funding for this in the British health care system are currently remote.

The role of the teacher in the adjustment of disfigured children is likely to be an important one. Teachers can help by being aware of the tendency for disfigured children to be left out in play sessions and of the possibilities of manipulating the classroom environment to prevent this. Counselling can be used to help teachers to realise that, through the sensitive use of information and by example, they are in a powerful position to counteract any stereotypes that children may acquire that could work to the detriment of the disfigured.

Counselling for staff

No discussion of the relevance of counselling and the disfigured would be complete without a mention of the need for the provision of counselling for staff involved in the care of disfigured people. This need is particularly pressing for those who care for patients horribly disfigured by accidental injury or by violence. In many cases these patients survive only as a result of the dedicated efforts of staff, yet the reward for this dedication can seem to be minimal, especially in burns care, where recovery is very slow. In burns care, the procedures (such as dressing changes) are vital, but often cause considerable pain. Patients are frequently abusive to staff, and it is not uncommon for patients to say they would prefer to be dead. Many staff find the intensive care of such patients (especially children) very stressful and frequently question why they are striving to keep such distressed and profoundly disfigured people alive.

Most staff realise that to allow their concerns and frustrations to be apparent on the ward can be detrimental for the patients, their families and other members of staff. Therefore, counselling should be offered individually and in private. This can give staff the opportunity to offload their concerns and worries in a supportive nonjudgemental setting, with subsequent benefits for all concerned.

HOW SHOULD CARE FOR THE DISFIGURED BE PROVIDED?

Variations in the provision of care are bound to occur between various health care systems, and between the public and private sectors. However, no matter what the health care system, counselling should ideally be offered as part of a multidisciplinary approach to care. Permanently established multidisciplinary teams have been shown to be beneficial in the care of burns and plastic surgery patients in the United States (Bernstein, 1976), and are used successfully and cost effectively in other areas of patient care in the UK, for example in pain and in diabetes. The provision of care through the medium of a multidisciplinary team may require a philosophical shift for some. Although some centres in the UK are convinced of the benefits of such an approach, the majority still design their service according to the medical model of care. As previously mentioned, this model favours a functional approach to disfigurement, and many of those whose problems are primarily to do with social difficulties are made to feel as if their needs are unimportant and secondary to those with physical impairments. This may be reflected in the allocation of a low waiting list priority, with patients made to feel like second class citizens. After their operations, patients are frequently discharged after the minimum period, with little consideration to long-term follow-up and support.

It is the opinion of the author that multidisciplinary teams should be established on a regional basis, and that a team approach to care should be adopted at all stages of assessment, treatment and follow-up. The involvement of counsellors and other health care professionals should begin at the time of initial assessment, with a multidisciplinary perspective brought to bear on the allocation of waiting list priority, treatment and discharge planning. Any time the patient has to spend on the waiting list for surgery could be used constructively by team members other than the surgeon, to tackle additional problems which will impact on the long term adjustment of the patient. In addition to addressing the medical aspects of the problem, treatment and discharge planning would become more closely attuned to the social and psychological needs of the patient. A follow-up service in which patients and their families could make appointments to see the counsellor or other team members when and if problems occur could do much to relieve the anxiety and stress so many experience after formal contact with the hospital has ceased.

Counsellors (preferably working as part of a multidisciplinary team) could also be used to provide advice and support for those people for whom hospital treatment is not necessary or desirable. Many of the problems commonly facing disfigured people occur whether or not a person wants surgery, and much of the advice and support is also necessary for those who would not normally be treated in hospital. For these people access to counselling at GP level could be beneficial, although it would be unrealistic to expect that all GP counsellors should acquire specialist knowledge of the problems associated with disfigurement. For those needing more specialist help, a system of GP referrals to the specialist counsellor and, if necessary, other members of the multidisciplinary team could be adopted.

If adequate funding were forthcoming, the team could consider holding 'open days', in order to give disfigured people, their families and colleagues open access to advice and support from members of the team. In addition, the team could act as a training resource and could also offer support to local branches of the two national organisations for disfigured people, both of whom have so eloquently demonstrated the need for the provision of help and support on a regional basis.

Some surgeons maintain that the areas outlined above are covered by existing service provision and that patients are 'counselled' adequately at present. However, such 'counselling' usually consists of bedside chats (when the hard pressed staff can spare a moment from their busy schedules) and the current superficial level of attention paid to the social and psychological problems experienced by patients simply is not adequate. Those units with truly adequate counselling provision are rare. The majority (often as a result of economic constraints) provide a service which may be excellent in terms of medical care, but is sadly lacking in its provision for the care and rehabilitation of disfigured people.

CONCLUSION

Disfigurement is a multidisciplinary problem and one for which counselling
has great relevance and potential. If it is approached from the standpoint of
the medical model, as is all too frequently the case at present, many aspects
of the problem will be overlooked.

For disfigured people, the provision of counselling is greatly needed, yet
sadly lacking. It is hoped that with a growing awareness of the problems
associated with disfigurement, this situation will be redressed in the not too
distant future. Even if additional funding is not forthcoming, much could be
achieved by an enlightened redistribution of existing resources. The regional
provision of counselling, preferably as part of a multidisciplinary team approach to care, would do much in the urgently needed move towards a
service which more adequately addresses the needs of the many disfigured
people in our society.

USEFUL ADDRESSES

'Let's Face It' Network for the Facially Disfigured, Christine Piff,
10 Wood End,
Crowthorne,
Berks, RG11 6DQ,
UK.

The Disfigurement Guidance Centre,
52 Crossgate,
Cupar,
Fife, KY15 5HS,
UK.

REFERENCES

Bernstein, N.R. (1976). *Emotional care of the facially burned and disfigured*. Boston: Little,
    Brown & Co.
Bernstein, N. (1988). Coping with Disfigurement. In N.R. Bernstein, A.J. Breslau and
    J. Graham (Eds), *Coping strategies for burn survivors and their families*. New York:
    Praeger.
Bull, R.H.C. and Rumsey, N.J. (1988). *The social psychology of facial appearance*. New
    York: Springer-Verlag.
Cahners, S. (1983). Personal communication.
Cash, T. and Cash, D. (1982). Women's use of cosmetics: Psychosocial correlates and
    consequences. *International Journal of Cosmetic Science*, **4**, 1–14.
Kalick, S. (1982). Clinician, social scientist and body image: Collaboration and future
    prospects. *Clinics in Plastic Surgery*, **9**, 379–385.
Lansdown, R. (1981). Cleft lip and palate: A prediction of psychological disfigure-
    ment. *British Journal of Orthodontics*, **8**, 83–88.
Macgregor, F.C. (1974). *Transformation and identity: The face and plastic surgery*. New
    York: Times Books.

Rumsey, N.J. (1983). *The psychological problems associated with disfigurement*. Unpublished doctoral thesis, North East London Polytechnic, London, England.

Rumsey, N.J., Bull, R.H.C., and Gahagen, D. (1986). A preliminary study of the potential of social skills training for improving the quality of social interaction for the facially disfigured. *Social Behaviour*, **1**, 143–145.

Trust, D. (1986). *Overcoming disfigurement*. Wellingborough: Thorsons.

7 Counselling in Head Injury

ANDY TYERMAN
Rayners Hedge, Croft Road, Aylesbury, Buckinghamshire, HP21 7RD

INTRODUCTION

Head injury may have devastating consequences for the individual, the family and for society as a whole. Whilst recovery may continue over many years, people with more severe injuries will face permanent disability. This may be physical, sensory, cognitive, emotional or behavioural. These changes have a marked impact upon the person and widespread social repercussions, precluding or threatening return to former work, family, leisure and social life.

The impact for the individual and family is magnified by the limited public awareness of the nature and effects of head injury. The public conception, fostered by the media, is that all will be well once the person has regained consciousness. This will of course bring immense relief to family members, but will also highlight the extent of physical and psychological disability and mark the start of a long struggle to regain lost skills. Counselling is a vital part of the rehabilitation process from acute care, active treatment and resettlement to long-term personal, family and social adjustment.

Outcome after head injury varies from complete recovery to profound disability, depending upon the nature and severity of brain injury. The severity of head injury is commonly defined by the duration of unconsciousness or post-traumatic amnesia (PTA), the latter being defined as the length of time from the accident until the return of some continuity of memory function.

This chapter will focus upon the counselling needs of those with severe head injuries (i.e. those unconscious for at least 6 hours and/or with a PTA of at least 24 hours) and their families. Reference will be made to the author's longitudinal study of self-concept and psychological changes amongst 60 people with very severe head injuries (PTA > seven days, median ten weeks) admitted to two specialist neurological rehabilitation centres (Tyerman, 1987).

Counselling and Communication in Health Care. Edited by H. Davis and L. Fallowfield
© 1991 John Wiley & Sons Ltd

EPIDEMIOLOGY

Incidence

In Scotland an estimated 1778 people per 100 000 attend hospital per annum with head injuries. This constitutes 11% of new attenders at accident and emergency departments (Jennett and MacMillan, 1981). Of these about two-thirds are male and over half are aged under 20 years. The annual admission rate of 313 per 100 000 in Scotland compares with an estimated 270 per 100 000 in England and Wales. Based on the depth of coma on admission about 84% of these injuries will be minor, 11% moderate and 5% severe (Miller and Jones, 1985). The annual incidence of severe head injury in the UK is therefore about 14 per 100 000, most of which arise from road traffic accidents.

Prevalence

The prevalence of serious disability after head injury in the UK is in the order of 100–150 per 100 000 (Medical Disability Society, 1988), or about 250–375 per average Health District of 250 000. An estimated 210 people are totally disabled and 1500 severely or profoundly disabled after head injury every year in England and Wales (Roberts, 1979). One family in 300 is thought to have a member with persisting disability after head injury (Lancet, 1983).

PATTERNS OF IMPAIRMENT

Physical disability

Many people with head injuries suffer transient physical disability, but persistent deficits are common after more severe injuries. Residual neurophysical disability includes paralysis, ataxia, dysarthria, inco-ordination, muscular weakness and fatigue, plus complications such as epilepsy and hydrocephalus (Jennett et al., 1981). In Tyerman's (1987) group with very severe injuries, 90% had some physical disability, with 28% totally dependent on others when admitted to the specialist rehabilitation unit.

Sensory deficits

Sensory deficits are a common consequence of severe head injury with 68% of Tyerman's (1987) group having cranial nerve deficits. Visual disturbances are the most common, primarily occulomotor deficits such as double vision or less often nystagmus, and occasionally visual field deficits. Somatosensory deficits, reduced taste and smell and hearing disturbances also occur (Jennett et al., 1981).

Cognitive impairment

Cognitive impairment after head injury tends to be of a generalised nature (Brooks, 1984). Primary problems lie with memory, especially learning and retention of new verbal information. Poor concentration, distractibility and a general reduction in speed of information processing are also very common, even after moderate injuries. Whilst marked receptive or expressive dysphasia affect only a minority, word finding lapses and difficulty in organising one's thoughts and structuring sentences are common complaints. Reductions in planning and reasoning ability are often evident on formal cognitive testing with specific spatial and constructional deficits affecting a small proportion. Many also suffer a loss of awareness of themselves and others, lacking insight into their cognitive and personality changes and insensitive to the views and needs of others.

All of those with moderate or severe head injuries are likely to have some impairment in the early stages of recovery, with more subtle changes after minor injuries. Those with more severe injuries face permanent functional disability. Tyerman (1987) found that 98% of his group showed evidence of reduced general intellectual ability, 8% had marked visuospatial/constructional deficits, 13% marked language dysfunction and all were impaired in memory and learning skills at the beginning of rehabilitation.

Personality change

Personality change embraces a wide range of emotional and behavioural sequelae, which reflect a combination of primary neurological damage and secondary psychological reactions to the initial trauma and long-term consequences of head injury. Primary changes such as irritability, impulsivity and disinhibition interact with secondary reactions such as frustration, loss of confidence and depression. These secondary reactions include the broad spectrum of responses seen in other injured, sick or stressed people but with additional responses specific to brain injuries (Bond, 1984).

A common change early in recovery is loss of behavioural control resulting in socially inappropriate or unacceptable behaviour, often of an aggressive or sexual nature. Other common changes include irritability, lack of initiative and egocentricity. Many people experience a loss of emotional control, and are subject to rapid mood swings and strong, unpredictable reactions. Common emotional responses include frustration, anger, anxiety and depression.

Such changes are extremely common in severe injuries. In Tyerman's (1987) group, 85% were considered by rehabilitation staff to demonstrate problems in social behaviour (although severe behavioural problems were noted in only a small number of cases) with 40% emotionally distressed on self-report scales of anxiety and depression. Overall 97% were noted to have some change in personality on the basis of self-report or staff ratings. In contrast with the gradual, albeit partial, recovery of functional skills after severe head injury, relatives report greater personality change and much more disturbed behaviour at five years than at one year post-injury (Brooks *et al.*, 1986).

Many with less severe injuries also experience personality changes often described as a 'post-concussional syndrome'. This consists of a constellation of subjective symptoms such as headache, dizziness, fatigue, irritability and poor memory and concentration. Such symptoms are generally short-lived, but may persist as a result of subtle changes in cognition and personality, of which only the person or close family members may be aware.

PERSONAL, SOCIAL AND FAMILY ADJUSTMENT

Life changes after head injury can be far-reaching. Whilst those with minor and moderate injuries will generally be able to resume their former lives, only a minority of those with severe injuries will do so. In a 1 to 14 year follow-up of 150 people with severe injuries (coma > six hours) Jennett *et al.* (1981) reported that 40% had made a good recovery (able to resume normal occupational and social activities), 40% had moderate disability (independent but disabled) and 20% severe disability (dependent in activities of daily living). Some degree of disability was evident in 97% of cases. Many face major changes in their work, leisure and social life, as well as in marital and family relationships.

Personal adjustment

Head injury often has a marked impact upon the person. Those with mild injuries may have the nagging doubt that they are not quite as before, whilst those with severe injuries are confronted by a confusing array of neurological disability, totally outside the realm of normal experience. Those with marked physical disability struggle to perform basic personal and domestic activities, whilst others feel frustrated and isolated by severe communication problems. Those with severe perceptual or visuo-spatial deficits face a confusing and bewildering world, and those with reasoning difficulties may find that life has become an insoluble puzzle. Marked impairment of memory will result in a disturbing lack of order and continuity to one's life. Changes in personality are profoundly disturbing, and the person is often unable to make sense of this confusion because of their limited insight, poor memory and reasoning problems.

Marked changes in self-concept were reported by Tyerman's (1987) group on admission to rehabilitation. They rated their current selves as more bored, unhappy, helpless, worried, dissatisfied, unattractive, forgetful, irritable, clumsy, dependent and inactive than they were prior to their injury. Such changes were, however, generally seen as transient, with ratings of the future no different from the past. The group continued to underestimate their problems at discharge, lacking insight into their cognitive and personality changes and maintaining unrealistic expectations. At follow-up 20 months post-injury, present self-concept remained markedly lower than the past, but the future was now viewed less positively, mid-way between the present and the past. This was paralleled by lower expectations of functional recovery. Many were beginning to appreciate the true extent of their restrictions at a stage when few were in contact with professional support. A higher proportion of the group were distressed at follow-up (44%) than on either admission or discharge.

Lack of insight and unrealistic expectations may initially protect people from depression and anxiety about the future. However, many are misled by their lack of insight, equating discharge from rehabilitation with recovery and expecting to resume life where they left off. On returning home they are confronted by the realities of their limitations. There may follow a gradual realisation of the extent and implications of residual disability. This provokes in some a period of depression, characterised by confusion, frustration and uncertainty. Others find it hard to acknowledge their limitations and respond with renewed determination to make a full recovery, setting themselves unrealistic targets which lead to repeated failure and despair. The limited occupational opportunities for people with head injury fuels a sense of hopelessness and futility.

Social adjustment

At the time of injury most adults are in full-time study, training or employment, to which those with severe injuries are often unable to return. For those able to return to work there is a tendency to rush back as soon as possible, underestimating the effects of fatigue and subtle cognitive changes. For others there may be prospects of work in a reduced capacity or of retraining for a different kind of work, but of those assessed at employment rehabilitation centres, few progress to training or work. Some may find sheltered work or attend a sheltered workshop, but suitable opportunities are very limited. Others may be offered a place at a day centre, but the programme is rarely stimulating for young people. Many people with severe head injuries are therefore left with no regular occupation.

Many with a less severe injury will resume former leisure and social activities. Those with more severe injuries, however, may no longer enjoy their former hobbies and sporting activities because of residual physical disability or a loss of interest or initiative. There is often a parallel reduction in social activities with complaints that, whilst a few friends remain loyal, most fade away. The cognitive and personality changes experienced by the person with a head injury are a major obstacle to making new friends, particularly new boy- or girl-friends.

A marked lack of social activities was reported by a group of very severely injured people (PTA > seven days) two years after injury. They had fewer interests and hobbies, fewer friends, less social and sexual activity and a more lonely life than a group with less severe head injuries (Weddell, Oddy and Jenkins, 1980). A dearth of social activities was still evident after seven years: half had very limited contact with friends and 60% had no boy- or girl-friend (Oddy *et al.*, 1985). Those with very severe head injuries, therefore, often become socially isolated. Families may be very resourceful in arranging leisure and social activities, but this poses an additional strain upon family members and relationships.

Family adjustment

Head injury is a major source of stress upon close family members. After the trauma of the initial injury and the anxious, seemingly endless, wait for signs of recovery the family share in the long struggle to regain lost skills. Throughout, the family is a vital source of comfort, support and reassurance. However, family members may also have to assume the role of carer for the dependent patient and later perhaps adopt the role of a therapist in home-based retraining. This change in roles may be a source of additional strain on families already under intense stress.

Ultimately, the family is faced with the task of adjusting to the many changes in the person with a head injury, especially changes in personality. The process of readjustment is especially difficult for spouses. They may find the role of carer or therapist irreconcilable with that of a sexual partner. They may find the altered personality and behaviour of the injured person no longer attractive or compatible with their own. All caretakers may feel isolated and trapped, but spouses may feel in a 'social limbo', still living with their partner, but with whom they can no longer enjoy their previous leisure, family, social and sexual lives.

Spouses with children may also find themselves torn between the needs of their injured partner and those of their children. They face the additional task of trying to cushion the children as far as possible from the worst effects of the head injury, whilst helping them to accept, understand and adapt to changes in their injured parent.

This strain does not diminish from 3 months to 12 months (McKinlay *et al.*, 1981) and tends to have increased markedly by five years (Brooks *et al.*, 1986). This leads to high levels of anxiety and depression amongst relatives, who may themselves suffer problems in marital, family and social relationships (Livingston, Brooks and Bond, 1985). Families therefore often experience a sense of social isolation comparable to that of the person with the injury.

COUNSELLING PEOPLE WITH A HEAD INJURY AND THEIR FAMILIES

The process of rehabilitation and counselling after head injury can be conceptualised as four interlinked phases: acute care, rehabilitation, resettlement and long-term adjustment.

Acute care

As people regain consciousness they usually experience a period of disorientation and confusion. They may become restless and agitated or exhibit disinhibited or aggressive behaviour. Staff need advice in the management of behaviour and in promotion of cognitive recovery through graded orientation exercises. As people become more aware of their circumstances they require repeated explanations of what has happened to them, starting simply and becoming more detailed in line with recovery.

A pressing need at this stage is the support and counselling of family members, who also need repeated and sensitive explanations of the injuries. Such information should be graded over time as relatives may only gradually be able to take in the details and implications of what they are told. Relatives vary in the level of knowledge they seek, with some craving detailed explanation of brain dysfunction in their struggle to understand and cope with what has happened.

Once the person's life is out of danger, relatives need opportunities to raise concerns about the likely course and extent of recovery. It is important to avoid short-term reassurance of an unwarranted degree of recovery, as this may cause problems later in rehabilitation when relatives may cling to early assurances of a full recovery. It is also distressing and singularly unhelpful for relatives to be told, as some report, that their loved one will remain a 'vegetable'. It is surely better to be honest about both the seriousness of current problems and the prospects for recovery. This usually allows for optimism about their being marked improvement but doubt about the extent of recovery.

Rehabilitation

As the person with the injury is often easily confused early in recovery, a primary need is for explanation of the nature and purpose of rehabilitation. Results of assessment should be discussed sensitively with the person to promote greater understanding, taking into consideration their cognitive and emotional state. As many have difficulties with insight and self-monitoring skills, it may help to provide an external illustration of problems: for example demonstrating poor gait in front of a mirror, tape-recording dysarthric or dysphasic speech, video-taping cognitive assessment or poor social skills. The rationale of the rehabilitation programme should be explained and treatment goals negotiated to take account of the person's own priorities. It is also helpful to provide the person with a record of problems, treatment programme and goals to compensate for memory difficulties.

The counselling needs of people with head injury are not, however, confined to education. As discussed above, the emotional impact of head injury can be devastating and many experience depression during the course of rehabilitation. In particular, parents may feel guilt and inadequacy in their inability to care or provide for the children, whilst young adults may rebel against the loss of independence. Where someone becomes distressed by the slow rate of progress early in recovery, it may help to focus upon immediate needs and short-term attainable goals in treatment. Regular counselling can play a crucial role in monitoring progress, reviewing treatment goals, and in promoting greater understanding and more realistic expectations of recovery. Formal re-assessment provides a framework through which to monitor recovery and help the person to moderate their expectations in line with recovery, as in the following example.

M.R. was a 27-year-old single man admitted four months after his injury for intensive rehabilitation. He presented with inco-ordination, a left hemianopia, memory and reasoning problems, severe visuo-spatial and constructional deficits and aggression. He was aware of his physical disability and his aggressive tendencies, but lacked insight into his memory and reasoning problems and was totally bewildered by his visuo-spatial deficits, which he found intensely frustrating. He was clearly distressed and reported marked changes in self-concept; compared with the past he saw himself currently as being more bored, unhappy, worried, dissatisfied, forgetful, irritable and dependent. However, he expected to return to his pre-injury self in almost all respects within a year. He required repeated and detailed explanations of the nature of his difficulties and the rationale of his treatment programme. The results of three repeat neuropsychological assessments provided the framework within which to explain and monitor cognitive recovery and to promote greater insight and a more positive attitude towards rehabilitation within a supportive counselling relationship. He made impressive gains during eight months of rehabilitation and viewed himself much more positively at discharge, rating himself as much more interested, happy, relaxed, satisfied, stable, mindful, calm, skilful and cooperative than on admission.

The family should be included as far as possible in the process of rehabilitation counselling, much of which can be undertaken jointly with the injured person. Relatives also need detailed feedback about the results of assessment, the nature and implications of disability and explanation of the rationale and goals of treatment. They frequently require advice about the management of cognitive and/or behavioural problems and may assume the role of co-therapist in reinforcing treatment strategies at home, in home-based retraining programmes or in the management of inappropriate behaviour. They also need guidance about future recovery, and support in making appropriate plans for resettlement.

Resettlement

Counselling on resettlement is essential as people with head injury tend to make unrealistic plans. They need information and advice about realistic options. This is not to suggest that they should give up hope of further recovery, but rather that they cannot afford to wait for it to happen and need to plan on the basis of current needs. Those capable of working may need advice about the timing of their return and the need for a supervised trial of restricted duties in the first instance. Those unable to return to work may initially resist the recommendation to consult a Disablement Resettlement Officer or complete an assessment at an Employment Rehabilitation Centre, clinging to the hope of an eventual return to previous employment. Those requiring sheltered work may not wish to take the step of registering as a disabled person. Similarly, people may initially be resistant to alternative leisure and social pursuits, and may need guidance and encouragement, especially if low in confidence.

Many people with head injury therefore leave rehabilitation dismayed by the extent of their residual disability and dissatisfied with the options immediately available to them. This is well illustrated by the following example.

B.J. was a 20-year-old single professional man who was admitted for rehabilitation 11 months after his injury. He had poor balance, inco-ordination, moderate cognitive impairment and mild changes in personality. He reported poor self-concept and depressed mood. He was anxious about the future but determined to regain lost skills. He made limited progress as he was discharged after seven weeks, which provided little opportunity to deal with his low confidence and self-esteem. He was referred to the Disablement Resettlement Officer on discharge. Six months later he was living in his parents' flat, working for his father's firm as a 'dogsbody', making tea and coffee, filing, taking messages and delivering post. He had been assessed at a training college for the disabled but rejected both the recommended course and the whole environment. He was now acutely distressed. He was asked to provide a number of self-descriptions, and used negative adjectives to describe himself, including 'twisted', 'warped', 'soured' and 'boring'. His current feelings included 'depressed', 'isolated', 'hopeless', 'frightened', and 'burdensome', and current behaviour was described as 'drifting' and 'stagnating'. Intervention aimed to promote a more positive attitude towards his 'new' self and provide a framework within which to help him to re-evaluate his life situation following his head injury, to identify his remaining strengths and consider practical options for the future. He learnt gradually to accept the present and plan for the future rather than dwell upon the past. At 18 months after discharge he was finally settled in a new job, independent of his family.

B.J. illustrates the need for regular counselling during rehabilitation and resettlement and for routine follow-up, especially as advice during rehabilitation is often not fully absorbed whilst hopes of a full recovery remain. Many benefit from a review of progress and advice about further therapy, occupational prospects and leisure/social pursuits. This is ideally undertaken within the security and trust of an established counselling relationship.

Long-term adjustment

People with head injuries are often devastated by the change in personal skills and social circumstances. Amidst the confusion of the present and the uncertainty of the future, they may cling to the apparent security of the past. Some struggle to carry on as before, not wishing to acknowledge the changes that have occurred and continuing to judge themselves inappropriately by the pre-injury standards that they can no longer meet. For others, their preoccupation with what they have lost clouds any appreciation of the positive attributes and potential that remains. Burr (1981) suggests that people with head injuries may be grappling with an altered perception of their own worth, their new-found social stigma as a handicapped person, their dependence on others, and their lessened freedom of choice. He suggests that they need supportive counselling to move from denial to acceptance, from a sense of loss to an appreciation of potential, from dwelling on the past to looking to the future, and from seeing themselves as sick to seeing themselves as different.

Counselling at this stage may need to take on a more psychotherapeutic approach, where the focus is less on the process of rehabilitation and more on the meaning of the injury and resultant disability for the individual person. The rehabilitation counselling described above concentrates on providing information and explanation, promoting insight and realistic expectations, and planning appropriately for resettlement. The need now is to assist people to re-appraise their new situation and achieve the difficult balance whereby they accommodate the consequences of their injury without also being governed by them.

A very important consideration for counselling is that people will often be restricted by their cognitive impairment. The counsellor can help the person to compensate for these difficulties by providing a clear structure for sessions and by acting as a 'surrogate information-processor' (Wexler, 1974). This may include helping people to maintain their train of thought, assisting their memory through detailed recording and prompting, and guiding their reasoning through structured problem solving techniques. Self-exploration techniques, such as self-descriptions and semantic differentials, also provide a structure within which people can explore changes in themselves and re-appraise their lives in the light of acquired disability. With support and guidance, they can often move forward to explore their 'new' selves, re-evaluate their strengths and weaknesses, review their plans and aspirations and find a new direction and purpose to their lives, as illustrated by T.E.

T.E., a 26-year-old sales executive, had mild weakness and inco-ordination, double vision, poor memory and mild personality change at three months post-injury. He made good progress and, after first returning to his old job, he completed a post-graduate diploma in journalism and launched himself into his new career. However, his need to prove he had made a complete recovery led to him driving himself hard. Changes in personality culminated in the breakup of a long-standing relationship with his girlfriend and his associated guilt and regret meant that he now avoided close relationships. He clung to his past, in his own words 'trapped in a melancholic longing for the way things were'. Changes in T.E. as a result of his head injury were explored through semantic differential ratings (present, past and future) and self-descriptions before and after his accident. This assisted him in both his awareness and acceptance of such changes. However, he still held a very negative view of himself and was unable to move forward to form new relationships. He was later asked to provide further descriptions of 'positive aspects of T.E.' and 'T.E. as I would like him to be'. Specific problem and desired behaviours were identified and a scaled-down version of fixed-role therapy was implemented (Bannister, 1974). This required T.E. to adopt an agreed role in social circumstances with the specific goal of getting to know new people. This helped him to let go of his past enough to enjoy making new relationships. At four years post-injury he was finally settled in a new relationship.

Families often face a similar process of re-adjustment. As the person with a less severe head injury improves, regains independence and resumes their former roles, family relationships may naturally resume their pre-injury pattern. However, for those with permanent disability, changes in family roles and relationships may be inevitable. Many families adjust well to such changes and some report that they are brought closer by the effects of the injury.

Where such changes do cause problems, counselling can help members to understand and resolve the conflicts that arise (Lezak, 1978). Help is especially important for marital relationships. Couples may strive to return to their previous interaction and need help to review and re-build their relationship in the light of the injury. Where families find changes too great to accommodate, family therapy can help them to understand the problems that have arisen within the context of the head injury. Where reconciliation is not possible, family members may need help to resolve the situation for all concerned with the minimum of recriminations and guilt, so they can re-build their own separate lives.

COUNSELLING SERVICES

People with head injuries and their families therefore have many complex educational and emotional needs. These can be met by regular counselling, providing information, guidance, support and continuity for the person and family throughout the course of rehabilitation. Inexplicably, counselling has rarely been seen as vital to the rehabilitation process after head injury, with a few notable exceptions (e.g. Muir and Haffey, 1984; Prigatano, 1986). Accordingly, very little is known about the efficacy of such counselling. In one of very few controlled studies, Prigatano et al. (1984) did find some advantages for a Neuropsychological Rehabilitation Program including educational, supportive and vocational counselling.

Tyerman and Humphrey (1988) stress the need to take account of the perceptions, aims and expectations of people with a head injury and for a more psychotherapeutic approach to aid long-term personal and social adjustment. It is suggested that people with head injuries are encouraged to 'co-manage' their own rehabilitation, within their cognitive limitations, through the support of ongoing counselling. This is most effective when fully integrated within the rehabilitation programme, through a combination of group work, focusing on education, goal setting and resettlement (Tyerman et al., 1987) and a network of individual key workers. Whilst a key worker system can enhance specialist regional rehabilitation centres, it is equally important in local district services which have a vital long-term coordinating role.

Given the central importance and the constraining effect of cognitive impairment, the clinical or neuro-psychologist should play a leading role in such a system. However, it would not be possible for the psychologist to be involved directly in counselling everyone, especially given the acute shortage of psychologists. There is much to be gained from selecting the key worker who is best placed to meet the particular needs of the individual: the speech therapist to counsel those with marked communication problems, the occupational therapist for those dependent in activities of daily living, the physiotherapist for those with severe physical disability and the social worker for those with financial or social problems. In the case of in-patient facilities key workers would ideally link with a network of primary nurses. The psychologist would then be free to take on those people with the most complex problems, to provide guidance and support when key workers run into difficulties and to set up training for all staff undertaking counselling.

Support is also available from self-help groups such as Headway (National Head Injuries Association) in the UK and parallel organisations abroad. Headway provides a newsletter and valuable information leaflets and booklets on many aspects of head injury. There are now over 80 Headway groups in the UK providing local information and support. All groups have local 'contacts' and there are plans to set up basic training in counselling on a regional basis so that all groups will eventually have someone offering 'counselling'. Some local groups independently arrange sessional work from professional counsellors and there is a counsellor on the staff of the national office. Headway fulfils a vital supportive role, often helping to compensate for the lack of rehabilitation services. This should not be seen as an alternative to counselling by professionals, rather as complementary to it in meeting the emotional needs of people with head injuries and their families.

In conclusion, counselling should be regarded as an essential component of rehabilitation for people with head injuries and their families. Counselling services should be provided throughout the rehabilitation process, from acute hospital care through to long-term community support, to facilitate optimal personal and family adjustment after head injury.

USEFUL ADDRESS

Headway
The National Head Injuries Association
200 Mansfield Road,
Nottingham
NG1 3HX
Tel: 0602 622382

REFERENCES

Bannister, D. (1974). Personal construct theory and psychotherapy. In D. Bannister (Ed.), *Issues and approaches in psychotherapy*. New York: Wiley.
Bond, M.R. (1984). The psychiatry of closed head injury. In N. Brooks (Ed.), *Closed head injury: Psychological, social and family consequences*. Oxford: Oxford University Press.
Brooks, N. (1984). Cognitive deficits after head injury. In N. Brooks (Ed.), *Closed head injury: Psychological, social and family consequences*. Oxford: Oxford University Press.
Brooks, N., Campsie, L., Symington, C., Beattie, A., and McKinlay, W. (1986). The five year outcome of severe blunt head injury: a relative's view. *Journal of Neurology, Neurosurgery & Psychiatry*, **49**, 764–770.
Burr, M. (1981). The rehabilitation and long-term management of the adult patient with head injury. *Australian Family Practitioner*, **10**, 14–16.
Jennett, B. and MacMillan, R. (1981). The epidemiology of head injury. *British Medical Journal*, **I**, 101–104.
Jennett, B., Snoek, J., Bond, M.R., and Brooks, N. (1981). Disability after severe head injury: observations on the use of the Glasgow Outcome Scale. *Journal of Neurology, Neurosurgery & Psychiatry*, **44**, 285–293.
Lancet (1983). Caring for the disabled after head injury. *The Lancet*, **II**, 948–949.
Lezak, M.D. (1978). Living with the characterologically altered brain-injured patient. *Journal of Clinical Psychiatry*, **39**, 592–598.
Livingston, M.G., Brooks, D.N., and Bond, M.R. (1985). Patient outcome in the year following severe head injury and relatives' psychiatric and social functioning. *Journal of Neurology, Neurosurgery & Psychiatry*, **48**, 876–881.
McKinlay, W.W., Brooks, D.N., Bond, M.R., Martinage, D.P., and Marshall, M.M. (1981). The short-term outcome of severe blunt head injury as reported by relatives of the head injured persons. *Journal of Neurology, Neurosurgery & Psychiatry*, **44**, 527–533.
Medical Disability Society (1988). A Working Party Report on *The Management of Traumatic Brain Injury*. London: The Royal College of Physicians.
Miller, J.D. and Jones, P.A. (1985). The Work of a Regional Head Injury Service. *Lancet*, **I**, 1141–1144.
Muir, C.A. and Haffey, W. (1984). Psychological and neuropsychological interventions in the mobile mourning process. In B.A. Edelstein and E.T. Couture (Eds), *Behavioral assessment and rehabilitation of the traumatically brain damaged*. New York: Plenum.
Oddy, M., Coughlan, A., Tyerman, A., and Jenkins, D. (1985). Social adjustment after closed head injury: a further follow-up seven years after injury. *Journal of Neurology, Neurosurgery & Psychiatry*, **48**, 564–568.
Prigatano, G.P. (1986). Psychotherapy after brain injury. In G.P. Prigatano (Ed.), *Neuropsychological rehabilitation after brain injury*. Baltimore: Johns Hopkins University Press.

Prigatano, G.P., Fordyce, D.J., Zeiner, H.K., Roueche, J.R., Pepping, M., and Woods, B.C. (1984). Neuropsychological rehabilitation after severe head injury in young adults. *Journal of Neurology, Neurosurgery & Psychiatry*, **47**, 505–513.

Roberts, A.H. (1979). *Severe accidental head injury: An Assessment of long-term prognosis.* London: MacMillan.

Tyerman, A. (1987). *Self-concept and psychological change in the rehabilitation of the severely head injured person.* Unpublished PhD Thesis, University of London.

Tyerman, A. and Humphrey, M. (1988). Personal and social rehabilitation after severe head injury. In F. Watts (Ed.), *New developments in clinical psychology Vol. II.* Leicester: British Psychological Society.

Tyerman, A., Rowland, D., Williams, J., Cranch, M., Bendall, J., Simonson, P., and Jenkins, D. (1987). *Proposal to coordinate and evaluate the Wolfson Cognitive and Communication Programme.* Unpublished manuscript available from the author.

Weddell, R., Oddy, M., and Jenkins, D. (1980). Social adjustment after rehabilitation: a two year follow-up of patients with severe head injury. *Psychological Medicine*, **10**, 257–263.

Wexler, D.A. (1974). A cognitive theory of experiencing, self-actualising, and therapeutic process. In D.A.Wexler and L.N. Rice (Eds), *Innovations in client-centred therapy.* New York: Wiley.

8 Counselling with Spinal Cord Injured People

PAUL KENNEDY

National Spinal Injuries Centre, Stoke Mandeville Hospital, Aylesbury, Buckinghamshire, HP21 8AL

JON'S NARRATIVE

Immediately Post-Injury: 'I felt little fear, just that something dreadful had happened and I could do nothing about it. There were few tears at this stage, probably due to the fact that I did not fully understand the consequences.'

First Few Weeks: 'A type of euphoria set in. Financial concerns were set aside. Hospital and tetraplegia were new experiences. Lots of plans and contingencies had to be made with my wife and parents. Lots of visitors. Spinal shock and some movement has returned. A lot of attention from medical and nursing staff.'

First Quarter: 'Gradually the realities of my condition dawned. Bed rest continued and provided security from the final condition in which I would find myself. There was still room for optimism.'

Second Quarter: 'Bed rest finished, depressed periods really start.'

Third Quarter: 'Getting up brings success in others' eyes but disappointment for me. Need to relate my condition to lying in bed not my pre-accident state. Horror that I can do absolutely nothing independently and precious little then.'

Last Quarter: 'Moving to the minimal care ward provides more social freedom. However, using the Bungalow (an independent living facility) highlights my dependence on my family. It's depressing and frustrating. Many decisions to be made which somehow make me less aware of my condition. I think that moving towards discharge is positive but community services don't appear to want me at home at their expense.'

At home: 'Acquiring a computer and telephone has enabled me to constructively engage in activity. Many, many people are coming and going, nurses, baby-sitters, etc. This has prevented the return to normality and privacy; am I realistic to expect this? I lose my temper, my wife helps with everything; she has suffered dreadfully.'

One year after the accident: 'I'm not surprised the way things are, the future doesn't look any more predictable. However, the reasons for continuing are as strong as ever despite the physical and emotional costs. I would like to be a part of a normal family again.'

June 1989
Date of Injury May 1988

THE SPINAL CORD INJURY

Few physical injuries have such sudden and devastating consequences as a spinal cord injury. The spinal cord is the main conveyance for sensory,

Counselling and Communication in Health Care. Edited by H. Davis and L. Fallowfield
© 1991 John Wiley & Sons Ltd

motor, and autonomic neural information. A spinal cord injury may involve losses of these functions and therefore, initially, people are thrust into a dependent high technology medical milieu. Later through rehabilitation they may return to the community. In Jon's moving narrative, the expression of his feelings, fears and thoughts demonstrates that the psychosocial management of this injury is vital.

The symptoms of spinal cord injury were first described 5000 years ago by an unknown Egyptian (Edwin Smith, Surgical Papyrus). It was almost certainly a fatal condition with an 80% death rate in the first few weeks (Guttmann, 1973). In fact, death was considered the best outcome in battle casualties (Gowland, 1941) until 1944 when Guttmann challenged this prevailing pessimism by establishing the first comprehensive rehabilitation programme for people with spinal cord injuries in Stoke Mandeville Hospital, England. Now, with life expectancy greatly enhanced and the availability of rehabilitation centres in most developed health systems, quality issues rather than basic survival have become the main concern.

Aetiology, incidence and prevalence

In industrialized countries road traffic accidents are the single major cause of spinal cord injuries, accounting for approximately 50%. Domestic and industrial accidents (including falls) account for 21%, and sporting activities register between 14% and 23%. Penetrating wounds, such as gunshot and stab wounds, are another cause, varying from 5% (UK) to 12.5% (USA) (Creek *et al.*, 1988; McCollough *et al.*, 1981).

There are approximately 250 000 people with spinal cord injuries in the USA (Young and Northrup, 1979) and an estimated 40 000 in the UK, not including people with non-traumatic injuries (such as tumours or infection) which would increase the estimates by 25%. In Britain the annual incidence is between eight and ten per million (Frankel, 1983). Almost 70% are under 34 years of age (Creek *et al.*, 1988) and the male to female ratio is 3:1 (Oxford Regional Health Authority, 1983). Life expectancy estimates suggest that people with spinal injuries will live most of their mature life with significant uncompromised loss of physical function.

Physical and neurological losses

An injury to the spinal cord is most often associated with a fracture or fracture dislocation of the vertebral column. The neurological impact will depend upon the damage to the cord, i.e. complete or incomplete, and the level of the injury. Cervical (neck) injuries may result in tetraplegia (quadriplegia) and injuries at the thoracic, lumbar and sacral levels (i.e. upper, middle and lower back) may result in paraplegia. A complete injury suggests a total loss of function below the level of the injury. Cervical injuries can impair motor function in the hands, arms, diaphragm as well as abdominal and leg muscles.

In paraplegia it is usually the lower trunk muscles that are impaired. As a rough guide injuries above the seventh cervical segment would usually preclude the possibility of independent living. In complete lesions the area of sensory impairment will generally match the area of motor loss, including the loss of touch or pressure, temperature, pain and position. Perhaps the greatest difficulties to bear are the loss of bladder, bowel and sexual functions.

Although some people have incomplete injuries, spinal cord neurons do not regenerate, and losses are permanent. The neurological damage affects not only the person's physical relationships with the world but also their self concept, intimate relationships, social and vocational roles and responsibilities, and independence. Additionally, the loss of pressure sensation and lack of movement can result in pressure sores (decubitus ulcers) which require long periods of treatment and bedrest. Involuntary and uncontrolled spasms can occur in the trunk, arms and legs and may restrict activities and require medication or surgery. Other complications include chronic pain, urinary tract problems, respiratory infections, blood pressure problems and contractures.

The management process

People are transferred to a specialist spinal rehabilitation centre as soon as possible after their injury. In the Acute Stage the main goal is to stabilize the spine. This may be done conservatively through bedrest, internally by surgery or externally with a brace. Once this has occurred, active rehabilitation begins. The person learns how to manage the bladder, bowel, skin care, wheelchair mobility, functional independence and strengthening. Counselling also occurs and may include such things as social skills training and family support, together with information about accommodation, finance and vocational issues. Most rehabilitation centres have a limited care ward and independent living facilities for use prior to placement in the community. For paraplegia the average period of hospitalization is four to six months and for tetraplegia six months to one year.

THE PSYCHOLOGICAL IMPACT

Such devastating physical changes require considerable psychological accommodation, which has been the focus of much research in the last twenty years. Early work suggested the need for a period of mourning (Siller, 1969; Hohmann, 1975), although the validity of this model has not been established (Trieschmann, 1980). Such notions do not account for individual differences and sometimes erroneously remove responsibility for adjustment from the individual and attribute it to members of the team. Shontz (1984) convincingly suggests 'that reactions to illness and disability are not responses to physical conditions but to the meanings of those conditions to the individual'. It is not what happens in life that is important, but what the individual thinks about it. A cognitive-behavioural approach, therefore, not only explains different psychological reactions, but also provides a framework for psychological interventions, without regarding people with disabilities as qualitatively different from others.

Anxiety, depression, cognitive impairment, chronic pain, sexual dysfunction and institutional dependency are the most adverse and notable aspects of psychological impact (Crewe and Krause, 1987; Brucker, 1983; Trieschmann, 1980; Siller, 1969). This is not to suggest illness in the psychiatric sense but that these psychological reactions are a normal response to the abnormal physical state. This requires recognition of the person's changed needs and the necessary coping processes. The changed needs include: the management of illness-related procedures such as self-catheterization of the bladder; renegotiating mobility such as independent wheelchair use; and the adaptation of current accommodation. The coping processes include: the negotiation of loss; the integration of information and conceptualization of the injury; challenging the prevailing negative beliefs about disability; maintaining a sense of self-competence and acquiring specific skills.

Emotional reactions

Shock and denial

The sudden onset of the injury is often associated with periods of shock, numbness, disbelief and denial. 'This isn't happening to me.' This confusion is often compounded by the difficulty of making a prognosis in the early period, particularly if the injury is incomplete. At this stage patients and relatives are often described as denying the consequences of the injury, or attempting to minimize the severity of an undesirable consequence (Janis, 1983). Caplan and Schechter (1987) conclude that this is often only verbal disavowal and does not usually subvert rehabilitation. It can be seen as an expression of hope allowing the person to acknowledge deficit gradually in manageable units. Although longer term denial may prevent accommodation to the injury, it is generally an adaptive response to the management of potentially overwhelming emotions. As one person with tetraplegia put it: 'Denial is one of the ways we get through hell'.

Depression

Beck (1976) suggests that depression can occur when a person perceives a significant loss to their personal domain. Since a spinal cord injury involves significant losses, depression may occur and some assume it to be inevitable (Siller, 1969). However, not every person gets depressed; estimates vary from 22% to 100%.

The depressed thoughts associated with losses can trigger off negative thinking patterns which distort current perceptions and expectations. These may lead to further negative thoughts resulting in depressed mood, helplessness, apathy and other symptoms of depression. Therefore, rather than being helpful in some people, this depression can acquire a momentum of its own, and if left untreated can be very destructive. Observation suggests that it often emerges in the later stages of rehabilitation and immediately post-discharge, perhaps because the true meaning of loss does not become apparent until the first time home.

Anxiety

If depression occurs when people believe their coping skills are exhausted in a current situation, then anxiety is a response to a perceived future inadequacy (Trower, Casey and Dryden, 1988). Again given the devastating physical changes, hospitalization and separation from loved ones, anxiety can be considered normal. Lack of information and comprehension of medical terminology, lack of control and predictability, all intensify fears for the future. Individuals may overestimate the severity of the injury and underestimate their capacity to cope.

In addition to hypervigilance, agitation, and loss of concentration the person may often alternate between approach and avoidance behaviours. Periods of active problem-solving and hopefulness alternate with periods of withdrawal and surrender. The anxiety reduction associated with avoidance often reinforces further withdrawal, resulting, for example, in selective attention to the rehabilitation programme, concentrating on safer, less threatening aspects, such as upper limb strengthening, as opposed to marital concerns. While most researchers highlight anxiety, its prevalence is difficult to measure because of the avoidance mentioned above. It is perhaps the most conspicuous reaction in the first few months of injury, and may help in the generation and mobilization of coping skills. However, prolonged anxiety can impair coping skills, lead to depression or precipitate the acquisition of maladaptive responses such as substance abuse or social isolation.

Indirect self-destructive behaviour

This includes the failure to relieve pressure, abusing alcohol and drugs, and refusing essential treatment, which may occur in up to 34% of patients (Nehemkis and Groot, 1980). Although largely preventable, Lawes (1984) found that 15% of patients were readmitted with pressure sores. The extent of substance abuse remains unclear, despite 60% of people with new injuries (Khella and Stoner, 1977) reporting a history of heavy drinking prior to the injury.

Parasuicide and pre-injury problems

Parasuicide is often an unreported cause of spinal cord injury. Kennedy (1989) found that 15% of admissions to a London spinal unit were the result of a suicide attempt, which is therefore an issue to be explored along with the other rehabilitation concerns. Nyquist and Bors (1967) found a suicide rate of 1.3% in 2011 patients with spinal cord injuries in a 19-year period. While the suicide rate is higher than in the general population, it is relatively rare, even though most contemplate it at some point. Although injury rarely precipitates psychotic breakdown, except in cases of extreme sensory deprivation, when it is transient, people with severe psychiatric difficulties do have spinal cord injuries and they do present a challenge to the rehabilitative team.

Behavioural impact

Leisure, social and vocational activity as well as personal care activity are initially altered, and, even in later stages virtually all behaviour is affected in some way. A previously accessible environment becomes formidable and in some cases insuperable. Rehabilitation is a learning process that requires new skills to be acquired, old skills to be re-established and compensatory skills to be developed. Institutionalization, passivity and social isolation are major concerns. Kennedy, Fisher and Pearson (1988) detailed the behavioural profile of patients during rehabilitation and found that they spent a considerable proportion of their time in solitary and disengaged behaviours. Cogswell (1968) found that upon returning home patients showed marked reductions in social contacts, the number of community settings entered and the social roles they played.

Cognitive impairment

It is unlikely that the spinal cord injury itself directly impairs cognitive functioning, but head injuries are the most common associated injury (Silver, Morris and Otfinowski, 1980). An estimated 15% have a major head injury and associated cognitive deficits, and between 40% and 60% have a mild head injury. Cognitive deficits include impaired speed of information-processing, and difficulties with memory, concentration, judgement, decision-making and social appropriateness. Such difficulties impede and complicate the rehabilitation process, and the individual's adaptation to the injury (Morris, Roth and Davidoff, 1986). Knowledge about the specific deficits helps to tailor the programme to the person's particular needs.

Sexual dysfunction

While the spinal cord injury often impairs the ability to move during inter-course, to feel in the genital area and to experience orgasm, it does not necessarily prevent the person from obtaining satisfaction or providing gratification. The extent of sexual impairment is dependent on the level and completeness of the injury. Most men lose the ability to produce a psycho-genic erection, although many retain a reflexogenic capacity, and women lose their vaginal responsiveness.

While women remain fertile post-injury, most men with complete injuries are infertile, although Brindley (1984) is pioneering research into this do-main using electro-ejaculation techniques and vibrators. It is important to distinguish between sexual function and sexuality, since the latter need not be lost after injury. For example, we found that 50% of patients reported levels of satisfaction, sensuality and activity comparable to the able-bodied. Couples often leave this intimate renegotiation to the later stages of their adjustment and may benefit from a counsellor facilitating discussion and offering advice regarding new positions or means of expressing their affec-tion and sexuality towards each other.

Chronic pain

Umlauf, Moore and Britell (1987) concluded that chronic pain is a prevalent and serious problem for the person with spinal cord injury. They found that 51% of their patients reported persistent problems and again this com-pounds the adjustment process.

Interpersonal, social and cultural impact

Perhaps the most common immediate concern for the patient after injury is the effect on major relationships. In addition to the personal adjustment, accommodation is necessary from family members and the social network. The impact of the injury on marriage has been the focus of much research. This not only shows little difference in the divorce rate from the general population (El Ghatit and Hanson, 1976), but that the injury may make marriages happier (Crewe, Athelstan and Krumberger, 1979). Nevertheless, previously unstable marriages are not helped by the injury.

In parallel to the personal adjustment, intimate relationships may require renegotiation of roles, responsibilities and decision-making, but often the trauma serves to increase family cohesion and there appear to be few effects of the disability on the children (Buck and Hohmann, 1981). Nevertheless, the burden of care falls on families, particularly the female spouse, and they are often unsupported by services in the community (Creek *et al.*, 1988).

Prevailing social attitudes towards disability often impair social interaction and expectations. Siller *et al.* (1967) found that the majority of reactions of disability were negative in tone and were often associated with strain and discomfort. They included social avoidance, pity, and patronising benevolence and clearly contributed to the social isolation experienced by many disabled people.

Employment is often used as an indicator of social reintegration and engagement and, irrespective of the level of their injury, people have successfully entered a wide range of occupations. Creek *et al.* (1988) found that while 91% of people were employed at the time of injury only 50% were employed in a long-term follow-up in Britain. In contrast, Jenik (1982) in a Swiss Study noted that 78% were working or had definite plans to do so.

Factors which hinder employment include inaccessibility, transport problems, economic disincentives and lack of vocational counselling. Perhaps the most striking cultural manifestation of negative attitudes towards disability is the architectural inaccessibility of shops, pavements, offices, theatres and public amenities. Despite legislation compelled by the independent living movement (Varela, 1983; Topliss and Gould, 1981) major problems remain. For example, public transport is particularly inaccessible and compounds the physical barriers and magnifies the social isolation and sense of exclusion.

PSYCHOLOGICAL INTERVENTIONS AND COUNSELLING

With traumatic injuries perhaps the most important feeling in the early stages once a period of consciousness has occurred is that of being safe and surviving. Consciousness is altered by associated injuries, shock, drugs, sleeplessness and pain. Then the patient becomes aware of the immobilization, hospitalization and symptoms. Clinical experience suggests that a return to consciousness and feeling secure helps people manage the immediate emotions, and this is aided in most cases by supportive counselling, emphasizing 'safeness', and listening.

The next major issue is the medical prognosis and awareness of the injury. Heilporn and Noel (1968) found that 53% of their sample were aware of paralysis at the time of injury. However, irrespective of personal perceptions, the provision of clear, accessible prognostic information is crucial. The delivery of this information varies with individual centres and medical practitioners, but most provide patients with their prognosis as soon as it is reliable and the patient is stable. This interview is only the beginning of the communication process which can continue for years before the consequences are fully conceptualized and integrated.

Patient reactions vary from total devastation to apparent calm. They often turn to nurses and physiotherapists for clarification and further information, but all staff should try to ensure that patients have the opportunity to express emotions, and permit them to decide with whom they feel most comfortable talking. Families, nurses, physiotherapists, doctors, social workers and psychologists are frequently involved at this time.

Psychologists can encourage and enhance the emotional responsiveness of the team by facilitating the following:

(a) Giving the patient permission to express concerns. Once rapport is established with a particular member of staff, that person should be available to listen to the patient's fears and anxieties. Little more can be done because the prognosis may not be clear.

(b) Giving clear information. Staff should be available to answer specific questions and respond in a clear and consistent manner.

(c) Cognitive restructuring and decatastrophizing. While the catastrophic elements have to be acknowledged, the staff must begin to emphasize management, and challenge some of the patient's more obvious negative beliefs. As this can so easily seem dismissive, staff training and support is necessary.

(d) Foster coping processes. Minimizing the seriousness of the crisis often maintains an individual's psychological well-being, and as previously mentioned, may be adaptive in preventing the person from being overwhelmed. Statements of future coping should be supported and encouraged.

Family support during this period is essential. Most spinal centres have a facility for accommodating families in the early stages to ensure that regular contact with the patient can be fostered. Staff may intervene if this contact is destructive and access should be decided by the patient. Whilst some centres have clinical psychologists who are routinely involved in every admission, most refer only the most disturbed for assessment and counselling. Generally, however, patients identify the psychologist as a person with whom they can discuss confidential information such as pre-injury problems and personal difficulties.

Cognitive-behavioural counselling for anxiety and depression

As previously mentioned, problems of anxiety and depression can be conceptualized within the cognitive-behavioural model (Crewe and Krause, 1987) which suggests that emotional reactions in spinal cord injury are governed by the same processes that account for emotional reactions in the general population. Trower *et al.* (1988) suggest that all forms of human interaction, including counselling, follow the same triadic structure of opening, interacting (exploring, influencing and monitoring) and closing.

Establishing contact

It is important that the provision of counselling does not convey an implication that, in addition to the physical problems, the person will lose control psychologically. Rather, counselling should be seen as a process which can help the person express concerns, resume control and begin to accommodate. This is a difficult start because it implies dealing with a future that includes permanent disability. Current concerns are an appropriate initial focus. Relationship enhancement skills have already been covered in the first section of this book. However, genuineness, openness to the expression of feeling and acceptance of personal worth are particularly important facilitative skills at this stage.

Exploring and influencing

This is the assessment and intervention phase. Thoughts and beliefs about the consequences of the injury are explored. Specific periods of emotional distress are examined; the antecedent events, thoughts and beliefs, and emotional and behavioural consequences are separated and their interrelationship discussed. Once specific negative thinking patterns and inferences are identified, related core assumptions are made explicit. By focusing on maladaptive and irrational patterns negative assumptions about the consequences of the injury can be challenged. The aim is to encourage people to respond to their injury in a rational and realistic fashion, and not simply to think positively.

Many people, in the initial period, assume an unsatisfactory quality of life post-injury, drawing on preconceptions about disability in the absence of evidence. In a recent study of the long-term implications of injury, Creek *et al.* (1988) concluded that most respondents were satisfied with the quality of their lives. Another common distortion is to magnify the injury into a disaster with which one can never cope. Yet Scott-Richards (1986) found that while people were significantly more depressed than able-bodied controls three months after injury, these differences disappeared by one year. Other common distortions include ignoring achievements, focusing on failures and expectations of helplessness.

Once these distortions are understood the process of change can occur. Self-observation and correction is often the initial strategy. The counsellor may challenge these distortions and negative thoughts using the following techniques:

Questioning: For example, 'What is the evidence that you will never be able to work?' This is one of the most effective ways of eliciting realistic thinking.

Information giving: As previously mentioned this can reduce anxiety and also provide alternative expectations.

Teach problem solving: This encourages control and can foster a sense of accomplishment (Spivack, Platt and Shure, 1976).

Model adaptive responses: Providing access to credible peer role models and information on their eventual adaptation allows patients to see the possibility of self-efficacy.

Time out from negative thinking: Whilst this does not facilitate rational thinking, short-term avoidance and distraction can help the person consolidate and maintain a psychological balance.

Graded exposure and behavioural experiments: Encouraging patients in small steps to confront situations which provoke anxiety, (e.g. going to a restaurant) can foster improved confidence and mastery. Success can also effectively challenge negative beliefs.

Structuring activity and feedback: Arranging the environment to be responsive to individuals' needs and recognizing achievements can enhance the sense of control and minimize negative emotions. The following are examples of the type of negative thoughts and responses to typical situations post-injury.

Philip

Philip was referred eighteen months after his injury because of severe depression. He had had an active job in the Fire Service prior to his paraplegia and had not worked since. He was reluctant to see the psychologist since he thought nothing could be done to help. Negative thoughts included: 'I'm just going through the motions of life', 'I can never mountaineer again so there's no point in going out', and 'No girl is going to find me attractive'.

He was encouraged to list the evidence for and against 'just going through the motions of life'. At first he could not identify one reason against. However, through questioning he began to acknowledge that perhaps he was doing much more than he acknowledged. While he missed climbing, he could still travel and enjoy the scenery. He also discovered an interest in water-skiing. He recognized that one reason for not having a girlfriend was not going to places where he might meet one. Also he would never ask a girl out as he assumed that he would be rejected. However, since fear of rejection had not stopped him before, an experiment was set up, and he asked out an acquaintance. She did not refuse, demonstrating that he could still develop relationships.

Philip thought he could only enjoy working for the Fire Authority, but when questioned he recognized friendship, a sense of accomplishment and serving the community, which were important issues to him could be provided by an alternative job.

Brendan

Brendan was injured in a major disaster six weeks before being seen in the Acute Ward. He still believed he was going to die from his injuries. The nursing staff reassured him by establishing a routine care plan and answering his questions carefully. However, he frequently hyperventilated and slept for a maximum of four hours. He would sometimes scream out but at other times appeared calm. He was taught to relax using autohypnotic methods and when relaxed was encouraged to talk about some of the most disturbing thoughts and images of the disaster. Within a few sessions he was able to talk about the disaster without losing control.

He then reported such thoughts as, 'I'll never be able to look after myself or enjoy my children growing up' and, 'A tetraplegic can never be in control of any aspect of living'. These global judgements were challenged by first separating feelings from probabilities and then highlighting his retained ability and potential achievement. This was aided by discussion of comparable peers. Whilst these discussions were at times challenging and confrontational, this was permitted by the supportive framework of the sessions. The provision of personal care attendants, in addition to family support, enabled Brendan to pursue training in information technology, and whilst he remained physically dependent he also remained in control of the routine and important decisions in his life.

Terminating

This is a gradual process arrived at by mutual consent once progress has been sustained. With the provision of feedback on what is happening between sessions the patient becomes more capable of analysing new situations and applying the model.

Goal planning, advocacy and teamwork

In response to the problems associated with institutional dependency and disengagement, I developed a goal planning, key worker system (Kennedy, 1989). The main objective was to maximize the potential of each patient.

The main strategies included:

(a) Patient involvement in decision-making.
(b) Identification of needs and recognition of personal assets.
(c) Breakdown of targets into manageable units.
(d) Specification of who will do what, under what conditions and the degree of success expected.
(e) Key workers appointed for each patient to co-ordinate, inform and advocate.

As a result, there was a significant reduction in time spent in the bed area or in isolated disengagement (Kennedy, in press), a reduction in perceived staff control and an increase in programme clarity. Key workers were drawn from all sections of the multi-disciplinary team (physiotherapists, nurses, social workers, psychologists, medical staff and occupational therapists) and trained in goal planning and basic counselling skills.

Chronic pain management

Chronic pain behaviour is a function of the interplay between organic and learning factors, including avoidance of social discomfort, absolution of responsibilities, negative prediction and expectation of pain. Again the cognitive-behavioural approach can be used to reduce pain behaviour (Turk, Meichenbaum and Genest, 1983) through contingency management (e.g. increasing behaviours incompatible with pain perception), relaxation training and cognitive restructuring (e.g. relabel sensations and challenging negative beliefs).

For example, Jane was a 35-year-old fashion designer who had had a thoracic spinal cord injury three years before whilst horse-riding, and who was experiencing chronic and severe pain below the level of the injury. She was provided with autohypnotic relaxation training and taught the self control model of pain, which aims to help the person develop strategies for controlling the consequences of pain in terms of activity levels and cognitive assumptions. A pain diary was used to demonstrate the ineffectiveness of passivity by highlighting how levels of perceived pain remained similar despite differences in activity. Negative beliefs including 'I've nothing to look forward to' and 'There's no point in doing anything because of pain' were challenged and behavioural experiments were organized. Pain behaviour was ignored and well behaviour was reinforced. The family were involved in the programme and were encouraged to stop her 'pain forecasting'. Self-coping statements such as 'a little at a time' were fostered.

Progress began with an increase in general social activity. She reported taking more control and feeling 'less fragile'. The family also reported her to be more in control and happier. While the level of perceived pain remained the same, her overall mood and general activity increased, demonstrating that the negative consequences of pain can be ameliorated, if not the pain per se.

Sexual counselling

A variety of approaches have been developed to help people manage their sexual concerns. One of the most flexible and useful is the PLISSIT model (Annon, 1974). This model had four levels of intervention, each increasing in sophistication, which allows counsellors to structure a programme according to their level of competence:

Permission giving

This relates to the general responsiveness within the rehabilitation context to the discussion of sexual issues and concerns. The legitimacy of continued sexual interest is acknowledged and questions are answered in a mature and matter of fact fashion.

Limited information

Once the person is aware that questions concerning sexuality are permitted and encouraged, they can decide when they require further information. The amount of information given is dependent upon the patient's abilities and level of concern, but most members of staff should be trained appropriately. A variety of published material may be useful and should be available to patients on request, but McKrell (1985) has produced a particularly well written handbook.

Specific suggestions

With this next stage, specific suggestions are offered to the patient and their partner. The counsellor should be comfortable communicating the specific techniques in a sensitive and open manner. Specific suggestions include advice on maintaining an erection, positioning, developing relationships and possible problems.

Intensive therapy

People with more complex sexual difficulties may require more intensive therapy, which may focus on sexual behaviour, for example 'sensate focus' (Masters and Johnson, 1970) or on communication. This should be provided by people trained in sexual counselling, but all staff should be encouraged to refer such people to suitable therapists.

Malcolm

Four years after his injury, Malcolm revealed that, whilst initially they had a good sex life, his wife had become disinterested and unresponsive. He was dissatisfied because of infrequency, and she, because she did not find the sexual contact sensuous.

Therapy began with a total ban on intercourse, which helped relieve anxiety. The couple subsequently began to work through the various stages of sensate focus, beginning with non-genital contact and finishing with intercourse. This process enabled the couple to relearn sexual responsiveness and communication of likes and dislikes, demonstrating that despite physiological compromise, normal levels of satisfaction can be obtained.

THE WIDER CHALLENGE

Many spinal cord injury rehabilitation centres provide access to trained counsellors, some offer a service to every patient, and others have sessional input. Referrals for specialist counselling are usually made by members of the rehabilitative team. However, trained counsellors can support and enhance the rehabilitative milieu by training nursing and therapy staff in counselling skills. The service is also enriched by the availability of peer counsellors both trained and untrained, particularly for group work to facil-itate community return. These are largely problem-solving and information exchange groups, but self-help and advocacy groups are particularly effec-tive. The Spinal Injury Association (Britain), American Spinal Injury Asso-ciation and various European cohorts not only provide welfare, access and resource advice, but they also arrange symposia and meetings addressing health professional issues.

It is also important to consider the societal context, within which counsell-ing occurs. The main objective of any intervention is to preserve social value, self-esteem and quality of life. Some of the approaches discussed have in-volved organisational change issues which are as distinctive as personal responses. Regular evaluation of service delivery and developments creates a climate of continued progress and responsiveness to developing needs. If, as a society, we take the responsibility of managing the acute physical prob-lems, then surely we must follow this through and respond to quality of life issues.

This holistic approach implies the integration and achievement of op-timum physical, psychological and social functioning. That individuals can achieve this after such a devastating physical injury is without question. Research, personal and clinical experience have shown that this is possible. What is questionable is our collective discernment to make the necessary accommodations, to ensure accessibility to our physical, health and social domains.

REFERENCES

Annon, J.S. (1974). *The behavioural treatment of sexual problems (Vol. 1)*. Honolulu: Enabling Systems Inc.

Beck, A.T. (1976). *Cognitive therapy and emotional disorders*. New York: International Universities Press.

Brindley, G. S.(1984). The Fertility of Men with Spinal Injuries. *Paraplegia*, **22**, 337–348.

Brucker, B. (1983). Spinal Cord Injuries. In T.G. Burish and L.A. Bradley (Eds), *Coping with chronic disease: Research and applications*, pp. 285–311. New York: Academic Press.

Buck, F. and Hohmann, G. (1981). Personality, behaviour, values and family relations of children of fathers with spinal cord injury. *Archives of Physical Medicine and Rehabilitation*, **62**, 432–438.

Caplan, B. and Schechter, J. (1987). Denial and Depression in disabling illness. In B. Caplan (Ed.), *Rehabilitation psychology*, pp. 133–170. Baltimore: Aspen.

Cogswell, B. (1968). Self Socialisation: Readjustment of paraplegics in the com-munity. *Journal of Rehabilitation*, **34**, 11–14.

Creek, G., Moore, M., Oliver, V., Silver, J., and Zarb, G. (1988). *Personal and social implications of spinal cord injury*. London: Thames Polytechnic.

Crewe, N., Athelstan, G., and Krumberger, J. (1979). Spinal Cord Injury: A com-parison of preinjury and postinjury marriages, *Archives of Physical Medicine and Rehabilitation*, **60**, 252–256.

Crewe, N.M. and Krause, J.S. (1987). Spinal Cord Injury: Psychological aspects. In B. Caplan (Ed.), *Rehabilitation psychology*, pp. 3–33. Baltimore: Aspen.

El Ghatit, A. and Hanson, R. (1976). Marriage and divorce after spinal cord injury. *Archives of Physical Medicine and Rehabilitation*, **57**, 470–472.

Frankel, H.L. (1983). Spinal Injuries units in England and Wales. *Estratto da Europa Medicophysica*, **19**, 31–32.

Gowland, E.L. (1941). Traumatic Paraplegia. *British Medical Journal*, **1**, 814.

Guttmann, L. (1973). *Spinal cord injuries: Comprehensive management and research.* Oxford: Blackwell Scientific Publications.

Heilporn, A. and Noel, G. (1968). Reflections on the consciousness of disability and somatognosis in cases of acute spinal injuries. *International Journal of Paraplegia*, **6**, 122–127.

Hohmann, G. (1975). Psychological aspects of treatment and rehabilitation of the spinal injured person. *Clinical Orthopaedics*, **112**, 81–88.

Janis, I. (1983). Preventing pathogenic denial by means of stress inoculation. In S. Breznitz (Ed.), *The denial of stress.* New York: International Universities Press.

Jenik, F. (1982). Social and vocational reintegration of paraplegic and tetraplegic patients in Switzerland. *Paraplegia*, **20**, 65–70.

Kennedy, P. (1989). Psychological approaches in the management of spinal cord injury. *British Journal of Holistic Medicine*, **4**, 169–176.

Kennedy, P. (In press). Goal Planning, Advocacy and Behavioural mapping. *Paraplegia.*

Kennedy, P., Fisher, K., and Pearson, E. (1988). Ecological evaluation of a Rehabilitative Environment for spinal cord injured people: Behavioural mapping and feedback. *British Journal of Clinical Psychology*, **27**, 239–246.

Khella, L. and Stoner, E. (1977). 101 Cases of spinal cord injury. *American Journal of Physical Medicine*, **56**, 21–32.

Lawes, C. (1984). Pressure sore readmission for spinal injured people. *Care Science and Practice*, **4**, 4–8.

Masters, W.H. and Johnson, V.E. (1970). *Human sexual inadequacy.* Boston: Little, Brown and Co.

McCollough, N.C., Green, B.A., Goldberg, M.L., and Klose, C. (1981). Spinal cord injury in South Florida. *The Journal of the Florida Medical Association*, **68**, 968–973.

McKrell, J. (1985). *Sexuality after your spinal cord injury.* Pittsburgh: Harmarville Rehabilitation Centre.

Morris, J., Roth, E., and Davidoff, G. (1986). Mild closed head injury and cognitive deficits in spinal cord injury patients. *Journal of Head Trauma and Rehabilitation*, **2**, 31–42.

Nehemkis, A. and Groot, H. (1980). Indirect self destructive behaviour in spinal cord injury. In N. Farberon (Ed.), *The many faces of suicide.* New York: McGraw-Hill.

Nyquist, R. and Bors, E. (1967). Mortality and survival in traumatic myelopathy during nineteen years from 1946 to 1965. *International Journal of Paraplegia*, **51**, 22–48.

Oxford Regional Health Authority (1983). *Use of resources for the care and treatment of patients with injuries to the spinal cord at the National Spinal Injuries Centre.* Report: Oxford.

Scott-Richards, J. (1986). Psychologic adjustment to spinal cord injury during the first post discharge year. *Archives of Physical Medicine and Rehabilitation*, **67**, 362–365.

Shontz, F.C. (1984). Spread in response to imagined loss: An empirical analogue. *Rehabilitation Psychology*, **29**, 77.

Siller, J. (1969). Psychological situation of the disabled with spinal cord injuries. *Rehabilitation Literature*, **30**, 290–296.

Siller, J., Chipman, A., Ferguson, L., and Vann, D. (1967). Attitude of the non-disabled toward the physical disabled. *Studies in reaction to disability XI*. New York: New York University.

Silver, J.R., Morris, W.R., and Otfinowski, J.S. (1980). Associated injuries in patients with spinal injury. *Injury*, **12**, 219–224.

Spivack, G., Platt, J., and Shure, M.B. (1976). *The problem solving approach to adjustment*. San Francisco: Jossey Bass.

Topliss, E. and Gould, B. (1981). *A charter for the disabled*. Oxford: Blackwell and Robertson.

Trieschmann, R. (1980). *Spinal cord injuries: Psychological, social and vocational adjustment*. New York: Pergamon.

Trower, P., Casey, A., and Dryden, W. (1988). *Cognitive-behavioural counselling in action*. London: Sage.

Turk, D., Meichenbaum, D. and Genest, M. (1983). *Pain and behavioural medicine*. New York: Guilford.

Umlauf, R., Moore, J., and Britell, C. (1987). *Prevalence and nature of the pain experience in spinal cord injured*. Paper presented at the 8th Annual Society of Behavioural Medicine conference, Washington D.C.

Varela, R. (1983). Changing social attitudes and legislation regarding disability. In N. Crewe and I. Zoh (Eds), *Independent living for physically disabled people*. San Francisco: Jossey-Bass.

Young, J.S. and Northrup, N.E. (1979). *Statistical information pertaining to some of the most commonly asked questions about SCI*. Phoenix: NSIC Data Research Center.

9 Counselling People with Multiple Sclerosis and Their Families

JULIA SEGAL

ARMS Research Unit, Central Middlesex Hospital, Acton Lane, London NW10 7NS

Multiple Sclerosis (MS) is a disease of the central nervous system which affects about one per thousand of the population. There is no cure and no known cause. Confirming a diagnosis may take years and involves enormous distress. MS affects people in a frighteningly random way and is extremely unpredictable. Some people have it for thirty or more years, and are scarcely affected except for tiring easily and gradually developing some physical or sensory abnormalities. Others deteriorate quickly and may die within ten years. Symptoms include fatigue, difficulty in walking, constant or intermittent pain, clumsiness, disturbances of vision and other senses, loss of sexual responses, speech or swallowing difficulties, and intellectual problems. Any of these may be temporary or permanent.

WHO NEEDS COUNSELLING

Before diagnosis

The uncertainty and anxiety generated by having no clear diagnosis is generally described as an experience far worse than knowing what is wrong, yet doctors often delay giving the diagnosis, ignorant of the trouble they may be causing. In the early stages of MS, symptoms are often mysterious and disturbing, giving rise to conflicts about being mad or about whether symptoms are 'real' or 'in the mind'. These conflicts may lead to extremes of bad temper, withdrawal, loss of self-confidence and fears of a revival of past disturbing situations. Social relationships at home or at work may be threatened. However, once the anxieties or the illness can be openly discussed, the situation may ease.

The way the diagnosis is given is often a source of short- or long-term difficulty for families and a source of worry for the doctor. There is real difficulty in deciding what to say. Since the doctor cannot cure MS and may

Counselling and Communication in Health Care. Edited by H. Davis and L. Fallowfield
© 1991 John Wiley & Sons Ltd

be most aware of people who are badly affected, the family may receive a strong message of hopelessness from the doctor, or be quite explicitly thrown back on their own resources.

Relations between patient and doctor may be improved in some cases if the doctor can be open about the possibility of MS before it is certain. Patients can be asked directly if they would like to know the main possibilities or if they would rather leave the worrying to the doctor. Asking what the patient thinks may be wrong can also be useful as the doctor may be able to offer more accurate information and reassurance.

Doctors are often unaware of the help they can give in terms of referral to ARMS (Action and Research for Multiple Sclerosis), the MS Society or the local library for information, to physiotherapy, for dietary advice, or for counselling. They may not ask what the family already knows about MS, even though this affects their understanding and their reactions. They may not recognize the value of friendly sympathetic encouragement to talk, and the need to check whether information has been understood. They may try to protect patients by concealing information, without realizing that they are leaving the family to make serious life decisions without relevant facts.

John gave up a secure job with a good pension for a new venture ten years after his doctor knew he had MS. The venture failed partly because he had a serious relapse which left him unable to work and which left his family dependent upon social security.

Part of the difficulty of having MS is the need to negotiate a new, more realistic view of the medical profession. A counsellor may help families express and bear the frustration, fury and suffering caused by inadequate or even damaging behaviour on the part of other professionals. This can be very uncomfortable, but it is important for future relations.

After diagnosis

Diagnosis may bring relief. It also brings new problems, and different anxieties, hopes and possibilities for action. The question of who to tell may be an issue for many people. Hiding the MS has its attractions, but it can cut off sources of support or information. It may be protective, when a mother with few symptoms decides not to tell her children until after their A-levels, but it can be patronizing. For example, a woman whose mother had always been a source of comfort did not tell her because she thought she could not cope with it. Discussing this kind of issue with a counsellor can either help the person in a stressful situation of concealment, or open up the possibility of more support from those around. The difficult question of what and how to tell, and the frustrations of failing to make people understand, may also be shared.

One consultation can enable someone to consider whether counselling could help or not, and if so when. Some prefer to 'go it alone' and a counsellor can acknowledge this, perhaps making an appointment for one year later. It is common for people to need two years or more before they really incorporate any serious loss or change into their basic assumptions about life. Some want to try their own methods of dealing with the illness first, before allowing anyone else to discuss it with them.

Other people realise there are long-standing problems in their lives which they now need to sort out and will be glad to use counselling. Grant *et al.* (1989) have recently found that in a sample of people with MS, 75% had suffered some seriously disturbing life event in the six months prior to the onset of symptoms. These events were not under the control of the person concerned, and left people seriously shaken emotionally. Such events may well be appropriate subjects for counselling. In particular, work on past griefs and the handling of helplessness may be relevant and productive.

Counselling for family members

Chapter 1 of this book describes vividly the experiences of one young man whose wife had a rapidly developing form of MS. MS can make difficulties for whole families, including children, parents and siblings. Love and affection may remain, but sometimes MS affects people so that they become difficult to love. Some give up their previous role in the family, because of the physiological effects of MS or for emotional reasons, or for social reasons to do with the way they are treated. This can leave family members feeling abandoned by the person with MS. As in any family, destructive and despairing feelings or actual violence may also be experienced at times, when the MS may add to the intensity of danger involved.

Children respond in different ways to their parents' MS. Many seem to feel an enormous sense of responsibility towards the ill parent, and desire to make them better. They work out their own explanations of what is happening, often including their own culpability. They may be relieved, therefore, to be offered the chance of a friendly exploration of the meaning of MS in their lives. Others reject any suggestion that they cannot handle everything themselves. Children living alone with a very disabled parent may be terrified of losing that parent if they tell anyone in authority anything at all.

ISSUES ARISING

Uncertainty and lack of control

The experience of MS is different for everyone. The symptoms themselves are variable and change over time; their meaning and the consequent emotional reactions also vary and change. No-one knows what causes MS, what course it will take or how it will affect a family physically, intellectually, psychologically or socially. Neither the person with MS nor anyone else may be sure whether a particular symptom is exaggerated or played down or whether it can be changed.

This ignorance leaves people making their own interpretations of events in the hope that they might be able to have some influence or control. People may decide that sex, pregnancy, getting upset, resting too much, or working too hard will make MS worse. The uncertainty about what causes or contributes to MS is replaced with a false certainty. Precipitate action taken on these beliefs may cause considerable trouble to the family concerned.

Sometimes people 'fight the disease' by insisting they can control it. Others give up too much, rather than struggle with the uncertainties of discovering exactly what can be salvaged. Rather than find out if he could still have children or a loving marriage, a young man gave up all sex and all demonstrations of affection the moment he lost an erection for the first time. A young woman decided that the diagnosis meant she should not get married; this removed the uncertainty of waiting to find out whether anyone would want her when disabled. Fifteen years later she was still walking around and working.

Family members (and professionals) often also come up with their own 'cures', because they cannot bear not knowing what to do for the best. An ARMS counsellor was told by a father, 'you must tell him he must make himself do something'. The son had MS and tired easily. The father 'knew' what his son needed and could not listen to his son or the counsellor saying something different. A woman with MS who wanted a second child said her doctor told her, 'you don't need children, you need to travel'.

Stress

Families often have problems related to the fear that stress of any kind is actually dangerous for someone with MS. Symptoms can get worse under all kinds of stresses, such as heat, cold, or tension, but this lasts only a few hours and involves previously damaged nerves. These effects are different from relapses which last days or months and in which new symptoms appear or old ones become worse (Burnfield 1985), but families may not distinguish them and may react in ways which lead to real, serious and unnecessary losses which threaten long-term relationships.

A man was asked by the counsellor whether his MS had affected his sex life. 'Oh, I gave it up,' he said. 'It made me worse.' The counsellor asked what his wife thought about this, and he said he did not know, he hadn't asked her.

A girl of 10 was told not to upset her mother because she had MS. Her mother was physically unable to do much, but was good at listening to and comforting her children. The girl felt she could no longer talk to her mother about her troubles at school because these might upset her and make her worse.

Fears about the future

Some fears about MS and the future are so frightening that people do not dare speak about them. They may fear that if they say something, it will happen, or that 'If I say that, you won't like me any more'. Such fears may be addressed with a counsellor, in a room which can be left afterwards, when they cannot be addressed with any other professional whose goodwill and respect is needed for other purposes. Examining such fears has important consequences: thoughts may become more realistic, and there can be a great sense of relief. The possibility and value of sharing real worries is demonstrated, and this can improve other relationships. It can also remove the feeling that worries are 'lurking', ready to emerge at unguarded moments. Where continual activity has been used to defend against frightening thoughts, examining fears can enable people to allow themselves to rest, which can be important in managing MS.

Grief and loss

Grief may be avoided or put off for some time with the use of denial partly in an attempt to keep control. Grief may be seen as 'giving in' and as the opposite of 'fighting the illness.'

It can be very painful to sit through some of the losses people need to share, with no means of doing anything to alleviate them. A counsellor found it almost unbearable when a father, who could scarcely move or speak, struggled to say, 'What I dread most is my children growing up with me like this'. But her presence made it possible for this thought to be formulated and shared, and gave some relief to the man and his wife.

Facing grief like this means being prepared to feel quite helpless and hopeless. Sometimes after such feelings have been held for long enough, possibilities for positive action may emerge. Counselling can help people to discover what they have really lost and to separate this from what they do not have to lose. It can help them to fight realistically rather than to fight reality.

Some losses involve illusions, especially about the self (Segal, 1987). The illusion of being totally independent is common and is challenged by MS which may symbolize becoming 'dependent like a child again.' People may need to be helped to see that a mature adult has to handle a mature kind of dependence on others.

Reactions to losses, or attempts to deal with them, can result in serious misunderstandings within relationships, already stretched by the losses themselves. Communication within the family may be badly affected, and counselling may be important in helping family members to speak to each other and to interpret non-verbal communication better. Communication can also be affected by sensory as well as physical losses, both of which can create a sense of strangeness and of loss of common ground with other people.

Intellectual problems

Intellectual problems are common. These vary from slight memory loss, difficult to distinguish from normal ageing, through difficulties in carrying on an argument, to a total inability to make rational decisions. Sorting out the details of what exactly happens can be very helpful for a family. The difficulties of facing yet another loss, the intellectual, on top of physical losses can be considerable. These difficulties may threaten the whole basis of a relationship.

Facing the fact that a husband or wife no longer has the ability to make certain decisions can be very painful and problematical in many ways. Not only does the partner have to take over some functions previously undertaken by the other, but they are often painfully aware that this may further disable the person concerned. There may gradually be a transition from wife or husband to nurse, with this role being happily or unhappily accepted. The worry about how children will cope with the condition of the one parent and the physical and emotional preoccupation of the other adds to the guilt and anxiety for the parent who has become a 'carer'.

Sexuality

Sexual activity may be affected by MS. The functioning and sensations of the penis and the vagina may be inhibited, but there may also be fear of causing damage. Loss of potency in men in particular can cause enormous problems, including loss of confidence at work and in general family life. Since difficulties in the emotional relationship may also be expressed sexually it can be important for a couple to explore what exactly is behind the sexual difficulties. Routine enquiries about sexual life can uncover such troubles and may bring relief, particularly where the couple did not know of the effects of MS on sexual responses and misinterpreted them as loss of love or affection.

Pregnancy and childbirth

It seems that in the long term MS does not seem to be affected by having children (Weinshenker et al., 1989), but many doctors still warn their patients against pregnancy. Some women with MS are suffering today from being pushed into abortion or sterilisation by their doctors twenty or thirty years ago. Even where the doctor tries to help the couple make their own decision and supports them in this, potential parents worry. These issues are examined in the ARMS booklet, 'Pregnancy and MS' (Forti and Segal, 1986).

Death and dying

Medical staff often worry that talking about the fears or realities of death or dying will make things worse. In fact sharing such feelings even about suicide can help reduce the sense of loneliness and abandonment described so clearly in Chapter 1. Other anxieties about death and dying may be ameliorated by discussion. It may be possible to help plan for a good death, or to uncover quite unrealistic fears or beliefs about dying. Even disturbing, realistic fantasies about death can seem better after being discussed.

People with MS who seem close to dying may live in a very disabled state for years. Family members, including young children, may need considerable support and help in talking about their fears and worries at this time. All the family may be faced with serious challenges to the sense of their own goodness, value, potency and importance. Love may sometimes seem to disappear, and duty be felt as a poor substitute. In other situations, love remains but either way, the pain of slow loss can be extreme.

Relations between people who have MS and people who do not

Identification with other people is a normal means of understanding their reactions. With MS this is complicated since people with MS have such different experiences from those without. Some nurses, for example, assume that patients with MS are 'attention-seeking' or 'being difficult' when they ask for a bedpan and are then unable to use it, or when they demand to have their legs moved in order to avoid bedsores. They do not recognize the confusing messages passed by the bladder to the mind and assume that this behaviour is caused as it would be in them, by the mind alone. They may not understand the experience of having paralysed legs, and may feel that the person with MS does not want to move them, or makes them stiffen up when they are being moved.

Professionals and family members often feel guilty that they do not have MS. Sometimes they feel they would hate others who could walk or work if they could not, and they assume the person with MS would rather not see someone else walking or working. This may inhibit them in both what they do themselves and what they say to someone with MS. People do sometimes hate others for being 'all right' when they are not, but not everybody feels like this all the time. The person with MS may feel even more excluded from normal life as a result of such awkwardness and concealment.

A woman was worried about telling her husband about hill walks which they used to do together and she now (less often) undertook without him. When the counsellor helped her ask her husband how he felt, he said he wanted her to tell him, because he felt he was 'up there with her' when she talked about it.

Living well with MS

It is possible to have a good life with MS.

Sally has had MS for more than twenty years. She has two adult children, a devoted husband, a good social life and a productive (part-time) work life. She is better dressed and more attractive than most women in spite of using a wheelchair most of the time. MS causes her trouble sometimes, and she gets depressed, but she recovers. She hates her wheelchair at times, but her sons now tease her about her latest acquisition, an electric buggy for going round the shops.

A close friend of hers is 70 and has had MS since she was 20. She has worked to support herself and her children all her life. She has 'funny turns' but appears otherwise unaffected. She enjoyed counselling and said it enabled her to ask her neighbours for assistance.

HELPING

One means of helping people with MS and their families is to offer an opportunity to explore the question: 'What does MS mean to you?' This may be particularly important before delivering the diagnosis.

Frances was irritated with the doctor's lecture on relapses and remissions. Her immediate thought on being told she had MS had been 'that's what cousin Maud had, and she died within five years'. She 'knew' the doctor was just being reassuring and felt patronized by him.

Stanley's family did not listen to the doctor except to hear that MS only affected you physically. They kept themselves going with the thought 'Stanley can now do the Open University course he always wanted to do'. When they discovered some time later that his intellect could be affected, they were devastated and furious with the doctor.

As the disease progresses the significance and meaning of MS for the family change, but the value and importance of enquiring about it at regular intervals remain. New fears may emerge and old ones lose their power. 'What is your greatest fear about MS?' may also be explored.

For Jane, the wheelchair was her biggest fear. It meant being 'pushed out of the way' by her husband in a divorce, and by her brother when she was a child. Marriage counselling helped her with these issues.

Professionals' emotional reactions

In order to examine such questions fully, it is necessary to be prepared to hear painful stories and to have very upsetting emotions evoked in both speaker and listener. Professionals, like others, often block attempts to relate distressing events because they are scared of their own or others' emotional reactions. This may be realistic, particularly if the professional knows they have no supervisor or consultant to give them support. Furthermore, some issues, such as incest, family violence or rape, may be so disturbing for both speaker and listener that they cannot and perhaps should not be spoken about within a relationship which has another purpose. The doctor or the physiotherapist may not be the person to hear a serious confession or a desperate cry of pain; it would be too awkward to return to a more 'ordinary' relationship afterwards. Sometimes a confidentiality far stricter than a doctor is believed to offer, and the security of being able to leave immediately afterwards may be necessary for very threatening issues to be handled. Counsellors who work to very strict times find they are told such things in the two minutes before the end of the session and believe that the time boundary facilitates the confession.

Janet felt her MS was a punishment for having had an abortion, which was then followed by two miscarriages. She spoke movingly of the three children she had lost. She had also been attacked sexually as a teenager and had tried to kill herself repeatedly. She had never told anyone until it emerged in counselling. As she listened to Janet, the counsellor found herself feeling invaded, angry, dirtied, helpless; she wanted to shout and scream, and get rid of Janet. This was extremely uncomfortable, but the counsellor understood it as a reflection of some of the feelings Janet had experienced at the time, and continued to see Janet. Janet said the sessions enabled her to begin to appreciate the children she had.

Professionals can be very disturbed by MS, because of the feelings such as helplessness, frustration and anger evoked in them, partly by identification with the patient, partly in response to the patient's own reaction to their MS. This can make them distort their perceptions, for example by being 'too nice'.

A psychologist said she felt terribly sorry for a woman with MS. In discussion she confessed that in fact the woman made her very angry but she thought it was wrong to feel this. Consequently she was unable to help the woman with her social problem, which involved irritating all those around.

It is common for professionals, as in this case, to distance themselves both from their own emotions and from the patient. Physiotherapy departments are often arranged so that intimate conversation is easily avoidable. Nurses may keep themselves busy. GPs can easily arrange their visits so that there is no time to talk.

Referral

Since it has to be accepted that some professionals are neither willing nor able to spend time exploring emotional aspects of MS with all their patients, referral to professional counsellors may sometimes be essential. Professionals may be most aware of this if an emotional or social difficulty is hindering their work. Sometimes a counsellor can help the professional to handle the situation themselves without the need for referral. However, a consultation with a counsellor can also be arranged as a matter of course, for the patient to explore their own reactions to MS and to give them the opportunity to discover what a counsellor can offer them. In this situation, particularly with a counsellor who specialises in MS, areas of ignorance about MS may be uncovered, and the patient's own strategies for handling it may be discussed.

Preparation for working with MS

Because the attitudes of professionals affect those with whom they work, it is important that they should spend some time thinking about their own attitudes (De Souza, 1990). Professionals need to sort out what they think their own reactions would be if they had MS. They need to consider their own worst fears, their reactions to it, the impact it would have on their relationships with others, and, for example, their occupational status.

As well as questions relating to the professional's identification with the patient, there are questions relating to the professional as an onlooker. How do they handle frustration and impotence? How do they react to other people's symptoms, such as tiredness or inability to walk (e.g. 'that's laziness'; 'it's mind over matter'; 'I wouldn't let it affect me like that')? How do they feel about being healthy when the other person has MS? How do they feel about people with MS getting married, having children, or wanting to commit suicide?

Professionals of all kinds could also probably improve their handling of any relationship with a family with MS by discussion with professional counsellors. Those who work with people with MS may be most helpful, but other counsellors may also have useful contributions to make. For doctors, the main difficulty may be to recognize that they cannot know how the patient understands their MS and feels about it unless they ask, but this implies a commitment to a situation which may be uncomfortable for the doctor and may involve them in considerable work.

IMPLICATIONS

Professional counselling and supportive professionals

It is important to distinguish between professional counselling and the emotional support which health workers and others can give to people with MS. Counsellors choose and are trained to work with emotions. Their experience, their work setting, their personal supervision and their closely defined task may enable them to work in considerable depth with some of the problems raised in this chapter. Other health professionals should have a choice in their willingness and ability to offer a sympathetic ear and understanding.

Professional counselling: what is available?

People seeking counselling are generally forced into the private sector, though some enlightened GPs are beginning to employ counsellors. A few counsellors offer a specialist service to people with MS, some in close relationships with ARMS. Elsewhere counsellors have to be sought through the British Association for Counselling. These may or may not know much about MS and may have difficulty facing some of the realities of it. ARMS provides a back-up service for these counsellors, sending literature and offering case discussion by telephone or in person with an ARMS counsellor.

The NHS provides virtually nothing in the way of professional counselling for people with MS, who are frequently told there is nothing they can be offered. They are not even put in touch with ARMS or the MS Society, where they can be given information about the disease and support or help in living with it. This is not satisfactory, and it adds to the sense of abandonment and the feeling of having lost social support and value.

Emotional support from professional health workers: What is available?

People with MS have to handle health workers who have considerable difficulties with MS. Professionals often misinterpret symptoms as intentional: they may feel 'she's attention-seeking' when bladder problems cause bedpans to be required repeatedly, for example; or 'she's not trying' when someone with MS cannot walk; or 'there's nothing wrong with her' when symptoms cannot be seen to correspond with brain-scans. They may feel blamed and guilty because they cannot cure the person, nor even help their symptoms. They may resent the patient for not getting better, for having a relapse when they seemed to be better, for not trying to be independent enough, or for being too upset or too demanding when there is nothing that can be offered. The value of sympathy and understanding is not recognized and there is a tendency to label people quickly as 'a difficult patient', 'hasn't come to terms with their disability' or 'managing well'.

Professionals, therefore, at present seldom offer much in the way of emotional support. There are of course exceptions, professionals who respect the patient's knowledge of their own body and their own MS. They make efforts to seek out what the patient knows and feels and wants and fears. They do not run away when emotionally upsetting issues are raised, and they can share the sense of frustration and impotence engendered by MS, in such a way that neither patient nor professional feel belittled.

Emotional support from professional health workers: What should be available?

Ideally all professionals should be warm and caring people, and well-supported so that their ability to care is not worn away by too many demands on them and by unrealistic expectations. However, they may or may not be good at handling emotional issues. Doctors, for example, may find it very difficult to admit that they cannot provide the support required by some of their patients, and see this simply as their failure. They may need to be more clear about the limits of their role with families where MS is involved. They also need to recognize that they cannot give emotional support without seeking it for themselves. The employment of counsellors in a practice is a recognition of the different roles. Where the two can discuss their work together, the doctor may be helped to face up to and perhaps improve his or her own treatment. Discussion groups for GPs, such as those run by the Tavistock Clinic in London, have helped many doctors to reduce their need to distance themselves from patients.

A further realistic option, chosen by some already, is to seek out a consultant, such as an experienced counsellor, who can help the professional to develop his or her interpersonal skills within their work. The aim is to help professionals do their job better, rather than to turn them into counsellors themselves. This kind of consultation may also counteract the risks of burnout.

Emotional support from non-professionals

Emotional support from non-professionals is available, both face-to-face and on the telephone, but it may take time before people discover it. ARMS and the MS Society offer the support of groups and individuals in many parts of the country. Local conditions vary. At their best, these local organisations demonstrate to people with MS that there are things one can do to alleviate the long-term effects of MS; that people with MS can be effective organisers, and can support each other in their struggle with MS and share their knowledge and experiences; and that life with MS does not have to be a disaster. At their worst, they offer visits by people who are patronizing and know-it-all, and who encourage very gloomy and depressing attitudes.

Other, non-specialized organizations may also offer emotional support to families affected by MS. Churches, carers' groups, classes and clubs of all kinds can provide friendship and relief. Unfortunately, relationships with friends and with churches in particular sometimes seem to be unable to withstand the strains put upon them by MS. These, perhaps, are the relationships where most is expected and where real people may fail to live up to the ideal.

CONCLUSION

This chapter has tried to show the enormous variation in the experience of MS, and the way in which reactions to the MS may be more socially damaging than the illness itself. These reactions can be modified by counselling and by supportive interactions with other people who understand something about MS and the changes and difficulties it can bring. At best, new possibilities for social relationships and perhaps work may open up; self-confidence and emotional maturity may grow; family misunderstandings may be cleared up; children may be helped to talk with their parents. At the very least, the sense of abandonment and isolation, as described in Chapter 1, may be reduced by a real attempt to understand.

MS affects not only patients and their families but also the professional, threatening sometimes their basic assumptions about themselves and their work. Professionals too may behave and feel better if they seek help to understand their own reactions to MS and to those who have it. Health care professionals should not only ensure that families with MS know about the sources of information and support available to them, but they should also look carefully, preferably with someone else, at their own behaviour and their own assumptions when faced with people who have MS. Professionals who consult an experienced counsellor or psychotherapist for this purpose will be better able to assess the value of such consultations and so to advise patients and their families on the basis of their own experience.

USEFUL ADDRESSES

ARMS: Action for Research into Multiple Sclerosis
4a Chapel Hill
Stansted
Essex CM24 8AG
Tel: (0279) 815553

BAC: British Association for Counselling
37a Sheep Street
Rugby CV21 3BX
Tel: (0788) 578328/9

MS Society, UK
25 Effie Road
London SW6 1EE
Tel: 071-736 6267

REFERENCES

Burnfield, A. (1985). *MS: A personal exploration*. London: Souvenir Press.
De Souza, L. (1990). *Multiple sclerosis: Approaches to management*. London: Chapman and Hall.

Forti, A. and Segal, J.C. (1986). *MS and pregnancy.* Stansted: ARMS.

Grant, I., Brown, G.W., Harris, T., McDonald, W.I., Patterson, T., and Trimble, M.R. (1989). Severely threatening events and marked life difficulties preceding onset or exacerbation of multiple sclerosis. *Journal of Neurology, Neurosurgery and Psychiatry,* **52**, 8–13.

Segal, J.C. (1987). Independence and Control: Issues in the counselling of people with MS. *Counselling,* **62**, 10–17.

Weinshenker, B. *et al.* (1989). The influence of pregnancy on disability from MS: A population-based study in Middlesex County, Ontario. *Neurology,* **39**, 1438–1440.

10 Infertility Counselling

PAULA SHAW

Ashburton Cottage, 43 North Road, Highgate Village, London, N6 4BE

INTRODUCTION

Pregnancy and parenthood are important social issues in all cultures. It has been well documented that substantial numbers of couples have difficulty in conceiving, although obtaining accurate figures has always proved problematic. Government statistics have been based on details of women who are past child bearing age without having produced children, but include those who have elected to remain childless for social and personal reasons. In 1972 it was estimated that 19% of the population were affected by infertility (Karahanasoglu, Barglow and Growe, 1972). Houghton (1984) proposed that one in seven and Menning (1984) one in ten couples experience involuntary childlessness. Hull *et al.* (1985) investigated a population in which one in six couples with a history of infertility of approximately 2½ years sought medical assistance. These particular figures may indicate that some people are encouraged by scientific advances and social attitudes to seek medical help for infertility, but not all who are childless will choose this avenue.

Historically, involuntary infertility has been viewed as a medical problem with medical solutions, and therefore diagnoses and investigations have been largely concerned with anatomical, physiological and pathological causes. However, as it became clearer that not all cases of infertility could be viewed in terms of organic origins, interest developed in the causal role of psychological factors in unexplainable infertility. In this chapter I consider the non-medical aspects of childlessness, in particular the psychosocial problems experienced by infertile people and the current and future place of psychological counselling in patient care.

THE PATIENT AND THE PROBLEMS OF INFERTILITY

A brief overview of infertility studies demonstrates the complexity of issues that have accompanied the patient's experience of infertility. In the last 40 years it has been widely reported that childlessness is associated with considerable personal distress. Coughlan (1965) found a high incidence of divorce in childless couples and Schellon (1957) made note of the increase in

Counselling and Communication in Health Care. Edited by H. Davis and L. Fallowfield
© 1991 John Wiley & Sons Ltd

frequency of suicide where couples were childless. The numerous papers and reviews that have addressed the emotional issues of childlessness have tended to take very different theoretical perspectives on infertility and display widely varying results.

Early research in the 1950s was primarily concerned with the female partner and her psychological profile and suggested that infertile women were fearful of childbirth, were in conflict about their femininity, and demonstrated psychosexual difficulties (Rommer and Rommer, 1958). Studies at this time however, produced conflicting conclusions, demonstrating poor methodology and inadequate scientific procedures. Subsequent studies attempting to refine this picture of infertile women reported evidence of raised levels of anxiety, neuroticism and dependency (Karahanasoglu et al., 1972; Harrison et al., 1984). Although Mai, Munday and Rump (1972) found these characteristics to be similar in fertile women, they noted that infertile patients had increased identity disturbance and ambivalent attitudes to having children. In general terms, female infertile patients during the 60s and 70s were depicted in the literature as emotionally immature, demonstrating personality difficulties and characteristics that would suggest a picture of considerable psychological disturbance.

As interest grew in the nature of infertility that could not be explained in medical terms (psychogenic infertility), scientific exploration during this period prompted studies that searched for psychological causes of infertility and examined the psychosocial responses to it. Clinicians and researchers debated the existence of a state of childlessness that was not elected or medically classified. This produced a series of options regarding unexplained infertility as a diagnostic category, an indication of the current limits in medical and scientific development, or as a psychosomatic response in patients who viewed childbearing and parenthood as particularly stressful (Jeker et al., 1988). A review of studies that attempted to estimate the incidence of unexplained infertility has shown figures which range from 6 to 60% (Templeton and Penney, 1982). Estimates of psychological causation are similarly variable, but have been reduced to approximately 18% as a result of more recent investigative and neuroendocrinological advances (Edelman and Golombok, 1989).

Edelman and Connolly (1986) reviewed a large number of previous studies in order to clarify a confused perspective of infertile patients and the characteristics of infertility. They concluded that patients with unexplained infertility did have higher levels of stress than fertile people. Comparisons between patients with unexplained infertility and those with an organically explained infertility did not provide substantial evidence of personality differences, although again there were signs that those people who had unexplained infertility were more anxious. These investigations clearly indicated that infertile patients could not be depicted as a group of psychologically disturbed people.

In general, retrospective investigations of the relationship between psychopathology and infertility have tended to ignore the relevance of the immense emotional strain and distress that patients associate with their infertility and the treatments that they undergo (Seibel and Taymor, 1982). This becomes clearer in data drawn from discussions and accounts in which patients invariably describe infertility as a major crisis that dislodges their life plans and views of their future. For some, the desire to have children can become so preoccupying that it is difficult to be interested or involved in anything other than the state of constant waiting and uncertainty. The medical intervention that many undertake tends to bring intrusion into a couple's intimate relationship and exposes their personal problems to outsiders. Frequent hospital appointments can require considerable absence from work and bring awkward questions that demand explanation. Infertility not only presents these patients with substantial personal and social dilemmas, but these problems make an impact on their lives for what is often a very long period of investigations and treatments. Friends and associates may be a source of help and sympathy, but their pregnancies and family life will also bring painful reminders of continuing childlessness.

Although current approaches emphasise the problem of infertility as that of the couple, frequently the female partner undertakes the burden of medical attention, even when the male may have an infertility diagnosis. Some women still feel responsible nevertheless, and see themselves as the cause of the infertility, a belief that is encouraged by women's keen awareness of their reproductive systems and their bodily functionings. (Pfeffer and Woollett, 1983). It is thus not surprising to observe the absence of research into the relationship between male infertility and psychological explanations.

Society expects that married couples will have children. Parenting is viewed as an important adult goal which, if impeded by the crisis of infertility, will have serious implications for later life (Menning 1977). Desiring children and becoming pregnant can thus be a major focus in a couple's relationship, although men and women experience infertility differently. For many women, becoming a parent is closely associated with the primary source of their identity and motherhood presents a public expression of this womanly role (Pfeffer and Woollett, 1983). The inability to demonstrate their identity in the creation of the mother and child relationship may evoke feelings of failure and a sense of being isolated from others who do not share the same experience. Women usually take the major responsibility for child care, and are therefore responsive to the inevitable reminders of children and motherhood from family, friends, new acquaintances, in work and domestic life. The pregnancies of others may therefore evoke unwelcome feelings of envy which can impede social relationships and increase their sense of isolation.

The traditional view of infertility as a woman's problem has had an impact on the role of men in the infertility experience and on the way in which they will participate in the investigation and treatment phases. As stated earlier, they are not the focus of medical management even when there is a male problem. Men have strong feelings about their capacity and wish to father children, but are less likely to be subjected to the same degree of pressure regarding their childlessness at work or in social contacts. However the close association between male potency and fatherhood fosters a belief that a child is the evidence of a man's virility, his ability to perform sexually.

Couples recounting their experience of infertility invariably highlight the challenge that occurs to sexual and marital functioning. Efforts to conceive emphasise performance and sex may be described therefore as mechanical, unspontaneous and inhibited. It is a rare couple who do not show some loss of sexual desire or capacity for orgasm during the investigations. Periods of impotence commonly occur, no matter which partner has been diagnosed and individuals can feel they do not deserve to enjoy sex if they are not managing to produce children. Because motherhood is such a central role for women, they particularly tend to disregard their feelings of anger and disappointment at what has become an unfulfilling sexual relationship (Mazor, 1979). From the moment that infertility is identified as a problem in the clinic, it is inevitable that the focus of sex shifts from gratifying intimacy to a preoccupation with the reproductive aspects of sex involving planned sexual activity that brings the tensions associated with passing or failing a test (Seibel and Taymor 1982).

The literature on infertility since the 70s, has made frequent references to the 'roller coaster ride of infertility', to describe the euphoric state associated with the possibility of pregnancy and the feelings of despondency when it fails to occur. On an interpersonal level, infertility can be destructive to the couple's relationships with their family, friends and job associates. Fear of disclosing the problem to others can lead to either 'withholding', or 'compulsive revealing' which are symptomatic of the sense of alienation that is intensified by infertility. When infertile couples or individuals most need support, they have described feeling separate from others whom they believe cannot understand the extent of their pain (Rosenfeld and Mitchell, 1979). Anger, rage and envy of those with children may provoke powerful and violent feelings towards others which in turn evoke a sense of self-disgust and a subsequent withdrawal from social contact. Ensuing guilt, failure, and shame have been acknowledged in anecdotal accounts in which patients have described themselves as having feelings of worthlessness, a sense of being different and defective, frustrated, despairing, and alone.

Awareness of patient needs and care in the last ten years has been stimulated by the advent of major developments in the form of new reproductive treatment techniques and technology. The procedures of in-vitro fertilization (IVF) and embryo transfer (ET) have brought fresh hopes for some childless patients but have also introduced additional complex psycho-

social considerations. By 1986 there were already more than 200 IVF clinics
world-wide, and it is estimated that in 1990 there will be 46 centres in Britain
alone (Voluntary Licencing Authority Report, 1988). In the absence of
further treatment options these procedures are considered by couples and
clinicians to be the 'end of the road' for infertile people, a theme which has
been much publicised in the media. Both IVF and GIFT (gamete intra-
fallopian transfer) programmes offer the potential for some couples to produce their joint biological child, often following a long history of extensive
and emotionally taxing methods of investigation and treatment. The procedure was initially developed as a treatment of infertility caused by
blocked fallopian tubes, but has broadened to include idiopathic infertility,
male sterility, ovarian dysfunction and uterine abnormality.

Although each clinic will have particular criteria for suitability and selection, there are inevitable intensive medical interviews and assessments, and
in some cases, surgical intervention before treatment can be undertaken.
Hospitalisation is required to retrieve the ova, followed by fertilization with
sperm in laboratory conditions before being returned to the uterus. Any of
these crucial phases of initial assessment, egg retrieval, fertilization and
transfer may fail (Johnston, Shaw and Bird, 1987). These procedures and the
uncertainty of the pregnancy test constitute stressful experiences for
patients. In the National Health Sector there is a lengthy waiting period
prior to treatment and patients describe their difficulties in maintaining the
demands of the programme which prompt some couples to withdraw after
one or two attempts.

Apart from the difficulties described, patients undertaking these particular treatments have to face the relatively low rate of success that accompanies this high profile medical technology. Soules (1985) estimated 13%
success on a single IVF attempt which was increased to 37% by Guzick,
Wilkes and Jones (1986) on the basis of three IVF treatment cycles.

DI (artificial insemination using donor sperm), as with IVF and GIFT, is a
medical means of aiding conception in cases of male infertility. Current
estimates of births from DI in Great Britain are about 2500 a year (Snowden
and Snowden 1984), with an overall success rate of approximately 75%.
Although it is a simple procedure, the couple and the clinic are confronted
by complex moral and psychological issues, particularly regarding the decision to undertake treatment. Clinicians and researchers vary in their criteria
for suitability. Some recommend evidence of a stable marriage, no psychiatric history and sound social relationships, although couples may in fact
screen themselves in the decision-making process.

Apart from selection issues, DI treatments highlight concerns about the
male's response to his infertility and the adjustment of the couple to the
hopes and motivations associated with having DI. Following this procedure,
only the biological identity of the female parent is known which may create
conflicts within the tripartite relationship of mother, father and child

(Edelman 1989). Whether, when and how to inform children of their origins are important issues for all couples.

COUNSELLING IN INFERTILITY

Introductory issues

Although sparse research material exists that shows the effectiveness of counselling, there is clearly a considerable consensus regarding the need for it in this field. Infertility counselling is a recent development and was given considerable impetus by the work and theories of Menning (1980). Subsequent counselling practice has been influenced by her conceptualization that predictable patterns of emotional responses occur during infertility, and that these involve phases of disbelief, denial, helplessness, anger, depression and guilt; a group of reactions that have been linked to the crisis of loss experienced in the mourning process.

Currently, counsellors in this field are concerned with the specific needs of people experiencing the crisis of infertility and the demands of investigations, diagnosis, treatments and outcome. As not all individual undergo the same degree of distress, it is important for clinic staff to be able to identify and predict those who most require counselling attention and the points at which individuals may feel most at risk. For some patients the point at which a diagnosis is given is particularly devastating, for others the approach of a treatment brings renewed stress and fear. Because the process of infertility is invariably lengthy and has fluctuating stages of intensity, counselling must address the many issues that accompany the individual's experience and difficulties.

Any discussion about counselling practice in infertility must begin with the acknowledgement that this is such a new counselling arena that little evaluation of techniques and approaches exist. It is therefore likely that where counselling has been introduced to the infertility treatment programme, the counselling itself is ad hoc and to some extent the counsellor will be gaining experience from within the work environment. Counsellors interested in this wide open field inevitably reflect a variety of backgrounds and disciplines. As with most specialized counselling, there are no specific modalities that have been isolated for greatest suitability with infertile individuals, but it is widely believed that counsellors require suitable characteristics, skills and training for the counselling task. Infertility counselling may be provided for individuals, the couple, or a group of patients, usually in the hospital or clinic offering treatment to patients.

Aims and applications

Regardless of the setting, a major counselling task involves the exploration of the psychological impact of infertility on the patient, the partner and on their relationship. Counselling aims to encourage individuals to express and accept the many feelings that accompany the crisis of infertility. Counselling theory supports the view that a successful resolution of a life crisis is achieved through the process of mourning. It is often difficult and confusing for patients to recognize their feelings of grief in the absence of a tangible loss on which to focus their disappointment. Therefore counselling techniques need to be sensitive to the complexity of the grieving experience and to the variations and reoccurrences that frequently take place. For example, patients describe their embarrassment at their sadness when seeing a new baby even though years may have elapsed. Others find birthdays painful reminders of passing time. Counselling offers patients a means of accepting and understanding these often uncomfortable and unwelcome feelings as part of the grieving experience.

In group counselling sessions for example, couples are relieved to hear the experiences and reactions of others, to feel they share a common predicament, and are not alone and isolated by a solitary preoccupation. A patient described her surprise at hearing that other wives had fears of being rejected and began to understand her own terror that being 'damaged goods' she 'would be replaced by a better model'. Counselling in a group environment particularly encourages improved social functioning and problem sharing so that individuals can feel that they are able to make valuable contributions to others and thus replenish the loss of self-esteem and worth they experience in the light of their infertility. Patients who have already undertaken treatments and investigations and have considered alternative options feel helpful as they share their experiences and knowledge with others.

Counselling in all forms offers an arena in which feelings of frustration, anxiety, anger and distress may be accepted as part of the infertility experience. As infertility is invariably a problem affecting the couple, it becomes important that the emotional reactions of each partner can be understood and expressed so that feelings of guilt and anger in the relationship can be reduced. When the couple attend sessions together, it is important that the counsellor facilitates freer communication of their negative and distressing feelings. Equally, counselling encourages each partner to renew interest in aspects of their lives that may have been neglected by the demands of and preoccupations with the infertility process. Although couples frequently undertake counselling together, in some cases one partner may express a particular desire for individual support. A patient described her husband's reticence to talk about his sexual difficulties for fear of being judged or blamed and sought help to encourage him to attend counselling also.

Psychosexual counselling and infertility

At various times during investigations counselling will inevitably focus on the psychosexual aspects of infertility. The counsellor needs to be sensitive to the quality of the sexual relationship while couples attempt to meet the sexual demands associated with infertility diagnosis and treatments. The counselling process may uncover sexual problems that existed prior to investigation. It is not unusual for previous experiences such as abortion, treatment for sexually transmitted diseases or promiscuity to evoke feelings of guilt and blame. References have also been made to 'sexual difficulties that masquerade as cases of infertility'. After more than ten years' medical treatment, a couple were referred for counselling during which it became apparent that unresolved psychosexual fears associated with intercourse had impeded proper penetration. Within three months of entering counselling, the couple were expecting their first child.

Counselling and psychopathology

The crisis of infertility can act as a trigger which exposes particularly sensitive or vulnerable aspects of the patient's early developmental experiences and history. In such cases, counsellors find themselves involved in the task of facilitating personal development by encouraging the individual to re-examine those difficult points which were not successfully negotiated or 'worked through' at an earlier time. This may prompt new decisions or choices regarding short or long term aims. For many years a husband had concealed his strong feelings about his own adoption, but during the infertility crisis, as these emotions were stirred, he began to doubt his parenting suitability.

Ambivalent feelings towards being a parent are not usually associated with those who are in the process of undertaking difficult and demanding treatments, and the counsellor needs to be sensitive to the complexity of emotional states that may hide beneath the attempts to achieve conception. Where there is severe psychopathological disturbance, more intensive psychotherapy may be advisable.

Counselling and life plans

As has been stated earlier, many couples expect that marriage will be followed by parenthood which, when thwarted, challenges their sense of being in charge of their life plans. Counselling assists individuals to feel more in control of themselves and their infertility by identifying and making choices. This encourages patients to make decisions about significant issues such as seeking treatment, withdrawing from the programme or considering other options and aspects of their present and future life style. For those who remain infertile, counselling provides a means of assisting individuals to develop a new identity as someone without children who can nevertheless accept the reasons and feelings that accompany their desire for children and parenthood.

COUNSELLING ISSUES RELATED TO THE NEW REPRODUCTIVE TECHNOLOGIES

IVF and GIFT

The recent interest in new medical approaches to infertility treatment has brought renewed questions about the nature of the counselling process and the skills, training and qualifications of the counselling practitioner, particularly where new reproductive technologies involving the use of human material may be involved. In such cases, a Government Bill, (Human Fertilization and Embryology Bill, 1989), has recommended that 'proper counselling' be provided as an integral feature of patient care. The Warnock Committee (1984) recommended that non-directive counselling by 'fully trained counsellors' be available to all infertile couples and third parties at any stage of treatment.

There are particular areas of concern for counsellors in cases of assisted reproduction. Because of the sensitive nature of treatments that may involve the use of donated genetic material and the relatively low success rate of IVF and GIFT procedures, counselling will provide support in what is a highly stressful situation. As considerable anxiety is associated with these procedures, participants benefit from the opportunity to extend and clarify their information and understanding of the procedures they are undertaking as well as their likelihood of achieving pregnancy and the much desired child.

A postal study to assess couples' experiences and counselling needs while awaiting IVF treatment for over 12 months, showed that 52% requested counselling and that men and women showed similar interest. The men desiring counselling were hopeful and optimistic about final success and described themselves as happily married, whereas the women were more anxious and lacking in self-esteem (Shaw, Johnston and Shaw, 1988). Group sessions with these couples revealed considerable agreement regarding the problems associated with IVF and childlessness generally. Regular counselling throughout the lengthy waiting period for treatment and availability of counselling as an integral part of the programme was requested by all.

DI (donor insemination)

Counselling in conjunction with artificial insemination treatment will be concerned with the man's adjustment to his infertility and the long-term impact of this medical procedure on the relationship between the couple and the child. There are important social and emotional issues for couples to confront. Counselling offers a medium in which they can examine the prospect and grief of childlessness as well as their motivations associated with choosing DI treatment. Counsellors frequently report that DI couples experience feelings of guilt in relation to the nature of their infertility and may be attempting to keep it a family secret.

In this field of infertility treatment there is an established approach to counselling that draws upon the experience of workers in the field of adoption and has encouraged a keen awareness of the implications for the child and family life where the child has been separated from its genetic origins. When DI takes place, the biological identity of only the mother is known and counselling needs to be sensitive to the potential conflicts that may arise within the mother, father, child relationship. Of equal relevance to a successful DI outcome to treatment will be the inevitable reminders to the father of his 'social' not biological fathering role. The dilemmas that surround the issue of informing children of their origins are important questions to be addressed in counselling sessions.

For some time counselling has been recognized as an appropriate forum in which to explore issues regarding the use of donor sperm. Currently, counsellors are alerted to questions deriving from the recent usage of donated gametes and embryos in infertility treatments.

Counselling and long term implications

In the counselling context, couples can consider the possible options and coping strategies that are available to them in the event of continued childlessness. In order to cope with taxing medical procedures and extended disappointments, supportive counselling may permit patients to redefine their goals from long term attainment of parenthood to the more immediate experience of their next treatment. Similarly, the counsellor may detect that the couple has become dislodged from their 'child goal' and become immersed in the momentum and aims of the treatment treadmill or current drug protocol. When ultimate failure of treatment occurs or a couple decide to withdraw from the programme, a reappraisal of their reality and identity as future parents is confronted by a new status of non-parenthood. To aid the couple's successful achievement of this transition, counselling will encourage them to acknowledge the sensation of loss in terms of their desired child and the mourning process that accompanies the grief experience.

In addition, longer term counselling has relevance and regard to the issues that accompany a successful treatment outcome. After protracted and arduous procedures with raised and dashed hopes, couples may feel that pregnancy and the arrival of their baby brings a reality that is different from their expectations.

The counsellor

The present source of personnel taking a counselling role may be drawn from nursing staff, social work departments, psychologists and from within the infertility clinics. Counselling suitability does not require that counsellors be infertile or have or not have children, but that they possess suitable characteristics, training and knowledge pertaining to the field. An anecdotal evaluation of counselling has declared it to be 'only as good as the counsellor', but where the counselling is practised in a specialised setting, the process cannot be effective without a body of ideas and skills. How this knowledge and skill is acquired becomes a vital issue in terms of the future development and integration of counselling in the field of infertility.

FUTURE IMPLICATIONS

The nature, place and context of psychological counselling in the investigation, treatment and care of infertile couples have been widely debated issues. It can also be seen that considerable confusion remains. One reason for this lies in the fact that the impetus of reproductive innovations has raced ahead regardless of the size and complexity of the psychological dimensions associated with the state of childlessness. These range from questions regarding the possible psychological causes of infertility, to concerns about the adjustment of those who remain childless, and to consideration for the psychic health and identity of parents and children following a successful outcome. In between, there exist all the aspects of the experience of infertility itself, the pressures of undertaking treatments, the effects of that pressure on the treatments, the impact of long periods of uncertainty and the demands of repeated and continued attempts to combat the state of infertility. The momentum of technology has highlighted the lag in psychological awareness and the present picture shows a rather disorganized and inadequate response to the emotional and social implications of these developments and to infertility generally. In addition the current attitude towards traditional treatments and approaches in infertility appears to be one of low priority and diminished interest.

On the one hand, medical advancement reflects scientific and technological development in society. At the same time it is evident that the advent of these innovations has heightened the anxiety of some doctors and clinics regarding the present stagnant state of thinking about the more conventional approaches to investigation and treatment, as these are still available and employed for many cases of infertility. This anxiety focuses particularly on issues of provision and allocation of resources to improve the care of those who are not able to participate in the new technological reproductive arena. There is currently very limited availability of counselling facilities in infertility centres, especially within the National Health Service. More often than not, doctors and nursing staff have been called on to be both medical and emotional caretakers in the absence of trained counselling professionals. With the acclaim that acknowledged the new technologies came recommendations for careful monitoring of their impact on patients and this prompted clinics to reconsider their facilities and in some cases arrange counselling provision in conjunction with treatments. IVF and DI treatments have tended to be viewed as priority procedures which are emotionally demanding for the couple, but clearly the state of infertility and all medical investigations are stressful. Certainly issues surrounding eventual outcome and continued childlessness are relevant for all.

A large part of the confusion in this area may be rooted in a counselling history that has not produced one clear and theoretically sound model that could be applied to the field of infertility and which would clarify questions of what constitutes appropriate counselling skills and where, when and with what aims it would be available in the treatment programmes. These are issues that are being addressed by the recently formed British Infertility Counselling Association (BICA) which is concerned with defining, developing and influencing the advancement of professional, qualified infertility counselling as a integral part of the infertility programme of investigation, treatment and patient care. At present there are few centres where counselling services have been established as a coherent response to either the recent technological developments or to infertility needs generally. This is partly a problem of training and coordination but also of availability of financial resources.

Management and allocation of these resources is complicated because patients tend to present themselves for investigation or treatment at different points in the evolution of their infertility, and their needs at each stage require a particular counselling awareness. As has been shown earlier, there are very specific emotional features and characteristics associated with infertility and childlessness, which have caused infertility to be referred to as an 'invisible problem' for the individual. Furthermore, clinics have clear criteria for what are considered to be successful and unsuccessful outcomes to treatment and infertility. However these may not necessarily coincide with the patient's outcome experience. Ambivalent attitudes to parenting, pressure from others to have children and 'be normal' may mean that unsuccessful treatment results are not inappropriate or necessarily unwelcome in the couple's life. Similarly, it is widely recognized that life difficulties can be 'wished away' in plans and thoughts about the advent of a baby, whose appearance fails to meet these often unrealistic expectations.

One area of action has been in the development of a 'self-help' approach to infertility distress, established by voluntary organizations such as the National Association of the Childless and CHILD, both of which provide support for their members. Some hospitals also have patient groups and meetings.

A plan for the future of infertility counselling would view all infertility technology and treatment as inseparable from a psychological dimension. The provision of appropriately trained counsellors in all infertility clinics would make it possile to have a counselling service fully integrated with the medical care available to all patients at all stages of infertility. This involves counselling in the initial decision-making process of seeking medical help, through the investigation, test, diagnosis, treatment and outcome phases of the whole experience.

It is clear that further research is required to evaluate the benefits and effectiveness of infertility counselling as part of patient care. There are also questions regarding the long-term impact of infertility treatment, not only for the couple, but in terms of the future adjustment of the child. In particular, there is little known about the nature of parent-child relationships, the child's psychosocial development and family life following infertility treatments, especially those which have been recently added to infertility programmes.

The Government Bill (1989) previously mentioned proposes that there be a Licensing Authority responsible for infertility investigations and treatments in the UK which will require that a code of practice document for counselling be devised and implemented. This would mean that all clinics undertaking infertility treatments would be required to provide suitable and available counselling facilities as stipulated, in order to meet the licensing criteria. In conjunction with this the Department of Health sponsored a report and investigation into 'The Nature and Provision of Infertility Counselling in the UK' in 1990. The progress of this and other studies which examine counselling methods and counsellor training will be of considerable interest to all who are involved in the infertility counselling field.

USEFUL ADDRESSES

CHILD,
Farthings,
Gaunts Road.,
Pawlett, Somerset.
Tel: 0278 683595

National Association for the Childless (NAC),
318 Summer Lane,
Birmingham B19 3RL
Tel: 021-359 4887

Relate,
76a New Cavendish Street,
London W.I.
Tel: 01-580 1089

British Infertility Counselling Association,
Department of Obstetrics and Gynaecology,
Hammersmith Hospital,
Du Cane Road,
London W12

REFERENCES

Coughlan, W.C. (1965). *Marital breakdown*. New York: Columbia University Press.

Edelmann, R.J. (1989). Psychological aspects of artificial insemination by donar. *Journal of Psychosomatic Obstetrics and Gynaecology*, **10**, 3–13.

Edelmann, R.J. and Connolly, K.J. (1986). Psychological aspects of infertility. *British Journal of Medical Psychology*, **59**, 209–219.

Edelmann, R.J. and Golombok, S. (1989). Stress and reproductive failure. *Journal of Reproductive and Infant Psychology*, **7**, 79–89.

Guzick, D., Wilkes, C., and Jones, H. (1986). Cumulative pregnancy notes for in vitro fertilization. *Fertility and Sterility*, **46**, 663–667.

Harrison, R., O'Moore, R.R., and Robb, D. (1984). *Stress in infertile couples*. Proceedings of the XIth World Congress of Fertility and Sterility.

Houghton, P. (1984). Infertility: The consumer's outlook. *British Journal of Sexual Medicine*, **11**, 185–187.

Hull, M.G.R., Glazener, C.M.A., Kelly, N.J., Conway, D.I., Foster, P.A., Hinton, R.A., Coulson, C., Lambert, P.A., Waall, E.M., and Desai, K.M. (1985). Population study of census, treatment and outcome of infertility. *British Medical Journal*, **291**, 1693.

Jeker, L., Micioni, G., Ruopa, M., Zeeb, M., and Campana, A. (1988). Wish for a child and infertility: Study of 116 couples. *International Journal of Fertility*, **33**, 411–420.

Johnston, M., Shaw, R., and Bird, D. (1987). 'Test-tube Baby' procedures: Stress and judgments under uncertainty. *Psychology and Health*, **1**, 25–38.

Karahanasoglu, A., Barglow, P., and Growe, G. (1972). Psychological aspects of infertility. *Journal of Reproductive Medicine*, **9**, 241–247.

Mai, F.M., Munday, R.M., and Rump, E.E. (1972). Psychiatric interview comparisons between fertile and infertile couples. *Journal of Psychosomatic Medicine*, **34**, 431–440.

Mazor, M. (1979). Barren couples. *Psychology Today*, **5**, 101–112.

Menning, B.E. (1977). *Infertility: A guide for the childless couple*. Englewood Cliffs, NJ: Prentice Hall.

Menning, B. (1980). The emotional needs of infertile couples. *Fertility and Sterility*, **34**, 313–319.

Menning, B.E. (1984). The Psychology of Infertility. In J. Aiman (Ed.), *Infertility, diagnosis and management*. N.Y.: Springer-Verlag.

Pfeffer, N. and Woollett, A. (1983). *The experience of infertility*. Virago Press: London.

Rommer, J.J. and Rommer, C.J. (1958). Sexual tones in the marriage of the sterile and the once sterile female. *Fertility and Sterility*, **9**, 309.

Rosenfeld, D.L. and Mitchell, E. (1979). Treating the emotional aspects of infertility: Counselling services in an infertility clinic. *American Journal of Obstetrics and Gynaecology*, **135**, 177–180.

Schellon, A.M.C.M. (1957). *Artificial insemination in the human*. New York: Columbia University Press.

Seibel, M.M. and Taymor, M.L. (1982). Emotional aspects of infertility. *Fertility and Sterility*, **37**, 175–182.

Shaw, P.D., Johnston, M., and Shaw, R. (1988). Counselling needs, emotional and relationship problems in couples awaiting IVF. *Journal of Psychosomatic Obstetrics and Gynaecology*, **9**, 171–180.

Snowden, R. and Snowden, E. (1984). *The gift of a child*. London: Allen and Unwin.

Soules, M. (1985). The in-vitro fertilization pregnancy note: Let's be honest with each other. *Fertility and Sterility*, **43**, 511–513.

Templeton, A.A. and Penney, G.L. (1982). The incidence, characteristics and prognosis of patients whose infertility is unexplained. *Fertility and Sterility*, **37**, 175–182.

Voluntary Licencing Authority (1988). *The third report of the VLA for human in vitro fertilization and embryology.*

Warnock Committee (1984). *Report of the committee of enquiry into human fertilization and embryology.* London: HMSO.

11 Pain in Gynaecology

ALEDA ERSKINE* AND SHIRLEY PEARCE†
*Department of Psychology, Royal Northern Hospital, Holloway Road, London, N7 6LD
†Department of Psychology, University College London, Gower Street, London, WC1E 6BT

INTRODUCTION

The experience of any pain, from a pinprick to appendicitis, is multidimensional and involves the inner world of thoughts and feelings as much as physiology and behaviour (e.g. Pearce 1986a). We cannot begin to understand gynaecological pain (pain that is located in the reproductive organs), let alone its treatment, without considering factors such as expectations, attributions and attitudes to women's bodies, femininity and sexuality.

Unlike pain in other functional systems, where one does not expect to experience discomfort normally, women learn from an early age that aspects of gynaecological functioning may be painful. The implications of this are only just beginning to be explored. There is no systematic research into the way little girls respond to their mother's menstrual cycle. However, Clark and Ruble (1978) found that premenarcheal girls together with boys of the same age believed that many symptoms are normally associated with the menstrual cycle. Ruble (1977) found that women led to believe that menstruation was due in one or two days reported a higher degree of physical discomfort than those who believed they were intermenstrual.

The force of such expectations is unsurprising given the evidence of widespread negative cultural and religious values surrounding menstruation and reproduction. Common euphemisms for menstruation such as 'the curse' or 'being unwell' are telling. Many religions, including Hinduism, Islam, and Orthodox Judaism teach that a woman is 'unclean' during her menstrual phase. In the Bible, the book of Leviticus (Chapter 15) instructs that the menstruating woman 'shall be put apart seven days and whosoever touches her shall be unclean until the even' (Quoted in Slade, 1987). Western women have not been secluded during menstruation but the taboo against sexual intercourse at this time is probably still powerful (Paige, 1973). In terms of childbirth, the story of another 'curse' ('In sorrow thou shall bring forth

Counselling and Communication in Health Care. Edited by H. Davis and L. Fallowfield
© 1991 John Wiley & Sons Ltd

children') in Genesis suggests an ancient association between notions of normative pain and women's defectiveness. In this context the Latin origin of the word pain, *poena* or punishment, seems particularly apt. At the end of the reproductive cycle, a pattern of negative, derogatory language and attitudes is again to be found:

We do not have 'testicular insufficiency' to match 'ovarian insufficiency' or 'senile scrotum' to match 'senile ovaries'. In the 'Merck Manual of Diagnosis and Therapy', the common physicians' handbook, in describing premature menopause, specific medical directions are given for 'preservation of a serviceable vagina'. Do you think there is equal discussion of a 'serviceable penis'? (Reitz 1981: 73, quoted in Ussher 1989).

One survey found that 49% of women believed the menopause was unpleasant and restricting and these views were particularly salient among pre-menopausal women (Neurgarten *et al.*, 1963, quoted in Ussher 1989).

Negative cultural stereotypes have always been counterbalanced by a tendency to idealise women's bodies, thus establishing an unreal and tyrannous norm of the body beautiful. The link between a woman's body as an object of scrutiny and her sense of self has been analysed by Berger:

To be born a woman has been to be born, within an allotted and unified space, into the keeping of men. The social presence of women has developed as a result of their ingenuity in living under such tutelage within such a limited space. But this has been at the cost of woman's self being split into two . . . *men act* and *women appear*. Men look at women. Women watch themselves being looked at. (Berger 1972: pp. 46–7, cited in Orbach 1986.)

Ussher (1989) traces a recurrent pattern of splitting within the self, throughout a woman's life cycle. She describes how women face impossible dichotomies such as good/bad, madonna/whore, feminine/career-oriented. This leads on to: 'the splitting in the adolescent, who cannot assimilate the changes in her developing body and thus separates them from herself, the splitting in the pregnant woman who is faced with the dichotomy of sexuality and motherhood, with the archetype of woman as mother; the splitting of the menopausal woman who cannot reconcile the archetype of uselessness and redundancy with her own experiences . . .'. These disjunctions between self, body, and sexuality have been explored by feminist psychodynamic writers who have located their earliest manifestations within the mother-infant girl interaction (e.g. Eichenbaum and Orbach 1985). They argue that mothers have internalised the 'feminine' values of deference to the needs of others and the subordination of their own needs. On the one hand, a mother will want to prepare her little girl to take up a similarly circumscribed role. On the other hand, she identifies with the little girl and, by so doing, may painfully confront the needy little girl in herself which until now has been overlooked. She may also find it hard to look at her child and her child's body with respect and acceptance because of her awareness of the second-class role which her daughter will assume. As a consequence of this, the growing girl will also find it hard to relate to her body, her sexuality and her self without ambivalence.

We have gone into some detail in outlining the complexities of social and intrapsychic attitudes to women's bodies and sexuality because we feel they are intrinsic to an adequate psychology of gynaecological pain. We shall describe the development of a biopsychosocial multilevel model of pain, which involves the conceptualization of a woman's subjective responses to her pain and to her body as part of the pain problem itself. Such a model allows us to avoid the dualities of biomedical reductionism on the one hand and social-constructionist or psychogenic explanations on the other.

Ussher (1989) examines the scientific evidence for the so-called 'syndromes' of pre-menstrual stress, post-natal distress and the menopause, all of which rest on a variant of the 'raging hormone' theory. She argues that these classifications are essentially catch-all descriptions of distress, which can work to explain and control women's deviant behaviour:

Women who complain of distress, of anger, of excessive libido; women who feel disenchanted following childbirth; women who feel disillusioned in their middle years can all be labelled ill, and so excluded and dismissed. (Ussher 1989: p. 136)

Tendencies among gynaecologists to resort to surgery too readily, for example in the case of unexplained pelvic pain (Arnold, Rogers and Cook, 1990), or to over-medicalise childbirth are further examples of reductionist approaches. In this context, it is important to note that gynaecology only emerged from general surgery in the early twentieth century and is still considered a primarily surgical specialty (Hunter 1989). It is also, of course, an overwhelmingly male profession with only 12% of its consultants being women (*The Guardian*, 14 November 1989).

At the other extreme, Lennane and Lennane (1973) have described how some common gynaecological conditions such as dysmenorrhoea, nausea in pregnancy and labour pain have often been dismissed as psychogenic, even though there is evidence of organic causes. They note the resulting damaging impact on diagnosis, treatment and research. Ussher (1989) also criticises the stance of some feminist writers who have argued that social-constructionist explanations alone are relevant to understanding negative experiences with menstruation.

In recent years, the development of investigative techniques such as the laparoscope, the ultrasound scanner and sophisticated hormonal assays have provided a spur to medical research into gynaecological pain. Perhaps equally important will be the collaboration of psychologists and gynaecologists in developing new ways of understanding and treating gynaecological pain based on a biopsychosocial approach. Such an approach would give full weight to the salience of cyclicity and reproduction in women's experience without neglecting the power of the attributional framework, the social constraints and psychosocial stresses in which that experience is lived.

Conventional surgical and medical techniques are particularly important in the management of acute gynaecological problems, although counselling methods are often invaluable adjuncts, for example in the provision of pre-operative preparation (Hunter, 1989). With chronic conditions, the lack of reliably effective medical treatment has given some urgency to the development of counselling approaches which enhance a woman's ability to cope effectively with pain. In this chapter we will discuss one such condition: chronic pelvic pain.

CURRENT THEORIES OF PAIN

Much still remains unexplained about the mechanisms by which pain is perceived. The simplistic view of early sensory physiologists that a 'direct line' transmission system exists between peripheral nociceptors and central brain areas has been replaced by complex models in which ascending and descending influences interact. The development of the Gate Control theory is described by Melzack (1983). This influential theory was an attempt to integrate the findings from psychological research with existing anatomical and physiological knowledge of pain. The essence of the theory is that afferent neural activity from peripheral nociceptors is modulated by, a) activity in other sensory afferent fibres e.g. from touch receptors and, b) descending pathways from central cortical areas. This provides a model of pain in which psychological factors such as attention, distraction, mood, expectations and personality were given a credible mode of action. Although certain aspects of the model have been questioned, the basic concept of modulation of sensory input by both ascending and descending cortical influences has remained unchallenged.

Despite the fact that it is many years since the Gate Control theory explicitly recognised the central role of psychological processes in the perception of pain, there has been relatively little attention paid to the development of further psychological models of pain. A number of writers have stressed the importance of viewing pain as a multidimensional experience with more similarity to emotional states than sensory processing. Melzack (1973) distinguished between the sensory and affective components of the pain experience. Others have included activity in physiological and behavioural systems as part of the pain experience (e.g. Fordyce 1978; Pearce 1986). Concordance between the three systems (physiological, subjective and behavioural) may vary.

This 'three systems' model of pain has been extended by Karoly (1985) to include two additional factors: a) 'lifestyle impact', for example, marital distress, vocational change; and b) 'information processing or central control', for example, coping styles, problem solving skills and health beliefs. He suggests that the different components of pain should be considered equally 'primary' to the experience of pain. Previous models have suggested that psychological and physiological factors interact such that psychological factors modulate physiological input. Karoly challenges this assumption and considers pain could be experienced even if all sensory afferent input could be blocked.

The development of a biopsychosocial model of pain goes some way to explaining how patients may have equivalent levels of pathology yet report very different levels of pain. Endometriosis with an equivalent degree of detectable organic pathology may, for example, result in extreme pain for one woman yet pass unnoticed by another. The identification of a particular form of pathology in gynaecological pain may indicate the appropriate intervention at a physical level. But it does not provide, in itself, an explanation for the pain. If the physical treatment is ineffective or partially ineffective, this may be because psychological or psychosocial influences have not been identified and altered.

CHRONIC PELVIC PAIN

Pelvic pain is one of the most common presenting problems among women attending a gynaecological clinic (Beard and Pearce, 1989). Chronic pelvic pain may arise from a number of benign causes and medical and surgical interventions are often either not appropriate or even counter-productive. Gillibrand (1981) showed that of 331 women presenting with pelvic pain, only 37% had any identifiable pathology. Recent studies by Beard *et al.* (1984) have suggested that a substantial proportion of these women may have pelvic venous congestion (engorgement of pelvic veins with blood).

The relationship between the extent of pathology and the experience of pelvic pain is complex. Where pelvic abnormalities can be found they are not necessarily causal. Likewise the demonstration of psychological abnormalities does not mean that these *caused* the pain problem. Considerable research energies have however been directed towards identifying the psychological characteristics of women with chronic pelvic pain. Typically, studies in this area compare patients with undiagnosed chronic pelvic pain with those without pain, using psychometric tests or psychiatric interviews. Discrepant findings have resulted. Gidro-Frank, Gordon and Taylor (1960) and Benson, Hanson and Matarazzo (1959) report a high incidence of psychiatric problems in women with unexplained pelvic pain, while others (e.g. Castelnuovo-Tedesco and Krout, 1970) fail to find such a relationship.

It has been suggested that the long term experience of pain, whatever the underlying organic pathology, causes psychological changes. Hence, studies investigating psychological factors that may have played a causal role should include comparison groups of women with clear pathology who have had chronic pain for an equivalent period of time. Pearce (1989) controlled for the duration of pain and found no difference on measures of mood and personality between women with or without organic pathology. Some differences on other psychological measures did however emerge. Women experiencing pain in the absence of observed pathology were found to have higher disease conviction scores on the modified Illness Behaviour Scale (Pilowsky and Spence, 1975). There was also a trend for the no-pathology group to have higher hypochondriasis scores than the pathology group. This suggests that women in the no-pathology group may be more concerned about their physical state and hence they may be monitoring bodily sensations more closely than the pathology group. It was also noted that women in the no-pathology group reported higher rates of serious illness and death of family members. Such exposure is not sufficient to *cause* unexplained pelvic pain, since many of the illnesses and deaths had occurred several years before the onset of the pain, but it suggests that exposure to serious illness may influence attitudes, causing closer monitoring of one's own bodily sensations and well-being. Given certain other conditions, such as a tendency to venous congestion, this may lead to the report of symptoms.

Some studies have suggested that attitudes to sex may influence the likelihood of reporting pelvic pain. Gross *et al.* (1980) identified early traumatic sexual experiences (incest) in 9 out of 25 patients with chronic pelvic pain. However, Petrucco and Harris (1982) found that seventy-two % of women with undiagnosed chronic pelvic pain were orgasmic and reported no sexual problems. More systematic investigation is required before concluding that sexual behaviour plays an aetiological role.

A model of chronic pelvic pain

The model presented in Table 1 suggests that women who develop pain associated with pelvic congestion have a biological predisposition to pelvic blood flow responses to stress that are either greater in magnitude, or take longer to return to baseline levels than normal. Hence, when exposed to psychological stressors, changes occur in the pelvis vasculature which lead over time to the development of chronically dilated pelvic veins. The abnormal sensory afferent activity from the pelvis is then attended to and labelled as painful by those women who are closely monitoring their physiological state, possibly as a consequence of concern about illness in general or pelvic dysfunction in particular. The experience of pain then leads to 'pain behaviour' which may be reinforced and maintained (Fordyce, 1978). For example, concerned family members may react to expressions of pain by discouraging the woman from social or domestic activities. Or the taking of 'sick leave' may bring coincidental welcome relief from burdensome responsibility. Feedback loops may arise at several of these levels of pain experience; for example, being in pain is likely to direct further attention to the pelvis and strengthen the *central schema* or expectation of pain.

COUNSELLING WOMEN WITH GYNAECOLOGICAL PAIN

The first assessment interview with a woman presenting with gynaecological pain can be difficult both for the counsellor and the patient. Many women will have been through a succession of lengthy investigations and failed treatments before being told that nothing further in terms of conventional medicine can be tried. The referral to the counsellor or psychologist may have been made with minimal explanation. As a result, the woman may feel ambivalent about the appointment and her first words and non-verbal behaviour can reveal puzzlement, apprehension, hopelessness, irritation or even hostility. It is also possible that negative or mixed feelings may be hidden under outward politeness or compliance, and it is important that they are quickly elicited. Here, the values and communication skills of the counsellor play a crucial role. The process of counselling women in pain rests on the same foundations of respect, genuineness and empathy which underlie any effective form of helping (Rogers, 1961). These values need to be translated into the kind of sensitive and accurate listening skills which facilitate the expression of doubts as well as hopes about counselling (Egan, 1986).

Case Example

Counsellor: Did Dr. X discuss the referral with you?
Helen: He just said he couldn't do any more and he'd send me to you
C: How did you feel about that?
H: (politely but looking angry) Well, I suppose he had his reasons.
C: You may well have felt taken aback.
H: I did feel surprised, but then he can't feel my pain.
C: It sounds as if you may have felt he disbelieved in your pain.
H: (hesitating) Maybe . . .
C: . . . and was sending you here for that reason. You may have had very mixed feelings about coming today.
H: Actually I might not have come if my husband hadn't insisted.

Further counselling with a patient such as Helen often shows that adherence to the medical model of illness is contributing to the ambivalence. Pain is either 'real' and 'in the body' or 'unreal' and 'in the mind': hence a psychological referral may feel tantamount to an accusation of malingering or madness. The fear of being labelled in this way needs to be acknowledged and discussed. Once this is done, we find an outline of the three systems model can be very useful, especially if the woman's own experience of pain is used to provide examples. The aim is to move the woman on from her view of pain as a unitary, physiological process, which is outside her control,

towards a multi-dimensional model which can validate a psychological interaction. This allows hopelessness about cure to begin to give way to a new
hope of rehabilitation. Failure to initiate this all-important process of recon-
ceptualization can often render subsequent assessment quite fruitless.

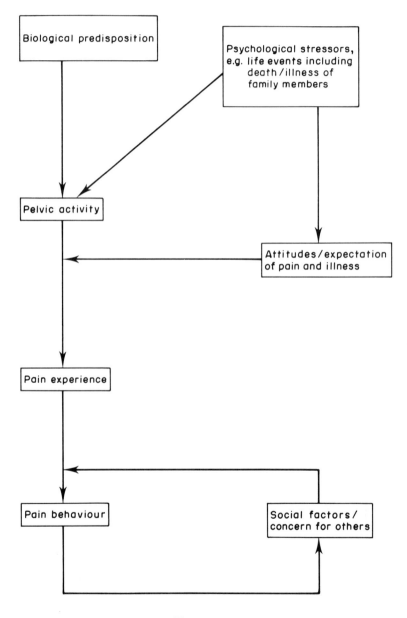

Figure 11.1

Once a shared model of pain is at least tentatively agreed, it is easier to take a case history. This should include attention to past episodes of pain and a psychosexual history. With some patients, it may be possible to start a functional analysis of the pain in the first session. This includes an assessment of precipitating factors, exacerbating factors, variations in time and place of pain episodes together with the attributions and reactions of the patient and significant others to the episodes. Indeed, all the components of pain described by Karoly (1985) should be investigated. The response of a partner or significant other may be one of the factors maintaining the pain, and interviewing the partner or significant other can be important. We also often ask the woman to keep a pain diary (e.g. Erskine and Williams, 1989) before the next session; this can pave the way for more detailed discussions of fluctuations of pain in relation to psychosocial changes. It can also provide a useful baseline to test the impact of future intervention. Karoly (1985) gives a full and critical account of multilevel assessment.

The initial assessment phase is not complete until the woman's own wishes about counselling are explored and these may well change over the course of the assessment. Only at this point can any decision about intervention be made. If the pain and pain management emerge as the main focus, a cognitive behavioural approach is likely to be the treatment of choice. It can, however, happen that the presenting pain problem becomes less salient as other problem areas such as depression, marital conflict, eating disorder or a history of sexual abuse are assessed. In such cases, non-directive counselling, cognitive therapy, marital therapy or psychodynamic counselling may become appropriate, either as an alternative or as an adjunct to pain management.

The cognitive behavioural interventions described below are structured, time limited and include the planning of behavioural tasks. However, we also take full account of the stressors linked to the pain and the woman's attributions. As our case history (see below) shows, the woman's perception of the factors which are relevant to the problem is another determinant of the eventual counselling programme. Invariably, that programme demands familiarity with cognitive techniques as well as behavioural methods, together with continuous attention to the building and maintenance of a good therapeutic relationship.

In outline, we suggest that a cognitive behavioural intervention is likely to include the following components:

1. The identification through discussion of a number of goals, which should be as specific and concrete as possible. These goals are likely to include the expansion of activities, including hitherto avoided activity. They will also include the development of coping strategies to deal with identified current stressors. Stressors may derive from relationships, from the home or working environment, or from intrapsychic processes such as negative expectations and attributions towards reproductive functioning, poor body

image or poor self-esteem. Graded progress towards these goals should be monitored and encouraged at every session.

Case Example

Helen's goals

(i) Take up a brisk walking programme three times a week starting from a 15 minute baseline.
(ii) Return to evening class.
(iii) Move back to full-time from part-time work.
(iv) Work on increasing communication with husband around mutual needs in the relationship.
(v) Learn to relax via autohypnosis.

2. Making a treatment contract (usually verbal) which includes the number of expected sessions, session duration and treatment methods. We never promise relief of pain intensity, but we do say that the distress caused by pain can be minimised and that patients can expect to feel in control of their pain by the end of the therapy.

3. Relaxation training, for example, through progressive muscular relaxation or hypnosis is an important tool for reducing the effects of stress. We use tapes to enhance home practice. After a few weeks daily practice, the relaxation can be applied to daily life and especially to pain episodes.

4. A graded, individual exercise programme. In a hospital setting it is sometimes possible to liaise with a physiotherapist. Failing this, a simple walking or swimming programme can be safely introduced, if need be in consultation with the medical referrer or GP. The principle of pacing activity needs to be emphasised. Some patients need gentle restraint from excessive effort, while others need equally gentle encouragement! Bedrest should be discouraged as a coping measure, while other forms of rest can be used as a time-limited reward for previous activity.

5. The identification and discussion of new strategies to cope with current stressors. Assertiveness training, non-directive counselling and anxiety management are all possible methods to help the woman avoid the stressors or work to reduce their impact.

6. The teaching of cognitive pain coping strategies. This involves: (i) the identification of negative or 'automatic' thoughts used in anticipation of, or during, a pain episode and the substitution of more adaptive self-statements (e.g. Beck *et al.*, 1979); (ii) the practice of additional strategies such as focusing on an engrossing pleasant image or distracting mental activity (e.g. making lists or mental arithmetic). Pearce and Erskine (1989) give a fuller account. To be successful, these strategies need to be carefully devised and planned with the patient and, above all, practised.

7. Setting weekly 'homework' tasks which enable the patient to progress towards their goals and generalize achievements made during sessions.

8.   Inviting the spouse or significant other to become a source of support for the patient in implementing the components above. This usually means educating the partner or friend about the programme and tactfully alerting them to their role as a powerful reinforcer of pain behaviour as well as of new and adaptive behaviours.

Patients will obviously vary in the relevance of each of the different components and we take care to tailor the programme to the individual woman's needs.

Despite evidence that the counselling approaches outlined here can be an effective means of managing pain (e.g. Pearce, 1986b; Germaine and Freedman, 1985), there are still too few pain clinics or departments of gynaecology in the UK which employ or liaise with a psychologist or counsellor. We would like to see a time when psychologists or counsellors were an accepted part of a multidisciplinary gynaecological team. As such, they would need to be in touch with the patient during the initial assessment and investigations as well as intervene subsequently when appropriate. In this way, the current unfortunate divide between medical and psychological approaches would be overcome.

CHRONIC PELVIC PAIN: SPECIFIC INTERVENTIONS

A prerequisite for any intervention is a credible model which the patient comes to share with the counsellor and we have found a version of the model of pelvic pain presented in Table 1 to be persuasive and more relevant to chronic pelvic pain patients than the Gate Control Theory.

Beard, Belsey and Liberman (1977) were among the first to mention the use of psychological approaches to chronic pelvic pain. They presented anecdotal evidence that some women responded well to relaxation training. Most subsequent studies also had methodological shortcomings (Petrucco and Harris, 1982; Pearce, Knight and Beard, 1982). The results of a recent controlled trial of two different methods provides firmer evidence that psychological interventions may be effective in the management of chronic pelvic pain, particularly in the long term. Pearce (1989), compared stress analysis and pain analysis with a minimal intervention control group. Women allocated to the 'stress analysis' group received a form of cognitive and behavioural stress management as well as relaxation training. Discussion of the pain was discouraged and the focus of counselling was directed towards current concerns apart from the pain. The 'pain analysis' group involved the patient in close monitoring of her pain and its associated antecedent and consequent events. Therapy was aimed at identifying patterns associated with pain episodes and teaching alternative strategies for avoiding or reducing pain. In addition, graded exercise programmes were instituted for each patient and spouses were encouraged to become involved in the exercise programme. A range of measures was used to assess outcome: these included ratings of mood, pain intensity, and behavioural disruption as well as 'blind' ratings by the gynaecologist of the extent to which the patient was affected by her pain. At six months follow-up, both treatment groups were significantly better than the controls on all measures of outcome.

Case History

Eileen R., a woman of 45, was referred by her gynaecologist with pelvic pain of five year's duration. The referral letter to the clinical psychologist described how a pelvic infection had been first diagnosed, but, despite a short period of pain relief following antibiotics, the pain soon returned. Two years later, a small cyst was discovered on the right ovary. The gynaecologist was unsure that this was the cause of the pain, but a right ovariectomy was performed. The pain was relieved for five months and then gradually built up again. The referral letter ended: 'Although no abnormal findings have been found, this patient is now urging me to perform a left ovariectomy. I have explained to the patient that she must keep her appointment with you before I can consider any further steps'.

The first thing Eileen R. said (politely but firmly) as she sat down in the psychologist's office was that whe was not sure why she was there. The psychologist responded by saying she understood how puzzling and perhaps frustrating the referral might seem and invited Eileen to describe further how it had come about. Information about Eileen's pain, albeit somewhat grudgingly given, led on to the counsellor commenting on how radically ideas about pain had changed in recent years. She then outlined a three system model of pain. Eileen was able to recall a time when she had tripped while running for a bus but had not noticed the resulting ankle cut for a good hour. The psychologist explained that such phenomena had led to the current theories of pain. By the end of the session, it was agreed that Eileen would keep a pain diary for the next two weeks.

In the course of the next session, the counsellor learned more both about Eileen's pain and her history. Rather to Eileen's surprise, the recorded levels of pain in the diary were usually low (2–3 on a 10 point scale), even though there was marked behavioural disruption. Eileen spent most of the day on a settee, avoiding activities for fear of increasing the pain. The diary also revealed that interacting with her 19-year-old daughter, Michelle, was a major source of stress. Michelle came home late at night, played loud music in her very untidy room and argued with Mr R., her stepfather.

The issue of asserting her needs and beliefs emerged as a common theme of difficulty experienced throughout Eileen's life. Her mother had been a controlling and obsessional woman who had instilled high standards of cleanliness and orderliness. She was slim and smartly dressed and Eileen, always on the plump side, had never felt she came up to her mother's unspoken expectations. She was all the more compliant to mother's expressed wishes. Father, a shopkeeper, emerged as a marginal figure who interacted more with Eileen's brother. Eileen believed her parents (now both dead) had had a perfect marriage. This gave her another reason to feel a failure since her first husband had left her when Michelle was six. That marriage was sexually unfulfilling and had been undermined by her partner's heavy drinking. Six years later she met and married Mr R., an easygoing, wealthy businessman. She was on the brink of feeling that she too, had achieved a perfect marriage when Mr R.

suffered a cardiac infarction and had a pacemaker fitted. Nursing him during the convalescence was all the more difficult because of the onset of her own pelvic pain.

Eileen made it very clear that she was not prepared to accept a link between broader issues of self-assertion and (in her words) her ovarian cysts. She did, however, concede that the difficulties with Michelle were a direct cause of tension and increased the pain. She also conceded that it might be risky to have surgery without seeing if she could 'do more despite the pain'. She was able to identify several goals and a hierarchy of tasks was drawn up ranging from walking to the local postbox to visiting her nearest shopping centre. Mr R. was interviewed and commented on how much better his wife's pain had been on their recent holiday abroad.

Over the next seven sessions, Eileen made steady progress with her hierarchy. She discussed and rehearsed new ways to confront her daughter's behaviour. One day she told Michelle that she would have to get a flat unless she met a limited number of conditions; the result was a marked reduction in noise and late night disturbances. The relaxation training she had also been undergoing helped Eileen in her effort to become more assertive. Eventually she managed her visit to the shopping centre. Soon after this major achievement she decided, without prompting, to go back to her old career as a secretary, which she had given up (at Mr R.'s suggestion) on their marriage. Her pain remained unchanged in intensity, but her enjoyment of life had increased and the surgical option was old history.

ACKNOWLEDGEMENT

We would like to thank Dr. Katrina Erskine, Senior Registrar in Obstetrics and Gynaecology, University College Hospital, London for all her help in the preparation of this chapter. We are also grateful to Mrs Lee Drew for her help and patience in the preparation of the manuscript.

USEFUL ADDRESSES

Endometriosis Society,
65 Holmdene Avenue,
London SE24 9LD

Pelvic Inflammatory Disease Support Group Network,
c/o W.H.R.R.I.C.,
52 Featherstone Street,
London EC1 8RT
Tel: 071-251 6332

Women's Health Concern,
317 High Holborn,
London WC1V 7NL
Tel: 071-938 3932

Women's Health and Reproductive Rights Information Centre,
52–54 Featherstone St.,
London EC1 8RT
Tel: 071-251 6332/6580

REFERENCES

Arnold, R.P., Rogers, D., and Cook, D.A.G. (1990). Medical problems of adults who were sexually abused in childhood. *British Medical Journal*, **300**, 705–708.

Beard, R.W., Belsey, E.N., and Liberman, J. (1977). Pelvic pain in women. *American Journal of Obstetrics and Gynaecology*, **128**, 566–570.

Beard, R.W., Reginald, P., Pearce, S., and Highman, R. (1984). Diagnosis of pelvic varicosities in women with chronic pelvic pain. *Lancet*, **2**, 946.

Beard, R.W. and Pearce, S. (1989). Gynaecological Pain. In P.D. Wall and R. Melzack, *The textbook of pain*, (2nd. Edn), London: Churchill Livingstone.

Beck, A.T., Rush, A.J., Shaw, B.F., and Emery, G. (1979). *Cognitive therapy of depression*. N.Y.: Guildford.

Benson, R., Hanson, K., Matarazzo, J. (1959). Atypical pelvic pain in women: Gynaecologic and psychiatric considerations. *American Journal of Obstetrics & Gynaecology*, **77**, 806–823.

Berger, J. (1972). *Ways of seeing*. London: B.B.C. and Penguin Books Ltd.

Castelnuovo-Tedesco, P. and Krout, B.M. (1970). Psychosomatic aspects of chronic pelvic pain. *International Journal of Psychiatric Medicine*, **1**, 109–126.

Clark, A. and Ruble, D. (1978). Young adolescents' beliefs concerning menstruation. *Child Development*, **69**, 231–234.

Egan, G. (1986). *The skilled helper*. California: Brooks/Cole Publishing Co.

Eichenbaum, L. and Orbach, S. (1985). *Understanding women*. Middlesex, England: Penguin.

Erskine, A. and Williams, A.C. de C. (1989). Chronic pain. In A.K. Broome, (Ed.), *Health psychology*. London & New York: Chapman & Hall.

Fordyce, W.E. (1978). Learning Processes in Pain. In R.A. Steinbach (Ed.), *The psychology of pain*. New York: Raven Press.

Germaine, L.M. and Freedman, R.R. (1985). Behavioural treatment of menopausal hot flushes: Evaluation by objective methods. *Journal of Consulting & Clinical Psychology*, **52**(6), 1072–1079.

Gidro-Frank, L., Gordon, T., and Taylor, H.C. (1960). Pelvic pain and female identity. *American Journal of Obstetrics & Gynaecology*, **79**, 1184–1202.

Gillibrand, P.N. (1981). *The investigation of pelvic pain*. Communication at the Scientific Meeting on 'Chronic Pelvic Pain – a Gynaecological Headache'. London: Royal College of Obstetrics & Gynaecologists.

Gross, R.J., Doer, H., Caldirola, P., Guzinski, G., and Ripley, H.S. (1980). Borderline syndrome and incest in chronic pain patients. *International Journal of Psychiatry in Medicine*, **10**, 79–86.

Hunter, M. (1989). Gynaecology. In A.K. Broome, (Ed.), *Health psychology*. London: Chapman & Hall.

Karoly, P. (1985). The assessment of pain: Concepts and procedures. *Measurement strategies in health psychology*. New York: Wiley.

Karoly, P. and Jensen, M.P. (1987). *Multimethod assessment of chronic pain*. New York: Pergamon Press.

Lennane, J.K. and Lennane, R.J. (1973). Alleged psychogenic disorders in women: A possible manifestation of sexual prejudice. *New England Journal of Medicine*, **288**, 288–292.

Melzack, R. (1973). *The puzzle of pain*. New York: Basic Books.

Melzack, R. (1983). *The challenge of pain*. Harmondsworth: Penguin Books.

Neurgarten, B., Wood, V., Kraine, R., and Loomis, B. (1963). Women's attitudes towards the menopause. *Vita Humana*, **6**, 140–151.

Orbach, S. (1986). *Hunger strike: The anorectic's struggle as a metaphor for our age.* London: Faber & Faber.

Paige, K.E. (1973). Women learn to sing the menstrual blues. *Psychology Today, 7*, 41–46.

Pearce, S. (1986a). A biobehavioural approach to chronic pain. In M.J. Christie and P.G. Mellett (Eds), *The psychomatic approach: Contemporary practice of whole person care*, 217–239. Chichester: John Wiley & Sons.

Pearce, S. (1986b). *Chronic pelvic pain: A psychological investigation.* Unpublished PhD Manuscript. University of London.

Pearce, S. (1989). The concept of psychogenic pain. An investigation of psychological factors in chronic pelvic pain. *Current Psychological Research and Reviews, 6*, 16–21.

Pearce, S., Knight, C.K., and Beard, R.W. (1982). Pelvic pain – A common gynaecological problem. *Journal of Psychosomatic Obstetrics and Gynaecology, 1*, p. 12.

Pearce, S. and Erskine, A. (1989). Chronic Pain. In S. Pearce and J. Wardle, *The practice of behavioural medicine.* Oxford University Press: British Psychological Society.

Petrucco, O.M. and Harris, R.D. (1982). A psychological and venographic study of women presenting with non-organic pelvic pain. paper presented at 8th New Zealand Congress, Auckland N.Z.

Pilowsky, I. and Spence, N.D. (1975). Patterns of illness behaviour in patients with intractable pain. *Journal of Psychosomatic Research, 19*, 279–287.

Reitz. R. (1981). *Menopause: A positive approach.* London: Unwin.

Rogers, C. (1961). *On becoming a person.* London: Constable.

Ruble, D. (1977). Premenstrual symptoms: A reinterpretation. *Science*, **197**, 291–292.

Slade, P. (1987). Menstrual cycle disorders: Psychological theories and the potential role of the clinical psychologist. In E. Karas, (Ed.), *Current issues in clinical psychology*, Vol. 3. New York & London: Plenum Press.

Ussher, J.M. (1989). *The psychology of the female body.* London & New York: Routledge.

12 Genetic Counselling

FIONA STEWART
*Department of Mental Health, University Medical Buildings,
Foresterhill, Aberdeen, AB9 2ZD*

INTRODUCTION

Genetic disorders not only cause considerable burdens to affected individuals but also to their families and health services. Two to five % of all liveborn infants suffer from a genetic disorder or congenital malformation. These disorders cover a wide spectrum of origin: chromosomal (e.g. Down's syndrome); single gene (e.g. tuberous sclerosis); multifactorial (e.g. neural tube defects) and those of somatic origin (e.g. neoplasia). They are frequently severe in nature and the majority are not amenable to treatment.

The localisation of the genes responsible for many disorders has been made possible through developments in molecular genetics and the rapidity of gene mapping. Awareness of these advances and of the association of genetics with disease is leading to an increase in demand for genetic counselling.

This chapter is concerned with the different kinds of problems presented by those who are counselled, and methods of counselling which can be used to help. Finally ways of improving the service are explored, including issues such as embryo research and genetic registers which have implications for the service.

PATIENTS AND PROBLEMS

Because genetic disorders are often severe and incurable, many of the problems are chronic. This section outlines some of the more common problems and the difficulties that can arise when trying to deal with them.

Misconceptions

Because of the specialised and highly complex nature of genetics, those seeking the help of genetic counsellors often have firmly held misconceptions. They may have received incorrect information from relatives, friends and health professionals, such as general practitioners and physicians. A

Counselling and Communication in Health Care. Edited by H. Davis and L. Fallowfield

commonly held misconception is that genetic disorders only affect male offspring. The well known pattern of inheritance of certain sex-linked disorders such as Duchenne muscular dystrophy and colour blindness, which are associated with males, has contributed to this confusion. Misconceptions can be reinforced by personal experience as in the case of a pregnant woman with a family history of Ectrodactyly or lobster claw. This dysmorphology affected all the females and none of the males in three successive generations of her family, although the disorder is equally likely to affect males. The patient went to her GP and requested foetal sexing in order that she might prepare herself for the birth of an affected baby if the foetus was found to be female. Counselling was ineffective in convincing her that either sex of baby was at a 50:50 risk of having the disorder, and in the event her suspicion was reaffirmed as the foetus was found to be both female and affected.

Attributing blame

Another widely held belief is that women transmit the disorders and they therefore carry the blame. In these cases the husband may only accompany his partner for counselling in order to discover the nature of his wife's problem and he may become hostile to any suggestion that he may be involved.

Similarly, it is common for people to feel that something, such as a misdemeanour committed earlier in life, has caused them to be ill. Rationalising the presence of illness by searching for a tangible and understandable cause has been termed 'effort after meaning' and is not specific to genetic disorders.

Social isolation

Many families with an affected member feel socially isolated. Parents may be embarrassed to tell others of their baby's disorder, or fear their reaction. Friends and relations may avoid them either because they feel at a loss for what to say or because they fear the disorder to be contagious.

Unrealistic expectations

People can have unrealistic expectations of genetic testing, sometimes believing that it is possible to have a complete 'genetic overhaul'. Such misconceptions may continue even after testing. For example, difficulties can be caused by the limitation that only tests which have been specifically requested are performed, as in the case of parents who opt for prenatal testing for one disorder and find that their child is born with an unrelated disorder. These parents may feel particularly cheated and misled, having made great efforts to ensure that their child would be healthy. Furthermore, there is a degree of error with some tests. Thus, the uncertainty of there being a disorder may not be entirely alleviated by testing, and people should be warned of this possibility before taking a test. Another related problem requiring sensitive counselling concerns the possibility of aborting a normal foetus which may be unacceptable to some individuals.

Need for information

Information about options

Frequently the counsellor deals with people who have little knowledge about their disorder and who seek information on which to base major life decisions. Couples for whom pregnancy carries a high risk of transmitting a heritable complaint may need to decide upon one of a variety of reproductive options. These could include prenatal testing with the option of elective abortion, artificial insemination by donor and adoption.

Understanding information

In the case of recessive disorders it is sometimes difficult for people to understand that they can carry the gene for a particular disorder (e.g. cystic fibrosis) without ever having symptoms of the illness. In the absence of any symptoms they may either be unaware of, or deny, their carrier status and proceed with a pregnancy to produce an affected child.

Timing of information

People may have difficulty absorbing information when they are in crisis. They may, for example, not pay attention to the risks for future pregnancies when they have just been told of a serious diagnosis in their baby. The timing of counselling sessions is therefore important.

Assessment of risk

Risk and types of disorder

An issue which is frequently central to counselling is the probability of transmitting a disorder. The risks vary with the many types of disorder. Single gene or Mendelian disorders, caused by mutant genes, carry a high risk of recurrence. Conversely, chromosomal disorders are unlikely to recur and many common disorders have no clear pattern of inheritance. Furthermore, the variable expression of some disorders can cause difficulties in assessing whether or not an individual is affected. This may lead to problems as in the case of a woman with no symptoms whose mother was affected by myotonic dystrophy and who presented to a genetics clinic to find out if she was at risk of transmitting the disorder to any prospective children. Recombinant DNA techniques can occasionally provide the answer in genetically informative families, but these were unsuccessful in this family. The woman was therefore left with the knowledge that, although clinically well, she could still be affected and, if so, any affected foetus would be at an increased risk of stillbirth or early death.

Risk and difficult situations

Complicating situations, such as people who have had children by previous partners, or as a result of a secret affair, can lead to problems in assessing who contributes the risk and may result in emotional problems for the family.

Estimating the risk of some disorders necessitates the cooperation of other family members in order to confirm a diagnosis. These relatives may have to give a blood sample when DNA analysis is required. At best this is a time consuming process. There may be particular difficulties in estranged families, when the individual who seeks counselling is adopted, when the hereditary pattern of the disease in the family is denied and when it is not possible to obtain informed consent to donate a blood sample from a key relative. Those affected by Huntington's Chorea, for example, often suffer from severe dementia and may be unable to consent to a blood sample for analysis which could be crucial in assessing the risk to another family member. In other cases, relatives who are unaware of their illness status may refuse to donate a blood sample, fearing that their sample may implicate them in having passed on a disease.

Meaning of risk

Few people easily grasp the meaning and implications of a risk figure when it applies to them directly. For example, is a 25% risk of transmitting a disorder an acceptable chance to take and a 50% chance unacceptable? Information about the severity of the disease can affect this type of decision, as can the options for prenatal diagnosis and whether the illness is treatable. However, no matter how small the risk figure, many will translate it into a 50:50 chance of having either an affected baby or an unaffected baby, despite having excellent recall of their actual risk figure. In a study of parents faced with this type of uncertainty the most common pattern was for parents to indicate that probabilities were not useful as a basis for action, and more important was to emphasise that no matter the size of the recurrence rate, something could happen (Lippman-Hand and Fraser, 1979). Similarly, given the option of prenatal diagnosis and therefore the knowledge that they will eventually be able to produce a healthy child, some will forget their risk figures as they no longer see them as relevant.

The news that one is at risk of having or transmitting a disorder can have diverse implications for different people. Those in continuous contact with a severely affected relative, for example, might be expected to react differently from those without this experience, as they will know what the future may bring.

Uncertainty

Living with uncertainty

Genetic disorders can vary between family members both in severity and, with some diseases, in the age of symptom onset. Thus, it can be difficult to give the family definitive information. For instance, the risk to children with a parent affected by Huntington's Chorea, decreases with age; at 30 years the risk is 50%, which declines to 10% by the age of 65 (Kingston, 1989). This type of uncertainty is difficult to come to terms with and often leaves people fearful of the unknown.

Particular problems can be experienced by those awaiting the results of an amniocentesis test and many try to cope by denial of their pregnancy. This can be a difficult period as they may reach the stage of pregnancy when they are able to feel their baby move and begin to doubt whether they could terminate the pregnancy if the result proved positive.

Ending uncertainty

Although testing for carrier status can have important benefits in conditions where prognosis is improved by early detection, prenatal and pre-symptomatic diagnosis of severe disorders (e.g. Huntington's Chorea) which are not amenable to treatment can cause immense emotional diffi-culties. Presymptomatic detection differs from other types of screening in that the individuals identified are not healthy carriers of the disease but will eventually develop the disease.

Learning that the illness is present ends the uncertainty and may come as a relief. However this news may arouse terrible fears for the future and cause feelings of anger, sadness and loss of self-esteem. With Huntington's Chorea, people may also have to live with the guilt of having transmitted the disease to their children and grandchildren. There will also be financial burdens for the family, such as the provision of care and supervision once the illness appears, particularly if the affected individual is the main wage earner. There are also difficult decisions involved when it is not considered to be in the best interests of an individual to undertake this type of test, for example, when he or she is thought to be suicidal.

Culture and religion

Cultural expectations within different communities or religious groups vary. Some are antagonistic to scientific evidence indicating that some diseases are explained by genetic theory. In some religious communities, consanguineous marriages are common and can contribute an increase in risk of having affected offspring. In addition, individuals may be under pressure to continue having children despite being aware of the risks. There may also be explicit objections to contraception and/or termination of pregnancies.

HELPING

Skills of counselling

In counselling, individuals often grieve for their present situation, such as the recent death of their affected baby, for the loss of a healthy future for themselves, their children and/or their prospective children. Counselling therefore involves more than the presentation of scientific and medical facts. The skills and the sensitivity towards moral, ethical, psychological, social and other related issues exceed the demands of everyday medical practice.

Role of counselling

The counsellor must impart complex genetic and technical information in an understandable form which does not lead to confusion, within an emotionally supportive environment. It is necessary to convey both the risk of transmitting or developing a disease and what this means, for example, in terms of the likelihood of producing an affected child and what problems that child might experience. The counsellor must help people adapt to such information and support them while they do so.

Setting

Counselling sessions should ideally be held in a room which is quiet and private. People need to feel able to discuss intimate matters and express intense feelings without being overheard. A bedside session on a hospital ward should be avoided at all costs.

Establishing rapport

It is helpful and often reassuring for the counsellor to begin a session by introducing himself or herself and how he or she fits into the system. Because of the complexity of the information to be imparted, it is preferable to counsel couples rather than individuals. This not only helps their memory of the information, but also helps prevent one individual being blamed.

Establishing a contract

There are a wide variety of motives for seeking counselling. Expectations of what counselling can provide also differ greatly. Some motives are vague and expectations may be unrealistic. This is largely due to the fact that genetic counselling is a relatively new service. An early explanation of what can be expected from counselling, including the tests which may be offered, can do much to alleviate anxiety.

Limitations of genetic testing

The limitations of testing must be explained early. For instance, it is not possible to have a complete 'genetic overhaul' to ensure that all genes are normal.

Misconceptions

The counsellor must deal with misconceptions and misinformation as soon as possible. For example, the man who has accompanied his wife to discover the nature of her problem may become angry and hostile at any suggestion that he is implicated. In this and most other counselling situations it is helpful to explore the issue directly to enable them to share the problem, to stop them blaming one individual and to help them communicate effectively.

Barriers to communication

At the beginning, people may fear bad news or feel that the counsellor will consider that their concerns and questions are stupid. This makes them less able to attend properly, understand and make informed decisions. To over-come these barriers the counsellor must listen to the individuals, explore the nature of any concerns and address any questions they may have. An emo-tionally supportive environment enables them to talk more freely and re-duces their fear of being considered stupid.

Information content

Avoiding jargon and pacing of information

The counsellor needs to check continually to see whether the individuals understand, and information often needs to be repeated. Some words may mean nothing, or have surprisingly different meanings to different people, or they may even be offensive or hurtful. Words such as 'malformed', 'abnormal' and even 'pedigree', can fall into this category. In order to avoid this, it is important to listen to individuals, use words tentatively and check their meanings. This process will also enable the counsellor to judge the pace at which to offer new information.

Giving children information

Before offering counselling to children either affected by a disorder or to those with an affected family member, it is desirable for a family member to have given the child some of the basic facts of the disease. The child may resent receiving this information from a counsellor, feeling that it is the duty of the family. The child's carer should be prepared for the distress and anger that the child may feel and it is therefore preferable for the carer to have already come to terms with the situation. It is also important to find out if the child has someone in whom they can trust and feel able to accept support. The counsellor should ask children what they have already been told, by whom and how they reacted. It is important to determine what they want to know and the nature of their concerns before imparting any information. This also helps to gauge the child's intellectual capabilities which influence the counsellor's mode of communication and the content of the information. The effect of genetic information must not be underestimated as it can lead to a poor sense of self-worth and attractiveness. For example, children may fear that no one will want to marry them. Children of 12 years and over are becoming independent from their family and developing their own opinions. It is therefore helpful to offer them some sessions separate from other family members.

Organization of information

Answers to individual's questions need to be built into the framework of the session in order that information is conveyed logically. A process which simply involves questions and answers can lead to an unstructured and incomprehensible session. The counsellor should acknowledge any questions and mention that they will be fully answered later, if it is not appropriate to do so at the time.

Number of counselling sessions

Ideally, counselling should consist of a series of sessions, yet all too often this does not happen. More than one appointment is usually needed to assimilate information and to enable the counsellor to check for understanding, to repeat or rephrase information and to address new concerns and questions. The number of sessions should be dictated by the individuals' needs and will vary greatly.

Structure of counselling

Exploring the medical and genetic impact

The counsellor needs to explore the medical and genetic history of the disorder in the family, as their experience of the disease is often important in assessing an individual member's risk of being affected or carrying a disorder, and in verifying a diagnosis.

Exploring the psychosocial impact

The psychosocial impact of the disease needs to be explored if the counsellor is to understand what the disorder means to the family. Different families with the same disorder can have varying concerns and therefore need to learn about different aspects of the illness. A thorough interview might also uncover hidden feelings such as anger and depression and may reveal important factors such as social isolation and financial strains. The counsellor may be able to help them resolve these problems. When people feel alone or ashamed of their problem it can occasionally be helpful to mention that others in the same position experience similar feelings. However, care must be taken not to normalise or minimise the enormity and significance of the problems to the individuals concerned. If this happens they may regret confiding in the counsellor and so become alienated.

Process of counselling

Exploration of options

Genetic counselling often involves a process of working through options and must therefore be non-directive. Difficult ethical issues are raised by those who support directive counselling for some individuals who are considered to be incapable of making responsible reproductive decisions because of mental handicap or lack of social responsibility. The counsellor should present all available options in a non-judgemental manner and help individuals reach their own informed decision, since they and not the counsellor, have to live with the consequences. People need to explore how they feel about all the options in order to work out how they might cope with each.

Given that such emotive issues are at stake, it can be difficult for the counsellor to avoid giving direct advice, as in the case of exploring the reproductive options available to a couple at risk of transmitting a disorder.

Prenatal testing, with the possibility of elective abortion, could be one option which may be abhorrent to the counsellor on religious or ethical grounds. Alternatively, counselling may involve helping a couple determine the risk that is acceptable to them of transmitting a disorder, when they may be prepared to take what seems to the counsellor an excessively high risk in order to have a much wanted child. The counsellor should therefore be aware that factual information is only partly related to the final decision, which will often be what is the most acceptable, as opposed to the optimal, decision. Furthermore, patients' attitudes to their genetic risks may change over time and in response to scientific discoveries (Harris, 1988).

The counsellor may also need to suggest and discuss the implications of a particular option, if the individuals themselves have not considered them. For example, in predictive testing for Huntington's Chorea, a positive result not only means that this devastating disease will develop later in life, but it can also affect premiums for life assurance, availability of mortgage facilities and employment. A negative result on the other hand can lead to feelings of guilt when relatives have not been spared. Similarly, the consequences of a positive prenatal diagnosis following an amniocentesis test will involve the mother undergoing an induced labour if she elects for a pregnancy termination. With a fuller picture of the possible consequences, those involved may view a particular option differently.

Difficulties in counselling

Genetic counselling can involve very painful work for the counsellor. For instance, the implications of a positive diagnosis can be devastating, not only for the individual concerned, but also for many members of the family, and there is usually no prospect of a cure. Counsellors have to face this situation time and time again, and have to deal with the fear, anger and despair of those seen. It contrasts dramatically, however, with the pleasure of reporting that a test is negative.

Referral to other specialities

Genetic counselling has its limitations, which must be recognised by the counsellor. The option of referral to another specialist service such as a psychiatrist or psychologist is useful in some cases, such as those who are possibly depressed or suicidal. In situations of financial hardship the counsellor may help by guiding them tactfully towards state benefits, or trust funds, who may be able to provide money or practical aids.

Voluntary agencies

Referral to one of the many self-help groups can provide a variety of assistance, such as jargon-free literature and the opportunity to talk to others in a similar position. It is helpful for the counsellor to have either an up-to-date list of organizations concerned with specific disorders, or a list of a few umbrella organizations which can put people in touch with groups that will best meet their needs. Without this information many experience difficulties finding a suitable organization, and organizations themselves often have to deal with the anger of those informed by health professionals that no such agency exists. Conversely, self-help groups are not suitable for everyone and therefore this option needs to be fully discussed.

Letter of summary

Although time consuming, a letter to the couple summarising the key points raised during sessions will help their recall and minimise misunderstandings. It should contain a clear diagnosis, mode of inheritance and derivation of risk figures. It should also address the individuals' concerns, using terminology which will be understood. Such a report can also act as a focus for the couple's own discussions and with other family members or friends.

Summary

The process of helping involves many skills, not the least of which are the abilities to listen, empathise and show respect for the individual. Within an emotionally supportive environment, the nature of any concerns should be explored, as should all the options which the service can offer. Finally, complex information must always be presented accurately in terms which are meaningful to those being counselled.

IMPLICATIONS

The demand for genetic counselling is increasing and it is important that the service is properly equipped to cope. This section looks at how the system can be improved, the necessary training and some wider implications for the service, including genetic registers and embryo research.

Service improvement

Health care for all?

A considerable number of individuals who are at risk from genetic disorders are not being reached. People who come forward for counselling tend to be a self-selecting population and are therefore not representative of the 'at risk' population. They are often articulate, and well educated, and have usually requested a referral to the genetics clinic from their GP. These people are likely to be familiar with the questions at stake and more comfortable in conversations with health professionals.

It is not clear how best to make contact with people who are not currently being reached. There are several options, including more effective health education programmes, tracing at risk individuals through genetic registers, or involving health professionals in the community and mental handicap services. Whether it is right to trace people is a difficult issue. It is costly to undertake extra testing and counselling, and there is often no cure for the illnesses which may be detected. However, it can be argued that a health service should make efforts to provide health care for all, and not only for those who are able to make their way to the service. In addition, efforts to trace at risk individuals may lead to an eventual reduction in those affected, and an improvement in the health of the community. Thus, a short term increase in costs may result in substantial long-term savings.

Referral system

People with genetic disorders may be seen by professionals from a variety of specialities in many different settings. A patient whose baby has congenital heart disease will probably learn of the risks for future pregnancies from her obstetrician, while a patient who has suffered a heart attack may learn of hereditary factors for ischaemic heart disease from the general practitioner. These professionals will be seeing patients with many types of problems, and only some with genetic problems. They may have poor knowledge of current genetic technology, and may not be the best qualified to help. Thus, not everyone will be offered appropriate counselling. All too often, individuals are offered factual and technical information by professionals who have little training in the skills of counselling and may have poor knowledge of the available options. In these circumstances it is likely that their distress will remain unrecognised. Routine referral to a genetic clinic where the counsellor can provide expert help and up to date information would alleviate these problems.

Training

In addition to an ability to listen, empathise, show respect and be caring, counsellors require other expertise. They must have a sound knowledge of the complex and technical aspects of many disorders. Moreover, they require a particular sensitivity towards moral and ethical issues which can exceed that necessary for other specialities. Although most of the professionals involved will have a medical degree, there is little provision within current medical training for the acquisition of the skills which are so vital to effective genetic counselling (Maguire, 1985). As the demand for counselling increases, there is a danger that unqualified people will adopt the role of counsellor. In the UK there is currently no specific qualification in genetic counselling, although a master's course is available in Canada and the USA. Many already involved in this service have attended general counselling courses, which may not include reference to the particular situations encountered in genetic counselling. It would be of benefit if courses and qualifications specific to this area became available soon.

Provision of staff support

It is inevitable that counsellors will experience difficulties in coming to terms with people's distress and they need to be able to discuss these feelings with colleagues in order to share the burden. Often, this support is not readily available, so the counsellor may begin to cope by a hardening of outlook in order to create a distance from the pain of counselling. Those who are not given supervision and support may begin to feel a sense of failure, because it is not acceptable for professionals to reveal their difficulties. They may become less effective and the ongoing strain might make them leave the profession. It is therefore important for those organising counselling services to recognise that counsellors experience difficulties and require support and supervision.

Genetics and medical education

Screening tests are being developed for more disorders and may be offered to select subgroups, such as older mothers, who are at particular risk, or to the general population. As mass screening becomes more routine, there is a danger that individuals will be unaware that they are being tested. It is therefore essential that there are adequate health education programmes and counselling services to back up the expanding potential for screening. Similarly, certain procedures, such as amniocentesis, carry risks, and test results may not be completely accurate. Individuals need to be made aware of these facts before deciding to undergo a test.

Respect for the individual

If testing and counselling are accepted, then the individual's views should be respected by the entire system of service. However, some hospitals will only offer prenatal testing after the couple agree to a pregnancy termination if the result proves positive, and many find this precondition unacceptable. Some may want to leave making a decision until they receive the test result, while others are adamant that they will not terminate a pregnancy regardless of the result. The latter want testing in order that, if necessary, they can prepare emotionally and practically for the birth of their affected baby, and a hospital which refuses to test them may be failing to provide a valuable service.

Consent and confidentiality

Where necessary, it is the job of the individual seeking counselling to obtain the cooperation of relatives. Occasionally, these may either decline to give personal medical information which would help in assessing the hereditary risks to the individual being counselled, or be too ill to consent to donate a blood sample for analysis. The choice between respecting the rights of un-cooperative relatives and making every effort to collect information that will benefit the individual can be difficult, as the necessary data could be obtained by examining medical records without the relative's permission or by taking a blood sample without informed consent. However, the counsellor must always obtain consent and respect the confidentiality of everyone concerned.

Similarly, divulging confidential information should not occur without consent, even when the aim is to help in some way. An example is the case of a health visitor who informed her patient that his neighbour also suffered from a type of dysmorphology, to the great distress of the neighbour. Such breaches of confidence do little to instil the trust which is vital to effective counselling.

Wider implications

Embryo research

Advances in the field of in vitro fertilisation may allow genetic disorders to be diagnised at a very early stage, before implantation has occurred. Thus, couples might be offered the option of having a risk free baby from the start of pregnancy. To many, this would end the distress of having repeated pregnancy terminations following positive prenatal test results. Questions concerning choices about human reproduction involve strong emotions and are laden with moral and ethical considerations (Fletcher, Berg and Tranoy, 1985). Indeed, the legality of this and similar research such as gene therapy, is the subject of much debate,and any future legislation will directly affect the service offered.

Genetic registers

The existence of genetic registers, which have been introduced by a number of health authorities recently, is a cause of controversy. They hold personal and medical information about affected individuals and their families, usu-ally stored in a computer. Their main aim is prevention, and they help to identify those at risk of either developing a disorder or transmitting it, so they can be made aware of the risks and the options available to them. In addition, registers can be used to monitor services, to provide a record of who might benefit from new tests or therapeutic advances as they become available, and for research. However, individuals are not always included on these registers with their full knowledge and consent. Given the sensitive nature of the information recorded, this situation requires remedy. Indeed, concerns have been expressed that these types of register are open to abuse, for example, by those who advocate that the quality of the human race can be improved by selective breeding, or by elements in the police, who claim that access to this information would aid crime prevention.

Summary

Genetics is a rapidly advancing field, and it is essential that the service is equipped to deal with the consequential increase in demand for counselling. Health education programmes and referrals to adequately trained staff will do much to help. It is also important to consider how best to contact at risk individuals, who do not present to the services, in order to inform them of the options that the service can offer.

CONCLUSIONS

Medical genetics is a complex and technical field. There are vast numbers of disorders for which there are rarely effective cures. They vary in their symptoms, severity, inheritance patterns and in the options that the service can offer. These factors contribute to the feelings of uncertainty which are so commonly experienced by those who are affected by a disorder.

Genetic counselling takes place in a variety of settings and involves a number of different health professionals. Counselling has a vital role to play by informing individuals of their diagnosis, risk of recurrence and by discussing the long-term medical and possibly educational implications of the disease. Counselling should also involve information about the options which are available, and deal with the distress and uncertainty caused by the disease. Failure to provide adequate counselling services will leave many fearful and confused.

VOLUNTARY AGENCIES

Association for Spina Bifida and Hydrocephalus,
22 Upper Woburn Place,
London WC1H 0EP
Tel: 071-388 1382

Contact a Family,
16 Strutton Ground,
London SW1P 2HP
Tel: 071-222 2695

Cystic Fibrosis Research Trust,
Alexandra House,
5 Blyth Road,
Bromley,
Kent BR1 3RS
Tel: 081-464 7211/2

Downs' Syndrome Association,
153–155 Mitcham Road,
London SW17 9PG
Tel: 081–682 4001

In Touch,
10 Norman Road,
Cheshire M33 3DF
Tel: 061-962 4441

Muscular Dystrophy Group,
Nattrass House,
35 Macaulay Road,
London SW4 OQP
Tel: 071-720 8055

REFERENCES

Fletcher, J.C., Berg, K., and Tranoy, K.E. (1985). Ethical aspects of medical genetics. A proposal for guidelines in genetic counselling, prenatal diagnosis and screening. *Clinical Genetics*, **27**, 199–205.

Harris, R. (1988). Genetic counselling and the new genetics. *Trends in Genetics*, **4**, 52–56.

Kingston, H.M. (1989). ABC of Clinical Genetics. Estimation of risk. *British Medical Journal*, **298**, 449–451.

Lippman-Hand, F. and Fraser, F. (1979). Genetic counselling: parents' responses to uncertainty. In C.J. Epstein, C.J. Curry, S. Packman, and B.D. Hall (Eds), Birth Defects, **15**, 325–339. Alan R. Liss Inc. New York.

Maguire, G.P. (1985). Training in genetic counselling. In A.E.H. Emery and I.M. Pullen (Eds), *Psychological aspects of genetic counselling*, Academic Press Inc., London.

13 Neonatal Intensive Care

HELEN BENDER
Department of Child Psychiatry, The London Hospital, Whitechapel, London E1 1BB

INTRODUCTION

The overall impression of neonatal intensive care is one of medical technology, where the small or sick newborn is subjected to increasingly intrusive and vigorous investigations and treatment. The main task in this field is the survival and care of the newborn, and the impressive fall in neonatal mortality of very low birthweight infants is to be welcomed. However, of growing concern is the fact that, although medical care has become increasingly sophisticated, preoccupation with the biochemical and physiological needs for survival does not mean that the emotions, anxieties and fears connected with life and death can be ignored. On the contrary, Minde *et al.* (1978) indicate that a mother's behaviour towards her infant correlates most highly with her perception of her infant's sickness, rather than its actual severity. This research gives credence to the view held by many psychoanalysts (Bender, 1981; Earnshaw, 1981; Szur, 1981; Freud, 1981) and other workers in this field, that a greater awareness of the psychological aspects of prematurity and a more integrated approach is necessary, to ensure the overall well-being of preterm infants, their caretakers, and families.

A large body of research has developed highlighting the effects of prematurity on babies and their impact on parents and staff. Follow-up studies raise concern at the extent to which Neonatal Intensive Care Units (NICU) may potentiate or create adverse conditions and a variety of problems which can persist for some years (Portnoy *et al.*, 1988). There is now an urgent need to alleviate the emotional crises which permeate the setting of the NICU. One is struck by the realization that there are many diverse and conflicting needs to be met in order to create optimum conditions. This involves recognition that there are three simultaneously 'at risk' populations: the babies, the parents and the staff. These groups form a closely interlinked system to be addressed at all, or any of the different points of entry.

This chapter will, however, mainly be confined to the parents, examining the *impact* of prematurity on the process of attachment, the problems arising

Counselling and Communication in Health Care. Edited by H. Davis and L. Fallowfield
© 1991 John Wiley & Sons Ltd

from this, and the parents' responses to the system in which they find themselves, and hence their counselling needs. The different forms of psychotherapeutic interventions of benefit in such a setting will be described, including the contribution and application of psycho-analytic understanding to this specialised area of work. It is increasingly difficult for medical and nursing staff to provide the emotional support needed by families, and more specialised help is appropriate.

THE PARENTS

Prematurity has been described as 'an accidental psychosocial crisis'. The different kinds of problems facing parents of premature infants and their responses to this situation may be determined by several factors:

Factors which pre-date admission

Parents of premature babies are often from socially deprived backgrounds. Low birthweight babies are more likely to be born to women who are already in stressful situations, and may be least able to cope with the additional strain. Many have had little or no ante-natal care. Gunter (1963) in a retrospective study of premature versus full-term births, found that mothers of the former reported twice as many stressful life events, including early neglect by their own mothers, deaths, desertions by husbands, financial difficulties, interpersonal problems and physical disabilities. Since a complicated obstetric history of infertility, habitual abortion, stillbirth, previous prematurity and neonatal death is also not unusual, parents may bring many pre-existing psychological conflicts to the intensely stressful situation of having a baby on such a unit. One mother, who had suffered several neonatal deaths, confided on the eve of taking her only surviving baby home, that she had had an illegal abortion many years previously, and believed that she was being punished with a succession of dead babies. Mothers often express feelings of low self-esteem and worthlessness. They experience what Solnit and Stark (1961) describe as a 'narcissistic blow'; a sense of failure that their bodies are inadequate containers, unable to grow and hold a baby to term. In an achievement orientated society, they feel that they have not produced 'as expected'. They require time to adjust to the reality, and mourn the loss of the idealised, hoped-for baby (Kaplan and Mason, 1960).

Mothers often express guilt at bringing a baby into the world early, and blame themselves for all the suffering that ensues. A mother whose baby was very ill with respiratory distress syndrome and heart-failure, sat crying next to her baby, talking about the pain he was undergoing and wondering how she could have been so selfish to want a baby so much, thereby putting him through such pain. Conversely, mothers may have very negative feelings towards their babies, blaming them for the bad delivery and the unexpected trauma.

Fathers too, report feelings of anxiety, depression and loss of concentration at work. They may experience disappointment and shame at having produced a puny, sick infant. This may constitute a blow to their virility in a society where weight is erroneously equated with quality. This may be especially acute because the father tends to have a more central (liaison) role, often being the first parent to see the baby, to speak to staff, and to liaise with the mother and relatives.

Emergency transfer

Regionalisation of NICU resources has added additional stresses. Families may find themselves far from home, and cut off from their own support systems. The mother may lose the staff she has come to trust during pregnancy, and find herself in an unfamiliar environment, with an entirely new set of caretakers. This can create practical difficulties for parents, who may be in conflict over their children at home, and a baby, far away, who does not *appear* to need them (McIntosh and Bone, 1984).

Factors associated with the pregnancy

Each baby's personal history from conception is unique, and parents of premature babies often recount intense preoccupation with prenatal fantasies and dreams. The relationship with the in-utero baby may already be influenced by the unconscious meaning this particular pregnancy has for the mother and her social and cultural background.

'The belief that external events can influence the unborn child, caused by such factors as magic, the gods and the planets, or by the infants' own actions, or by events experienced by the pregnant woman, has been held throughout all of recorded history, in all cultures' writes MacFarlane (1977). This appears particularly so in prematurity, where parents strive for reasons to explain the baby's early arrival. They frequently question the relationship between the maternal state of mind and foetal sensitivity, wondering whether negative or ambivalent feelings they may have had, could have influenced events.

A young West Indian mother whose marriage was collapsing, felt lonely and isolated, and clung to the fantasy that her baby would somehow replace her missing husband, completing the family triangle in a more gratifying relationship. She recounted several powerful dreams foretelling doom. At 21 weeks she dreamt that her grandfather (who had been dead for many years) appeared to her as a dead man, accusing her, 'You killed the Picknay' (meaning baby). In Jamaican folklore, a dream about 'old dead' meant that someone new could die. Although she tried to disregard these dreams as primitive, her son was born two weeks later, (at 23 weeks gestation) and lived for only eight months.

Mrs B.'s pregnancy was punctuated by a recurring dream about her obstetrician. In reality, he had assured her that all was well, but he appeared in her dreams, almost nightly, confessing that a grave error had been made, and telling her that her baby had already died in utero. She gave birth at 24 weeks to a deformed child who lived for only a few hours. At the unconscious level, she appeared to be aware that something was very wrong, despite reassurances to the contrary. Although it is difficult to understand the mechanism by which information about the body is held in the unconscious, the frequency of such reports and the way in which parents' and siblings' dreams reflect the medical condition is striking (Bender, 1989). Verny and Kelly (1982) hypothesize an 'organismic memory' that allows even a single cell to carry memories, and link it to the Jungian concept of the collective unconscious.

Factors associated with the birth

In general there will have been emergency aspects of the delivery, involving a transfer of hospitals, perhaps with little time for explanation. The experience of childbirth may remain confused, in the parents' minds. The birth experience itself may have been traumatic, or totally unavailable to consciousness (in the case of a Caesarian section), or partially so as a result of a protracted labour and the use of analgesic drugs. This, together with the period of separation which follows, increases the parents' anxiety about what they will discover upon seeing the baby.

With pre-term infants, the third trimester of pregnancy is missed, which according to some workers is the phase in which the mother-to-be is most able to familiarise herself with her infant, attribute gender, and endow the baby with traits (Rafael-Leff, 1982). Hence, not only is the baby premature, but so are the parents. Denied the necessary transitional stages, they are prematurely jettisoned into parenthood, having to deal with the consequences of giving birth too soon, often to a seriously ill baby. In addition, parents often report incredulity upon seeing a baby born by Caesarian section for the first time: 'She might have been a fairy child . . . for all I know she might not even be mine!'

Factors associated with the baby's appearance and the NICU

There are a variety of factors that may obstruct the process of attachment. For example, the first exposure to the baby's unexpected foetal appearance and small size can be shocking. The pre-term infant is bony and has transparent gelatinous skin which reveals the body contents. Occasionally, the baby is badly bruised after a difficult birth, or severely jaundiced. 'Baby bird', 'drowned rat' and 'bald monkey' are common descriptions given by parents conveying a sense of the baby belonging to a different, alien species. Because of all the equipment, and the thermal wrapping and bonnets, very little of the baby can actually be seen. It thus becomes difficult for parents to recognise the unique personal characteristics which identify the baby as theirs.

This first precious encounter takes place in an environment which is un-familiar, hot and unwelcoming. It is dominated by complex equipment, which appears to be assaulting the baby's every visible orifice and body surface. In addition to strange appearance and unexpected size, the parents are faced with a baby who spends most of its time sleeping. It is unrespon-sive and unpredictable. To what extent these long sleep periods are due to physiological needs, or an expression of conservation and withdrawal, is difficult to assess. Recent research has placed greater emphasis on minimal handling of the very low birthweight baby, who sometimes needs resuscita-tion after handling (Wolke, 1987).

The implication of this conflicts with parental needs and the observation that babies open their eyes more in response to parental handling (Minde *et al.* 1978). In other words, there has to be someone there to provide the baby with an incentive to open its eyes. The fact that an infant *can* discriminate the parent's touch and presence is testimony to the pre-term infant's sophistication.

The baby's and parents' experience is *qualitatively* different from the healthy newborn. Intensive care, by definition, means that the infant re-quires more than parental care. The task is not one of plumping up and nurturing a rather undersized infant, but frequently involves inflicting pain-ful procedures (arterial catheterisation, heel pricks) on an infant whose future life and development is, at best, uncertain.

In the incubator, babies are exposed, unheld, with few good experiences. They have no rights and little ability to influence the world. Attention is given because of their immaturity and the demands of an externally en-forced timetable, not because *they* have expressed a need. Their own needs for consistency and uninterrupted deep sleep are often not respected by the professionals. The sense of impotence, so frequently described by parents in this situation, surely mirrors that of their infants. They often feel envious of the capable nurses and potent doctors, contrasting their own feelings of inadequacy and their sense of being peripheral to their baby's needs. One mother, in describing her sleeplessness night after night, suggested that lying awake *thinking* about her baby was all she felt she could offer, as she felt so peripheral to his care. 'He needs doctors to save him, not parents to mess things up!' Furthermore, it is difficult for parents to develop sensitivity to their incubator baby's needs, since a major channel of communication, the mother's body, which carried the communication during pregnancy, is de-nied, and parents have to balance the need for contact with the fear of distressing the baby, or dislodging some essential piece of equipment.

In response to the fear that their baby might die, parents exhibit all the features of grief: depression, sadness and crying, loss of appetite, sleep disturbances and even phobic symptoms. Their distress may take the form of somatic symptoms such as shortness of breath, palpitations and tighten-ing in the throat. These symptoms are neither uncommon, nor pathological, but may be considered as healthy responses to the *pathology of circumstance*. At the unconscious level, these may be understood in terms of the parents' identification with their sick baby, for whom respiratory problems are a major concern. Parents often express the desire to take on the pain instead, thereby alleviating their infant's condition. To preserve a sense of parenthood under these conditions and retain a sense of the uniqueness of each baby must be a priority.

Moving on

It is important for staff to concentrate their awareness and efforts upon the aim of moving parents and baby on from the trauma, so that they can build a core of benign experiences together. However, the need to respect parental defences is important, particularly in those parents who have difficulty adapting to this situation. Over-enthusiasm to promote togetherness and attachment opportunities can turn into persecutory zeal and have the opposite effect. It must also be understood that attachment difficulties (e.g. a mother's unwillingness to visit) do not necessarily signal lack of love, but may be due to the baby's failure to engage her, or her need to stay away from a deviant or disturbing baby, or her fear of becoming attached to an infant who might be damaged or die.

If physical contact between the parent and baby can be initiated and fostered with sensitivity, then a benign cycle may be set in motion. For example, a mother was afraid to touch her infant, despite continued reassurances from the staff. It emerged that the parents had suffered a neonatal death a year earlier, and had the new child on the first anniversary of this death. I commented to her parents on her vigorous sucking movements, and the following week I was greeted by delighted parents holding and cuddling their baby. The mother had again noticed the baby sucking the corner of the cot sheet. Needing 'official' confirmation of her perceptions, she called one of the nurses, who suggested putting Lisa to the breast. Encouraged and supported, the mother did so, and at 30 weeks gestation she gained the distinction of being the youngest baby on our unit to become fully breastfed.

Where handling a sick newborn is ill-advised for medical reasons, thinking about the baby, holding it with one's thoughts, may provide the only medium for contact, until the condition improves. Daws (1989) suggests that this thinking may be perceived as a way of keeping the fragile baby alive. As long as parents do this, they feel that the baby cannot slip away. Daws explains that many parents are unable to stop this intense thinking and looking, and switch to more active caretaking, even after the baby is brought home. Still fearful, they neither expect, nor allow their baby to settle or sleep, often resulting in subsequent sleep problems.

COUNSELLING

Identifying therapeutic needs

Crisis is often a useful point for intervention; parents are most needy at such times and more receptive to therapeutic intervention.

Airing anxieties and irrational fears

In crisis, rational thought is often suspended, and unconscious feelings move to the fore. These must be understood before parents can take in the reality. Irrational fears can colour the parents' perception, persisting despite repeated reassurances, and obstructing the mother's desire to be in contact with the baby. Particularly prevalent are worries about damaging the baby. These may stem from a mother's feeling that she is bad or inadequate, and they are often based on guilt.

Mrs A. was reluctant to handle her daughter. In talking to the Unit psychotherapist, it emerged that she yearned to hold her baby, but had been warned by her own mother of the dangers of infecting such a tiny baby, and she therefore stifled her longings. She also revealed that she had suffered a neonatal death a year earlier, during a time when the dustmen were on strike, and somehow she retained the fantasy that the dirty environment outside the hospital had given rise to the fatal infection.

Another mother who had suffered two stillbirths and a neonatal death was understandably terrified when her daughter was born at 28 weeks gestation. She found that the iron tablets she had been prescribed gave her diarrhoea. This, together with a nervous rash that she developed, increased her anxiety, and convinced her that she had infected her baby with some life-threatening disease. She insisted that the paediatricians check her baby twice daily.

It is important that parents are able to express such feelings, but without the worry that they will be considered unfit or mad by staff, in whose possession the baby seems firmly placed. Some parents are reluctant to share their anxieties for this reason, imagining that if they reveal their inadequacies they will not be allowed to take their baby home.

Someone needs to understand this unconscious dimension. He or she needs to listen to, and contain, the powerful unconscious feelings which are evoked and associated with these circumstances. Parents need an opportunity to explore and discuss the kinds of feelings described above, preferably with someone who does not have responsibility for their baby's medical care.

Observation

Psychoanalysts have long emphasized the value of attentive observation and reflection as part of the healing process. Others maintain that sharing babies' observable behaviour reactions with the parents can become a powerful technique for establishing a good working relationship with them (Brazelton, 1978). Closely observing their baby can confirm parents in their parenting abilities, since with encouragement they may be ready to interpret their observations, and to explore intuitive feelings. This may help draw attention to the baby in a new way. Observation can also provide the first safe stages towards initiating physical contact through touch, which will, in turn, initiate further and deeper feelings of attachment. It can also link parents back into the prenatal communication system which had been disrupted by the early birth, and which needs to be maintained as part of the 'perinatal continuum' (Freud 1988). Time given to listening to parents' observations can provide a contrast with the medical model of 'doing', but also complements and augments the bank of knowledge that exists about their baby, and helps the parents to begin to identify their infant's distinctive qualities and needs.

Assimilation and integration

The experience of childbirth may remain confused, unresolved and unassimilated in the parents' minds. Because of the attendant life and death issues, recounting the birth experience to the paediatric staff can appear irrelevant and inappropriate. The counsellor, by providing the opportunity for going over the unique details of the birth, allows the parents to integrate the experience, enabling them to move on and to attend to the physical and psychological demands of being parents. Through discussion they can re-experience what was wholly or partly missed, gain new perspectives and assimilate undigested experiences, which may become more bearable (Bender and Elkan, 1980). It is interesting to consider whether parents who are able to work through this trauma, may provide, in parallel, an integrative function for their premature infant, whose own capacity for integration at a crucially formative stage is surely overtaxed by the onslaught of stimuli (light, noise, pain and a multiplicity of handling) that are all too common in the NICU.

The complex dynamics of the relationship between staff and parents is explored elsewhere (Bender and Swan-Parente, 1983). However, the parents, struggling with their impotence, may not feel able to speak on their baby's behalf, in the face of the seemingly omnipotent doctors and nurses, with their impressive god-like powers of life and death. For this reason a genuine partnership needs to be fostered, so that both groups work together and contribute to the successful outcome. This is another area where the counsellor may play a useful role as facilitator. From individual work with parents, information often emerges which can alter the staff's distorted perception of the family, and help to endow the infant with a history which makes it a unique individual.

In the face of increasing technology, it becomes important to emphasize the role of the parents as necessary for the baby, and complementary to medical intervention. Unfortunately the status of parents often remains anomalous. They are not the *patients*, yet staff frequently regard them as such, treating them with the tacit assumption that they are not really 'good enough' parents (or they would not be in this situation).

Groups

Groups, for staff and parents, may provide an effective utilisation of the counsellor's time. For those unable to articulate their difficulties, much can be gained by listening to others, and thereby dealing by proxy with their own problems. Frequently the group fosters mutual support, and helps parents build up a network. Groups have been found to have a more positive effect when a veteran parent is included, presumably because this generates a hope of survival, and a future beyond the present trauma. Minde *et al.* (1978) reported that parents who participated in self-help groups visited their infants in hospital significantly more than controls.

The drawbacks must also be considered. For some parents extensive use of denial is necessary to survive, and they are unable to tolerate another's pain as well as their own. Parents may also be at different stages of their baby's illness, and find the preoccupation of the group 'out of synch' with their own needs. Ethnicity has also been an issue, for example, when trying to find a common language.

The counsellor's role

Ideally as a counsellor one would wish to see all parents upon admission. This would both convey a sense of an integrated approach to the infant's care, and identify the person to whom they can turn at time of crisis.

From contact with parents, either routinely or in response to referral, individually or in groups, the counsellor is in a position to take on many roles — parent advocate to staff; interpreter of concepts to parents; spokesman for the baby and his or her psychological and emotional needs amidst a setting dominated by technology; a coordinator of the staff's efforts at emotional support, as well as a supporter of the staff's work-related problems; and grief counsellor.

Parental support requires individuals trained to understand the *dynamics* of perinatal crisis. They may come from a variety of backgrounds, such as psychotherapy, psychology, or social work, but they should be unencumbered by medical responsibility for the babies.

Suggestions and attempts to alleviate the stresses of the NICU have been diverse, but features recur as important and beneficial, both for parents and staff:

1. There is a need for quiet, reflective moments within a setting where action sometimes takes the place of, and inhibits, thought.
2. There must be a neutral person to whom both the parents and the staff (not necessarily together) feel free to speak.
3. Time must be given to the interpretations of observations, and opportunities must be created to explore and encourage intuitive feelings.

To deal exclusively with anxieties surrounding serious illness, death and handicap, is extremely stressful, and therapists engaged in this work should ensure that they themselves receive adequate supervision and support from colleagues.

WEAK POINTS IN THE SYSTEM

Many of the difficulties encountered by the parents of low-birthweight babies are created or exacerbated by hospital practices, which could be altered. It is therefore important to identify which aspects cause or contribute to distress.

The current system is far from ideal. It is characterised by separation of the infant from its parents. Such separation, like illness and prematurity, can never be totally eliminated. Its damaging effects can, however, be minimised. In a speciality which is still young, a successful outcome often remains uncertain and parents may be left with anxiety about abnormality for some time into the future.

Staff rotational policies and the shift system militate against *the formation of close attachments* to babies and parents. This also allows staff to maintain a distance, and appears to protect them from distress and the pain of loss. The system also ensures that during their stay, babies will be handled by innumerable caretakers, each with their own style, hence delaying the baby's capacity to build up a consistent picture of his or her environment.

Staff are susceptible to the same factors that are associated with the infant's immaturity and illness, and that cause parents to approach or withdraw from the babies. Add to this responsibility for the lives of numerous seriously ill infants, the impact of repeated loss through death, or the pain of handicap, and it is not surprising that staff burnout (i.e. low morale and absenteeism) has become a common feature in this field. Staff despair and hopeless feelings are transmitted. As a result, the infant's health may be affected by its early interactions with the doctors and nurses, as well as with its parents.

The question of whether one can achieve a balance between heightening sensitivity and maintaining the need for defences necessary to survive the work remains unresolved. If staff are not sensitised to the issues, they risk becoming mechanistic in their care, working 'only from the eyebrows up' as one nurse pointedly told me, and becoming unable to care appropriately for the parents.

Growing research into the pre-natal period has raised awareness of babies' abilities, and is increasingly creating greater conflict for the staff. To closely examine the baby's needs for contact and continuity means confirming the baby as a thinking and feeling person, with all that this implies for the way in which the staff proceed with interventions and treatments.

For some years now, some doctors and nurses have suggested that trying to identify how the baby experiences the NICU is a way of ensuring that stresses are minimised and that the infant is treated with more respect. For example, staff must reflect on the effect of routine practices (Taylor 1982), evaluating the timing and sequencing of these procedures, and respecting deep sleep states in older premature babies. As staff often become models for inexperienced parents, rigid and insensitive practices may represent a considered, expert view of how parental relationships are best conducted.

To address the problem of inconsistency of handling, and to promote a closer relationship between parents and staff, primary care nursing (the appointment of one or two key workers for each baby) could be implemented, provided staff feel able to take on this level of involvement. For the parents, it is usually valuable to have known workers with whom to share their observations and experiences.

Individual and/or group counselling should be available to both parents and staff to promote better understanding of all the elements described in this chapter. Above all, additional training for both the nurses and doctors should include a fuller understanding of the psychological aspects of neonatal care.

CONCLUSIONS

Nurses and doctors not only represent authority figures but also, at an unconscious level, they may represent the combined parent and by their behaviour can convey parental approval. Therefore, in addition to physical care, they have a major role to play in welcoming the baby, especially a very sick or damaged baby, who may never survive to live in the outside world, and who therefore only exists in the minds of the parents and caretakers.

By caring for the parents, we nurture the infant. It is they who will carry the responsibility for rearing the child in the future. The perinatal period can therefore present a valuable opportunity for intervention, particularly where there has been a cycle of deprivation and bad mothering. Therapeutic intervention on a NICU may be regarded as the earliest intervention among a population of babies who have long been recognised as having more than their fair share of behaviour problems and emotional adjustment as they grow up. It is preferable that help be offered during this initial crisis period, rather than much later when the traumatic evidence of failure may be a battered child, or one who fails to thrive.

We must, however, also address ourselves to the needs of the staff. It has been said that as mothers are mirrors for their infants so, too, staff often reflect parental concerns. These concerns have largely been written up by doctors as highly intellectualised professional concerns, emphasizing such issues as the ethical and legal dilemmas faced on such units. Nurses, presumably because of their closer identification with mothers, have been less reticent in exploring the emotional impact, in contrast to the medical emphasis placed on the stresses resulting from the NICU hi-tech environment.

Over the years changes have occurred in the emphasis placed on different problems with the NICU baby. Initially the focus was on the problems of separation. The work of Bowlby (1958) and Klaus and Kennell (1982) was extremely valuable in contributing to the understanding of the attachment process, and how it can be facilitated or disrupted by many aspects of hospital routine. From this arose work focused on parents' needs and responses, demonstrating the vulnerability of social relations to interference. Only more recently have workers begun to explore the concept of the premature baby as *a different kind of child*, a pre-natal baby, and the impact that the babies themselves have on those who care for them. Klaus and Kennell (1983) reviewed various interventions aimed at reducing parental anxiety and developing more positive environments for both parents and infants. They concluded that even the most sensitive interventions may fail if the parents view their infant as weak and likely to die. This confirms the central importance of exploring and working with the parents' *inner* perception, and no other member of the neonatal team is trained to do this, apart from the psychotherapist.

Surely we have now attained that state of knowledge where we are sufficiently aware of the needs of all three groups within the system, to begin to synthesize and integrate applications into an improved working model of neonatal intensive care. To attain this synthesis will surely facilitate the baby's precarious course from traumatic and unexpected birth, through to the homecoming and integration into the family. Parents' needs have been neglected in the past, and unfortunately in most institutions continue to be so. To save the life of a pre-term baby at the expense of the relationship with the parents represents little advance. Counselling should be recognised as an essential and integrated component of neonatal intensive care, and not as a fringe luxury. Work which does not take cognisance of new developments in the field of prenatal and perinatal psychology and medicine will ultimately lead to a diminished experience of childbirth and child care, for both parents and the professionals in this field.

USEFUL ADDRESS

BLISS Link,
17–21 Emerald Street,
London WC1N 3QL
Tel: 071-831 9393/8996

REFERENCES

Bender, H. and Elkan, J. (1980). *Unconscious aspects of communication about the birth.* Unpublished paper.

Bender, H. (1989). On the outside looking in: sibling perceptions of the premature infant. Paper presented at a congress of the International Society for Pre- and Perinatal Psychology and Medicine, in Jerusalem.

Bender, H. and Swan-Parente, A. (1983). Psychological and psychotherapeutic support of staff and parents in an intensive care baby unit. In J.A. Davis, M.P.M. Richards, and N.R.C. Roberton (Eds), *Parent–baby attachment in premature infants.* London: Croom-Helm.

Bowlby, J. (1958). The nature of the child's ties to his mother. *International Journal of Psychoanalysis*, **39**, 350–373.

Brazelton, T.B. (1978). Future care of the infant. *Birth and the Family Journal*, **5**, 242–5.

Daws, D. (1989). *Through the night: helping parents and sleepless infants.* London: Free Association Books.

Earnshaw, A. (1981). Action Consultancy. In colloquium: Hospital care of the newborn: some aspects of personal stress. *Journal of child psychotherapy*, **7**, 17–20.

Freud, W.E. (1981). To be in touch. In colloquium: Hospital care of the newborn: some aspects of personal stress. *Journal of Child Psychotherapy*, **7**, 7–9.

Freud, W.E. (1988). Prenatal attachment, the perinatal continuum and the psychological side of neonatal intensive care. In P.O. Feydor-Freybergh and M.L. Vanessa Vogel (Eds), *Prenatal and perinatal psychology and medicine encounter with the unborn*, pp. 217–234. New York: Parthenon Press.

Gunter, L. (1963). Psychopathology and stress in the life experience of mothers of premature infants: a comprehensive study. *American Journal of Obstetrics and Gynecology*, **86**, 333–40.

Kaplan, D.M. and Mason, E.A. (1960). Maternal reactions to premature birth. *American Journal of Orthopsychiatry*, **30**, 359–364.

Klaus, M. and Kennell, J. (1982). *Maternal–infant bonding* (2nd Edn) (St. Louis; C.V. Mosby).

Klaus, M. and Kennell, J. (1983). An evaluation of interventions in the premature nursery. In J.A. Davis, M.P.M. Richards and N.R.C. Roberton (Eds), *Parent-baby attachment in premature infants.* London: Croom-Helm.

Macfarlane, J.A. (1977). *The psychology of childbirth.* Fontana: London.

McIntosh, N. and Bune, C. (1984). Dilemma of perinatal intensive care. *British Journal of Hospital Medicine*, Feb, 145–148.

Minde, K., Trehub, S., Gorter, C., Boukydis, C., and Celhoffer, J. (1978). Mother–child relationships in the premature nursery. *Paediatrics*, **61**, 373–379.

Portnoy, S., Callas, M., Wolke, D., and Gamsu, H. (1988). Five year follow-up study of extremely low birthweight infants. *Developmental Medicine and Child Neurology*, **30**, 590–598.

Rafael-Leff, J. (1982). Psychotherapeutic needs of mothers-to-be. *Journal of Child Psychotherapy*, **8**, 3–11.

Solnit, A.J. and Stark, M.H. (1961). Mourning and the birth of a defective child. *Psychoanalytic Study of the Child*, **16**, 523–528.

Szur, R. (1981). Infants in hospital: In Colloquium: Hospital care of the newborn: some aspects of personal stress. *Journal of Child Psychotherapy*, **7**, 3–6.

Taylor, P. (1982). Some Perspectives on neonatal intensive care. *Australian Nurses' Journal*, **11**, 35–37.

Verny, T. and Kelly, J. (1982). *The secret life of the unborn child.* New York, Summit Books.

Wolke, D. (1987). Environmental and developmental neonatology. *Journal of Reproductive and Infant Psychology*, **5**, 17–42.

14 Counselling Families of Children with Disabilities

HILTON DAVIS
Academic Unit of Psychology, The London Hospital Medical College, Turner Street, London E1 2AD

The sight of an ill or disabled child elicits powerful and complex feelings of alarm, sadness and anger, along with the desire to help, comfort, and protect. An immediate reaction is an urge to make the child better. These are strong feelings for an onlooker, but so much more powerful, even desperate, for the child's parents. Such feelings have been portrayed forcefully by MacKeith (1973) who made the point that parents and professionals may experience similar reactions, which may also contain an ambivalent or negative component (e.g. revulsion).

A major problem in this context is that cures are not forthcoming. The 'magic bullets' (Underwood, Owen and Winckler, 1986) of heroic medicine are not in the armoury of this area. Professionals who expect to solve problems and cure disease will be in difficulty, and this may explain the low popularity of this specialty amongst medical practitioners. It is also a problem for parents, who, like all other parents, cannot remedy every difficulty, and must learn to suffer *with* and not *for* the child. For parents of a child with a disability, however, this is a vital issue and only one of the many that influence their adaptation to parenthood.

It is essential that parents adapt to their situation before effective help can be made available to the child. If the parents are distressed, have no clear idea of the benefits of what the professional advocates, cannot work with the child for whatever reasons, or do not want to, then all other efforts will be attenuated. This is not to say that parental adaptation is ever absolute, only that it is a vital process that must be considered explicitly by all professionals at all times, if they are to be of benefit not only to the child but also to the family as a whole.

DISABILITY

Disability refers to normally available abilities being absent or significantly reduced. This arises from diverse sources, ranging from specific genetic

Counselling and Communication in Health Care. Edited by H. Davis and L. Fallowfield
© 1991 John Wiley & Sons Ltd

conditions and intrauterine circumstances, such as placental dysfunction, infections and drugs, to peri-natal trauma. The term includes sensory dysfunction (e.g. deafness and blindness), motor difficulties such as cerebral palsy and spina bifida, and delays or deficits in the development of cognitive skills. A significant number of children experience disability simultaneously in more than one of these areas.

There are a large number of children in all societies with disabilities. The most recent survey estimated there to be approximately 360 000 children under 16 years with disabilities in Britain (Bone and Meltzer, 1989). Lewis (1987) concluded that as many as one in ten children in the Western world are so disabled as to have very reduced or no prospect of employment as adults. The size of the problem is doubled if one also considers children with less severe difficulties; Warnock (1978), for example, concluded that as many as 20% of children would have special educational needs at some point in their school lives.

THE CONCERNS OF PARENTS

It is impossible to provide a comprehensive list of concerns, as families and parents are unique, and experience situations specific to themselves regardless of the problem. What parents present as problems are not necessarily static. Regardless of the help available to them, most parents continuously adapt or 'metamorphose perpetually' as one mother remarked. Their concerns change and evolve as a function of changes in their children, their family, social and material circumstances, and perhaps above all in their views of themselves. As one mother said, 'I am not the person I was five years ago. When she was born, I was desperate to make her better and I put all my trust in the people at the hospital. I did everything they said and neglected the others (*her husband and two other children*). When she didn't improve, I blamed myself and tried even harder with the exercises. I was driven and . . . now I know . . . isolated and cold. She's never going to be independent, but she will be happy, because I realised just in time that it is our relationship as a family that is most important for us all'.

The child and the disability

Learning that there is something wrong with a child is a profound crisis for parents. Literally, this means a point of change, a turning point, a time for decision. They have to adapt to a sudden occurrence that has serious long-term implications, which are probably far beyond their previous experience. They begin the process of losing their images of the non-disabled child and start to build a new set of constructs to enable them to anticipate their child's behaviour and the disability (Davis and Cunningham, 1985). This ongoing process has been conceptualised by various authors as having phases of shock, emotional reaction, adaptation and orientation (e.g. Cunningham and Davis, 1985a), which signal the turmoil of change in the parents' understanding of their world.

The process has been likened to bereavement or a grief reaction. That they are similar in involving major upheaval and change is indisputable. That they differ, however, is clear, since the process is not only one of adaptation to loss, but to gaining a child with a disability. One mother, whose good looking, intelligent and gentle three year old became spiteful, destructive, disfigured and unpredictable as a result of an accident, described the two pictures she continued to hold in her head years later: the one confronting her daily, and the beautiful one from the past that she allowed herself to see when 'depressed and hidden under the bedclothes'.

Initially, making sense of the disability is a central concern for parents. Most seek to understand its extent, severity, aetiology and prognosis. This is not a simple task since such knowledge may be limited even for the paediatrician, who may not know the cause or be able to forecast the future. It is, however, made more difficult by the fact that parental understanding of technical terms and psychological processes is likely to be limited. Parents may not know of the existence of chromosomes, let alone be aware of the effects of deviant changes. This may be complicated by conceptual differences, as in a multi-cultural context where a parent from, for example, Bangladesh may have a concept of disease more related to the spiritual than the physical realm. Furthermore, the ability to take in information about the disability may be initially hindered by the emotional arousal engendered in the communication of the diagnosis.

It is not uncommon at the initial diagnosis for the full understanding of the implications of the disorder to take several sessions even when the professional is a skilled communicator. It may take much longer, or never happen at all, without adequate communication. In one parent support group, it became apparent that none of the mothers understood the I.Q. figure quoted for their children despite their awareness of the diagnosis of intellectual impairment for at least 18 months.

Perhaps the most important question parents face is what can be done to help their child. The possibilities vary enormously from the medical to the behavioural, including help with health problems (e.g. infections), orthopaedic difficulties, specific skill deficits, sensory disorder, general developmental delay, and behaviour problems. Many professionals are involved, including dieticians, psychologists, physiotherapists, OTs, speech therapists, paediatricians, GPs, health visitors, social workers and teachers. They provide advice of many kinds, but frequently specify developmental programmes to be carried out by parents, despite the absence of evidence for effectiveness (e.g. Palmer *et al.*, 1988) and often without discussion of outcomes. This is partly a result of the therapist assuming validity without requiring evidence, partly the difficulty of admitting their ignorance, and in part a response to the very strong desire in parents to remove the disability immediately.

Parents differ enormously in whether they have or even want realistic information about the future. Some desperately want to know the future exactly. However, as one mother said, 'I don't want to know what's going to happen; I just take each day as it comes'. Others will construct a future whether accurate or not: 'I know exactly what's going to happen; she'll be with us for as long as we can manage, but she'll end up in an institution'.

The question of whether parents should undertake enormously time-consuming procedures, such as those advocated by Doman-Delacato based approaches (Scotson, 1985), must be taken seriously. They require help to decide what they want to do within the context of what they expect to achieve, considering the whole family and their wider social situation. For one family regular exercise routines may fulfil the desire 'to do something' or 'to try everything'. For another, such programmes just emphasise the futility of the situation confronting them. These feelings are closely related to the ever present experience of helplessness, of not being able to take away the child's pain, disability or disfigurement.

For some families the question is not whether they want or can afford (financially or otherwise) to seek particular treatment options, but whether the options are available. Resources are frequently short in inner-city and rural areas, and potentially beneficial services may either not exist or be so under-funded as to be inaccessible. This is a source of irritation at best, and desperation at worst, and is not helped by the failure of statutory services (health, education and social) to cooperate, coordinate and advertise appropriately.

Another important problem is the decision about whether to pursue treatment options at all. Should they actively treat a sick child or let him or her die as peacefully as possible, when life is threatened? For how long should they allow invasive investigative procedures, when the outcomes are unlikely to suggest treatment measures? They have to face questions about whether to agree to potentially fatal procedures (e.g. cardiac surgery) with a chance of improvement, or to risk the possibility of death more quickly, because of the failure to treat the problem.

A final issue is the confusion of the child and the disability. Professionals may do this by referring to 'the autist' or 'the Downs', but parents may confuse their irritation/anger at the disability with their feelings for the child. Diamond, (1981) illustrates, from her own experience of growing up with a disability, how parents can lose sight of the needs of the child for contentment or play in their constant desire to improve, change or 'therapise'. The subtlety of this has been shown in maternal speech being much more directive to children with disabilities even in free-play (Davis, Stroud and Green, 1988).

This confusion may result in parents treating the child less consistently and firmly, with consequent discipline problems. Some may be so anxious and protective that the child does not experience appropriate independence, especially where the situation may be psychologically hurtful. It was agony for one mother when her son with spina bifida was either not invited to parties, or was unable to join in when invited. She also discussed her intense guilt at feeling angry with him when he was as irritating as any other three-year-old. Another mother discussed whether to stop her son, with mild hemiplegia, playing football in a primary school team. She knew this would hurt him, but wanted to spare him the pain of criticism and rejection as his disability became more evident compared to the rapidly increasing skills and competitiveness of the other children in the team. The impossibility of protecting him weighed heavily upon his mother, until she saw that all children were hurt at some point and necessarily so as part of growing up. She therefore decided to respect her son's independence by not intervening, and was rewarded a little later by him discussing his own similar worries and deciding to give up football. Ironically, he selected karate as an alternative!

Parental self-perceptions

Parental concerns about their children cannot be divorced from their constructions of themselves as people and parents. All actions and decisions in relation to their child reflect upon themselves. The question of their own adaptation is ever present. How they will cope with the child is one of the first questions parents ask themselves. They ponder their ability to cope with their distress, sadness, disappointment, and anxiety. They fear the stresses on them, and question their ability to meet the demands of the child and treatment schedules. Many parents explore their role in the aetiology of the disorder, to see if it was their fault and whether it could have been avoided. As a result of such deliberations some parents decide not to keep their child, but the decision is not taken lightly and requires enormous courage.

The same issue is present for some parents in their vigilance for any indication that they are failing as a parent or rejecting their child. For example, parents may find it impossible to accept respite care even for a short time, but most, at least initially, have considerable reservations (Green and Evans, 1984). It requires great staff sensitivity to facilitate the use of such a resource, especially for leisure purposes. Their feelings vary, but include fears about the child feeling rejected, guilt, anxiety about their own failure to cope, embarrassment at what others will think of them, and concerns about whether the child will receive adequate care.

Most parents, in fact, cope admirably with whatever happens, but not without considerable self-doubt and pain, as a result of lost independence or changing career ambitions. Some derive greater purpose in life than they had previously, and religious beliefs may become strengthened. Many, however, face the constant dilemma of whether they are meeting the needs of the child with the disability to the exclusion of other family members, let alone their own needs for personal space, achievement and interest. Parents of pre-school children have a particularly heavy work-load, which can be enormously increased in the case of a child with a disability by the demands made, for example, by regular home teaching programmes.

The parent's task can also be made more difficult by the many appointments with the various professionals involved in their child's care. These put considerable pressure upon the mother, who has to forgo other activities, make childminding arrangements for other children, occupy the child in the less convenient environment of the clinic, and still get home in time to shop, cook and do all the other things expected of her. The situation is made worse if the appointments take much longer than necessary, are not controlled by the parent and are not perceived as fruitful. 'I might as well camp in the hospital, I am here so often. And you know it's for at least a morning or an afternoon because the waiting rooms are always full.'

It is not surprising under such circumstances that some parents question what they personally achieve, what enjoyment they obtain and their own value. Such doubts are also exacerbated by our society's tendency to diminish the role of mother, construing it as simple and of relatively little value compared to other careers. This frequently means for example that they will see themselves as inferior to the professionals with whom they interact.

Family relationships

Family relationships are central concerns for all, but can be a source of particular worry for parents of children with disabilities. One frequently hears mothers' anxieties about neglecting their husbands and especially their other children. They may have to spend a great deal of time in hospital with one child, and they certainly spend much more time on caretaking, supervision and therapeutic activities. Many, therefore, may not be able or have the energy to spend time with other children, and parents do bemoan the loss of time spent as a family in leisure activities (Byrne, Cunningham and Sloper, 1988).

Of particular importance is the relationship between husband and wife. This changes inevitably with the birth of any child, and may change much more in the context of disability. However, there is no simple pattern. Some relationships are strengthened by the crisis, and some are weakened. The incidence of divorce does not appear to be significantly greater than in other families, and it is probably the case that the situation precipitates prior difficulties. Nevertheless, although the problem may not be any greater than in the general population, a substantial number of parents do experience difficulties with their partner. Mothers may complain of the lack of support, physically or emotionally, provided by their husbands. Fathers may complain of their wife's obsessional focus on their child and there may also be sexual problems.

Wider social relationships

Many families are well supported by relatives, neighbours and friends. Others do not have such support or lose it as a result of the situation of having the child. For example, they may have little time or energy for social occasions, and this, coupled with other people's anxiety about the problem, may result in their relative isolation. This can be further exaggerated by the fact that some parents find it difficult or embarrassing to take their child into public places, particularly, for example, if the child has behaviour problems. These reactions are related to the stigma experienced by people in the context of disease and disability. Parents may perceive people to be reacting differently to the child and themselves. They may feel that people are hostile towards them, and lose self-esteem as a result. Occasionally, families react by trying to hide the problem completely, as in the case of a Bangladeshi family who refused all professional help on the basis that it would signal a problem to other members of their family and cast a slur on them. This is an extreme reaction, but avoiding taking the child into public places or indiscriminate explanation of the child's difficulties are not uncommon, and parents say the problem is exaggerated when their child is disabled, but normal in appearance.

Although such strategies are a reflection of the parents' own adaptation, and they might misinterpret interest for criticism, nevertheless they do have to deal with obvious public reactions. These vary from people deliberately avoiding them, to openly staring ('I often think I'll put a large sign on the wheelchair, "YES! SHE IS STRANGE" '). Some parents react with aggression ('I just ask them what they're staring at'). Others feel anxious and hurry about their business, and some do not care, feeling that the people they meet cannot be expected to understand. Although people do talk to them expressing encouragement, concern and respect, the remarks remembered and recounted later are usually those that are hurtful, even if unintentional. A stranger's reference to her daughter, who was extremely intelligent but physically disabled, as 'mental' in a sympathetic comment hurt one mother deeply, such that she still exploded into tears weeks later. On the other hand, a question about whether her son with epilepsy was 'apoplectic' sent another mother into fits of laughter.

Explaining the disability to others is a problem for all family members. After the diagnosis the parents have to tell their other children, doting grandparents and their own brothers and sisters. This can be equally as difficult as the situation confronting the paediatrician when breaking the news to the parents. One woman was unable to tell her own parents about the diagnosis for more than 18 months after she had been told. It remains a problem, however, in that parents do feel obliged to explain their child's appearance and behaviour and yet do not want to overelaborate, bore or confuse the other person. Even so, it is clear that they do not expect the other person to understand in any depth, and it is interesting to listen to their clipped and clinical descriptions, that belie the seriousness of the problem and the depth of their feelings.

Other concerns

There remain many other potential concerns for parents including financial problems, practical modifications needed in their homes, necessary equipment (e.g. hoists and wheelchairs) and transportation. They are also not immune to all the other crises or life events that afflict everyone, including bereavements, illness, accidents, and occupational redundancy. These all arise as subjects in the counselling situation. Most families develop strategies to cope like anyone else, but such difficulties are additional stresses that further stretch the families' resources in situations that are already difficult.

Professional behaviour

Ironically, a difficulty that parents frequently raise in counselling relates to the behaviour of professionals. Needless distress is caused by some professionals, varying from remarks that are as hurtful as those made by ignorant strangers (e.g. 'She's weird, isn't she?') to an automatic and unconscious manner that undermines and belittles the parent: 'The doctors were marvellous. They saved her life and I'm grateful. But, then they put me down. It wasn't anything obvious, just that they ignored my questions or acted as though I were stupid'.

The evidence for dissatisfaction with professional communication was cited earlier in the book. In a recent survey of 60 mothers of children with various disabilities, including cardiac problems, epilepsy, spinal dysfunction and learning difficulties, I found that none of them were completely satisfied with professional behaviour and only 30% were moderately satisfied. When asked how they wanted their doctors and others to behave, there was unanimous agreement. They wanted to be treated respectfully, as intelligent adults. They wanted the professional to listen to them, and acknowledge their expertise. They wanted a caring, not a patronising attitude. They requested knowledge and information to be shared with them in ways that would enable them to be in control and to make informed decisions. They wanted professionals to treat their children respectfully as individuals, and to consider their whole family. They valued honesty, encouragement and the time to communicate.

It was clear from these mothers that few of their requests were being met currently. Furneaux (1988) also found that, although there were examples of superb professional skill and care, 58 of the 64 couples who were informed of the diagnosis by medical personnel felt they had not been given help or proper information. The need for someone to talk to and listen to them was strongly felt in this survey and echoes the thoughts of many I see in clinical practice. Other studies have demonstrated that overall satisfaction with disclosure averages around only 50% or so (e.g. Cunningham and Sloper, 1977). That this can be done well and that dissatisfaction is not inevitable, as some would argue, is demonstrated by Cunningham, Morgan and McGucken (1984) who found a 100% satisfaction rate when the paediatrician used a model procedure to tell parents their children had Down's Syndrome. Such dissatisfaction is significant in itself, because poor communication is distressing, demeaning and unhelpful. It does nothing to ease the burden on families in general, nor provide them with the help they need.

Professional behaviour and parental adaptation

Poor professional communication is not only unsupportive, it may hinder parental adaptation (Woolley *et al.*, 1989). Since this is such an important point, some explanation is warranted. Currently parents are regarded as crucial to the education of their child and a partner with professionals in this endeavour (Cunningham, 1985). Whether they all want this, or whether it is just an additional burden is a subject of considerable debate (Turnbull and Turnbull, 1982). Nevertheless, parents do mediate all help, which cannot operate without their commitment. A mother who is desperately distressed by her child's disability, with difficulties in relating to her husband and with doubts about herself, it is unlikely to relate well to her child and will not be committed to imposed treatment regimes. This mother is also more likely to attract professional disrespect, which in itself will not help her.

Parent adaptation, therefore, is crucial and complex. It is not a matter of adjustment–maladjustment, but a natural and continuous process of making sense of events. Davis and Cunningham (1985) used personal construct theory to view the process as an exploration (albeit painful) to discover, test and build up a conceptual model (a construct sub-system) of the child and the disability, now and in the future. This allows the parents to understand and anticipate events and, therefore, to institute appropriate action as necessary. Getting information about the disability, seeing other children, talking to other parents, considering taking the child's life and questioning in many other ways are all part of this process.

However, this construct sub-system and the resulting understanding is affected fundamentally by the whole of the parents' construct system for anticipation of all aspects of their psychological world. This includes their partners, other children, wider family and friends, material circumstances and values. Most important, I would argue, is the set of beliefs parents hold about themselves. At a recent conference a mother (Krins, 1989) said, 'One day the verdict (i.e. diagnosis) cuts through the heart like a steel knife . . . All parents become sad and shocked . . . Their situation is untenable and they will therefore change, but they need to find their own self-confidence'.

These self or core constructs are central to the adaptation process, determining both direction and motivation. Parents' constructions of their own value, or self-esteem, and constructions of their own abilities, or self-efficacy to use Bandura's concept (1989), are fundamental aspects of behaviour. Parents who are confident in themselves and have realistic beliefs in their own abilities to manage are likely to work more effectively, and to be of more benefit directly and indirectly to both the child and their family as a whole.

These core constructs may be largely determined by the support provided by the social environment, as demonstrated by Dunst, Trivette and Cross (1986) who found significant relationships between social support, parental well-being, their behaviour towards their child and the child's adaptation. If these assumptions are correct, then disrespectful professional behaviour, which puts the parent into an inferior position will not be supportive or enhance parental self-esteem. On the contrary, it is likely to threaten self-esteem, particularly if the parent construes the professional as of a high status, prestigious, and expert and therefore an important source of help.

Many parents in this position, especially if well supported from other sources, quickly realise the inadequacies of those professionals who communicate poorly, and simply ignore them. Unfortunately, although this may afford protection for their own self-concept, it does deprive them of potential help. Luckily most families find for themselves people to support them properly, but it is sad to see how often the distance between professionals and parents is large, and to realise, therefore, how much professionals are contributing to their own inefficacy and hence the availability of help for families. For example, in a recent study we explicitly asked mothers to describe the most helpful professional they knew (we stressed the word professional). Ten of the 20 mothers interviewed described a member of the family or a friend!

EFFECTIVE HELP

It follows from what has been said that the basis of all help is counselling. Immense improvements in available help would be predicted if all professionals understood and used the process and· skills of counselling. This would involve adopting a partnership with parents and negotiating all actions and assumptions, as opposed to imposing them. The foundation of this would be to provide the circumstances in which parents could express themselves openly, where professionals give respect, listen actively, genuinely attempt to understand the world from the parents' perspective and do not immediately try to solve all the problems they present. The process is one of helping parents themselves to explore, clarify and possibly change their perspectives, so that they can decide their goals and determine the way to pursue them. These points are explored further by Cunningham and Davis (1985b).

Such an approach would reduce the complaints levelled at professional behaviour, since parents would be treated respectfully as they request. They would have someone with whom they could talk and would be able to address the issues that concerned them, not just those thought to be important by the helper, whether professional or voluntary. The provision of appropriate information would be facilitated, including the disclosure of the diagnosis, because the professional would gain a greater awareness of the knowledge and understanding already available to the parent. Parents would be supported and helped to confront and explore any or all of the concerns described earlier. They would therefore be in a better position to decide aims and plan action. Their ability to choose between various options would be increased, and they would be more able to adapt to circumstances in which solutions are not possible (e.g. the child's death or deterioration).

Parental involvement in the whole process would in itself facilitate their self-esteem and belief in their own efficacy, and would act as a coping mechanism. Respect given to them by the professional would also increase their self-respect and confidence, and any improvements in their situation would be at least partly attributable to their own, as opposed to the professional's expertise. Increases in self-esteem might not always occur, but certainly parents would not be undermined.

An example

A mother was referred to a psychologist for the developmental assessment of her 4-year-old son. The assessment was carried out, involving the mother at all stages including decisions about the child's competence. The results were then discussed fully with the mother who was so upset at the severity of her son's delay that a second session was arranged for the next day.

This session began with some reticence on the mother's part. She described her shock, but knew that the results were valid as she had been involved completely in the assessment process. She then cried and began to pour out her thoughts and feelings. She described how she had been trying to deny her son's delay, and the knowledge that he would die soon as a result of his medical problems. She cried while listing all the medical and surgical procedures that had been carried out on the child in the last four years. Many of these were purely investigative and had been of little value in retrospect. She described her child's resulting fear of doctors and his pleading and screaming. She discussed her fears of questioning the paediatrician, whom she saw as distant, uncaring, poor at communicating and not telling her everything she needed to know.

She discussed her desire to stop all treatment procedures unless they were clearly beneficial. She wanted to stop trying to prolong the child's life at all costs. She described her neglect of her other children and her husband's obsession with curing the disorder at all cost. She also hinted at other difficulties with her husband. Finally, with considerable shame she told how her oldest son had just been caught stealing at school and attributed this to emotional neglect.

She poured out concerns, one after another. She had not talked to anyone before, even though seemingly well supported by both family and professionals. Sharing her burdens in this way was in itself beneficial, but further exploration of each of the concerns enabled solutions to several problems. She arranged to see the paediatrician, openly shared her concerns and asked pre-prepared questions. She found she had misjudged him, since he immediately responded to her distress with open expression of his thoughts and feelings, and they agreed about what treatment would be allowed and what would not. She became more assertive, and made sure that her son spent much more time with the family at home and not in the hospital. She used the experience of disclosing her own feelings to understand her older son and was able to help him to talk and change. Her relationship with her husband improved, again because she was able to listen to him, 'like the counsellor listened to me'.

The major problem was not removed, in that the child deteriorated and eventually died. However, the five sessions with the counsellor were perceived by her as a turning point. She valued the interaction not for the information, techniques or direction they gave, but because, 'It made me value myself. I stopped relying totally on the experts and began to trust myself. I decided that I was capable of making decisions and could be as effective as anyone else'.

ORGANIZATIONAL IMPLICATIONS

Counselling is a prerequisite of all help from the point at which a problem is suspected. All families should have access to a skilled counsellor who should be available to them on as regular a basis as parents need. Consistency is important as the essence of support is getting to know, respect and trust the person who attempts to help. Changing over from one professional to another should be managed appropriately with warning and careful preparation.

The need for counselling does not necessarily imply the creation of a new profession. On the contrary, the size of the problem requires the help of all people working in the area of disability. The ideal system would be for all professionals to be trained in basic counselling and to expect to engage in a supportive and effective dialogue with all the families they see all the time. Such training can be done effectively and cheaply, as shown by Davis and Rushton (1989), and a training manual is available (Davis, Buchan and Clemerson, 1987). However, to ensure that families are given appropriate support, each professional should take on responsibility for liaising with a small group of families on a regular basis regardless of their specific needs. Once a good relationship has been established, it may be sufficient to meet the family once a month to once every six weeks. Each worker would take on a role akin to that of the 'key worker' or 'named person', but would have the proper skills to do so. Such a system could also be intimately related to systems of voluntary help, including parent-to-parent support schemes or self-help groups.

These developments necessitate changes in health care systems and policy. Explicit policy statements would have to specify skilled communication and psychological care as priorities. Job descriptions would have to include time to establish relationships with parents. Professional attitudes would have to change to view their specific areas of expertise within the context of the whole family. Organisational procedures would be required to ensure cooperation and coordination of the various services (health, education and social). Administration would be necessary to implement the scheme, to allocate families, make changes as necessary and monitor the system. There would have to be a supervisory system to provide support for all professionals working in this format. There would also have to be specialist counsellors to pick up problems beyond the capacity of the professionals trained in basic counselling support. Such specialists, would also have a responsibility for training, supervising and advising the service generally.

On theoretical grounds such a system would be beneficial, given the full range of professional resources and treatment and educational options. Empirically this system has been shown by the Parent Adviser Scheme (Davis, 1985; Buchan, Clemerson and Davis, 1988) to be successful in meeting the needs of families from widely varying socioeconomic and cultural backgrounds. This research (Davis and Rushton, 1991) is described in Chapter 18.

CONCLUSIONS

From available evidence, the plethora of concerns described by families of children with severe disabilities are not well addressed by present service systems. This is largely because the focus of most professional work is on the child or part of the child and not on the family as a whole. Even where the intention is appropriate, very few professionals have either the time and, more important, the education to add the dimension of skilled counselling that is a prerequisite of all help from the moment a problem is suspected in the child. Such skills are essential in aiding parents to come to terms with the situation confronting them, to address effectively specific issues related to the child, their personal feelings, family situation and wider circumstances. These skills are also important in facilitating the strength, resources, independence and skills of parents themselves by reinforcing, or at least not undermining, their beliefs in themselves.

ACKNOWLEDGEMENTS

I am indebted to Dr Cliff Cunningham, Ms Caroline Philps and Ms Philippa Russell for reading and commenting upon a draft of this chapter.

USEFUL ADDRESSES

Contact a Family,
16 Strutton Ground,
London SW1P 2UP
Tel: 071-222 2695

Down's Syndrome Association,
153–155 Mitcham Road,
London SW17 9PG
Tel: 081-682 4001

Mencap,
117–123 Golden Lane,
London EC1Y ORT
Tel: 071-253 9433

Spastic Society,
12 Park Crescent,
London W1N 4EQ
Tel: 071-636 5020

REFERENCES

Bandura, A. (1989). Perceived self-efficacy in the exercise of personal agency. *The Psychologist*, **12**, 411–424.

Bone, M. and Meltzer, H. (1989). *The prevalence of disability: OPCS surveys of disability in Great Britain*. London: HMSO.

Buchan, L., Clemerson, J., and Davis, H. (1988). Working with families of children with special needs: the Parent Adviser Scheme. *Child: Care, Health & Development*, **14**, 81–91.

Byrne, E., Cunningham, C., and Sloper, P. (1988). *Families and their children with Down's Syndrome: One feature in common*. London: Croom Helm.

Cunningham, C. (1985). Training and education approaches for parents of children with special needs. In H. Davis and P. Butcher (Eds), *Sharing psychological skills: training non-psychologists in the use of psychological techniques*. Leicester: British Psychological Society.

Cunningham, C. and Davis, H. (1985a). Early parent counselling. In M. Craft, J. Bicknell and S. Hollins (Eds), *Mental handicap*. London: Bailliere-Tindall.

Cunningham, C. and Davis, H. (1985b). *Working with parents: Framework for collaboration*. Milton Keynes: Open University Press.

Cunningham, C. and Sloper, P. (1977). Parents of Down's syndrome babies: their early needs. *Child: Care Health & Development*, **3**, 325–347.

Cunningham, C., Morgan, P. and McGucken, R. (1984). Down's Syndrome: Is dissatisfaction with disclosure of diagnosis inevitable? *Developmental Medicine and Child Neurology*, **26**, 33–39.

Davis, H. (1985). Counselling parents of children who have intellectual disabilities. *Early Child Development and Care*, **22**, 19–35.

Davis, H., Buchan, L., and Clemerson, J. (1987). *The Parent Adviser Scheme: Manual for training counsellors to work with families of children with special needs*. London: LHMC.

Davis, H. and Cunningham, C. (1985). Mental Handicap: people in context. In E. Button (Ed.), *Personal construct theory & mental health*. London: Croom Helm.

Davis, H. and Rushton, R. (1989). An evaluation of basic counselling training. *Counselling*, **68**, 1–8.

Davis, H. and Rushton, R. (1991). Counselling and supporting parents of children with developmental delay: a research evaluation. *Journal of Mental Deficiency Research*, **35**, 000–000.

Davis, H., Stroud, A., and Green, L. (1988). Maternal language environment of children with intellectual impairment. *American Journal of Mental Retardation*, **93**, 144–153.

Diamond, S. (1981). Growing up with parents of a handicapped child: a handicapped person's perspective. In J. Paul (Ed.), *Understanding and working with parents of children with special needs*. New York: Holt, Rinehart & Winston.

Dunst, C., Trivette, C., and Cross, A. (1986). Mediating influences of social support: personal, family and child outcomes. *American Journal of Mental Deficiency*, **90**, 403–417.

Furneaux, B. (1988). *Special parents*. Milton Keynes: Open University Press.

Green, J. and Evans, R. (1984). Honeyland's role in the pre-school years: II Patterns of use; and III Factors inhibiting use. *Child: Care, Health and Development*, **10**, 81–98.

Krins, A–M. (1989). *The role of the parents*. A paper presented at the Second European Conference of the International League of Societies for Persons with Mental Handicap, Brussels.

Lewis, V. (1987). *Development & handicap*. Oxford: Blackwell.

MacKeith, R. (1973). The feelings and behaviour of parents of handicapped children. *Developmental Medicine and Child Neurology*, **15**, 24–27.

Palmer, F. *et al.* (1988). The effects of physical therapy on cerebral palsy. *New England Journal of Medicine*, **318**, 803–808.

Scotson, L. (1985). *Doran: Child of courage*. London: Collins.

Turnbull, A. and Turnbull, H. (1982). Parent involvement in the education of handicapped children: a critique. *Mental Retardation*, **20**, 115–122.

Underwood, P., Owen, A., and Winkler, R. (1986). Replacing the clockwork model of medicine. *Community Health Studies*, **10**, 275–283.

Warnock, M. (1978). *Special educational needs: Report of the committee of enquiry into the education of handicapped children and young people*. London: HMSO.

Woolley, H., Stein, A., Forrest, G., and Baum, J. (1989). Imparting the diagnosis of life threatening illness in children. *British Medical Journal*, **298**, 1623–1626.

15 Paediatrics

JACK A. CADRANEL
Department of Clinical Psychology, St James's University Hospital, Beckett Street, Leeds LS9 7TF

Counselling, a process which facilitates normal coping and adaptation, is an integral part of the practice of paediatrics, indeed of medicine in general. After all, people do not usually consult their doctors when they are feeling well. They seek help from doctors when they have problems and are worried about what is happening to them. In paediatrics the situation is more complicated. Problems are often defined and described by someone who is not the identified patient, usually by the child's parent. Children are dependent on families which exert powerful influences on them and which, in turn, are influenced by them. They are constantly changing and developing. At times only their behaviour will give clues to how they are feeling or what they are thinking. Each family member's perspective must be taken into account alongside physical and social factors in coming to an understanding of the problem. The paediatrician has to communicate that understanding to the child and family in appropriate ways, providing enough structure and support to enable them to consider possible courses of action.

CHRONIC AND LIFE-THREATENING ILLNESS

This process is at its clearest and most important in work with children with chronic and life-threatening disorders. The possibility of the death of a child is extremely frightening. The uncertainty makes it so difficult for a family to mobilize its resources.

Childhood cancer, cystic fibrosis and end-stage renal failure were, until the past few decades, fatal disorders of childhood. For the majority of children suffering from them care was, at best, palliative. Medical advances now enable many of these children to survive into adulthood. This success, achieved by the use of aggressive and technological treatment regimes, has given rise to new problems. The quality of cure is being examined. Hammond (1986) discussing improvements in the survival of childhood cancer patients points out that one component of cure '. . . connotes the restoration of health, including physical, developmental, functional and psychological.

Counselling and Communication in Health Care. Edited by H. Davis and L. Fallowfield
© 1991 John Wiley & Sons Ltd

In achieving this kind of cure we fail often. Perhaps we have not yet achieved that kind of cure for the majority of patients.' Reinhart (1970), in a different field, had anticipated the problem. 'Progress of dialysis and renal transplantation for children should be carefully evaluated in terms not of gross survival but in parameters of meaningful growth and development—living.'

The lesson has been learned. In all these fields treatment regimes are being evaluated not only in terms of survival rates but also of quality of survival. Increasing emphasis is also being placed on providing psychosocial care to facilitate adaptation and adjustment to disease and its treatment.

Cancer

Cancer affects one in 600 children. Until the 1960s the vast majority of these children died. Today 60% of newly diagnosed childhood cancer patients can expect to attain long-term survival. One in six of these survivors will have some degree of handicap or disability. The therapeutic regimes can be prolonged (up to two years) and may involve surgery, radiotherapy and multidrug cytotoxic chemotherapy. Painful medical procedures such as bone marrow aspirations, lumbar punctures, injections and blood tests are regular accompaniments to treatment. The possibility of relapse or of metastatic disease is a lasting source of anxiety. Common side-effects of chemotherapy and radiotherapy include nausea, vomiting and hair loss. Although these are transient and have little significance for the physical health of the children, they are distressing and hamper their adaptation to treatment and reintegration into school and social life. Hair loss particularly is a visible sign of a child's loss of health. One sixteen-year-old said:

Losing my hair was a hard thing to put up with. I looked at myself and thought 'Wow! there is something' and everyone else looked at me and said 'Yes, there is something seriously wrong with him.'

Repeated hospital admission for treatment of the disease, or of infections, which may themselves be severe or fatal in immunocompromised children, disrupt family and peer relationships.

Some unwanted effects are longer lasting. Surgery, for example, may result in disfigurement or some degree of disability. Some effects do not become apparent until long after the treatment has taken place. Impairment of intellect following cranial irradiation in young children, and impairment of growth and endocrine function are examples of these.

Cystic fibrosis

Cystic fibrosis affects approximately one in 2000 children. It is the most common fatal inherited disorder in childhood. It was not recognized until

1939. In 1972 few patients with cystic fibrosis lived to adolescence. By 1981 50% were living into their 20s and 25–35% to age 30 (Matthews and Drotar, 1984). The disease results in a thickening of the mucus throughout the body. The major effects are on the lungs and the digestive system. The smaller bronchial tubes tend to become blocked with thick, sticky mucus, impairing breathing and forming a ready site for lung infections. The children wheeze and cough and have difficulty in keeping up in games which involve running or climbing. Mucus also blocks the ducts from the pancreas so that enzymes needed to digest fats and starch do not reach the gut. Untreated the children fail to thrive and excrete foul, smelly stools. Treatment must begin early in life and involves three major components. A high protein diet and the taking of pancreatic enzymes during meals aids digestion and promotes growth. High doses of antibiotics prevent or treat lung infections. Breathing exercises and physiotherapy to the chest two or three times daily help to keep the lungs as clear of mucus as possible. There is no cure for cystic fibrosis. Treatment is for life and is a constant battle against a potentially declining picture. Good compliance with treatment is important to maintain optimum health. It can be difficult for children to keep up their motivation when they can see no improvement in their condition. Special problems for parents are the guilt that surrounds an inherited disease and the knowledge that further children have about a one in four chance of being affected.

End-stage renal failure

Until the development of haemodialysis only conservative treatment was available for children in end-stage renal failure. Kidney transplant is the ultimate goal for these children but not all grafted kidneys survive. Haemodialysis is time-consuming and restricting. It involves the child's blood-supply being connected to a kidney machine so that over a period of time waste products can be removed by an artificial kidney. If the family home is suitable or can be adapted or extended a kidney machine can be installed there and dialysis can take place overnight. If not the child must travel to hospital for treatment three times a week missing out on school and social activities.

Where haemodialysis takes place at home parents and children need the skill and the confidence to maintain the machine and to insert needles into the child's shunt or fistula in order to connect the blood supply to the machine. Continuous ambulatory peritoneal dialysis (CAPD) is an alternative to haemodialysis and uses the peritoneum as an artificial kidney. There is less equipment to maintain, less restriction on the child but an increased risk of infection. Dialysis regimes, especially haemodialysis, impose restrictions on fluid intake (for some as little as 500 ml per day) and restrictions on foods which are rich in sodium, potassium and proteins. This affects a range of foods of which children are particularly fond, e.g. snack foods, 'fast foods' and chocolate. Most children cheat at some time.

Kidney disease delays growth and sexual maturation of the children. Most children are chronically anaemic and lack stamina. All these factors affect the child's view of themselves and particularly their body image. Whilst other children are growing larger, stronger and more capable, they remain small, somehow incomplete and dependent on technology for a basic bodily function.

SOME COMMON THEMES

Although each of these disorders is different there are common threads which run through the experience of children and families faced by any one of them. Many aspects of the experience of chronic illnesses are determined not so much by the particular disease as by developmental, family and social issues.

PARENTS

Accepting the diagnosis

There is no easy way for parents to learn that their child is seriously ill. A diagnosis of life-threatening illness shatters the dreams and plans they had for themselves and for their child. Suddenly their world is bleak and uncertain. Their sense of shock and numbness is much like the experience of bereavement, of mourning for the healthy child they had known or hoped for. Denial, anger and guilt, and despair in varying degrees may all play a part in this initial period of adjustment.

For some parents diagnosis will come as confirmation of fears they have harboured for some time. They may have taken their child to the doctor only to be told that they were over-anxious. For some of these parents the comparative certainty of a diagnosis brings a degree of relief. It can precipitate others into disabling guilt and despair. Those who feel in some way responsible for their child's illness or for the delay in diagnosis are particularly vulnerable.

Margaret knew that there was something wrong with her twin daughters almost as soon as they were born. She took them repeatedly to her family doctor and to paediatricians over a period of three years. During that time she was described as neurotic and even admitted to a psychiatric hospital for treatment of 'her illness'. Eventually the girls were diagnosed with a rare metabolic disorder. They died when they were eight years old.

Elizabeth was 12. For two years her lethargy and lack of growth had worried her parents. They read an article about kidney disease in a magazine and showed it to the family doctor. They were told not to worry, that it was normal for young teenagers to be listless. When Elizabeth's poor growth could no longer be ignored she was referred to a paediatrician who diagnosed renal failure. She was quickly admitted for haemodialysis to be started in hospital. Her father was overwhelmed by guilt and despair. He became severely depressed and had to be admitted to a psychiatric hospital.

In time most families reach a sort of equilibrium, a degree of acceptance which enables them to function again. Even then it can be difficult to cope with any but the most immediate concerns. One father of a three-year-old recently diagnosed with leukaemia said: 'I'm all right today. Don't ask me about tomorrow. All I can say is that he's all right today so I'm all right today'.

With increasing acceptance comes a need for more information about the child's illness and its treatment. Information may have to be given over a period of time and more than once. Much of it will scarcely have been heard or absorbed during the early stages of shock.

Uncertainty

The most difficult part of adapting to life-threatening illness is coping with the uncertainty which inevitably accompanies it. Initially it is all-encompassing. It is never lost completely but it can be contained by familiarity with the illness and its treatment routines. As far as possible parents need to know what to expect. Even short-term treatment plans can help to bring some order out of the chaos and enable them to function. They need time to adjust to what is happening and a foundation on which to build the next phase of care.

The information parents are given must be honest and consistent. They will seek confirmation from other members of the team, from their own observations of their child and of others, from family and friends, from pamphlets and books. They have to be able to trust the staff who are caring for their child. They need to know that their questions will be answered and their concerns taken seriously.

Helplessness and a sense of loss of the ability to care properly for their child are common experiences of parents. One of the best aspects of current paediatric practice is the extent to which parents are seen as partners in the care of sick children. Taking control is the best antidote to helplessness, loss of hopes and unpredictability (Johnson, 1984). This is not an easy path. Burton (1975) quotes the mother of a child with cystic fibrosis.

Sometimes I get wearied out looking after him, but I would want to be caring for him myself. It would be a lot harder for me if I wasn't caring for him. I would worry too. I just love him and like doing things for him.

Balancing the needs of the family

Illness takes its toll on all aspects of family life. Specialized treatment centres are often far from home. It takes time and a great deal of organization to attend out-patient clinics or to visit or stay with a child during hospital admissions. One or both parents may lose time at work or have to give up employment to care for the sick child or to look after other children in the family. There is increased financial pressure and a loss of the time that is necessary to maintain family activities and relationships. The disease can become an overwhelming preoccupation to the detriment of all else in family life.

The parents concur that the most difficult task they face is walking the narrow line between the amount of time spent focusing on the disease and its treatment, and the amount of time spent on one's spouse and other children, on the continuation of life and living (Spinetta and Deasy-Spinetta, 1986).

Brothers and sisters of the patient are potential casualties of these changes in the pattern of family life. With attention focused on the sick child it is easy for them to feel jealous and neglected. Sourkes (1980) points out that siblings may feel frightened of developing the same disease as the patient, or guilty that they escaped the disease, or shame at having a child in the family who is ill, disfigured or dying. Balancing the needs of sick and healthy children is a formidable task for parents whose resources are already stretched.

If parents are to rise to this challenge they must also look after themselves. Those who adapt best are able to communicate openly with each other, especially about the illness, share responsibility for caring for the child and have broadly similar coping styles. They are often strengthened by willing support from outside the family (Burton, 1975).

CHILDREN

Understanding what is happening

. . . there is an appropriate version of any skill or knowledge that may be imparted at whatever age one wishes to begin teaching—however preparatory the version may be (Bruner, 1965).

Bruner was writing about schools and education but his statement is no less true of illness, especially the child's illness. Parents and professionals may worry about how a child will cope with distressing news. As important a question is how that child will cope with the absence of news when the situation is already distressing. Children are acutely aware of the situation around them. They can sense when their parents are tense and anxious. When they are being subjected to unfamiliar procedures in strange surroundings, all but the youngest children need information to understand what is happening to them and to make sense of their feelings. Their phantasies about what is happening may be as distressing to them as the reality.

Developmental issues

Age and developmental stage influence the impact of serious disease on children in at least two important ways. Eiser (1985) has reviewed the development of children's ideas about illness. Young children understand illness in terms which are concrete, global and magical. They often give explanations of illness which involve contagion. A significant number seem to believe that illness is in some way a punishment for bad behaviour. Older children understand that illness means that some part of their body is not working properly. Adolescents are able to appreciate that illness results from an interaction of factors inside and outside the body. Even their understanding is constrained by their limited knowledge of the structure and function of their bodies.

Serious illness disrupts development. The developmental tasks appropriate to the age of the child are most vulnerable to this disruption. Pre-school children are busy gaining increasing mastery over their own bodies and their environment. They are becoming increasingly independent and beginning to socialize outside the family as well as learning about roles within the family. Repeated admissions to hospital, malaise and lack of stamina, increased dependence on staff and parents and the restrictions imposed by treatment pose a threat to much of this.

For ten or more years of their lives school is the major social and educational setting for children. Most sick children miss significant amounts of schooling. They fall behind in their work and catching up becomes an added burden to them. They are often separated from their friends. Many find it hard to keep up in games or activities which require physical fitness or stamina. They stand out from their peers at a time when being just like everyone else is important.

Adolescence

Adolescence is a period of great change, of intense activity and keenly felt emotions. Its developmental tasks are a challenge even for healthy young people. They include adapting to physical maturity, developing identity and an adult sexual role, establishing independence and planning for the future. Serious illness forces adolescents to become emotionally and physically dependent on their parents and hospital staff. It cuts them off from their peer group and restricts their activities. Planning becomes difficult when faced with an uncertain future. Cancer, cystic fibrosis and renal failure each have an effect on the development of body image. All bring a sense of

imperfection. Renal failure, for example, impairs growth and sexual maturation and involves the loss of the basic bodily function of passing urine. Even
successful kidney transplantation can bring its own problems. One successful transplant patient expressed fears that she was no longer the same person she had been before the operation. She worried that she would begin to
take on the characteristics of her donor.

Despite all this, most adolescents have the resilience to cope with their
disease remarkably well. Those who have difficulty in adjusting to it often
give rise to great anxiety amongst their families and the staff who care for
them.

> Sarah was 13 when she joined a hospital dialysis programme. She loved sports and
> had many friends. Her mother always accompanied her to hospital and they kept
> themselves to themselves. At first she seemed to cope well with her treatment. After
> three months her health began to deteriorate. She was often overloaded with fluid
> and the staff became suspicious that she was drinking far more than her allowance.
> This was hotly denied by Sarah and her mother who insisted that the tests must be
> wrong. As her condition deteriorated her family and the hospital staff became in-
> creasingly worried. In a meeting with her parents Sarah's difficulties in coming to
> terms with her illness became clear. She had only attended a few days of school since
> she had begun dialysis. She had withdrawn from contact with her friends. If they
> called to see her, she would beg her parents not to let them in or curl up silently in a
> corner and wait for them to go. She had only once cried and talked about her illness.
> She had told her parents that she had spoiled the family's life by becoming ill. She
> had lost hope of ever being fit and happy as she had been before her illness.

Living with treatment

Most common children's illnesses resolve quickly with treatment. Chronic
illnesses require long-term treatment which may not produce immediate
benefits, which may mainly be designed to prevent further deterioration and
which may have unpleasant side-effects (Varni and Wallander, 1984). It is
small wonder that for many children the treatment seems worse than the
disease. Young children especially find it bewildering that they can go into
hospital feeling comparatively well 'to be made better' and be made to feel
worse by their treatment. Lansdown (1980) quotes a five year old child,
'Hospital is a place where they snatch you up and hurt you'.

Painful medical procedures, cytotoxic chemotherapy and radiotherapy
which produce nausea, vomiting and hair loss, malaise and headache following dialysis, the constant grind of physiotherapy for children with cystic
fibrosis all contribute to the unpleasantness of living with chronic disease.

Coping with the attitude of others

Life-threatening disease is fortunately rare. One consequence of this is that,
whilst the child and immediate family become more familiar with the

disease, for others it can remain a frightening mystery. The wider family, friends and the community may offer invaluable support, but often their attitudes impose a further burden on the child and family and increase their sense of isolation and difference from the rest of the world. Grandparents may shower the child with expensive presents. Teachers may reduce their expectations of the child and become excessively protective. Friends may find it so difficult to talk about the illness that they avoid the family altogether. Others may be overwhelmed by pity.

David, looking back on his experience of cancer treatment, said: 'You learned pretty quickly who your friends were. People who you thought were your friends, it turned out that they weren't because they didn't want anything to do with you. That was a hard thing to put up with'.

One mother of a sick child encountered radically differing attitudes. 'I didn't like to go out with him. People would cross over the road to avoid meeting us. I couldn't stand that. I would stay in when I could. Some people would call at the house. I opened the door one day. There was a woman on the doorstep holding a bunch of flowers with tears streaming down her face. She just gave them to me and ran down the path'.

Another said: 'There's almost no-one I can talk to about her. Sometimes I get so cross with her I want to hit her. But you can't say that to people. They think "How can you feel that when she's so ill?" I met a mother on the ward. She had a girl with a brain tumour. We could talk. We could tell each other just how we felt.'

Religious belief

Many families struggle with religious belief at times of crisis. Some lose their faith. They find it hard to understand how a merciful God could inflict such illness on their child. Many wonder why they have been singled out to be tested or punished in this way. Some turn to religion for the comfort and support which faith and a religious community offer. This can be a source of great strength but occasionally the attitudes of religious advisors can be bewilderingly harsh or unrealistic. One mother, coming to terms with the imminent death of her adopted son, received letters from two church ministers. One reminded her of the power of prayer and begged her not to give up hope for her son's life. The other admonished her for collaborating with the doctors in treatment and 'opposing God's will'.

APPROACHES TO COUNSELLING

Some basic themes

Counselling and the psychosocial care of sick children and their families draw on a wide range of approaches but are based on some common foundations.

The family is the unit of care. The child and family are intimately bound together; what happens to one member of the family reverberates through the family system and ultimately affects the child's response to treatment.

Every family will make its own adaptation to living with illness. This will reflect relationships within the family, its history and culture. What works for one family may not work for another. An important aim of counselling is to enable families to identify and mobilize their own coping mechanisms. It takes time for them to do this and to adapt to changes during the course of the disease.

Effective coping does not imply the absence of personal pain and distress. These are normal and inevitable consequences of living with life-threatening disease. Accepting these feelings is part of the process of adaptation.

Cure is not the only measure of successful care. It is an unattainable goal in the care of some children. Good quality care is an attainable goal even when it has been accepted that a child will die.

The whole team is involved

The care of children with life-threatening disease requires the combined skills of a multidisciplinary team. Every member of the team plays a part in the psychosocial care of the children and their families, though some will have more clearly labelled psychosocial roles than others. Every contact with the team from the initial consultation and diagnosis through treatment to discharge and follow-up or terminal care is loaded with significance for each child and family. Difficult questions, angry outbursts or overwhelming anxieties must be responded to when they occur by the person on the spot.

Key workers

Ideally each family will be introduced to one key worker offering explicit psychosocial support as soon as possible after diagnosis (Lansdown and Goldman, 1988). This will often be a social worker or a liaison nurse who can offer continuous care from diagnosis, through treatment to discharge or terminal care and beyond. They act as guides and supports during the crisis surrounding diagnosis and at other major turning points in the care of the child. They clarify misconceptions about illness or treatment and interpret medical information. They help families to explore their feelings and emotions and to recognize and foster effective coping. They offer all-important practical help and support. They may liaise with agencies in the family's community. They interpret family functioning to other members of the clinical team and may act as advocates for the family.

Helping children understand

Helping children accommodate to the hospital setting and to anticipate and understand what is happening to them may take many forms. Most centres make it possible for parents to stay with their children in hospital. The security of having a parent nearby makes an enormous difference to an anxious child. It also affords the parents the opportunity to meet other families facing similar problems. Often this is a source of great support, and networks of families are established through which they keep in touch.

Play, for the child who feels well enough, can be a necessary refuge from the concerns of illness. It is also a medium through which children may be prepared for medical procedures by rehearsing them with teddy bears and toy equipment. Sometimes children will use play to come to terms with experiences that have been frightening or baffling. Re-living the experience, sometimes over and over again, enables children to come to their own understanding of what has happened.

Reducing the stress of side-effects

Painful procedures and unpleasant side-effects commonly accompany the treatment of these life-threatening diseases. A range of approaches has been developed to reduce pain and procedural distress. Jay *et al.* (1984) for example, developed a cognitive-behaviour therapy treatment package to reduce distress in children undergoing bone marrow aspirations. The package included stress-inoculation training, distraction, relaxation, altering attributions, emotive imagery and rehearsal/practice. Hypnosis and attention-distraction have both been shown to reduce anticipatory and post-chemotherapy nausea and vomiting in children with cancer (LeBaron, Zeltzer and Zeltzer, 1983). What many of these approaches have in common is that they place new skills and increased control in the hands of the child.

All these are adjuncts to talking with children, not substitutes for it. Children need the reassurance of understandable information from their parents and professional carers and the opportunity to ask questions even if they don't take advantage of it.

Communication with the community

Lansdown (1980) writes: 'As a general rule of thumb, the more an observer knows about a condition, the less likely he is to come out with an insensitive comment. The more we know, the less we fear and the more we can see through to the normal bits of the person underneath'.

More than anyone else a child with a chronic or life-threatening disease needs to be able to develop those 'normal bits of the person'. Ignorance or fear amongst school-teachers, family doctors and the wider family can be cruelly inhibiting of that development. Time spent explaining to them the nature of the disease, its implications, what they can expect and what they should not expect is time well spent in the child's interests.

When children die

No piece of writing about children with life-threatening diseases can omit a mention of death. A proper treatment of it would require a chapter or book of its own. What it is possible to say here is that the death of a child does not mark the failure of the team to provide proper care, nor does it signal the end of the team's duty of care to the family. Such care would include, minimally, the opportunity for the parents to visit the hospital a few weeks after the child's death to discuss any doubts or anger or fears they may have about how their child died. These visits have other roles. If serious illness is isolating, the loss of a child is doubly so. Ideally families would be offered bereavement counselling and continuing visits or contacts with a familiar member of the team. These contacts may be especially appreciated at times of the year which evoke emotionally loaded memories, such as the child's birthday or the anniversary of the child's death.

Caring for the carers

Caring for children with life-threatening disease is stressful for professional staff. It is always distressing when a child dies. For the staff it may arouse feelings of failure and guilt, or anger, or overwhelming sadness at the loss of a familiar and much loved young patient. Nurses offer such personal care to the children that they are specially vulnerable to these feelings. The vulnerability of doctors is rather different. It arises because, traditionally, they are not supposed to display such emotions. If burnout is to be avoided there must be care of the carers (Maslach, 1982). The basis of this sort of care lies in the atmosphere of the team itself. Acceptance of grief, anger and exhaustion amongst the team and the opportunity to discuss these feelings are the foundations of mutual support.

REFERENCES

Bruner, J.S. (1965). Education as social invention. *Journal of Social Issues*, **20**, 21–33.
Burton, L. (1975). *The family life of sick children*. London: Routledge and Kegan Paul.
Eiser, C. (1985). *The psychology of childhood illness*. New York: Springer-Verlag.
Hammond, G.D. (1986). The cure of childhood cancers. *Cancer*, **58**, 2, 407–413.
Jay, S.M., Elliott, C.H., Katz, E.R., and Siegal, S.E. (1984). *Stress reduction in children undergoing painful medical procedures*. Paper Presented at the Annual Meeting of the American Psychological Association, Washington D.C.

Johnson, R.S. (1984). The role of the social worker in the management of the child with E.S.R.D. In R.N. Fine and A.B. Gruskin (Eds), *End-stage renal disease in children*, pp. 560–573. Philadelphia: Saunders.

Lansdown, R. (1980). *More than sympathy*. London: Tavistock.

Lansdown, R. and Goldman, A. (1988). The psychological care of children with malignant disease. *Journal of Child Psychology and Psychiatry*, **29**, 5, 555–567.

LeBaron, S., Zeltzer, L., and Zeltzer, P.M. (1983). *The effectiveness of behavioural intervention for reducing nausea and vomiting in children and adolescents receiving chemotherapy*. Abstracts of the 25th Annual Conference of the International Society of Paediatric Oncology, York, U.K.

Maslach, C. (1982). *Burnout, the cost of caring*. Englewood Cliffs, N.J.: Prentice Hall.

Matthews, L.W. and Drotar, D. (1984). Cystic fibrosis: a challenging long-term chronic disease. *Pediatric Clinics of North America*, **31**, 133–152.

Reinhart, J.B. (1970). The doctor's dilemma. *Journal of Pediatrics*, **75**, 505.

Sourkes, B.M. (1980). Siblings of the pediatric cancer patient. In J. Kellerman (Ed.), *Psychological aspects of childhood cancer*, pp. 47–69. Springfield: Thomas.

Spinetta, J.J. and Deasy-Spinetta, P. (1986). The patient's socialization in the community and school during therapy. *Cancer*, **58**, 512–515.

Varni, J.W. and Wallander, J.L. (1984). Adherence to health-related regimens in pediatric chronic disorders. *Clinical Psychology Review*, **4**, 585–596.

16 Counselling Patients with Cancer

LESLEY FALLOWFIELD

Academic Unit of Psychology, The London Hospital Medical College, Turner Street, London E1 2AD

The fact that you've got the dreaded big C, that you've got to have an operation, wear a bag and you might die anyway, that's not the worst of it you know. It's being treated like a changed person and not being able to talk about it. Everyone sort of clammed up or they were so overly nice it drove me crazy. I just wanted to be me; to cry about it; be angry about it; say how scared I was, and sometimes even be brave about it, but no one wanted to listen. They all just wanted me to be a good patient. I had to listen to them talking about how lucky I'd been, that they'd caught it early, what a good surgeon Mr. X was and don't forget all those endless conversations about the bloody weather or my nice flowers and cards when they changed the dressing. Did they really think that could make you feel better about it all? Then everyone who visited did the same sort of thing—this great big game of pretence. I just wanted someone to ask me how I felt, I didn't want to play let's pretend this nasty thing hasn't happened. It had and it was real for the rest of my life and no one could help. I've never felt so alone.

Almost a quarter of a million new cases of cancer are registered in the UK each year and in 1986 nearly 160 000 people died of the disease. It has been estimated on the basis of current incidence rates that one in every three people will develop cancer at some time in their life. Despite the fact that heart disease is responsible for more deaths each year in this country than any other illness, few diseases are regarded with as much universal dread as cancer. Most lay populations consistently overestimate the mortality from cancer. Wyler, Masuda and Homes (1968) asked subjects to rate the seriousness of 126 different diseases and found that cancer came top of the list. In another study by Jenkins (1966), subjects consistently rated cancer as the most prevalent disease, responsible for most deaths and associated with the most pain. It is not surprising therefore that some writers have described the reactions of people receiving a diagnosis of cancer as tantamount to receiving a death sentence. (McIntosh, 1974). One of the reasons why cancer is regarded with so much fear is due to it being such an enigmatic disease; the aetiology and biology of most of the common cancers are still poorly understood, consequently people harbour some apparently irrational notions about causal factors, all of which may have unpleasant implications for the unfortunate victim. For example, many people believe that cancer is

Counselling and Communication in Health Care. Edited by H. Davis and L. Fallowfield
© 1991 John Wiley & Sons Ltd

contagious, thus they may avoid contact with a sufferer at precisely the time that the love and support of friends and family is so vital for a sense of well-being. (Fallowfield, 1988; Peters-Golden, 1982). Most of us have an implicit faith in a 'just world', hence the victims of cancer may feel blamed for having 'caused' their own illness (Lerner and Miller, 1978). Although this is seen most often in those cancers where a direct causal link between behaviour and the disease has been established (e.g. smoking and lung cancer), this feeling of responsibility can occur in individuals with cancer of almost any site. For example, it is not uncommon for patients with cancer to feel that the disease is their punishment for real or imagined improprieties. The publicity given to the small link between early sexual experience and cervical cancer provides a good illustration. Revelations such as these impose a further burden, that of guilt, to the plethora of other emotional difficulties with which sufferers must cope.

The primary problems that patients with cancer experience can be discussed most easily under two main headings: those problems provoked by the knowledge that one has a potentially life-threatening disease, and the problems associated with the unpleasant treatments which must be endured. These knowledge related and treatment related difficulties are summarised in Table 16.1.

Most patients with cancer experience periods of anxiety, depression, helplessness, sexual dysfunction, relationship difficulties and cognitive impairments at some time during the course of their illness. Fortunately many of these difficulties are overcome as patients learn how to adjust and cope with the fact of their disease. However for a significant minority these psychosocial problems remain severe and are unremitting without help. Derogatis *et al.* (1983) used a standardised psychiatric interview with 215 newly diagnosed patients admitted to hospital with cancer. They found 44% of the sample to be suffering from adjustment disorders with depression and/or anxiety as a central feature. In another study reported by Bukberg, Penman and Holland (1984), 62 patients were interviewed and of these 24% were rated as severely depressed, 18% moderately depressed and 14% mildly depressed. A study of 97 patients with advanced cancer of various types reported by Plumb and Holland (1977) showed that 23% of patients were either moderately or severely depressed and according to the Beck Depression Inventory.

Despite the large volume of research work demonstrating the psychosocial trauma provoked by cancer and its treatment, clinicians are not very good at recognising symptoms of psychiatric morbidity (Maguire, 1985). Even those who do find evidence of anxiety and depression may fail to treat the problem appropriately or be reluctant to refer the patient on to a psychiatrist or psychologist on the grounds that such reactions are only normal. The attitude that prolonged psychological distress is 'normal' in cancer and does not therefore merit treatment, is as illogical as stating that as pain is a

Table 16.1. Problems experienced by patients with cancer

---

1. Knowledge of the diagnosis
   - inadequacy of information
   - uncertainty about prognosis
   - guilt about causality
   - stigma of cancer
   - fear of a painful and undignified death
   - worries about reaction of family and friends.

2. Treatment side effects

   - *Surgery* is often mutilating and can cause:

     body image problems
     loss of physical function
     loss of sexual function.

   - *Radiotherapy* can cause:

     nausea and vomiting
     lethargy
     skin irritation
     anxiety and depression

   - *Chemotherapy* can cause:
     (Hormonal or Cytotoxic)

     nausea and vomiting
     alopecia
     mouth ulcers

     leucopenia
     cardiotoxicity
     hirsutism or feminisation
     hot flushes

---

normal reaction postoperatively in cancer then analgesia should be withheld!

Sometimes doctors fail to pick up the psychosocial morbidity because they lack the skills necessary for effective communication with their patients. Others may use distancing tactics as a means of avoiding too much involvement with their patients' distress which might otherwise compromise the doctor's own emotional survival (Maguire, 1989). Some doctors deliberately evade discussion about psychological issues on the grounds that such problems are not part of their responsibility. Whatever the reason for this evasion and avoidance, patients are quick to realise that physical complaints receive attention and that references to their psychological problems are largely ignored. Unless patients are given permission to talk about their concerns their needs go unrecognised and unmet. It is clear that properly trained oncology counsellors have a vital role to play in the care of people with cancer provided that clinicians acknowledge their importance as part of the team and give them the appropriate resources and support needed to help patients most effectively.

WHAT ARE THE COUNSELLING NEEDS OF PATIENTS WITH CANCER?

Inadequacy of information

Top of the list of potential problems experienced by patients shown in Table 16.1 is 'inadequacy of information' and this is probably one of the most frequent complaints that patients make of their doctors whatever the medical specialty in question. Although the numbers of doctors who deliberately withhold the diagnoses of cancer have declined over the past decade, there is plenty of evidence to suggest that many patients with cancer in this country feel inadequately informed about the details of their illness and the treatments they must face. Worrying about the implications of symptoms, tests and treatments does not help an individual to cope with or adjust to their cancer, it just increases the anxiety and stress. In the words of Charles Fletcher 'No news is not good news, it is an invitation to fear'. The following quotation is taken from an interview with a woman aged 72 who had discovered a breast lump after a fall. She herself was aware of the sinister implications of the lump and was most resentful and angry about the way in which the doctor discussed or rather failed to discuss the results of her mammogram and cytology report.

He was rather vague really, looked awfully uncomfortable about it all which started me off worrying that it might be something even worse. He kept on talking about a few abnormal cells, never said the word cancer at all, but you don't take a breast off for just a few abnormal cells do you? I'm not sure if he thought he was being kind or something or whether he thought I was too stupid to realise what was going on. The nurse who does the breast clinic was the only one I could get anything sensible out of. I don't know what I'd have thought or done without her.

This quote also demonstrates the usefulness of having a qualified specialist nurse counsellor on hand to fill in the important informational gaps or correct misunderstandings which may have arisen during the interview. In fairness some of the apparent dissatisfaction with information giving is not always due to the doctor avoiding a truthful consultation, it may also reflect the underlying anxiety of the patient or a patient's reluctance to accept the bad news. The overly anxious patient may need more than one consultation, extra help from a trained counsellor, and/or supplementary material in the form of information booklets. Providing patients with cancer with audio-tape recordings of their consultation with the doctor may also be helpful (Hogbin and Fallowfield, 1989).

The number of people who genuinely prefer not to be given any information which is potentially upsetting is very much smaller than some doctors would like to believe. In a study by Jennifer Hughes (1985) involving 50 patients with inoperable lung cancer, 60% expressed full satisfaction with the amount of information given. Only three patients said that they had not wanted any further information and nine of the fully satisfied patients had in fact been told very little. Sixteen patients (32%) said that they would have liked more information. Of these some clearly had been misinformed including one women with a bad prognosis who had been told that her biopsy report had been lost. Some patients who wanted more information had been reluctant to ask on the grounds that they would have been wasting the doctor's time. Not one patient in the study was dissatisfied because they felt that they had been told too much and none regretted knowing the diagnosis!

In another study of 269 women with early breast cancer, women who perceived their information as inadequate were significantly more likely to be anxious and/or depressed at 12 months post treatment. Those women in whom anxiety was a characteristic trait (as identified by the Spielberger STAI) were more likely to feel poorly informed (Fallowfield et al., 1990). What this study demonstrated was the need for some form of screening before patients see their doctor. This might enable the counsellor to identify those women at risk for whom extra counselling support would be beneficial. Furthermore the doctor could be alerted to the fact that he or she might need to spend more time with such patients to ensure that they have really understood what has been discussed.

Another point worth mentioning here is that far too often untrained and unskilled counsellors confuse the provision of information giving and/or advice with counselling. While it can be an important part of the counselling process, it is not the sole purpose of the exercise. Often the information giving is all one way, that is from counsellor to patient; of equal importance is the information that the patient can provide about thoughts, feelings, worries and social circumstances. The quotation at the beginning of this chapter revealed graphically the frustrating sense of isolation experienced by patients who feel that no one wishes to listen to them.

Uncertainty about prognosis and fear of death

Despite the scenarios portrayed in drama or popular literature of patients with cancer requesting and being given information as to how long they have left to live, few people actually do ask the doctor. (Hogbin and Fallowfield, 1989). Even if patients do enquire, only the unwary clinician, given the vagaries of the disease, would make anything other than a rather vague prediction; for example weeks rather than months or months rather than years. Handing out an exact prophecy is akin to issuing the patient with a death sentence; the relatives may be triumphant if the patient exceeds the time 'given' by the doctor or angry if he or she is proved wrong.

This does not mean that patients themselves do not worry about their future and uncertainty about the prognosis can compound the anxiety experienced. Indeed some patients can become so scared about dying that they cease living the life left. Others may engage in hypervigilant monitoring of bodily aches and pains fearing that every change or discomfort must herald the dreaded recurrence of cancer and death. What patients do need is an honest and realistic appraisal of the staging of their disease to enable them to make appropriate decisions about their future. A lie to a patient with evidence of advanced disease may seem to bring short-term comfort, but does nothing to help adjustment and coping when the fact of approaching death becomes inevitable.

Many more people die in hospital these days. Consequently few lay people have ever seen a dead person, and many harbour strangely romanticised images or horrors about the process of dying. Such topics are treated as taboo in our society thus patients may find it difficult to raise the subject with family or friends. Most doctors rarely have the time, and others may lack the inclination or skills to conduct discussions about death; consequently the counsellor can be extremely useful in facilitating open discussion about the thoughts and fears that patients have about death especially if he or she can disabuse patients of myth that death is inevitably painful and undignified. For those patients who have early stage disease or cancers in which cure is a realistic aim, it is important nevertheless to allow them also to express their fears. In such a situation it is pleasing to be able to offer honest reassurance. The emphasis here is on honesty; false reassurance only serves to destroy trust when things go wrong.

Guilt about causality and stigma

I have already mentioned the fact that many lay theories about the causal factors associated with cancer can create further guilt and/or stigmatisation of the unfortunate sufferer. Counsellors may find themselves in a priest-like role receiving the confessional from those patients who feel that their cancer is some sort of punishment or divine retribution for past misdeeds. This can be seen in the following quotation from an interview with a 69-year-old woman with breast cancer:

Patient: 'When I found the lump I knew exactly what it was and I thought this is my punishment at last for what I did. You see I had an illegitimate baby when I was 19 and I kept her. You didn't do things like that in my day, although it seems all right to be an unmarried mother nowadays. Anyway, I've always lied and told everyone that my husband was dead.'
Interviewer: 'I'm sorry that this is distressing you so much but would you like to talk to me a little more about this?'
Patient: 'Yes, I've never told anyone else about it in 50 years.'

This particularly sad woman saw herself as so entirely sinful that she had also considered refusing any treatment for the cancer.

Some of the popular alternative cancer therapies can also promote guilt within patients. Those that assert that individuals can combat cancer through various dietary and psychological means can be extremely damaging. If one can cure one's cancer through imaging or by developing a fighting spirit, an obvious implication for most patients is that one may have caused the cancer in the first place. Encouraging patients to take control and assume too much responsibility for the outcome of their disease can serve to compound the guilt at having caused the cancer by a faulty lifestyle or personality. For example, this past decade has seen an increasing interest in the so-called type C personality (Morris and Greer, 1980; Temoshok and Fox, 1984). The primary characteristic displayed by type C individuals is 'emotional containment' in that they do not appear to be able to express emotion, particularly anger, very easily. While of theoretical interest, it is uncertain that changing an entrenched personality style (always assuming that this is possible) would necessarily make any difference to the patient's survival chances. What is clear is that some patients may find the added burden of feeling that their own personality putatively caused the cancer too much to bear. Maguire (1989) quotes this poignant example from a woman with breast cancer: 'It's bad enough having cancer and knowing that I could die before my time. But to be told that it is because I have type C personality is no help at all. I am 55 years of age. There is no way I am going to change the kind of person I am now.' Maguire also points out that whilst some patients are helped by the knowledge that there is something that they themselves cn do which might affect their chances of survival, sudden changes from quiet introversion to over-assertiveness may well seriously undermine their relationships with all the other people on whom they will depend for help and support. Counsellors need to familiarise themselves with the literature and the psychological interventions of which patients may have been made aware through the media, and offer appropriate help and support to those who wish to attempt some major life change as a result of their cancer.

One factor that contributes to the stigma associated with having the disease is the use of the word 'cancer' as a metaphor for anything unpleasant, invasive or growing and seen to be destroying cherished social structures or challenging societal norms. Football hooligans are sometimes described as a cancer on society', corrupt ideals may 'spread like a cancer' throughout an organisation. Such phases only serve to further sinister and pejorative attitudes all of which contribute to the stigmatisation of cancer sufferers. Counsellors can assist their patients greatly by exploring an individual's own feelings and attitudes towards the cancer and then helping to allay any fears that the disease is a punishment or that the likely outcome of treatment is dependent on some rational appraisal of individual worth or goodness. Many patients express their anger at what they see as the unfairness of getting cancer as can be seen in the following extract.

I just keep on thinking 'Why me? What have I done to deserve this?' I've always put in a good day's work, never claimed any benefit and I think I did my fair share with the kids when they were small. I've never gone off with other women and apart from the odd beer after football or to be sociable I haven't been a bad husband. She never went without because I'd spent all my pay-packet. It just doesn't seem fair to me at all.

Patients, such as this man who had stomach cancer, need the help of a counsellor, firstly to assist them in expressing and ventilating their anger, and then to help them find some way of accepting the fact that cancer is indeed unfair and whom it afflicts is entirely random. Without such counselling support these patients can become so consumed with their 'Why me?' thoughts that they become depressed, socially withdrawn and resentful of the seemingly undeserving well world.

Worries about reaction of family and friends

Many patients are deeply concerned about the impact that the news that they have cancer will have on those close to them. Not only do they wish to spare their loved ones the upset and distress that the diagnosis of a life-threatening disease provokes, but some patients are deeply anxious that family and friends will abandon them. The fear of abandonment is not mere paranoia; in an interesting study by Peters-Golden (1982) healthy adults were asked about their attitudes to people with cancer. A disturbing 61% of her sample stated that they would avoid a friend with cancer. In the same study more than half the women with cancer said that people were avoiding them and 72% of patients felt that lack of understanding by family and friends was contributing to their feelings of social isolation.

In view of the findings that perceived social support is so vital if patients are to adapt satisfactorily to their disease (Bloom, 1982) it is important that the oncology counsellor gives the patients' providers of social support an opportunity to discuss their fears and worries. Some avoidance behaviour on the part of family and friends can be ameliorated if fears of contagion are countered. A surprising number of lay people consider that cancer may be infectious and others do not like to touch patients who are receiving radiotherapy for fear of radiation contamination. However, one other reason for avoidance of people with cancer is the fact that many individuals find it deeply distressing to watch someone that they love suffer pain. Likewise it is hard to witness the profoundly changed appearance of a loved one which may arise as a result of multilating surgery or chemotherapy. Some of the emotional distancing by relatives and friends that can result for reasons such as these above may also be ameliorated or prevented if a trained counsellor is available for the family of a cancer patient. The spouses of patients who have undergone surgery for cancer often experience emotional difficulties and also report an increase in diffuse somatic complaints such as headaches when the patient returns home from hospital (Oberst and James, 1985). Group counselling for patients and their spouses which included such things as a relaxation and anxiety management programme together with information about coping with cancer, had beneficial effects on couples (Heinrich and Schag 1985).

Coping with treatments

Many of the therapeutic endeavours used in the treatment of cancer can be extremely unpleasant and may cause a variety of physical and psychological side-effects (Fallowfield, 1988). The most common and troublesome of these side-effects are shown in Table 16.1. Too often clinicians pursue aggressive treatment regimes in an attempt to prolong survival with scant regard for the deleterious impact such therapy may have on a patient's quality of life (Clark and Fallowfield, 1986). Where cure is a realistic aim no one would deny that the potential benefits may well be worth the unpleasantness of such things as nausea and vomiting or hair loss. However, when the patient has advanced, metastatic disease curative treatment is doomed, and the only criterion of benefit should be enhancement of the quality of the remaining life, good symptom control and psychological support. Counselling for both the family and the patient facing the terminal stages of cancer is a vital part of care and the hospice movement has demonstrated the value of good symptom control and appropriate counselling support at this time (Saunders, 1978).

For patients about to undergo active therapy with curative intent the counsellor has an important role to play in helping them to achieve satisfactory adjustment to their altered body-image, physical and sexual functioning, and to talk through the effects that all these things may have on patients and their relationships with others.

Surgery

This worries many but pre-operative informational counselling has been shown to assist in post-operative recovery (Johnston, 1980) and increases the satisfaction patients report about their treatment (Ley, 1976). When cancer patients have recovered from the physical trauma of surgery and the immediate threat to life has passed, other emotional difficulties may surface, as this quotation from a 42-year-old woman who had recently undergone extensive surgeryy for gynaecological cancer reveals.

The period while I was in hospital was fine. I felt that everything that could be done to cure me was being done and I was so wrapped up in ordinary physical things like trying to walk upright, not cough or laugh, that I didn't really consider what the future held. Since I've been at home, I've been very depressed and very anxious. I feel very different; I am still a cancer patient. I'll never have quite the same attitude to life. They've removed a lot of what made me a woman. I didn't want to have any more children at this age but I'm very aware now that I couldn't. I'm also rather worried about my husband. He has been very good, very understanding, but – well, I just wonder what this has done to us. You don't think about these things at first; you just want to do anything to help you live longer.

Surgery is often mutilating and patients may need considerable help to cope with their changed appearance (see Chapter 4, Rumsey). Self-image may well be affected by procedures such as limb amputation for bone sarcoma or mastectomy for breast cancer, but there is a considerable body of evidence suggesting that for many people the fact of having cancer exerts a greater impact on quality of life than the surgery (Fallowfield, 1988; Fallowfield *et al.*, 1990).

Chemotherapy

Some patients may have to undergo chemotherapy with or without surgery and cytotoxic chemotherapy which kills all rapidly dividing cells, not just cancer cells, has a fearful reputation. Patients who undergo this form of treatment may have to pay a high price for survival in terms of side-effects. The counsellor who is able to offer psychological interventions such as relaxation therapy and stress management can do much to assist the individual through their treatment, (Burish and Lyles, 1981). Not all chemotherapy is cytotoxic. Hormonal chemotherapy may produce side-effects such as hirsutism in women or feminisation in men and alterations to body shape. These symptoms may be devastating for a patient who has already suffered an assault to body-image from mutilating surgery. The counsellor may be able to help such patients find ways of enhancing their self-image and self-confidence, if these have been badly affected.

Radiotherapy

Certain forms of cancer can only be treated by radiotherapy and it is sometimes given as an adjuvant to surgery and chemotherapy. patients with metastatic disease may have radiotherapy as palliative treatment where it is particularly useful in lessening the pain experienced with secondary deposits in the bone. Anxiety and depression are common psychological problems during and following radiotherapy as well as the other physical side-effects mentioned in Table 16.1. The apparent paradox that something known to cause cancer is being used to cure it may be very disturbing. A counsellor who is able to dispel the myths and mystery surrounding radiotherapy may help reduce the anxiety some patients have. One further problem patients experience is an extremely debilitating tiredness which follows treatment. Some patients feel worse at the end of their course of radiotherapy than they felt at the beginning; consequently this enervating fatigue may reawaken fears that the cancer is still present and that their condition is deteriorating. A well-informed counsellor who can provide knowledgeable reassurance may well beable to help such patients.

DOES COUNSELLING PATIENTS WITH CANCER WORK?

I have made many assertions that counselling for patients with cancer is valuable, but mere opinion rarely convinces the cynics or produces the financial resources to fund an oncology counselling service. So what is the scientific evidence for its efficacy?

In fact the evidence that patients who receive counselling derive thera-peutic benefit is equivocal. The difficulties of evaluating counselling in can-cer are highlighted in Watson's authoritative review (1983). She found that many studies which purported to evaluate counselling were metho-dologically unsound; most failed to have a control group, lacked stand-ardised, objective measures, or had the same person counselling and assessing the patients. Interested readers are referred to her review, and Massie, Holland and Straker (1989) is also recommended for a more recent update describing methodologically sound work.

It is often rather difficult to determine precisely what outcome measure should be used to assess counselling. Below I give a sample of some of the work that has been done using a selection of different outcome measures. As anxiety and depression are such common sequelae to a diagnosis and treat-ment for cancer, many studies in this field have looked at the impact that counselling has on psychiatric morbidity. For example, Linn, Linn and Ham-mis (1982) measured the effect of counselling in men suffering from late stage disease in five different cancer sites. Patients with cancer of the lung, colon, stomach, pancreas and prostate were divided into a crisis intervention counselling or control group. No evidence of any benefit to counselled patients in terms of survival was found but the number of cases of depres-sion was significantly lower in the counselled group. In another study Gor-don et al. (1980) described the work of a team of oncology counsellors with 308 women who had newly diagnosed melanoma, breast or lung cancer. Affective disorders declined more rapidly in those given counselling.

Rather different outcome measures were used in a study reported by Capone et al. (1980), who found that women who received individual crisis intervention counselling had a better self-image, returned to work more quickly and showed less sexual dysfunction than the non-counselled group.

Whilst the general principles of good counselling remain the same what-ever the stage of disease or treatment that a patient may be undergoing, there are of course times when certain counselling styles are more appropri-ate. Cancer represents an existential crisis. The components of this crisis include: lack of information in a completely new situation of which the patient has had very little previous experience which would enable adequate coping; a profound sense of isolation and lack of support; and finally a feeling of loss of control. One of the skills in counselling patients with cancer comes with knowing whether patients require, for example, more informational as opposed to confrontational or supportive help. An interesting study by Cain *et al.* (1986) compared the outcome of three different interventions in 80 women with gynaecological cancer. Patients were randomised to received either eight sessions of what the authors describe as standard counselling or eight sessions of 'structured thematic counselling' which had a strong informational component discussing such things as diet, exercise, emotional reactions, physical problems and sex. Some patients received this 'structured thematic' counselling on an individual basis others in group sessions. Women assigned the 'structured thematic counselling' sessions, be that on an individual or group basis, were less anxious and depressed, had fewer sexual problems, were more aware about their illness and reported better relationships with their care-givers than those who received 'standard' counselling.

WHO SHOULD DO THE COUNSELLING?

Fortunately the growing awareness of the psychosocial distress provoked by cancer and its treatment, together with consumer demand, has resulted in the establishment of a variety of self-help or support groups and led to the appointment of oncology counsellors, liaison psychiatrists with a special interest in cancer and specialist nurses. All of these people and groups may offer forms of counselling support although the standard, quality and ability of some of the 'counsellors' would not match up to the descriptions of counselling described in earlier chapters of this book. The notion that any kindly well-motivated person can counsel, especially if they have had personal experience of cancer is too common. There is steadily accumulating evidence to suggest that 'victim-counsellors' may be psychologically damaged by their activities (Mantell, 1983) and that counsellors who lack appropriate training experience more difficulties with their work than those who have successfully completed recognised training courses. (Fallowfield and Roberts, 1990). A nurse-counsellor who has spent an interesting one-day or weekend training course is not equipped to counsel patients with cancer. (Fielding and Llewelyn, 1987).

The absence for so long of any formal counselling service for patients with cancer and their families led to the establishment of various self-help organisations. Some of these were ad-hoc, locally based groups led by an ex-patient, a relative or a motivated health-care professional. Others developed into big national associations with charitable status such as the Mastectomy Association (now known as the Breast Care & Mastectomy Association) or

Cancerlink. More recently charities such as BACUP (British Association of Cancer United Patients) have provided a valuable phone-in counselling and information service. The evolution of such groups from smallest to largest showed how many important psychosocial needs of both patients and their families were not being met by the hard-pressed, and inadequately re-sourced NHS. Included in lack of resources is the dearth of adequate train-ing for doctors and nurses to provide counselling.

Unfortunately some of the volunteer counsellors, despite their motivation and great dedication, are not able to cope with the huge emotional demands that effective counselling places on individuals. Many worked without any training or supervision and paid a heavy price in terms of emotional burn-out. Whilst the insight that actual experience of having had cancer provides is considerable, it is an entirely personal insight which might not be appro-priate for all other patients. Below is a description given by a woman await-ing breast cancer surgery, of a visit from a volunteer counsellor who had herself been treated for breast cancer.

Well she just swept the ward in a very matter-of-fact way carrying those horrible false breasts in a plastic bag for everyone else to see. I felt so ashamed. She then proceeded to tell me how there was nothing to worry about, and how marvellous her own husband had been. Then to cap it all she unbuttoned her blouse and showed me her reconstructed breast. I thought it looked horrible and just asked her to go away. She probably meant no harm but I was very upset by the visit.

I keep stressing the importance of adequate training for work in oncology and this applies as much to professionals as it does to volunteers. The following extract from an interview shows how inexperienced 'counselling' can dismally fail to help a patient with real concerns. This 46-year-old woman was awaiting surgery for primary breast cancer and was deeply anxious about her future; of particular concern was the impact that breast loss might have on her relationship with her husband.

Patient: 'I was so upset the night before the operation that they called in a nurse who specialised in breast cancer to speak to me.'
Interviewer: 'Did this help?'
Patient: 'No. She made things even worse.'
Interviewer: 'In what way?'
Patient: 'Every time I said anything like I was really frightened, she said something like, That's silly. When I said that I was worried about my husband's reaction, she said that was silly too, as I'd still be the same woman underneath even with only one breast. What a stupid thing to say – she knew nothing about the problems that we've been having lately – he's had an affair you know. When I said that I was scared stiff of dying from cancer, she just said that lots of women live for more than five years with breast cancer. Well that's not much comfort is it, if you're lucky you might live for five years. I watched my mother die from bowel cancer so I know what dying from cancer is like.'

An important aspect of counselling is that of challenging the negative attributions that patients may have about themselves. However, it is all too easy to convey an impression of dismissiveness about a patient's worries if the counsellor has not been well trained as the previous quotation demonstrated.

Likewise a little training (some courses last less than a week) is hardly adequate for someone who wishes to be a counsellor. Indeed a little knowledge could be very damaging to some patients as the example that follows demonstrates. The quote is from an interview with a patient who was awaiting surgery for breast cancer. She was visited by a nurse-counsellor who had some interesting ideas of the application of various psychodynamic approaches mixed in with some grief counselling.

Well I'd been doing quite well really considering what was going to happen to me in the morning. My family had all visited and that nice Mr X (the surgeon) came and sat on the bed and talked to me for ages, so I felt quite calm and cheerful even. Then the counsellor came and without a word pulled the curtains round my bed, sat herself down and said that she wasn't leaving until we had cried for my lost breast. When I pointed out that I hadn't lost it yet, she asked if I always denied things that were too painful to think about. I just couldn't believe what was happening to me, my husband was absolutely furious when he found out.

One would like to believe that such horror stories are rare but they do demonstrate the need to ensure that counsellors are properly trained and supervised.

It is clear that counselling is only as good as the person doing it. Some volunteers may possess skills which enable them to help patients more effectively than those people who may have a professional label but have not been given adequate training. This issue applies to all medical specialities not just oncology.

ISSUES SPECIFIC TO ONCOLOGY COUNSELLING

The oncology counsellor, to be effective, besides possessing good counselling skills, should know something about the disease and treatment options and side-effects. It is important to be able to understand the information regarding such things as treatment and prognosis. This allows the counsellor to provide realistic reassurance to patients who may have pessimistic fears about the disease. Sometimes those counsellors who come from a mental health background know little about the way in which cancer of different sites is treated or its likely effectiveness. Occasionally this may lead counsellors to adopt an overly optimistic approach which patients rapidly identify as inauthenmtic (Peters-Golden, 1982) or they may, through lack of knowledge, have as negative views about outcome as their parents.

Counselling anyone with problems can be distressing especially if one identifies too closely with the client; thus counselling patients with cancer who become seriously ill and seem likely to die may be particularly stressful for the 'victim-counsellor' who may fear that she too will share a similar fate. Another major difference from counselling healthy individuals is the fact that serious illness may impose a time-limit on the counselling process. Not only is the timing of sessions likely to be dictated by treatment times and/or how ill the patient is but the counsellor also has to conduct them at a rather different pace. Sourkes (1982) captures the problem succinctly when discussing the difficulty of conducting traditional psychotherapy with cancer patients. 'Letting a process emerge at its own pace and time is a luxury precluded by the very nature of the life-threatening illness. Its immediacy demands a focus on the present, framed by the themes of separation and loss'.

Cancer is a very cruel disease and it causes considerable physical and emotional pain to sufferers, their families and friends. Work with this group of people is often challenging and distressing, but it can also be immensely rewarding.

USEFUL ADDRESSES

BACUP – British Association of Cancer United Patients and their families and friends,
121/123 Charterhouse Street,
London EC1M 6AA
Tel: 071-608 1661

CANCERLINK,
17 Britannia Street,
London WC1X 9JN
Tel: 071-833 2451

Macmillan Nurses (Cancer Relief),
Anchor House,
15/19 Britton Street,
London SW3 3TY
Tel: 071-351 7811

Breast Care & Mastectomy Association of Great Britain,
26a Harrison Street,
Kings Cross,
London WC1 8JG
Tel: 071-837 0908

REFERENCES

Bloom, J.R. (1982). Social support, accommodation to stress, and adjustment to breast cancer. *Social Science & Medicine*, **16**, 1329–1338.
Bukberg, J., Penman, D., and Holland, J.C. (1984). Depression in hospitalised cancer patients. *Psychosomatic Medicine*, **46**, 199–212.

Burish, T.G. and Lyles, J.M. (1981). Effectiveness of relaxation training in reducing adverse reactions to cancer chemotherapy. *Journal of Behavioural Medicine*, **4**, 65–78.

Cain, E.N., Kohorn, E.I., Quinlan, D.M. *et al.* (1986). Psychosocial benefits of a cancer support group. *Cancer*, **57**, 183–189.

Capone, M.A., Good, R.S., Westie, S., and Jacobsen, A.F. (1980). Psychosocial rehabilitation in gynaecologic oncology patients. *Archives of Physical Medicine & Rehabilitation*, **61**, 128–132.

Clark, A.N. and Fallowfield, L.J. (1986). Quality of life measurements in patients with malignant disease: a review. *Journal of the Royal Society of Medicine*, **79**, 165–169.

Derogatis, L.R., Morrow, G.R., Fetting, J. *et al.* (1983). The prevalence of psychiatric disorders among cancer patients. *Journal of the American Medical Association*, **249**, 751–757.

Fallowfield, L.J. (1988). The psychological complications of malignant disease. In S. Kaye, (Ed.), Complications of Malignant Disease. *Bailliere's Clinical Oncology*, **2**; 2, 461–478.

Fallowfield, L.J., Baum, M., and Maguire, G.P. (1986). Effects of breast conservation on psychological morbidity associated with diagnosis and treatment of early breast cancer. *British Medical Journal*, **293**, 1331–1334.

Fallowfield, L.J., Hall, A., Maguire, G.P., and Baum, M.J. (1990). Psychological outcomes of different treatment policies in women with early breast cancer outside a clinical trial. *British Medical Journal*, **301**, 575–580.

Fallowfield, L.J. and Roberts, R. (1990). National survey of oncology counselling. *Psychology and Health*, in press.

Fielding, R.G. and Llewelyn, S.P. (1987). Communication training in nursing may damage your health and enthusiasm: some warnings. *Journal of Advanced Nursing*, **12**, 281–290.

Fletcher, C. (1980). Listening and talking to patients. *British Medical Journal*, **281**, 994.

Gordon, W.A., Freidenbergs, L., Diller, M., *et al.* (1980). Efficacy of psychosocial intervention with cancer patients. *Journal of Consulting & Clinical Psychology*, **48**, 743–759.

Heinrich, R.L. and Schag, C.C. (1985). Stress and activity management: group treatment for cancer patients and spouses. *Journal of Consulting and Clinical Psychology*, **53**, 439–446.

Hogbin, B. and Fallowfield, L.J. (1989). Getting it taped: The 'bad news' consultation with cancer patients. *British Journal of Hospital Medicine*, **41**, 330–333.

Hughes, J. (1985). Depressive illness and lung cancer: 11. Follow-up of inoperable patients. *European Journal of Surgical Oncology*, **11**, 21–24.

Jenkins, C.D. (1966). The semantic differential for health: A technique for measuring beliefs about disease. *Public Health Reports*, **81**, 549–558.

Johnston, M. (1980). Anxiety in surgical patients. *Psychological Medicine*, **10**, 145–152.

Lerner, M.J. and Miller, D.T. (1978). Just world research and the attribution process: looking back and ahead. *Psychological Bulletin*, **85**, 1030–1051.

Ley, P., Bradshaw, P.W., Kincey, J., *et al.* (1976). Increasing patients' satisfaction with communication. *British Journal of Social and Clinical Psychology*, **15**, 403–413.

Linn, N.W., Linn, B.S. and Harris, R. (1982). Effects of counselling for late stage cancer patients. *Cancer*, **49**, 1048–1055.

Maguire, P. (1985). Improving the detection of psychiatric problems in cancer patients. *Social Science and Medicine*, **20**, 819–823.

Maguire, P. (1989). Breast conservation versus mastectomy: psychological considerations. *Seminars in Surgical Oncology*, **5**, 137–144.

Mantell, J.E. (1983). Cancer patient visitor programs: a case for accountability. *Journal of Psychosocial Oncology*, **1**, (1) 45–58.

Massie, M.J., Holland, J., and Straker, N. (1989). Psychotherapeutic interventions. In J.C. Holland and J.H. Rowland (Eds), *Handbook of psycho-oncology: The psychological care of the patient with cancer*. New York: Oxford University Press.

McIntosh, J. (1974). Processes of communication, information seeking and control associated with cancer. A selective review of the literature. *Social Science and Medicine*, **8**, 167–187.

Morris, T. and Greer, S. (1980). A 'Type C' for cancer? Low trait anxiety in the pathogenesis of breast cancer. *Cancer Detection & Prevention*, **3** (1) abstr. 102.

Oberst, M.T. and James, R. (1985). Going home: Patient and spouse adjustment following cancer surgery. *Topics in Clinical Nursing*, **7**, 46–57.

Peters-Golden, H. (1982). Breast cancer: varied perceptions of social support in the illness experience. *Social Science and Medicine*, **16**, 483–491.

Plumb, M.M. and Holland, J. (1977). Comparative studies of psychological function in patients with advanced cancer. *Psychosomatic Medicine*, **39**, 264–276.

Saunders, C.M. (1978). *The management of terminal disease*. London: Edward Arnold.

Sourkes, B.M. (1982). *The deepening shade: Psychological aspects of life-threatening illness*. Pittsburgh: University Pitts. Press.

Temoshok, L. and Fox, B.H. (1984). Coping styles and other psychosocial factors related to medical status and to prognosis in patients with cutaneous malignant melanoma. In B.H. Fox and B.H. Newberry (Eds), *Impact of psychoendocrine systems in cancer and immunity*. Toronto: Hogrefe.

Watson, M. (1983). Psychosocial intervention with cancer patients: A review. *Psychological Medicine*, **13**, 839–846.

Wyler, A.R., Masuda, M., and Homes, T.H. (1968). Seriousness of illness scale. *Journal of Psychosomatic Research*, **2**, 363–374.

17 Counselling in Heart Disease

PAUL BENNETT* AND TONY HOBBS†

*School of Psychology, University of Wales College of Cardiff, P.O. Box 901, Cardiff CF1 3YG

†Dudley Clinical Psychology Services, Cross Street Health Centre, Dudley, West Midlands DY1 1RN

The World Health Organization defines ischaemic heart disease (IHD) as 'the cardiac disability, acute or chronic, rising from reduction or arrest of the blood supply to the myocardium in association with disease processes in the coronary arteries'.

Ischaemic heart disease may present in a symptomatic form as myocardial infarction (MI: heart attack), angina pectoris, or cardiac arrythmia, or without symptoms, diagnosed from ECG abnormalities or sudden death. It is the single greatest cause of death throughout the industrialised world. In the UK the disease accounts for 40% of deaths in men, and 10% of deaths in women, aged between 45 and 64 years. Mortality rates, however, are not constant, with them falling in many countries (those which arguably have adopted more 'healthy lifestyles', such as the United States, Japan, and Switzerland) and rising in others (such as Poland, Bulgaria, Ireland). This chapter will consider the need for counselling, and the issues for patients, throughout the disease process: prevention, acute care, rehabilitation and chronic disease.

PREVENTION

The potential for disease reduction by appropriate lifestyle change has resulted in a number of preventive health interventions targetted at the reduction of risk factors for IHD. Some, such as the Stanford (Farquhar *et al.*, 1985) and North Karelia (Puska *et al.*, 1985) projects are aimed at whole populations, whilst others focus more on the individual. In the UK, which has a well-organised primary care system, preventive screening for risk factors may be through systematic invitations from family doctors to attend screening sessions, usually conducted by a nurse (Fullard, Fowler and Gray, 1983). Where such an accessible system is not in operation, more entrepreneurial means of recruitment of patients have been developed, such as advertising

Counselling and Communication in Health Care. Edited by H. Davis and L. Fallowfield
© 1991 John Wiley & Sons Ltd

or conducting screening in public areas. Screening typically comprises a 20 to 30 minute interview plus brief physical check. Dietary, smoking and exercise habits are recorded and blood pressure and body mass index determined. Where risk factors are identified, patients may be referred to their doctor or receive counselling augmented by literature from the nurse. Counselling following screening is typically brief, although patients may be recalled and their progress monitored should this be necessary.

Relatively high levels of risk factors may be identified through such a screening process. In the South Birmingham Coronary Prevention Project (Bennett et al., 1989), for example, combined data from twelve GP practices gathered over one year found the following prevalence levels in attenders at health checks: hypertension (newly identified), 18%; obesity, 42%; raised serum cholesterol (> 6.3 mmol/litre), 27%; and smoking, 33%.

Despite such high levels of potentially modifiable risk factors, most people are aware of the primary causal factors implicated in heart disease. It is not lack of knowledge that prevents them adopting more healthy lifestyles. Some problems hindering positive change may be easily identified (though not easily resolved) such as low income, inadequate shops and little time to prepare healthier food. Other more fundamental difficulties may also interfere, such as women who use smoking as a means of coping with the stress of running a family, often in adverse social and environmental conditions. They are generally aware of the dangers associated with smoking, but they place their health lower on their list of priorities than other issues. Stopping is, therefore, not a simple unidimensional matter based on personal health issues. Psychological factors may also underlie such apparently unhealthy behaviour. Each one of us is capable of attempting to deny conscious realisation of a particularly worrying threat to ourselves and this enables some to discount standard health education messages as personally irrelevant.

Effective intervention in such instances entails the health check moving from a didactic, expert, provision of information to a more exploratory discussion in which the patient becomes an equally responsible partner. A problem-solving approach in which patients are helped to devise their own solution to particular obstacles to their own behaviour change is necessarily the most appropriate form of counselling. The professional must relinquish the expert role and recognise that the patient can be responsible for his or her own decision-making and eventual action. This runs counter to the ethos of attributed responsibility in medical and para-medical training, and many practitioners encounter difficulty achieving this essential change of direction. Mearns and Thorne (1988) and Egan (1982) provide substantial guidance to those developing counselling skills in a general health care context.

The majority of attenders find health checks useful. They are either reassured, if found to be 'healthy', or problems can be more fully discussed with appropriate advisory counselling should they choose. However, a minority of those found to be at increased risk find this information rather alarming. Raised serum cholesterol and hypertension, for example, are usually symptomless and screening may be the first time an individual becomes aware of them. This knowledge may raise considerable anxiety. It may be evident by what the person says or by over-adherence to recommended behavioural change and noticed, for example, through unwarranted weight loss following advice to reduce intake of animal fats. However, it is not just those found to be 'at risk' who may become anxious following preventive screening. There may also be the danger of making people already anxious unnecessarily alarmed, as in the case of those found to have high blood pressure on the first of three readings only, and who become highly anxious and/or depressed about their health and blood pressure in particular (Bloom and Monterossa, 1981).

Since health checks can be potentially disturbing, any information on a patient's personal risk should be explained carefully in a manner which is sensitive to the person's emotional response. There should also be time to discuss the implications. The relative importance of suggested lifestyle changes and likely positive effects on health need also to be discussed. Even moderate levels of anxiety, which can be expected after receiving unwanted information, may interfere with memory. Therefore, to maximise understanding, retention of information, and compliance with advice, there should be a follow-up session shortly after the initial check.

Case history 1

F. was a 38-year-old man, who attended screening for heart disease risk factors. Until then he considered himself to be relatively healthy. It was therefore something of a shock for him to be told by the health check nurse that he had raised serum cholesterol. He was told his level was high, (7.3 mmol/litre) but was not told the normal levels. He was also given some advice on how to reduce his cholesterol, by reducing his dietary fat, and given a list of low fat foods with some menu suggestions. His emotional reaction to this news was not explored.

At a routine follow-up session with a counselling-trained worker a month later, he had lost about two stones, and was continuing to lose weight despite not having been previously overweight. He looked haggard, and his clothes were hanging off him. He reported that he was living almost entirely on salads. He felt unable to eat any food he thought contained a significant amount of fat, and his wife was experiencing considerable difficulty accommodating the various family demands in her meal preparation.

F. reported extreme anxiety about his health in general and his cholesterol levels in particular. He experienced many intrusive worries during the day, particularly at meal times and when he heard people discussing health matters. After gentle facilitation to talk more freely, he became able to confide that he strongly believed that unless he made such radical lifestyle changes he feared that he would die within the next few years because he had read that high cholesterol 'is a killer'.

The dietary changes he was making were placing a considerable strain on him and his family, and had not helped to reduce his anxiety at all. Some ways round this problem were therefore explored during this session. The first, and probably most important part, of the discussion was to put the risk attached to his serum cholesterol level into a realistic context through the provision of basic information. Explanation was given about how much his cholesterol level was raised compared to the average, and he was reassured that with only one risk factor amenable to change the risk of developing heart disease was far lower than he had feared.

He nevertheless, quite appropriately, wished to reduce his risk as much as possible. By his own admission, his present attempts were unrealistic, and in exploring the situation a much wider range of foods than he had previously eaten was quickly agreed, and he was able to acknowledge, with relief, that any diet need not be followed slavishly and that treats were allowed. Furthermore a number of alternative approaches to controlling his cholesterol were considered. Since it was explained to him that exercise can help reduce cholesterol, he decided to cycle to and from work each day, as this would increase his fitness, and help control his cholesterol, without intruding too much into his daily routine.

F.'s cholesterol levels were measured about two months after this meeting, and they were within the normal limits. He had made the agreed changes almost immediately, but it had taken some time for his anxiety concerning his health to decrease. Appropriate and sensitive counselling at the initial screening would almost certainly have picked up F.'s sense of alarm and the implications for him of the news so that considerable distress could have been averted.

ACUTE CARE

Myocardial infarction

Experiencing a heart attack is a devastating physical event. It is frightening, involving an immediate threat to life and loss of self-control, and it can be extremely painful. Sufferers may be rushed dramatically to hospital where they lie surrounded by modern medical paraphernalia, constantly monitored by ECG, routinely observed by nurses and given pain killing drugs that sedate and may confuse. Although the patient is often cocooned within a Coronary Care Unit (CCU), they can usually see other patients and what they see may not be reassuring, as about 20% of those entering a CCU are likely to die.

Initial fears for survival are soon joined by concerns related to work, home, spouse and children. Often resentment of becoming ill is experienced and this may be directly expressed towards the staff. Longer term worries concerning future life plans may begin to come to the fore within the first day or two in the CCU and continuing symptoms including breathlessness, chest pain and weakness may also evoke high levels of anxiety.

The most common initial reactions to MI are anxiety, fear, anger (which can be internalised, contributing to depression), and feelings of hopelessness, helplessness and worthlessness. For example, Hackett, Cassem and Wishnie (1968) found evidence of anxiety in at least 80% of patients in CCU, and 58% were depressed. Although such feelings have been described as evidence of inadequate coping, it is more appropriate to view them as the initial phase of coming to terms with an enormously traumatic event that is likely to have adverse effects on the individual for a considerable time, if not for life.

There are, however, a substantial minority of patients who do not have such reactions, perhaps actively influenced by a CCU atmosphere in which the unspoken expectation of patients is that they do *not* express upset, anxiety, or fear. Croog, Shapiro and Levine (1971) found 20% of MI patients denied their medical status at 18 day and one year follow-up. Although this may involve a defence against overwhelming stress, the consequences of such a reaction may be disastrous in that people may disregard potentially fatal symptoms, refuse appropriate medication and continue smoking.

Understanding such a reaction is important for health carers. Anxiety can present with a rise in pulse rate or blood pressure for which there is no direct medical explanation, whilst the patient appears overconcerned with their symptoms, bodily functions or medication. Anxious patients may appear overdependent, demanding immediate attention and care. They may also appear hostile toward staff. The depressed person on the other hand may appear to be a model patient, compliant, well-behaved and accepting treatment without question when they are, in reality, sad, disinterested, and despondent about the future, foreseeing high risks of further infarction and unemployment.

Family, friends and relatives are all touched to some extent by myocardial infarction. Anxiety in the spouse may exceed that of the patient and continue well into the convalescence period and beyond. Thus counselling has an important role to play in either preventing or ameliorating psychiatric morbidity and in facilitating adjustment in patients and their families.

Counselling in CCU

A small percentage of patients within CCU will at some time require specialist treatment for emotional problems. However, all patients would benefit from help in reducing psychological stress and in promoting healthy psychological adjustment during their stay in the CCU. This may have two major advantages. It may positively affect the individual's physical and psychological state in the Unit and benefit subsequent rehabilitation. Secondly, there are financial considerations since counselling may reduce the average time spent within the Unit.

The main aims of counselling are to help individuals explore and express feelings concerning the heart attack, thus facilitating active adjustment and reductions in anxiety, depression and denial, and to help regain feelings of control over their future health and life. Such targets can be achieved in a number of ways, including:

(1) The development of a safe clinical environment which reassures the patient of the Unit's ability to cope with any medical problems.
(2) The provision of adequate formal and informal counselling opportunities during the acute phase (this has obvious staff training and support implications).

(3) Giving realistic and appropriate information concerning the nature of heart attack, its treatment, and the patient's prognosis, even at this early stage.
(4) Organising the environment to optimise perceptions of self-control.
(5) Providing opportunities and encouragement to allow patients to distract themselves from worries or boredom.

Although some professionals fear that information given at the acute phase may be harmful, Cromwell and Levenkron (1984) have demonstrated that it aids psychological adjustment if given carefully, sensitively, with opportunities for self-control over care, and the opportunity for distraction. Adjustment takes time, in which there is a need for relaxation and distraction from provided information; time to gain confidence in coping with their condition by actively putting this information to use. It is important that all information and explanation be given at the right time and at a level that the patient can understand. It may also have to be repeated often, because pain killing drugs, anxiety, and low mood all impair memory.

Counselling in this context is not simply a separate activity. Rather, it determines an overall style of approaching and interacting with patients. Gruen (1975) noted a number of key factors in such interactions that were related to positive outcomes in and beyond the CCU. These included:

(1) The development of a relationship allowing the individual to talk about genuine concerns in a non-judgemental, accepting atmosphere.
(2) Reassurance that the expression of so-called negative emotions is normal, acceptable and desirable.
(3) Encouragement of the patient's own coping resources.
(4) Acceptance of the individual's preferred coping style (denial was not challenged unless this interfered with medical care).
(5) Feedback of feelings and conclusions the person appeared to be experiencing.
(6) Feedback of the counsellor's faith in the patient's ability to cope.

This combination of techniques was found to reduce psychological distress, and to influence recovery in time spent on a cardiac monitor, in intensive care and in hospital.

Deep muscle relaxation is a specific and relevant coping strategy, appropriate even at an early stage. It can help the individual to deal with the immediate stresses of the CCU, and those they face in the future. It also provides a method by which individuals can regain some control over their lives, and begin the process of rehabilitation.

While training in relaxation helps the patient cope with pain, discomfort, and anxiety-related tension, counselling involving cognitive restructuring (Meichenbaum, 1988) can be most effective in minimising psychological distress and maximising the patient's ability for physical and psychological self-care. The negative impact of ruminations ('It hurts when I breathe. I must be dying'; 'I feel so weak I'll never get better at this rate'), which may adversely affect both mood and rehabilitation can, for example, be countered by rehearsal of positive, but realistic, alternatives ('These feelings are natural. The doctor has assured me they are not impeding my progress'; 'The doctor told me I'd feel weak for a while; it's all part of the healing process').

Beyond the CCU

Many patients feel reassured by their stay in the CCU. They feel relatively safe in the knowledge that should something go wrong, they are surrounded by competent staff, and the appropriate medical equipment. Moving from the CCU to the open ward, however, can provoke anxiety. Although it usually resolves within 24 hours, it does suggest a transition for which patients need to be adequately prepared and reassured. Further, it is essential that the staff in the new setting possess the knowledge and skills to maintain a focus on the psychological processes addressed in the CCU, and to maintain continuity of psychological and physical care.

Coronary by-pass surgery

The patient entering hospital for coronary by-pass surgery is likely to be less anxious or depressed than someone in acute care following MI. Many are optimistic that the operation will relieve symptoms suffered for a number of years. Confidence is also boosted by favourable publicised results and the knowledge that mortality is low. However, such optimism may be, at least partially, unfounded. Despite some contrary results, there is increasing evidence that emboli occurring during surgery and resulting haemodynamic changes may cause persisting neurological impairment in a significant percentage of patients. Problems, for example of impaired memory and concentration, may be sufficient to be noticeable in daily life (Newman, 1989). Full consent for an operation should not be given without these implications being discussed fully with patients and their family.

Patients may also be prepared in a number of ways prior to surgery in order to reduce post-operative anxiety and enhance immediate rehabilitation (Matthews and Ridgeway, 1984). The provision of information is reassuring, although a small minority may not find it so and their wishes should be acknowledged. Procedural information outlines what will happen in the immediate pre- and post-operative periods. Sensation information ('You may feel a pain across your chest where the incision was made—this is normal'), and behavioural information ('Try to exercise your legs every hour or so, to keep the circulation as good possible') are particularly beneficial.

Relaxation training and cognitive restructuring may also be useful in combination with appropriate information in preparing patients for the variety of smaller, pre-operative, investigations that patients have to endure. Cardiac catheterisation can be at best unpleasant and mildly anxiety provoking. At worst it can generate high levels of anxiety that may be inappropriate to the degree of risk or discomfort involved.

A small number of patients may develop acute confusional symptoms during the immediate post-operative phase as a result of the deep anaesthesia used during operation. Techniques for coping with this are described by Holden and Woods (1982). They include the provision of simple information aimed at reassurance (e.g. who you are; where you are; what has happened) repeated frequently and patiently. The reassurance of touch and a quiet, calm and confident voice all contribute to significant reductions in confusion and any associated anxiety. The majority of patients who suffer such difficulties immediately after the operation appear to have no long-term symptoms and this should be conveyed to anxious relatives.

REHABILITATION

Managing anxiety and depression

Anxiety, low mood, guilt, anger or distractibility are all components of psychological adjustment to major loss, in this case the loss of health and perceived safety. The counselling requirements of the acute stage are still necessary at the rehabilitative stage. Attentive listening and responsive information provision will still contribute to some patients' mood, as will encouraging further regular use of relaxation skills and cognitive strategies.

A common cause of depression is apparent lack of progress, usually as a result of overambitious expectations. At worst, this may result in complete hopelessness and a failure to engage in the rehabilitation process ('I'm not going to get back to my previous activities, so there's no point in trying'). At best it may simply be evident from compliance with a rehabilitation regime, but with no apparent spirit. Particularly useful here is cognitive restructuring ('OK I'm not improving as fast as I would like, but at least I *am* improving. It will only take a little longer than I was hoping.') and engaging the patient in appropriate goal setting. This involves them in planning their own rehabilitation in conjunction with the therapist, with an emphasis on setting meaningful and achievable goals, in order that the person is rewarded by success. The efficacy of general counselling is demonstrated by Frasure-Smith and Prince (1986) to be described in a later chapter on evaluation.

Formal therapeutic interventions

The relevance of stress and aspects of type A behaviour are increasingly recognised in heart disease. There is mounting evidence that stress management and reduction of type A behaviour decreases the risk of initial and recurrent MI

(Bennett and Carroll, 1990). Type A behaviour (typified as extremes of time urgency, hostility, and impatience) is highly prevalent after MI, and many patients attribute the onset of their MI to chronic or increased stress.

As a result, many also welcome the opportunity to take part in stress management groups. These teach techniques that can be used to reduce stress that may have contributed to the disease, and can help the individual cope better with the stresses resulting from it. After such training, patients report feeling less depressed, tense, fatigued, and more in control of their future life (Revel, Baer and Cleveland, 1988). They are also at less risk of re-infarction (Bennett and Carroll, 1990).

The core contents of stress management training includes:

(1) Education regarding the nature of stress and its role in the aetiology of MI and any symptoms that may persist (e.g. angina).
(2) Relaxation and/or meditation training.
(3) Anger management principles (Novaco, 1978).
(4) Cognitive methods of dealing with stress.
(5) Approaches to the modification of type A behaviour, focusing on time management and appropriate goal setting.

Typically groups meet on eight occasions, although some group members continue meeting afterwards. Many are fairly brief in-patient groups. However, weekly meetings on a post-discharge basis are ideal since patients can practice the use of stress management skills in their own environment, allowing them to discover problems during the life of the group, and not when help is unavailable.

Informal interventions

A percentage of patients express a need for continuing informal, or self-help groups, after the life of any formal intervention. These would appear particularly appropriate for MI patients or those with chronic angina. Short-term formal intervention may prove inadequate or fail to provide sufficient longer term help for both patients or their families. Self-help groups can fulfil these functions. Crucially, they provide help from people with a great deal of insight into the problems an individual faces or may face in the future. An important 'intervention' for any counsellor should be to help set up a network of small self-help groups. These may need professional help in becoming established, but this can be gradually withdrawn as the group develops.

Counselling in angina

Angina pectoris is a painful and potentially debilitating condition which can arise on its own or following MI. It can be triggered by exercise, stress and extremes of emotion both positive and negative. It varies in intensity from a mild ache to excruciating pain mimicking the pain of a heart attack.

A number of psychological factors are linked to the development of angina including affective lability, neuroticism, type A behaviour, anger and hostility. The continuing experience of angina can lead to depression and anxiety, particularly where attacks are difficult to control or occur frequently. Where the symptoms are acute, severe, and mimic a previous MI, anxiety can be extremely high and result in admission to hospital. Furthermore, anxiety and type A behaviour can all impair patients' functioning independent of the physical restrictions imposed by angina.

Consequently, counselling is important and must address certain key areas: (a) reduction of psychological factors that predispose to heart disease and angina, particularly type A behaviour and hostility; (2) the development of strategies for increasing control over physical symptoms; (c) counselling for lifestyle changes such as stopping smoking and changing diet; and (d) coping with loss.

The practice of relaxation and stress management techniques can reduce the risk of MI by fostering a calm approach to dealing with everyday life, and reducing emotional lability and anger, which can precipitate an angina attack. During an episode of angina, rapid relaxation can also be used to reduce the sympathetic activity and physical demands that may have precipitated the attack, and thus reduce its severity.

Cognitive techniques are also powerful aids during an acute episode. If a person believes the symptoms they are experiencing are those of a heart attack, they may become fearful, and increasingly aroused, promoting exacerbation of the angina that may result in unnecessary admission to hospital or at least some minutes of acute psychological and physical distress. A realistic appraisal of such symptoms ('This pain is the same as the last angina I had which went reasonably quickly after I took my medication') will result in less distress. A crucial exercise for those patients who have had a previous MI is to attempt to identify how their present symptoms differ from their MI, to be able to monitor their angina attacks and to use these differences as a method of increasing their ability to cope with them.

Other psychological issues also need to be addressed with these patients. Since angina is a debilitating and chronic condition, people have to come to terms with psychological loss and the prospect of future losses (health, financial, independence and so on), and counselling focusing upon such issues, may be useful whether or not the person has experienced the trauma of MI.

Counselling in a post-discharge rehabilitation programme

Far too frequently patients and their families on discharge from hospital are left feeling psychologically abandoned, with no-one to turn to for objective support at times of uncertainty or fear. During out-patient appointments, doctors may not appear to have either the time or the inclination to encourage patients to relax sufficiently and to be confident enough to express any feelings of psychological vulnerability, uncertainty, or fear. If patients have been treated in an overly 'positive' hospital setting, where acknowledgement of anxieties and fear is blocked or otherwise discouraged, they will remain unwilling to admit to uncertainties, and they will be left with no formalised support.

The more fortunate will be offered a short series of meetings which are a well-intentioned attempt by concerned hospital staff, working within their limited budget, to offer on-going support and help in continuing recovery beyond the hospital ward. These sessions often take the form of didactic teaching, followed by an exercise class and relaxation session. A small minority of patients have more extensive, and considerably more beneficial, opportunities open to them, such as provided by the Exercise Rehabilitation Association. This is based in Dudley (Dugmore, Bone and Kubik, 1986) and provides tremendous support to people with cardiac problems and is strongly recommended as a paradigm for developing programmes. It includes a long-term carefully and individually graded exercise programme, with supportive counselling and stress management. It aims to be a forum for mutual advancement, physically and psychologically, and provides ready access to professionals from a range of disciplines for advice, reassurance, and support as required. Patients are encouraged to retain a supportive contact with the Association over a period of years, and those who are willing are helped to achieve full realisation of their physical potential.

Case History 2

J. had his first heart attack at the age of 60 whilst out walking his dog. He became very dizzy and developed severe chest pains, prior to collapsing. He was hospitalised for ten days, but made a good recovery, returning to work within eight months without worrying about his future.

Sixteen months after his first attack, J. woke during the night and on the way to the bathroom collapsed in pain, experiencing great breathing difficulty. Several times he tried to pick himself up, but fell against furniture before eventually passing out. Four months later he was referred for specialist psychological help as he had begun to suffer panic attacks, at the onset of which he believed himself to be having a further heart attack. In addition, he had become housebound as a result of severe agoraphobia, and was experiencing considerable anxiety in his home. If he needed to go to the bathroom at night, after several hours restlessness, he would inch his way slowly along his now unfurnished landing leaning against the wall all the way, lest he fell and injured himself. If turning his gas fire off, he would crawl on hands and knees lest he collapse and fall onto the fire unconscious. On the rare occasion that he ventured out of his home he avoided crowded areas, or places reminding him of his first attack.

During psychological assessment J. reported having lost confidence in junior medical staff and the medication which they prescribed him. He also believed he ought to have been fitted with a pacemaker, and that the only reason that this had not been done was because the NHS was so short of money. He complained that he had not received sufficient counselling following his heart attacks. The assessment revealed the debilitating extent of J's anxiety based behavioural limitations, his desperation to understand why he had suffered both heart attacks, why his medication (in his perception) was being so frequently altered and why he was not urgently being fitted with a pacemaker. It also came to light that his mother had died of a second heart attack nine years after her first, within a few weeks of a change in her medication. Assessment also revealed his considerable concern regarding his wife's well-being, as she had recently become very low in spirits.

Had J. been provided with adequate opportunity to take part in counselling of sufficient breadth on his second admission, it seemed very likely that each of his concerns could have been appropriately and adequately addressed, thereby avoiding or at least greatly reducing his later psychological distress and suffering.

Treatment for J. comprised full discussion of the likely causes of both heart attacks, his subsequent medical treatment and how his case differed from that of his mother, and how he could minimise the likelihood of future difficulties. He was taught and supervised in the use of relaxation, and he quickly became able to function normally within his home. Owing to the severity of the agoraphobia, he required a few sessions of supported systematic desensitization to enable him to walk at ease with his dog through the woods and past the bus stop where he had collapsed initially. Once J. had begun to re-develop confidence in his abilities, his wife's mood improved and he willingly accepted referral to an Exercise Rehabilitation Programme with the intention of both improving his physical well-being and continuing to boost his personal confidence in his ability to live his life as fully as possible.

SUMMARY AND IMPLICATIONS

Many patients suffering from, or found to be at heightened risk of developing, heart disease require appropriate counselling if effective psychological and behavioural adjustment is to be made. Both formal and informal counselling have been shown to be pertinent at *each* stage of the health care process. Sensitive and accurate listening, help to allay fears, provision of factual information (or informed opinion) in a supportive manner, as well as teaching specific psychological skills all contribute to the full care of the individual. They maximise patients' development and acceptance of an appropriate personal health responsibility. Further, they can facilitate the reduction of psychological distress and any adjustment to loss, improve the course of emotional and physical recovery and subsequent rehabilitation, and optimise the appropriate future use of health service resources.

The key providers of such care must necessarily be those who come into daily contact with these patients: doctors, nurses, and other paramedical personnel. This has a number of major implications both for the delivery of any service and the training of workers to maintain it.

From a training perspective, increased emphasis needs to be placed on developing an understanding of psychological processes related to hospitalisation, the effects of acute or chronic illness, and facilitating behavioural change. These issues should form the core of any psychological teaching given to all healthcare workers. Further, they should be central to any curriculum, not simply a fringe component, as is often the case at present.

A higher priority should also be given to the training of counselling skills as part of all teaching programmes for medical and para-medical workers. Opportunities to attend counselling training courses should be given to established staff, and continuing programmes of post-qualification training established. Clinical psychologists, and others trained in counselling techniques (for example, some health psychologists) could provide such training.

From a service delivery perspective, psychological as well as physical health needs to become a focus of care planning, particularly in acute and rehabilitation settings. This has to be given support by any relevant managers. Time, space, and an appropriate level of resources need to be allocated. The full development of a 'key worker' system in acute and rehabilitative settings, where one member of staff is responsible for the primary counselling task with a number of designated patients, must be considered essential if effective counselling is to be provided. These key workers should have direct access to counselling specialists for advice or further referal where necessary. There *are* examples of excellence at all stages of the health care process and these should be disseminated.

REFERENCES

Bennett, P. and Carroll, D. (1990). Stress management approaches to the prevention of coronary heart disease. *British Journal of Clinical Psychology*, **29**, 1–12.

Bennett, P., Blackall, M., Clapham, M., Little, S., Player, D., and Williams, K. (1989). South Birmingham Coronary Prevention Project: a district approach to the prevention of heart disease. *Community Medicine*, **11**, 90–96.

Bloom, J.R. and Monterossa, S. (1981). Hypertension labelling and sense of well-being. *American Journal of Public Health*, **71**, 1228–1232.

Cromwell, R.L. and Levenkron, J.C. (1984). Psychological care of acute coronary patients. In A. Steptoe and A. Matthews (Eds), *Health care and human behaviour*. London: Academic Press.

Croog, S.H., Shapiro, D.S., and Levine, S. (1971). Denial among male heart patients. *Psychosomatic Medicine*, **33**, 385–397.

Dugmore, D., Bone, M.F., and Kubik, M. (1986). The organisation and implementation of a cardiac rehabilitation programme in the District General Hospital. In R.H. Fagard and I.E. Bekaert (Eds), *Exercise in health and cardiovascular disease*. Berlin: Martinus Nighoff, Dordrecht.

Egan, G. (1982). *The skilled helper: Models, skills, and methods for effective helping*. Monterey: Brooks/Cole Publishing Co.

Farquhar, J.W., Fortmann, S.P., Maccoby, N., Haskell, W.L., Williams, P.T., Flora, J.A., Taylor, C.B., Brown, B.W., Solomon, D.S., and Holley, S.B. (1985). The Stanford Five-City Project: design and methods. *American Journal of Epidemiology*, **122**, 323–334.

Frasure-Smith, N. and Prince, R.H. (1986). The Ischemic Heart Disease Life Stress Monitoring Program: 18-month mortality results. *Canadian Journal of Public Health*, **77**, Suppl 1, 46–50.

Fullard, E., Fowler, A., and Gray, J. (1983). Facilitating prevention in primary care. *British Medical Journal*, **289**, 1585–1587.

Gruen, W. (1975). Effects of brief psychotherapy during the hospitalization period on the recovery process of heart attacks. *Journal of Consulting and Clinical Psychology*, **43**, 232–233.

Hackett, T.P., Cassem, N.H., and Wishnie, H.A. (1968). The coronary care unit: an appraisal of its psychological hazards. *New England Journal of Medicine*, **279**, 1365–1370.

Holden, U.P. and Woods, R.T. (1982). *Reality orientation: Psychological approaches to the 'confused' elderly*. London: Churchill Livingstone.

Matthews, A. and Ridgeway, V. (1984). Psychological preparation for surgery. In A. Steptoe and A. Matthews. *Health care and human behaviour*. London: Academic Press.

Mearns, D. and Thorne, B. (1988). Person-centered counselling in action. London: Sage.

Meichenbaum, D. (1988). *Stress inoculation training*. New York: Pergamon.

Newman, S. (1989). The incidence and nature of neuropsychological morbidity following cardiac surgery. *Perfusion*, **4**, 93–100.

Novaco, R. (1978). Anger and coping with stress. Cognitive behavioural interventions. In J.P. Foreyt and D.P. Rathjen (Eds), *Cognitive behaviour therapy*. New York: Plenum.

Puska, P., Nissinen, A., Tuomilehto, J., Salonen, J.T., Koskela, K., McAlister, A., Kottke, T.E., Maccoby, N., and Farquhar, J.W. (1985). The community-based strategy to prevent coronary heart disease; conclusions from the ten years of the North Karelia Project. *Annual Review of Public Health*, **6**, 147–193.

Revel, K.F., Baer, P.E., and Cleveland, S.E.(1988). Stress management in cardiovascular disease: postmyocardial infarction patients. In M.L. Russell (Ed), *Stress management for chronic disease*. New York: Pergamon.

EVALUATION AND ORGANIZATIONAL IMPLICATIONS

18 Evaluating the Effects of Counselling and Communication

Having criticised modern health care and presented many examples of how counselling may be useful, it remains to address the question of whether improved communication and counselling can be shown by research to be beneficial in the health care context. As Martin (1988) has argued, when resources are scarce the wide scale adoption of counselling is unwise without first establishing its effectiveness. We shall do this by first summarising the theoretical benefits for health care to be predicted from using more adequate communication skills and a systematic counselling approach to complement the organic. Secondly, we will explore the research literature to discover to what extent our predictions are supported empirically.

ANTICIPATED EFFECTS

We are going to make a number of predictions about changes that are likely to occur in the circumstances of adding counselling and counselling skills to the usual health care context, where impressive specialist knowledge and skills related to the organic aspects of disease are already manifest. Although discrete hypotheses will be proposed, in reality most of them are highly interrelated. Problems of training and the organizational requirements of such changes will be taken up in the next chapter.

Professional satisfaction

If professionals acquire a greater understanding of communication and the necessary skills, we predict that they would be more satisfied with what they do and less stressed. A major problem for all professions is what has been called burn-out (Maslach and Jackson, 1981). As discussed by Kobasa and Kash (1987) the enormous stresses on health care professionals can eventually reduce motivation such that they care less, work less hard, feel incompetent, become more anxious and give up. Since problems of communication with both patients and other professionals (e.g. Gerrard, Boniface and Love, 1980) are a significant source of stress, then improved training in this area should be beneficial.

Counselling and Communication in Health Care. Edited by H. Davis and L. Fallowfield
© John Wiley & Sons Ltd

Specifically we would expect increased satisfaction, greater confidence, and reduced burn-out on a number of grounds. First, an adequate framework for understanding communication serves as a guide to the individual and may therefore increase confidence and decrease anxiety. Secondly, better skills within such a framework would improve communication and therefore the effectiveness of professionals, with resulting increases in patient outcomes generally and thence greater professional satisfaction. Thirdly, a counselling approach would change criteria of success, so that satisfaction may be derived from helping people in a broader sense and not just from solving their problems or curing them. Although senior physicians realistically claim that they rarely cure people and are only likely to ease suffering, they do not succeed in imparting this to their students. Many may not realise, therefore, that the ability to respect patients in ways that give dignity to their pain and indeed to their death can be a source of enormous satisfaction. Silence and avoidance are signs of discomfort, reflecting inability, and it is predicted that these would be radically altered by an explicit role endorsing psychological as well as medical support. Finally, if professionals themselves had an appropriate system of support, as advocated by the counselling approach, they would have the opportunity to discuss problems, develop alternative perspectives, and therefore function more happily.

Diagnostic adequacy

To the extent that communication is improved, we predict that diagnoses will be more adequate and accurate. Improvements in relating to patients, in respecting and soliciting their viewpoints and expectations, and in providing the opportunity for them to contribute should increase both the accuracy and breadth of diagnoses. Multiple problems would be elicited, allowing the opportunity for understanding the relationships between them, judging priorities, and deriving appropriate action for each. It also follows that there would be a reduction in the degree to which psychosocial problems are neglected.

Patient satisfaction

As professional communication is a major source of patient dissatisfaction, the skilled implementation of a counselling approach should increase patient satisfaction. The increased ability to elicit the needs and expectations of the patient not only enables them to be met more effectively, but also permits discussion and negotiation, with the possibility of agreeing realistic goals. Basic counselling skills would aid patients' satisfaction in making them feel respected; they would feel understood and part of the whole process, not an object of study. They would be more aware of what is happening, and more knowledgeable about the problem. They would feel less intimidated and belittled. These have obvious implications for patient satisfaction with professional communication, but also for their satisfaction with all aspects of health care, given improved diagnostic formulation, more appropriate treatment implications and better outcomes.

Treatment adherence

The adoption of basic counselling in the health care context is likely to reflect positively upon treatment adherence. Patients are much more likely to carry out the treatment or advice prescribed, when they are more satisfied with professional communication and the resulting therapeutic relationship. Patients will listen more to a professional they respect and who has a greater understanding of the problems and difficulties from the patient's viewpoint. Improved communication, resulting in clearer, more agreed aims, and better knowledge of the disease and treatment regimes will all contribute to the accurate adoption of and commitment to treatment plans, with fewer errors.

Psychological consequences

Improved communication skills and counselling would certainly be predicted to have important benefits for patients' psychological well-being. This would involve both direct positive effects and the avoidance of needless distress caused by inappropriate communication.

Positive effects

Given that improved communication would increase the likelihood of patients indicating their worries more clearly, then the professional will be in a better position to reassure appropriately. The presence of psychological and social difficulties would be identified more effectively, as well as the organic. The professional would, therefore, be more able to institute appropriate intervention, such as dealing quickly with severe anxiety and depression.

Professionals with supportive counselling skills will be able to help the psychosocial functioning of the individual in all ways. Personal adaptation to difficulties, including illness, is to some extent a function of self-perception. Individuals who feel strong, have high self-esteem or self-efficacy, are more able to take problems in their stride. Although some individuals may be naturally high in self-esteem, most are affected by other people. One or more truly supportive relationships will at the very least maintain the individual's self-esteem, and at best enhance it. Being respected and valued enhances our self-respect. This is as true for the professional–patient relationship as for others. If the professional acts with the utmost respect, valuing the individual, assuming his or her strength and therefore communicating honestly and openly, then the possibility is that the person will feel supported and valued no matter what the prognosis. The professional who is respectful, genuine and empathic is more likely to be valued by the patient and respected in return. It is likely, therefore, that communication will improve, the professional will be more understanding and more able to support positive adaptation appropriately.

We would also predict that such respectful interaction stands a greater chance of fostering independent behaviour in the patient. People who have self-esteem are more likely to be self-reliant and self-sufficient. They are, therefore, more likely to adapt better generally, but also to rely on their own resources, thus making fewer demands upon the professional. This would also be enhanced by improvements in the professional's ability to impart information more effectively.

Avoidance of the negative

Counselling skills would be expected to reduce the extent to which patients are distressed unnecessarily. Hurtful miscommunication would be much less likely. For example, improvements in the skills of disclosing diagnoses will not take away the basic trauma of receiving bad news, but it would not be tainted with needless hurt or exaggerated by the professional's own feelings getting in the way.

The removal of the communication gap would be expected to have general consequences reflecting upon the adaptation of the patient. The patient would not feel put down or that the professional was being disrespectful. The patient would feel less alienated and therefore more receptive to the clinician's help. It would prevent the situation of the patient suddenly discovering that information has been withheld. Patients may rightly take this as disrespectful, because it implies they cannot handle such information, and are weak, in need of protection and not worthy of respect, even if it is the clinician's caring paternalism that motivates the omission.

Understanding, memory and skills

We would predict that improvements in professional communication skills will be correlated with increases in the information patients remember about their illness, their general understanding, and the skills to cope with it. We would expect, therefore, a more effective relationship with the professional where patients are better educated. Clinicians with good counselling skills will listen better, acquire a greater understanding of the patient's knowledge and skills and, therefore, be more able to provide appropriate information at the right time and in the right way. They will know how to give information that is understandable and not forgotten, and evaluate the effects of the information so as to continue building on the patient's knowledge, or to take action to remedy a misunderstanding or misconception.

Improved physical outcome

What follows from many of the points already made is that the physical outcome of treatment should be better in circumstances incorporating basic counselling skills. We would expect people to improve to a greater extent and faster. With improved communication leading to improved diagnostic accuracy, then treatment will be more appropriate and therefore more effective. Greater adherence, as a result of increased satisfaction and better understanding on the part of the patient, will mean that treatment advice is carried out more appropriately and therefore to better effect. With better personal adaptation, greater self-esteem, and fewer other problems, then again it must be assumed that treatment procedures will be more effective.

We should like to argue for improvements in cost-effectiveness, and this may well be the case. However, counselling cannot be regarded as a cheap option. There are costs involved in training, in the increased consultation time that may be necessary for each patient, and in the employment of specialist counsellors. Considerable resources are necessary to produce the situation that we envisage. On the other hand, the benefits to the whole person are undoubtedly greater, but obviously difficult to cost relative to the present situation. It may be, for example, that a patient would require more time from one professional, but would as a result need much less time from all the other members of the clinical team.

Prevention

A basic counselling approach should facilitate the prevention of disease and the consequences of it. Specifically we would argue that such skills would provide professionals with the means by which they can enable effective behavioural change that would reduce the risk factors associated with disease, including, for example, smoking, alcohol, lack of exercise and diet. This would occur as a consequence of a more respectful working relationship, more open communication, greater ability to impart information appropriately, and a greater awareness of the factors inhibiting the adoption of more healthy living. Egan's model (1982) on its own, for example, would have benefits in that the need to negotiate goals and to foresee difficulties to an action plan are highlighted, thus countering the common strategy of imposing an authoritative global restriction.

Once disease exists, it can be predicted that improved communication would help to prevent unnecessary consequences. Better information and better general communication between professionals and patients should decrease unnecessary distress, anxiety and depression, as argued earlier. Counselling would increase personal adaptation, and therefore prevent family and relationship difficulties and social isolation. Greater knowledge generally of the present situation and the future consequences of a disease will prepare people to act more appropriately, help them to notice dangerous side-effects earlier, and enable greater control (as in diabetes) hence avoiding secondary problems.

EVIDENCE

Having made this series of predictions, we should now like to explore the evidence for them. This is not an exhaustive review; it is meant to be illustrative. There are many relevant publications, but relatively few that are methodologically sufficiently good to enable conclusions. In selecting studies we have generally adopted the criteria of having appropriate controls and measures, except where a study has something of particular interest to contribute to the debate. We have, however, cited reviews by other authors, especially meta-analyses, where a much wider range of studies have been included than we have the resources to cover.

Professional satisfaction

Our prediction that the adoption of a counselling approach to health care would increase professional satisfaction and decrease burn-out has some support. In a recent UK survey of people engaged in oncology counselling, Fallowfield and Roberts (1990) found that although very few had a qualification in counselling, the majority (77%) had attended some type of training course. In comparing those with and without training, it was found that the latter tended to derive less personal benefit from their work. Higgins (1990) exposed medical students to empathy training and found not only increases in empathy (as assessed by the students, observers and patients) but also significant decreases in perceived stress when interviewing emotional patients.

Davis and Rushton (1989 and 1991) trained experienced health care professionals in the basic skills of counselling families of children with disabilities. The effectiveness of the training is documented in the next chapter. However, it is relevant to note here that there were significant changes in the ways the trainees construed themselves and their role as a result of their course. Assessed by an independent researcher before and after training, the trainees came to construe counselling as a more essential aspect of their role, and as more facilitating in the helping process. It helped them to understand the parents more and to help the parents understand their situation. They came to see themselves as more able and more confident in communicating with families, and less anxious. The majority claimed that the addition to their role of an explicit counselling approach made their work more enjoyable. They also wished that all their work, besides the two families to whom they acted as Parent Adviser, allowed time for counselling.

Diagnostic adequacy

Rutter and Maguire (1976) provide evidence for the prediction that improvements in the ability to communicate are likely to improve diagnostic formulations. In a well designed study they trained medical students in history-taking using a specifically prepared handout, discussion and feedback on a videotaped recording of an interview conducted by the student. Those trained derived almost three times as much information relevant to the diagnosis compared to the untrained students. Specifically, they gained significantly more information about symptoms, the course of the present illness, previous episodes, the effects upon the patient's adjustment, and the patient's current treatment.

A further study by Maguire *et al.* (1978) evaluated the benefits to be derived from different teaching methods. Improvements in diagnostic adequacy were again indicated. The trained groups, and particularly those exposed to videotape and audiotape feedback, improved significantly in the amount of information they elicited during their interview and the histories they wrote subsequently. Similar results were also found by Maguire, Clarke and Jolley (1977).

Maguire *et al.* (1980) demonstrated improved diagnostic ability as a result of the work of a nurse counsellor. Working with women who had had a mastectomy, the counsellor was able to identify 89% of the patients who had psychiatric difficulties, and referred 79% of these appropriately. In the control group, only 22% of those with psychiatric problems were identified by the usual services and only 14.5% were referred for psychiatric advice.

Patient satisfaction

There is considerable evidence from a variety of different sources to indicate that improved communication is associated with increased patient satisfaction. Cunningham *et al.* (1984) developed a model procedure for the initial disclosure of the diagnosis of Down's syndrome, and trained staff accordingly. The parents were informed by a paediatrician and a specialist health-visitor as soon as possible, together, in private, with the child present. They were told in an unhurried, honest, balanced and empathic manner, responsive to the reactions of the parents. They were then left in private without interruption for as long as they needed. A follow-up interview was arranged within 24 hours to help them begin to further explore what had happened, and arrangements were made for subsequent meetings with the health-visitor. All the parents treated like this expressed complete satisfaction with the procedure when interviewed six months later, in comparison with a satisfaction rate of only 20% in parents not involved in this service. That this skilled counselling also had wider consequences is implied by the author's remark that 'The positive attitude and confidence expressed towards the service was particularly striking'.

Although not the main focus of their study, it is relevant to note that Hughes and Lieberman (1990) found that 50% of their families of children with cancer had considerable dissatisfaction with out-patient but not with in-patient services. A major difference was that the latter had a system of care that allocated one member of staff to take responsibility for generally supporting a particular family. Although it was not clear whether the staff were specifically trained for the role of key worker, the parents felt that information, advice and reassurance was readily available.

Anderson and Hasler (1979) assessed patient attitudes towards counselling in a general practice. The results suggested high levels of satisfaction in that 85% of the respondents to their questionnaire said that counselling should be available in the practice; 78% that they would use the service again; 83% that they would recommend it to relatives and friends; and 87% said that they would not have preferred to see the GP. Unfortunately the absence of a control group prevented testing the hypothesis that a counselling service will increase levels of satisfaction. It was also not clear whether the data was independently derived.

Egbert *et al.* (1964) evaluated a situation in which preoperative patients were given information and reassurance about the pain to be experienced after abdominal surgery. Very few of the patients treated like this had complaints about the information they had been given, in comparison with randomly allocated controls, who complained frequently of the lack of information about the expected pain.

Ferlic, Goldman and Kennedy (1979) found that patients who were newly diagnosed as having metastases and had group counselling sessions were significantly better adjusted to the hospital situation and more confident in communicating with staff than controls. The results are not conclusive, because of the absence of information about the selection of controls and the independence of the assessment. However, in another study of patients with cancer, Cain *et al.* (1986) using independent and blind assessment found that those given counselling were significantly more positive than controls in attitude towards the health care staff both at the end of the intervention period and at follow-up.

Ley (1988) has argued that if one attempts to increase patients' understanding and memory for information, then their satisfaction will also be increased, and cited two studies to this effect. He compared patients given extra visits by a physician to ensure their understanding with those given extra visits involving discussion of general topics and a group given the usual care. The former were significantly more satisfied with communication than the other two groups. In a study comparing patients given information in a single presentation with patients asked to repeat back to the doctor the information presented to them, so that it could be corrected as necessary, Bertakis (1977) found that the latter not only recalled significantly more of the information, but they were also more satisfied.

In relation to non-specific minor disorders, Thomas (1987) found that a positive approach involving a firm diagnosis and reassurance was associated with significantly greater patient satisfaction with their consultation than those in which the doctor was negative. Maguire *et al.* (1977) also found that students who had had appropriate training in history-taking were rated more favourably by patients than those taught by the more traditional methods.

Treatment adherence

Again there is abundant evidence to support the prediction that improved communication and counselling is associated with increased compliance. McKenney *et al.* (1973) showed that brief advisory counselling by a pharmacist made significant improvements to compliance with the treatment of essential hypertension. That this was to some extent a function of personal support is indicated by the fact that compliance decreased greatly once the service was withdrawn, despite significant increases in the patients' knowledge of their condition and its management in comparison with randomly allocated controls.

Very similar results were found by Inui, Yourtee and Williamson (1976). Physicians given a tutorial on hypertension and compliance based upon the Health Belief Model had patients who were significantly more knowledgeable about their treatment, and had more appropriate beliefs about the severity of their complaint, their susceptibility to complications and the effectiveness of the treatment than patients of untutored physicians. These patients also complied more with their treatment and had better blood pressure control.

In his review of this area, Ley (1988) cites several studies in which attempts have been made to communicate in such a way as to improve treatment adherence. The findings, including studies concerned with the provision of written information, give clear support for the conclusion that compliance is increased by improved communication. Ley's analysis also demonstrates the extent to which compliance relates both directly and indirectly to satisfaction, understanding and memory. It can also be argued that the effects indicated are underestimates, in that if attempts to improve compliance are individually tailored by face to face communication, greater compliance would occur as a result of consideration of the differences between people, in terms of, for example, intentional and unintentional compliance.

The conclusion of a strong relationship between communication and adherence is endorsed by the meta-analyses of Mazzuca (1982) and Mullen, Green and Persinger (1985). The latter surveyed 70 studies on a range of disorders, including hypertension, diabetes and asthma, and found impressive support for a significant decrease in drug utilisation errors as a result of diverse psychological interventions, including individual and group counselling, behavioural methods and written material. The best predictor of effect was the quality of the intervention, and particularly whether the method was tailored to the individual and included explicit feedback and reinforcement.

Psychological consequences

Before considering work specifically related to the general health care context, we should quickly summarise the general literature on the evaluation of counselling or psychotherapy. Early reviews were negative. Authors like Eysenck (1952) and Rachman (1971) concluded that there was no evidence for its effectiveness in comparison with untreated control. Bergin (1971) provided a more favourable review, but argued that there was evidence for people being made worse. In contrast, Meltzoff and Kornreich (1970) and Luborsky, Singer and Luborsky (1975) found considerable support for the effectiveness of psychotherapy.

According to Smith *et al.* (1980) the explanation of this inconsistency derived at least in part from the subjective nature of reviews of this kind. Results are easily biased at all stages of the review process by arbitrary judgements, preconceived notions and ideology. They implied, for example, that Eysenck was more concerned about advocating a behavioural approach than evaluating psychotherapy. In contrast, Smith, Glass and Miller (1980) published the results of a meta-analysis of 475 psychotherapy research studies. The conclusions were clear. The mean effect size of 0.85 indicated that the average patient treated by psychotherapy is better than 80% of untreated controls at the end of intervention. There was little evidence of patients being made worse, or that any specific type of therapy was superior. Measures of anxiety and fear were particularly prone to show improvements, and patients with phobic and depressive symptoms responded the most. The effects in general were equivalent to drug treatments, although a combination of the two was most effective. Other findings were that individual and group methods were equally effective, and that duration was not a significant variable, nor the experience of the therapist.

In a subsequent review of the more recent literature including several further meta-analyses, Lambert, Shapiro and Bergin (1986) confirmed the benefits of psychotherapy, even in comparison with placebo and pseudotherapy controls. The previous conclusions were generally supported, except that although differences between methods were not prominent, cognitive-behavioural approaches were somewhat more effective with phobias and compulsions. They also felt that there was some evidence for negative effects, although most patients were helped. The tendency is, therefore, by these and other reviewers, to emphasise the commonalities between approaches in terms of counsellor characteristics, the counsellor–patient relationship, the mechanism of effect and patient characteristics. We have discussed much of this in Chapter 2, but would like to list the kinds of processes for change that are suggested, including: persuasion, hope arousal, increasing self-esteem, stirring emotion, encouraging honesty and self-scrutiny, interpretation, strengthening social support, providing models and manipulating rewards.

To turn to the health care context specifically, we will consider the evidence for the effectiveness of counselling in relation to different specialties, beginning with general practice.

General practice

There has been considerable discussion on the use of counselling within general practice. In an early review, Wyld (1981) concluded that in spite of the absence of controlled experimentation, a number of advantages had been demonstrated by counsellors from diverse non-medical professions, in many different practices, using a variety of different theoretical approaches. There seemed to be a consensus that patients with psychosocial problems benefited. Other general conclusions were that counsellors from social work, psychology, and marriage guidance were more appropriate than medical personnel, that the stigma of a psychiatric referral was reduced, that patient scepticism was reduced by GP endorsement of counselling, and that continuity of support was ensured by attachment of counsellors.

These conclusions have generally been validated as experimental studies have begun to appear. For example, Cooper *et al.* (1975) found that chronic neurotic patients, who worked with a psychiatric social worker in primary care, improved more on independent psychiatric and social ratings than controls, even though the latter were referred more frequently to a psychiatrist. They were also significantly more likely to be taken off psychotropic medication.

In a relatively large study, Waydenfeld and Waydenfeld (1980) made an attempt to evaluate the effects of counselling with voluntary counsellors, trained in marital work and using a predominantly psychodynamic model. The patients had mainly anxiety and relationship problems. The authors concluded that counselling was a valuable facility in general practice and filled a definite psychological need. They presented data showing a 31% decrease in surgery attendance following counselling, a 30% decrease in psychotropic drug prescriptions and a 48% decrease in other prescriptions. Approximately 80% of their sample were rated as very much or somewhat improved after counselling, using ratings from the GPs, the counsellors and the patients themselves, all of which were in general accord. However, although suggestive, these results must be taken cautiously, as the authors acknowledge, because of the absence of a control group, sample attenuation, non-independent evaluation, and the lack of statistical comparison.

Anderson and Hasler (1979) reported a similar study based upon the work of one counsellor. The patients who took part were described as having a variety of stresses and relationship problems. According to GP ratings, the majority of the patients benefited. The patients themselves were not quite so enthusiastic, although there was evidence of change in their ratings. For example, 49% reported feeling more confident, 71% felt more capable of dealing with mood changes, 45% had found improvements in their friend-ships and 47% in close relationships, and 43% felt they were sleeping better. As in the previous study, there was a reduction in medical consultations, and in the use of psychotropic drugs, with 54% of those who had been on such medication before counselling either reducing or stopping. Again the results are optimistic and suggestive, but they are not conclusive, because of the same kind of methodological difficulties, compounded by the failure to provide relevant detail.

Earll and Kincey (1982) evaluated the use of what appears to be a cognitive-behavioural approach with patients who largely had anxiety and relationship problems. Methodologically the study was somewhat better because of the inclusion of a randomly allocated control group. As in the previous studies, the treatment group had significantly fewer prescriptions for psychotropic medication during the treatment period. Eighty-five percent of the patients rated themselves as helped by the intervention, and a relatively independent rater provided comparable results. Overall, there-fore, the study supports the predicted benefits of counselling despite the methodological faults that would have had the effect of preventing the detection of benefits. These included the very limited assessment of psycho-logical variables not specific to the presenting problems, the failure to assess immediately after the treatment period, the absence of pre-intervention mea-sures, and the inclusion in the treatment group of people judged to be unsuitable for the intervention and therefore not seen.

A similar study of clinical psychologists in general practice was carried out by Robson, France and Bland (1984). Although the assessment was not blind, some of the ratings used in the study were compared to those of a blind rater and were not significantly different. The design included a ran-dom control group. Measures included ratings of severity of problem, effects upon patient and household, satisfaction with outcome, the need for further treatment, the number of visits to the GP, and the cost of drugs. Both groups improved, but the changes were significantly greater and faster on all the ratings for the treatment group and maintained in some cases up to 12 months. Where the difference was not maintained it was because the con-trols continued to improve and caught up to some extent. The controls visited the GP significantly more often during and after the study and cost significantly more in psychotropic drugs. Anxiety problems seemed particularly amenable to the intervention, but relatively few sessions were involved (a mean of 3.7 per patient).

Although there is strong evidence for the effectiveness of specialist counselling in these studies, questions remain. As Freeman and Button (1984) have suggested, the use of gross measures and consultation and prescription rates may give a false impression of outcome without considering the general trends in the practice and the natural history of psychosocial problems. In a six-year period they found generally decreasing trends in the number of consultations for psychosocial issues and in the prescription of psychotropic drugs. They also showed a strong tendency for psychosocial consultations to cluster into relatively short periods, presumably because they are mainly related to stress events that are resolved within a finite period. Taking these factors into account means that the measures of the kind used in outcome studies will naturally show improvements. Random control design allows for this, but the implication is that intervention is only accelerating a natural process, as opposed to making qualitative changes. There are also questions about the representativeness of the patients used in general practice studies and about how to predict individual treatment options and outcome.

Much more detailed research is needed incorporating more elaborate measures of psychological functioning in relation to careful specification of counselling methods. These questions are to some extent addressed by Milne and Souter (1988) who assessed levels of stress, coping strategies adopted by the patient, and personal strain or distress in the form of the General Health Questionnaire. They also used patients as their own controls by incorporating a waiting period before counselling began. They found significant increases in the use of active cognitive coping skills and decreases in the level of strain experienced as a result of intervention. The findings were not simply the result of crisis resolution, as the group with the most chronic problems developed more adequate coping skills whilst at the same time showing increased stress scores. Those who improved showed significant reductions in treatment costs in terms of drugs, GP visits and hospital referrals. This study therefore does provide even stronger evidence of the effectiveness of counselling of a cognitive-behavioural variety.

A study by Holden, Sagovsky and Cox (1989) overcomes another of the criticisms mentioned earlier, by being problem specific. Women who had major and minor depression in the postpartum period were counselled by health visitors specifically trained in a Rogerian approach. The study was well designed including random allocation to groups, independent and blind assessment before and after the intervention. The recovery rate in the counselling group was significantly greater than in the control group (69% versus 38%), and there were significant decreases in all the measures of depression in the treatment group, in contrast to controls who did not change significantly. The study therefore appears to give convincing evidence of the benefits of counselling even after a training period that amounted to approximately six hours, albeit for very experienced health visitors. It would be very interesting to know the mechanism by which the changes occurred. The assumption that it was the support deriving from active listening and encouragement of self-decision could be tested very easily.

Cardiovascular problems

An extensive review of this area has been recently published by Bundy (1989) and a good summary by D. Johnston (1990). Both conclude that psychological methods have clearly demonstrated benefits in relation to the prevention of heart disease, intervention in the acute phase following myocardial infarction, and in rehabilitation. They report the use of a variety of methods, ranging from the psychodynamic to the cognitive-behavioural.

To illustrate prevention work, a large study by Farquhar et al. (1977) found that a community-based intervention, including media education, personal counselling and behavioural skills training were successful in altering the population's knowledge and behaviour, thus reducing heart disease risk factors. However, it is interesting to note that personal counselling was necessary to decrease smoking.

A study by Gruen (1974) demonstrates the possibility of benefit for patients in the acute stage. He randomly allocated patients admitted to an intensive care unit following myocardial infarction to daily counselling while in hospital or to standard care. In nurse records the controls were more frequently noted to be tired, and the medical staff judged them to be depressed more frequently. On various psychological measures the counselling group were significantly more vigorous in mood, felt more social affection and were less depressed. Four months later they were rated as significantly less anxious and as having returned more quickly to normal activity, although these final measures require caution because they were not collected independently.

A number of studies illustrate the effects of rehabilitation. For example, Frasure-Smith and Prince (1986) monitored patients on discharge from hospital and counselled those identified as highly stressed. They found significant reductions in stress levels compared to controls, who were not monitored in this way. Burgess et al. (1987) also found that cognitive-behavioural counselling and support for families and work colleagues resulted in less psychological distress and less dependence in patients who had suffered a myocardial infarction. The suggestion that benefits may derive from including the family in the intervention is also illustrated by Mayou et al. (1981) whose rehabilitation study appeared not to be generally successful. However, the men given advisory counselling with their wives were significantly less protected by their families at three months post discharge, had greater overall satisfaction with outcome at 18 months, spent more hours at work, and had sexual intercourse more often.

A final point to be made here is to indicate the benefits to be derived from preparation for invasive investigations such as cardiac catheterization. There is conclusive evidence for such preparation (D. Johnston, 1990). For example, Kendall *et al.* (1979) randomly allocated patients to one of four groups, which included cognitive-behavioural intervention, an education group, an attention placebo, and non-intervention. Both the intervention conditions were associated with reduced anxiety both before and during the catheterization procedure, with the cognitive approach the most effective.

Cancer

Watson (1983) reviewed the area of psychosocial intervention for patients with cancer and concluded that there was evidence that counselling was beneficial. She remained cautious, however, as a result of the lack of research and the difficulties in comparing available studies. There appeared to be particular benefits for patients who had difficulties in coping with stress, but quite long-term help was needed for the benefits to become apparent. Immediate benefits of short-term help may not be obvious, because many people in both intervention and control groups will adapt relatively quickly, leaving those in particular difficulty without sufficient time or help to have shown effects. She also concluded that no particular method of intervention had been shown to be more effective than another. These conclusions were essentially endorsed in a subsequent review by Massie, Holland and Straker (1989).

Early cancer: Capone *et al.* (1980) found no effects on mood disturbance three months after the diagnosis and treatment of gynaecological cancer as the result of a very short period of counselling during their stay in hospital. Nevertheless, they did show significantly less confused self-concept than the control group at three months after treatment and were significantly more likely to have returned to their usual frequency of sexual intercourse. The results of this study, however, do have to be taken cautiously as it is not clear whether the assessment was independent, how the groups were selected, nor their comparability.

   Gordon *et al.* (1980) found a significant decline in negative affect compared to controls in people with newly diagnosed cancer as a result of counselling support for six months after the diagnosis. Maguire *et al.* (1980) found no effects of a nurse counsellor on psychiatric morbidity at three months after mastectomy compared to a random control group. However, at 12 to 18 months the intervention group had significantly less psychiatric morbidity, perhaps because many more of the intervention group were quickly referred to a psychiatrist, who used what was described as a combination of brief psychotherapy and antidepressant medication. The effectiveness of the counsellor was endorsed in a following paper (Maguire *et al.*,

1982) where the costs of the intervention were carefully considered. The total costs were almost exactly the same for both intervention and control groups, with the extra costs of the counsellor being offset by the greater costs of psychiatric intervention in the controls and the losses resulting from the time taken off work by their relatives. The authors in fact concluded that the costs for the controls were probably greater than those found in the study, largely because more control than intervention patients refused to participate, and these tended to be the people with the more severe psychosocial problems.

Watson *et al.* (1988) also evaluated the work of a nurse counsellor, who aimed to provide both emotional support and information and advice before and after mastectomy. The group receiving counselling were less depressed than controls at three but not 12 months, had a greater internal health locus of control, and changed significantly on a measure of vigour. The authors, therefore, concluded that counselling is beneficial in speeding up the process of adaptation, but there were few significant changes overall, which may be the result of a number of factors including small sample size and the absence of pre-intervention assessment.

Bloom, Ross and Burnell (1978) found that an intervention group counselled at all stages of their illness, as an integrated part of their total care, were higher in internal locus of control at two months after their operation than controls. It was not clear how the intervention patients were selected, nor whether the assessment was independent, so that some doubt must be cast on the study. Nevertheless, as predicted, the patients in the intervention group were significantly *more* anxious, more depressed, less vigorous and more confused than the controls one week after surgery. This was predicted on the basis that denial is a common feature of adaptation to disease and that active counselling might initially change this, facilitating more overt emotional expression. It may be, therefore, that counselling is not necessarily an easy activity, but may make people think about things that are difficult to confront initially but which may have positive effects subsequently.

Worden and Weisman (1984) randomly allocated patients judged to be at high risk of poor coping to one of two types of intervention, a more psychodynamic and a cognitive didactic approach. Compared to controls, who were reasonably well matched, from a previous study, both types of intervention resulted in lower emotional distress, measured independently on a number of scales, and better problem resolution.

Forester, Kornfeld and Fleiss (1985) completed a study in which weekly counselling was carried out during the six-week period when the patients were undergoing radiotherapy and four weeks afterwards. They used an individual approach, which was non-directive and included supportive, informational, interpretative and cathartic elements. All assessment procedures were carried out independently and without knowledge of the patients' treatment status. Benefits were evident from the reduction in psychological symptoms in the intervention group compared to randomly allocated controls during the radiotherapy. The two groups differed significantly at the end of their radiation treatment, and diverged further by the end of the counselling period as the intervention group continued to improve.

Cain *et al.* (1986) randomly allocated women with gynaecological cancer to one of three conditions: routine care, individual structured thematic counselling or group counselling. Both intervention conditions involved information provision, emotional expression and instruction as appropriate in relation to a number of major themes, including the nature of cancer, its causes, the impact of treatment, relaxation, diet and exercise, relating to caregivers, family and friends, and goal-setting. The results derived from a blind and independent assessment were quite conclusive. Although all three groups improved in adjustment, the results favoured the counselling groups in that they were significantly less anxious, in the case of individual counselling, and significantly more knowledgeable about the disease and more positive towards the professionals. These differences, however, had become much greater six months later, when both intervention groups were significantly less depressed and anxious, better adjusted to their illness, more knowledgeable, and positive towards the staff, more involved in leisure pursuits, and with fewer sexual difficulties. The degree of change was also significantly greater in the intervention conditions.

Overall, therefore, there does appear to be general support for the benefits to be derived from counselling in relation to early cancer. Many questions need to be explored by research, and changes are not always dramatic and easy to achieve. Nevertheless, it is interesting to note a study by Holland *et al.* (1987), who worked with patients identified as highly distressed. They were either given a single session of relaxation training, which they were asked to carry out three times a day subsequently, or psychotropic drugs. Ten days later both groups were found to be significantly less anxious and depressed. Also, Burton and Parker (1980) studied the effects of a single preoperative interview with a psychologist, or the same interview followed by one session with a surgeon, who either simply had a friendly chat or employed Rogerian counselling. All three interventions resulted in significantly better psychological adjustment at both three months and one year post surgery for women undergoing mastectomy.

People with advanced cancer: Spiegel, Bloom and Yalom (1981) evaluated the effectiveness of support groups for women with metastatic breast cancer by randomly allocating patients to a counselling or control group. The results showed clear benefits for the counselled group, although it was not stated whether the assessment was independent. There were significant differences between the groups when those who survived 12 months were compared: the counselled group were significantly less tense, less depressed, and less confused. They were more vigorous, and less fatigued. They had less mood disturbance overall and showed fewer maladaptive coping responses and fewer phobias. When the degree of change was considered, the treatment group changed significantly over the period of the intervention in overall mood disturbance, anxiety and phobias, in maladaptive coping responses, vigour, fatigue and confusion.

The possibility that it is damaging for patients to be exposed to people who are dying was addressed by Spiegel and Glafkides (1983). A content analysis of one of their groups over a ten-month period showed that the presence of a person who was deteriorating or dying did affect the topic under discussion, in that death and dying were discussed significantly more frequently. Nevertheless, the emotional state of the group members and the tone of the group was not changed in comparison with conditions in which members were either unchanged physically or improving. The comments of the group were very favourable and indicated that the sessions were not only not damaging, but were helpful in enabling them to face and deal with their own related problems. It is important to note that the groups were run by experienced staff and consisted of people who became very close over a relatively long period of time.

Watson (1983) cited an unpublished study by Weisman, Worden and Sobel in which two types of group therapy were evaluated. One was concerned to identify problems and allow emotional expression and the other was a more didactic approach in which relaxation methods were frequently used. Both were found to result in less distress at follow-up than controls.

Ferlic et al. (1979) found that group work with both educational and supportive components was beneficial for people newly diagnosed as having metastases. These patients were found to be significantly better adjusted to group situations and to the hospital, to have more knowledge of their disease and to be better adjusted to the notion of death than controls. They were also found to have higher self-esteem. The intervention group changed significantly more than the controls on these measures, despite the fact that the intervention consisted of only six sessions in a two-week period. However, the results must be regarded cautiously as the method of patient allocation was not described, nor whether the assessment was independent.

Grossarth-Maticek et al. (1984) argued on the basis of survival studies that the aim of intervention should be to attempt to increase the will to live, self-esteem, and the expression of emotion, while reducing feelings of hopelessness. They evaluated these hypotheses by implementing psychotherapy with these specific aims, and found not only that survival time increased significantly, but seemed to do so via the predicted changes in psychological characteristics.

Linn, Linn and Harris (1982) worked with men who were in the late stages of cancer until their death, and in some cases continuing to support their families afterwards. The design of the study included random allocation to

the control group, independent and blind assessment, and explicit hypotheses. They found no differences between those counselled and controls
initially or at one month after the intervention had begun. There were,
however, significant differences between the groups at three months and
thereafter. At three months the intervention group were less depressed than
the controls, although the latter caught up at six months and beyond. The
people who were counselled were also more satisfied with life from three
months onward and had greater self-esteem. It was not clear from the report
whether the differences were significant, but the intervention group were
less alienated and felt more in control from three months onward.

Childhood disability

There has been much less attention paid to the area of disability, and most of
the studies have focused upon training the children. However, Davis and
Rushton (1991) focused upon the parents, predicting that counselling support would be beneficial both for the parents themselves and indirectly for
the child. Parent Advisers, trained in basic counselling skills, worked with
families of children with moderate to severe intellectual or multiple disabilities. They worked with the parents at home on a weekly basis initially,
decreasing the frequency gradually over a 15-month period. The aims were
to establish a close and respectful relationship with the family, to support
them, to help them explore whatever problems were relevant to them, and
to help them develop appropriate strategies as necessary. A major underlying goal was to facilitate the family's own resources, and particularly to
increase the parents' feelings of self-esteem and self-efficacy.

The results showed the intervention to be highly effective with very deprived immigrant families in comparison with a randomly allocated control
group, who received the usually available services. Although there were few
differences between the groups before intervention, the families in the control group changed very little, whereas the intervention group changed
significantly on many variables and were significantly better at the end of
the research. The mothers felt much more supported both socially and professionally as a result of the intervention. They felt more able to help their
children and less concern about whether they were doing enough to help.
They felt that there was less stress in the family, more joy in caring for the
child, and less neglect of their other children. The mothers developed many
more social contacts, felt much more positive about their child, and about
themselves and their husbands, and there was evidence that they felt significantly better about family relationships. What is perhaps more important is
that it was not just the mothers who changed; there were also significant
changes in the children. They progressed in all aspects of development and
changed significantly more than the children in the control group in both
developmental and behavioural terms.

Conclusions

To conclude our discussion of whether counselling has psychological benefits in the medical context, the results do appear to parallel the general
counselling situation described at the beginning of this section. There is
considerable evidence from a number of different areas that counselling can
alleviate distress and significantly facilitate psychological adaptation. This
does not happen magically and instantaneously, but usually requires time
and appropriate effort. It is also true, however, that much more extensive
research is necessary to answer many remaining questions about what kind
of intervention is particularly beneficial to what patients at which stage in
their illness and why. This requires detailed consideration of patient characteristics, such as the nature of and reasons for their problems, the extent of
distress, their prior coping strategies, and their family and social situation.
The point of intervention and the type of illness needs to be explored further. Consideration needs to be given to the characteristics of different methods of counselling and the attributes and experience of counsellors, as well
as theorising and investigating the many different ways in which psychological change may occur in different individuals.

Understanding, memory and skills

The prediction that there are benefits for patient knowledge and abilities to
be derived from improved communication is supported by a number of
studies. For example, McKenney *et al.* (1973) evaluated a project in which a
pharmacist monitored the response of hypertensive patients to their treatment, and provided appropriate information in a structured and individualised way. As a result the patients acquired significantly better knowledge
about their condition, adhered more to the treatment regime and gained
better blood pressure control. Inui *et al.* (1976), as mentioned earlier, also
found better knowledge in patients of physicians who were more aware of
the psychological determinants of compliance. Ferlic *et al.* (1979) found that
patients with newly diagnosed metastases had developed a better understanding of various aspects of their disease following counselling than
controls. Cain *et al.* (1986) found the same in patients with gynaecological
cancer.

It is clear from the work of Ley (1988) that clinicians can affect the understanding and recall of their patients, if they improve their communication
skills. There are a number of specific methods for doing this and a variety of
studies to indicate their success. The research will not be described here,
because this has already been done thoroughly and convincingly by Ley.
Instead the major conclusions will be summarised. In relation to the specific
content of consultations, it has been demonstrated that instructions and
advice that are either given first or are stressed as important are better

recalled. In relation to overall recall of information, all the following have been shown to significantly improve retention: using shorter words and sentences, explicit categorization before providing information, repetition either by the clinician or the patient (Bertakis, 1977) and making the instructions specific. As an example of this work, Ley (1988) described a study in which a manual was given to four medical practitioners explaining all the communication techniques listed above. Patients seen before the introduction of the manual averaged between 52–59% recall of the information provided during the consultations. Once they had read the manual the recall rate rose significantly to between 61–80%.

In a previously cited meta-analysis, Mullen, Green and Persinger (1985) found clear evidence of improved knowledge as a result of a range of intervention strategies. The most effective method appeared to be one-to-one counselling, and not surprisingly the quality of the intervention was the best predictor of outcome. In particular it was the extent to which the method individualised the intervention, and provided explicit feedback and reinforcement that predicted the effects best.

The argument that giving patients extra information about their condition and treatment may have adverse effects has also been discussed by Ley (1988) with reference to the disclosure of bad news, the possible side effects of drugs, and the risks of investigative procedures. The major conclusion from his review is that adverse effects are unlikely. He found that the majority of patients involved in the studies believed that such information should be provided for all patients. This data therefore indirectly supports an increase in patient satisfaction as the result of improved communication. In one of the studies quoted there was also evidence suggesting improved adaptation in a group given the diagnosis of inoperable cancer in comparison with those who were not informed (Gerle, Lunden and Sandblom, 1960).

Physical outcomes

Again there appears to be considerable support for the prediction that counselling and communication have effects upon outcome in organic as well as psychological ways. In a review of 27 studies concerned only with chronic disease, Mazzuca (1982) found that there were significant effects upon a variety of diseases achieved by methods concerned to communicate better with patients. This meta-analysis indicated superior effects for people in the intervention groups in comparison with controls given routine medical care, both in terms of specific therapeutic goals (e.g. blood pressure and blood sugar control and weight loss) and in long-term outcomes such as return to work or hospitalisation. For example, the average effect size for behavioural approaches in relation to specific goals was 0.74, indicating that the intervention group were better than about 78% of controls.

Schlesinger *et al.* (1983) used insurance claim data to evaluate the relative costs in four chronic diseases of what they called mental health treatment. The diseases included were diabetes, ischaemic heart disease, hypertension and airflow limitation. The results of the study suggested improved physical outcomes in that patients who had more than seven visits to mental health facilities had significantly lower medical costs in the third year after the diagnosis. The savings were largely in relation to in-patient treatment, and over the three years amounted to the cost of about 20 mental health visits.

We will again illustrate the research findings with reference to a number of specific disease categories.

Cardiovascular disease

The research in this area has been summarised by Bundy (1989) and indicates that significant benefits in physiological outcome do derive from counselling interventions. For example, Gruen (1975) found that patients who were randomly allocated to daily counselling following myocardial infarction stayed on cardiac monitors for less time, remained both in the intensive care unit and the hospital for shorter periods, had less congestive heart failure, and fewer arrhythmias than controls.

Although Cromwell and Levenkrom (1984) did not study counselling, the importance of psychological factors in the treatment and outcome of acute myocardial infarction is inescapable from their results. They investigated a complex set of variables including personality characteristics and intervention strategies related to information provision, participation in treatment and attention diversion in the acute phase of the illness. Although the psychological intervention did not predict death or reinfarction within 12 weeks, it did predict the length of stay in the coronary care unit and the hospital. The pattern of results, however, are of interest in that information provision alone did not predict early discharge unless it was coupled with the means by which patients could do something about their disease (i.e. participating in their treatment or being distracted from it). The implication is that information in this situation is only of benefit if the patient is also helped to consider and implement potential solutions as would be the case in any adequate counselling situation.

Pozen *et al.* (1977) allocated patients on a random basis to intervention, which consisted of individual daily sessions with a nurse rehabilitator while in the coronary care unit, supplemented by group sessions on alternate days in the convalescent period and weekly contact by telephone or in person after discharge. The role of the nurse included imparting information as well as discussing plans for return to normal life and helping to minimise anxiety. Although the assessment was not independent and some of the results are suspect, the intervention group at the six-month follow-up were significantly more likely to be working, and of a higher functional status generally.

Frasure-Smith and Prince (1986) monitored the stress levels of patients monthly after discharge from hospital. This was done by telephone using Goldberg's General Hospital Questionnaire (1972). Those identified as experiencing increased stress were visited at home by a nurse, who provided individually tailored help, which included teaching and support components. At 12 months the randomly allocated treatment group were not only less stressed than their controls, but showed a significantly higher survival rate, which was even more significant at 18 months. Given that these patients were all also being treated by appropriate medicine, these survival figures are even more impressive.

McKenney et al. (1973) trained a pharmacist to provide what amounted to advisory counselling for patients with essential hypertension. This began with a 25-minute session in which a pharmaceutical history was taken and the service explained. Subsequent sessions lasted six minutes on average and involved the evaluation of therapeutic response and discussion of problems. The patient's understanding of their problem and treatment was evaluated and information given as necessary in an individualised and structured way. As a result patients showed significant improvements in blood pressure (recorded independently) compared to random controls, had fewer adverse drug reactions, more knowledge of their condition, and became significantly more compliant for the period of the intervention. The fact that compliance and blood pressure reverted to the lower pre-intervention levels once the service stopped demonstrates the need for more than information, but for social support from someone prepared to listen to the patient.

As mentioned earlier Inui et al. (1976) found that 69% of patients treated for hypertension by physicians tutored about the psychological determinants of compliance had good blood pressure control in comparison with 36% of patients whose physicians had not had such teaching. The implication, supported by the results of this study, is that the physicians had improved their communication because of the tutorial, and had therefore not only imparted more information to their patients, but had affected their rate of compliance and hence the physical outcome of improved blood pressure.

Cancer

Several studies of counselling intervention with patients who have cancer have already been described in relation to the evidence for psychological effects. However, these also provide some evidence that there are physical effects of a beneficial nature. Forester et al. (1985) found that counselling significantly reduced the symptoms of anorexia, fatigue, nausea and vomiting in comparison with controls. Spiegel and Bloom (1983) found that the women with metastatic breast cancer in supportive counselling groups did not change over the 12-month period of the study in their ratings of pain and associated suffering, whereas the control group reported significantly increasing levels of both. The effects were further enhanced when the group included an element of self-hypnosis. Spiegel *et al.* (1989) subsequently followed up the patients from their previous studies, and found that the women in intervention groups survived about twice as long as controls on average, although the difference between the groups did not become apparent until eight months after the intervention period.

Grossarth-Maticek *et al.* (1984) also looked at the effects of psychotherapy upon the survival time of women with advanced breast cancer and found similar results. Thirty sessions of therapy were found to increase survival significantly and to the same extent as chemotherapy. A combination of the two, however, appeared to be particularly effective, resulting in fewer negative side-effects of chemotherapy and improved immune response. What is particularly interesting about this study is that the patient characteristics (including the will to survive, hopelessness, self-esteem and the expression of emotion) predicted to be significantly affected by psychotherapy may also have mediated the length of survival. The only problem with this, however, was that the authors did not state the extent to which the measures were independent.

This study also compared different methods of psychotherapy, and most benefit derived from the cognitive-behavioural method specifically formulated and implemented in the study by Grossarth-Maticek himself. The same was true in a second study, where only the people seen by Grossarth-Maticek had significantly increased survival rates compared to controls. Depth psychotherapy based upon classical psycho-analysis conferred no survival benefit in the first study and in the second was associated with reduced survival, although the sample size was relatively small.

Results are not unanimous in supporting an effect upon survival. Linn *et al.* (1982) in a study mentioned earlier, found no effects of counselling upon either functional status or survival. However, the situation must be explored further, because differences could be explained, for example, in terms of the type or intensity of the intervention, the possible mechanisms by which change occurs, or even in relation to the characteristics of the counsellors. Very little work of this kind has been described in this review, as most studies have focused upon outcome and not the processes involved. It could be that here is another demonstration of the importance of the counsellor. Could it be the charisma and reputation of the powerful hero-innovator, such as Grossarth-Maticek, that affects the patient's will to live and other characteristics, which in turn relate to survival? The fact that the characteristics predicting survival changed in one of the Grossarth-Maticek studies before the counselling had begun properly gives weight to this hypothesis. Just as Leshan (1990) aimed to help patients have enthusiasm for living, to find their own 'special song to sing', in the belief that this related to survival, so it may be that it is the counsellor's zest and enthusiasm, coupled with respect for the individuality of the person and encouragement of autonomy, that helps the patient.

Post-operative recovery

Egbert *et al.* (1964) considered the effects of what they called 'superficial psychotherapy' on post-operative recovery. The anaesthetist visited patients just before abdominal surgery and gave information about the pain to be expected as a result of the operation with relevant explanation. Suggestions were also given on how to control the pain (e.g. relaxation). The aim was to provide information and reassurance, and several follow-up visits were made post-operatively to reinforce this. As a result patients not only requested approximately 50% fewer narcotic drugs than randomly allocated controls in the first five days after the operation, they were also judged by independent and blind observers to be in significantly less pain, and were discharged 2.7 days earlier on average.

The intervention described was complex and included several aspects, which could be effective in isolation or in combination. Johnson, Morrissey and Leventhal (1973), for example, explored the provision of two types of information for patients who were to undergo endoscopic examination, either information about the procedure or information about the experiences they could expect (sensory information). This was done by audiotape in both cases and compared with a control group in which no such information was provided. This very simple endeavour produced significant effects, in that both intervention groups had to be given less diazepam. The sensory information group were also less tense during the examination. In a further study, Johnson *et al.* (1978) looked at all combinations of instruction versus no instruction and procedural information versus sensory information versus neither, before major abdominal surgery. All three factors were found to have a significant effect upon the post-operative mood of those patients who were particularly fearful beforehand. Sensory information was also associated with increased recovery rate in terms of length of post-operative stay in hospital and time before venturing from home once discharged.

These are examples of a few of the many studies carried out in this area using a variety of different psychological intervention methods. All the reviews of the area have been unanimous in the benefits of such intervention. Mathews and Ridgeway (1984) concluded that information, instruction and training in cognitive coping techniques were beneficial, particularly if sensory information was included. They also found that patients who were highly anxious were especially likely to benefit from such pre-operative preparation. More recently M. Johnston (1990) also concluded on the basis of an extensive review of 35 randomized controlled trials that psychological methods 'have been shown to be effective in reducing pain, reducing analgesic use, reducing patient distress and increasing patient satisfaction with care' (p. 8).

A meta-analysis by Mumford *et al.* (1982) supports and further illustrates the conclusions of the more subjective reviews. The results indicated consistent effects of a range of interventions from the psychotherapeutic to the educational upon a range of variables from pain and physiological indices, to drug administration, post-operative complications and speed of recovery. The overall mean effect size of 0.49 suggests that the average intervention patient is better off as a result than approximately 67% of controls. Of particular interest was the finding that in the ten studies that measured length of hospital stay, intervention groups remained in hospital for just over two days less than controls on average. Although psychotherapeutic approaches were found to be the more effective in general, with effect sizes of 0.41 as opposed to 0.3 for the educational, the most beneficial was a combination of the two (effect size 0.65).

Asthma

There have been a number of studies of different kinds of counselling in relation to both children and adults with asthma. Eleven controlled outcome studies were found by Smith *et al.* (1980) and included in a meta-analysis. The outcomes most commonly used in the studies were frequency of attacks, emergency hospital visits, medication and lung function. All the effect sizes were positive indicating that in all cases the people in the intervention group benefited in comparison with their respective controls. The mean effect size for all the studies was 0.82, which means that those who underwent psychological intervention were better off than 79% of controls at the end of the treatment period. Even when studies using very specific techniques were removed from consideration (e.g. hypnosis and relaxation) the mean effect size rose somewhat to 1.08.

Prevention

Bereavement counselling can be seen as a particularly important area of medicine concerned with the prevention and amelioration of both physical problems and distress. Parkes (1980) reviewed this area and found several studies indicating the preventive effects of counselling. Raphael (1977) showed that at a thirteen month follow-up widows who had one or more interviews with a psychiatrist within twelve weeks of their bereavement experienced significantly fewer new or worsening symptoms that necessitated consulting their physician than a matched control group, who were not supported in this way. This was especially true for those who were in the more difficult situation of having families they rated as unhelpful.

In a similar study by Gerber *et al.* (1975) people supported by a social worker or a psychiatric nurse for up to six months after bereavement had significantly fewer prescriptions, fewer medical consultations and reported feeling ill less often, when assessed at five and eight months post bereavement, in comparison with unsupported controls. A study by Polak *et al.*

(1975) did not confirm the differences between supported and unsupported people, but this was probably because they did not take account of their pre-bereavement state of health, and because the groups were not well matched. The controls were not as closely related to the dead person and suffered less financially as a result of the death. Even so, there was some evidence of a greater increase in psychiatric disturbance in the controls than in the group who were supported.

Jones in an unpublished study cited by Parkes (1980) found no differences in health or psychological state between bereaved people who attended a support group for eight weeks and controls. However, those who were considered to be at high risk, in feeling guilty or blaming themselves, did show significant improvements on several measures in comparison with low risk people and controls.

Parkes (1980) cited another unpublished study by Cameron of a volunteer counselling service. Twenty bereaved families from a palliative care unit were compared to twenty from other wards in the same hospital. The former, therefore, were exposed to a supportive family care situation both before and after the death of the ill person. At 12.5 months the people who were counselled showed less deterioration in health and had fewer sedatives and tranquillisers. Psychologically they were better adjusted, less preoccupied by thoughts of the dead person, less angry and less guilty. It is important to note, however, that there is the possibility of a systematic bias in the results in that the experimental and control groups were not allocated randomly. The fact that they were selected for different wards when the person was dying may have a role in explanation of the results.

Parkes (1979) also studied a voluntary counselling service and found beneficial effects. Relatives of patients who died at a hospice were randomly allocated to a support service or a control group. All were assessed as being of high risk and therefore in need of support. At 20 months after bereavement, the supported group were in overall better health than the controls, had fewer new or worsening autonomic symptoms and had increased their consumption of drugs, alcohol and tobacco less.

Vachon *et al.* (1980) evaluated a service provided by widows themselves who were trained to help the newly bereaved in both a one-to-one and group situation. Although there are some methodological concerns about this work in matching and sample attenuation, overall there were no differences in psychological state between the supported and unsupported at 6, 12 and 24 months. Nevertheless, at 12 months the supported group showed evidence of psychological change in a beneficial direction. Again, however, when only those considered to be at high risk a months after bereavement were compared, the people who had support were better psychologically than controls at both 6 and 24 months.

Parkes (1980) concluded his review of these studies with the view that both professional counselling services and voluntary or self-help services supported by professionals were able to reduce the risk of psychiatric and psychosomatic disturbance typically associated with bereavement. He concluded that this was especially true, however, for people who were particularly at risk of such disorder for whatever reason.

CONCLUSIONS

The research surveyed in this chapter clearly supports the predictions made and therefore indicates the importance and effectiveness of communication and counselling in all aspects of health care. The statements made about the validity of counselling in all the earlier specialist chapters not only make rational and human sense, but are also demonstrated empirically by the findings presented in this chapter. Counselling and communication can improve professional satisfaction, patient satisfaction, diagnostic accuracy, and treatment adherence. They have very obvious benefits to the psychological care of patients, are associated with improvements in the patient's understanding and retention of information about their illness and treatment, have significant effects upon the physical outcome of disease, and have demonstrable preventive effects.

The validity of these results is difficult to refute even though we have not reviewed all the available studies in all areas of medicine. The fact that there may be research not showing positive effects for counselling does not refute the conclusions we have drawn. What it does is to simply indicate our continued ignorance. Negative results may occur because of methodological reasons, and this is an important source of error, but the other sources are our lack of understanding. We have yet to fully understand psychological processes and the ways in which people change. We need to know more about counsellor characteristics and how they have their effect. We also require much more information about how such attributes interact with patient characteristics. We need to understand more about what kinds of counselling methods are appropriate for which patients at what point in their history. We must explore how these methods have their effects, so that we can begin to make individual predictions about outcome.

What we do know, however, is that communication and counselling must be made a priority in health care now. The question is not whether this is true, but how it can be achieved. We will, therefore, address these problems in the next chapter.

REFERENCES

Anderson, S. and Hasler, J. (1979). Counselling in general practice. *Journal of the Royal College of General Practitioners*, **29**, 352–356.

Bergin, A. (1971). The evaluation of therapeutic outcomes. In A. Bergin and S. Garfield (Eds), *Handbook of psychotherapy and behaviour change*. New York: Wiley.

Bertakis, K. (1977). The communication of information from physician to patient: a method for increasing retention and satisfaction. *Journal of Family Practice*, **5**, 217–222.

Bloom, J., Ross, R., and Burnell, G. (1978). The effect of social support on patient adjustment after breast surgery. *Patient Counselling and Health Education*, Autumn, 50–59.

Bundy, C. (1989). Cardiac disorders. In A. Broome (Ed.), *Health psychology: processes and applications*. London: Chapman & Hall.

Burgess, A., Learner, D., D'Agostino, R. *et al.* (1987). A randomised control trial of cardiac rehabilitation. *Social Science & Medicine*, **24**, 359–370.

Burton, M. and Parker, R. (1990). *A randomized controlled trial of preoperative psychological preparation for mastectomy*. Paper presented at the International Conference on Communication in Health Care. St. Catherines College, Oxford.

Cain, E., Kohorn, E., Quinlan, D., Latimer, K., and Schwartz, P. (1986). Psychosocial benefits of a cancer support group. *Cancer*, **57**, 183–189.

Capone, M., Good, R., Westie, K., and Jacobson, A. (1980). Psychosocial rehabilitation of gynecologic oncology patients. *Archives of Physical Medicine and Rehabilitation*, **61**, 128–132.

Cooper, B., Harwin, B., Depla, C., and Shepherd, M. (1975). Mental health care in the community: an evaluative study. *Psychological Medicine*, **5**, 372–380.

Cromwell, R. and Levenkron, J. (1984). Psychological care of acute coronary patients. In A. Steptoe and A. Mathews (Eds), *Health care and human behaviour*. London: Academic Press.

Cunningham, C., Morgan, P., and McGucken, R. (1984). Down's syndrome: is dissatisfaction with disclosure of diagnosis inevitable? *Developmental Medicine & Child Neurology*, **26**, 33–39.

Davis, H. and Rushton, R. (1989). An evaluation of basic counselling training. *Counselling*, **68**, 1–8.

Davis, H. and Rushton, R. (1991). Counselling and supporting parents of children with developmental delay: a research evaluation. *Journal of Mental Deficiency Research*, **35**, in press.

Earll, L. and Kincey, J. (1982). Clinical psychology in general practice. *Journal of the Royal College of General Practitioners*, **32**, 32–37.

Egan, G. (1982). *The skilled helper*. Monterey: Brooks/Cole.

Egbert, L., Baittit, G., Welch, C., and Bartlett, M. (1964). Reduction of postoperative pain by encouragement and instruction of patients. *New England Journal of Medicine*, **270**, 825–827.

Eysenck, H. (1952). The effects of psychotherapy: an evaluation. *Journal of Consulting Psychology*, **16**, 319–324.

Fallowfield, L. and Roberts, R. (1990). Cancer counselling in the U.K. *Psychology and Health*, in press.

Farquhar, J., Maccoby, N., Wood, P. *et al.* (1977). Community education for cardiovascular health. *Lancet*, **1**, 1192–1195.

Ferlic, M., Goldman, A., and Kennedy, B. (1979). Group counselling in adult patients with advanced cancer. *Cancer*, **43**, 760–766.

Forester, B., Kornfeld, D., and Fleiss, J. (1985). Psychotherapy during radiotherapy: effects on emotional and physical distress. *American Journal of Psychiatry*, **142**, 22–27.

Frasure-Smith, N. and Prince, R. (1986). The Ischemic Heart Disease Life Stress Monitoring Program: 18-month mortality results. *Canadian Journal of Public Health*, **77**, suppl. 1, 46–50.

Freeman, G. and Button, E. (1984). The clinical psychologist in general practice: a six-year study of consulting patterns for psychosocial problems. *Journal of the Royal College of General Practitioners*, **34**, 377–380.

Gerber, I., Weiner, A., Battin, D., and Arkin, A. (1975). Brief therapy to the aged bereaved. In B. Schoenberg and I. Gerber (Eds), *Bereavement: its psychological aspects*. New York: Columbia University Press.

Gerle, B., Lunden, G., and Sandblom, P. (1960). The patient with inoperable cancer from the psychiatric and social standpoints. *Cancer*, **13**, 1206–1211.

Gerrard, B., Boniface, W., and Love, B. (1980). *Interpersonal skills for health professionals*. Reston, Virginia: Reston Publishing.

Goldberg, D. (1972). *The detection of psychiatric illness by questionnaire*. London: Oxford University Press.

Gordon, W., Freidenberg, I., Diller, L., *et al.* (1980). Efficacy of psychosocial intervention with cancer patients. *Journal of Consulting and Clinical Psychology*, **48**, 743–759.

Grossarth-Maticek, R., Schmidt, P., Vetter, H., and Arndt, S. (1984). Psychotherapy research in oncology. In A. Steptoe and A. Mathews (Eds), *Health care and human behaviour*. London: Academic Press.

Gruen, W. (1975). Effects of brief psychotherapy during the hospitalization period on the recovery process in heart attacks. *Journal of Consulting and Clinical Psychology*, **43**, 223–232.

Higgins, H. (1990). *Empathy training and stress: their role in medical students' responses to emotional patients.* Paper presented at the International Conference on Communication in Health Care. St. Catherines College, Oxford.

Holden, J., Sagovsky, R., and Cox, J. (1989). Counselling in a general practice setting: controlled study of health visitor intervention in treatment of postnatal depression. *British Medical Journal*, **298**, 223–226.

Holland, J., Morrow, A., Schmale, L. *et al.* (1987). *Reduction of anxiety and depression in cancer patients by alprazolam or by a behavioural technique.* Proceedings of the Twenty-third Annual Meeting of the American Society of Clinical Oncology, 6: 258 (Abs No. 1015).

Hughes, P. and Lieberman, S. (1990). Troubled parents: vulnerability and stress in childhood cancer. *British Journal of Medical Psychology*, **63**, 53–64.

Inui, T., Yourtee, E., and Williamson, J. (1976). Improved outcomes in hypertension after physician tutorials: a controlled trial. *Annals of Internal Medicine*, **84**, 646–651.

Johnson, J., Morrissey, J., and Leventhal, J. (1973). Psychological preparation for an endoscopic examination. *Gastrointestinal Endoscopy*, **19**, 180–182.

Johnson, J., Rice, V., Fuller, S., and Endress, P. (1978). Sensory information, instruction in a coping strategy, and recovery from surgery. *Research in Nursing and Health*, **1**, 4–17.

Johnston, D. (1990). The prevention of cardiovascular disease by psychological methods. In P. Bennett and J. Weinman (Eds), *Proceedings of the Second Conference of the Health Psychology Section. Occasional Papers*, 2. Leicester: British Psychological Society.

Johnston, M. (1990). Counselling and psychological methods with postoperative pain: a brief review. *British Psychological Society Health Psychology Update*, Issue 5.

Kendall, P., Williams, L., Pechacek, T., Graham, L., Shisslak, C., and Herzoff, N. (1979). Cognitive-behavioural and patient education interventions in cardiac catheterization procedures. *Journal of Consulting and Clinical Psychology*, **47**, 49–58.

Kobasa, S. and Kash, K. (1987). Stress in oncology staff: measurement and management. In J. Holland, M. Massie, and L. Lesko (Eds), *Current concepts in psycho-oncology and AIDS*. New York: Memorial Sloan-Kettering Cancer Centre.

Lambert, M., Shapiro, D., and Bergin, A. (1986). The effectiveness of psychotherapy. In S. Garfield and A. Bergin. (Eds), *Handbook of psychotherapy and behaviour change*. New York: Wiley.

Leshan, L. (1990). Setting the scene: a new paradigm in the counselling and support of the somatically ill. In H. Balner (Ed.), *A new model: a challenge for biomedicine?* Amsterdam: Swets & Zeitlinger.

Ley, P. (1988). *Communicating with patients: improving communication, satisfaction and compliance*. London: Croom Helm.

Linn, M., Linn, B., and Harris, R. (1982). Effects of counselling for late stage cancer patients. *Cancer*, **49**, 1048–1055.

Luborsky, L., Singer, B., and Luborsky, L. (1975). Comparative studies of psychotherapies. *Archives of General Psychiatry*, **32**, 995–1008.

Maguire, P., Clarke, D., and Jolley, B. (1977). An experimental comparison of three courses in history-taking skills for medical students. *Medical Education*, **11**, 175–182.

Maguire, P., Pentol, A., Allen, D., Tait, A., Brooke, M., and Sellwood, R. (1982). Cost of counselling women who undergo mastectomy. *British Medical Journal*, **284**, 1933–1935.

Maguire, P., Roe, P., Goldberg, D., Jones, S., Hyde, C., and O'Dowd, T. (1978). The value of feedback in teaching interviewing skills to medical students. *Psychological Medicine*, **8**, 695–704.

Maguire, P., Tait, A., Brooke, M., Thomas, C., and Sellwood, R. (1980). Effects of counselling on the psychiatric morbidity associated with mastectomy. *British Medical Journal*, **281**, 1454–1456.

Martin, E. (1988). Counsellors in general practice. *British Medical Journal*, **297**, 637–638.

Maslach, C. and Jackson, S. (1981). *The Maslach Burn-out Inventory*. Palo Alto, CA.: Consulting Psychologists Press.

Massie, M., Holland, J., and Straker, N. (1989). Psychotherapeutic interventions. In J. Holland and J. Rowland (Eds), *Handbook of psycho-oncology*. New York: Oxford University Press.

Mathews, A. and Ridgeway, V. (1984). Psychological preparation for surgery. In A. Steptoe and A. Mathews (Eds), *Health care and human behaviour*. London: Academic Press.

Mayou, R., MacMahon, D., Sleight, P. and Florencio, M. (1981). Early rehabilitation after myocardial infarction. *Lancet*, December 19/26, 1399–1401.

Mazzuca, S. (1982). Does patient education in chronic disease have therapeutic value? *Journal of Chronic Disease*, **35**, 521–529.

McKenney, J., Slining, J., Henderson, H., Devins, D., and Barr, M. (1973). The effects of clinical pharmacy services on patients with essential hypertension. *Circulation*, **48**, 1104–1111.

Meltzoff, J. and Kornreich, M. (1970). *Research in psychotherapy*. Chicago: Aldine.

Milne, D. and Souter, K. (1988). A re-evaluation of the clinical psychologist in general practice. *Journal of the Royal College of General Practitioners*, **38**, 457–460.

Mullen, P., Green, L., and Persinger, G. (1985). Clinical trials of patient education for chronic conditions: a comparative meta-analysis of intervention types. *Preventive Medicine*, **14**, 753–781.

Mumford, E., Schlesinger, H., and Glass, G. (1982). The effects of psychological intervention on recovery from surgery and heart attacks: an analysis of the literature. *American Journal of Public Health*, **72**, 141–151.

Parkes, C. (1979). Evaluation of a bereavement service. In A. DeVries and A. Carmi (Eds), *The dying human*. Ramat Gan, Israel: Turtledove.

Parkes, C. (1980). Bereavement counselling: does it work? *British Medical Journal*, July 5, 3–6.

Polak, P., Egan, D., Lee, J., Vandenbergh, R., and Williams, W. (1975). Prevention in mental health: a controlled study. *American Journal of Psychiatry*, **132**, 146–149.

Pozen, M., Stechmiller, J., Harris, W., Smith, S., Donna, F., and Voigt, G. (1977). The nurse rehabilitator's impact on patients with myocardial infarction. *Medical Care*, **15**, 830–837.

Raphael, B. (1977). Preventive intervention with the recently bereaved. *Archives of General Psychiatry*, **34**, 1450–1454.

Robson, M., France, R., and Bland, M. (1984). Clinical psychologist in primary care: controlled clinical and economic evaluation. *British Medical Journal*, **288**, 1805–1808.

Rachman, S. (1971). *The effects of psychotherapy*. Oxford: Pergamon.

Rutter, D. and Maguire, P. (1976). History-taking for medical students: evaluation of a training programme. *Lancet*, September 11, 558–560.

Schlesinger, H., Mumford, E., Glass, G., Patrick, C., and Sharfstein, S. (1983). Mental, health treatment and medical care. *American Journal of Public Health*, **73**, 422–429.

Smith, M., Glass, G., and Miller, T. (1980). *The benefits of psychotherapy*. Baltimore: Johns Hopkins University Press.

Spiegel, D. and Bloom, J. (1983). Group therapy and hypnosis reduce metastatic breast carcinoma pain. *Psychosomatic Medicine*, **45**, 333–339.

Spiegel, D., Bloom, J., Kraemer, H., and Gottheil, E. (1989). Effect of psychosocial treatment on survival of patients with metastatic breast cancer. *Lancet*, October 14, 888–891.

Spiegel, D., Bloom, J., and Yalom, I. (1981). Group support for patients with metastatic cancer: a randomised prospective outcome study. *Archives of General Psychiatry*, **38**, 527–537.

Spiegel, D. and Glafkides, M. (1983). Effects of group confrontation with death and dying. *International Journal of Group Psychotherapy*, **33**, 433–447.

Thomas, K. (1987). General practice consultations: is there any point in being positive? *British Medical Journal*, **294**, 1200–1202.

Vachon, M., Lyall, W., Rogers, J., Freedman, K., and Freeman, S. (1980). A controlled study of self-help intervention for widows. *American Journal of Psychiatry*, **137**, 1380–1384.

Watson, M. (1983). Psychosocial intervention with cancer patients: a review. *Psychological Medicine*, **13**, 839–846.

Watson, M., Denton, S., Baum, M., and Greer, S. (1988). Counselling breast cancer patients: a specialist nurse service. *Counselling Psychology Quarterly*, **1**, 25–34.

Waydenfeld, D. and Waydenfeld, S. (1980). Counselling in general practice. *Journal of the Royal College of General Practitioners*, **30**, 671–677.

Worden, J. and Weisman, A. (1984). Preventive psychosocial intervention with newly diagnosed cancer patients. *General Hospital Psychiatry*, **6**, 243–249.

Wyld, K. (1981). Counselling in general practice. *British Journal of Guidance and Counselling*, **9**, 129–141.

19 Organizational and Training Issues

Although this book has not attempted a comprehensive review of counselling in all the possible areas of health care, the 15 applied chapters preceding this one demonstrate in a disturbing manner the clear neglect of communication and counselling in the practice of modern medicine. There is little cause for optimism that the situation might be any better in most of the other specialities not covered by the book, although consumer demand for more humane health care has resulted in better provision for patients in certain areas. For example there is much more counselling support given now to patients with AIDS.

Unfortunately much of the counselling that is available for patients and their families only exists because of the initial lobbying and efforts by committed individual health professionals, volunteers, self-help groups and charitable bodies, rather than from any initiatives within the NHS. Given the obvious needs expressed by patients and their families for good communication and better counselling support, the current situation represented in this book reveals a rather sorry state of affairs.

It should also be fairly clear to the reader by now that even if the resources were made available, the answer to the problems is not merely to train more and more counsellors. The most effective means of helping more of the people who have to use the health care system is to provide training in communication skills for all members of the health care team. Better communication in itself probably exerts a prophylactic effect on patients' well-being and care, but particular emphasis needs to be given in training doctors and nurses to elicit, understand, recognise and integrate with biological factors any signs of psychosocial distress. These health care professionals also require training in how to ameliorate those problems and difficulties that are uncovered by adopting a more empathic, skilled consulting style. Furthermore if we truly expect doctors, nurses and others to get closer to the psychosocial concerns experienced by patients as a result of illness and its treatment, then we must equip them with the means and skills to cope with the emotionally challenging results of their enquiries. This includes training in the personal development of humanistic values such as those described by Gorlin & Zucker (1983). Incorporating humanistic factors in

Counselling and Communication in Health Care. Edited by H. Davis and L. Fallowfield
© 1991 John Wiley & Sons Ltd

medical treatment programmes can promote more beneficial and satisfying outcomes for both the patient and the doctor, but thorough training and support is imperative. Lipkin, Quill and Napodano (1984) have commented that asking doctors to be constantly 'patient-centred' without focusing time and energy on their own personal development is unrealistic and unwise. All this means diverting time and money to more appropriate medical education and to effective staff support services, and there is little evidence that this is happening. For example, despite the fact that the Briggs Report in 1972 recommended that all nurses should have access to a counsellor, very few hospitals appointed any staff counsellors (Banks, 1989). This seems curious when one considers that universities have had counselling departments for years and that companies in the private sector have acknowledged that the improvements to staff welfare are worth the financial outlay. The health service appears to care very little about the psychological welfare of its own members which must in turn influence the ability of health professionals to respond empathically to their patients.

Even assuming that adequate training were made available in counselling and communication skills, there are still major barriers to overcome in organizational terms. Most of the medical care system is conducted at a pace and under physical conditions that defy any attempts by doctors and others to adopt a more patient-centred approach. There is the hard-pressed doctor working in ancient, ill-maintained out-patient departments (which sometimes appear purposefully designed to discourage privacy and dignity during consultations), the GP with appointments scheduled every five minutes, the nurse with reports and nursing process forms to fill in as well as meeting the more physical needs of his or her patients. None of these people are going to be able to put into practice their new found consultation and counselling skills within the current organization of care delivery. Indeed Maguire has shown that teaching ward nurses counselling skills is of limited value if they are not given the time by other senior staff when they return to the wards to 'just sit and talk to patients'! Simply changing the behaviour of individuals within the health service through better training without attending to organizational issues is insufficient. Milne (1985) has also shown how the changes brought about in nurses during a good training programme were rapidly nullified or reversed the moment that the nurses returned to their routine organizational environments.

This chapter will deal with training and organizational issues separately and in more detail but it is worth bearing in mind that both need drastic revision together if communication in general and the psychosocial concerns of patients are going to be satisfactorily addressed.

ORGANIZATIONAL ISSUES

There are probably three important questions concerning the organization of counselling in health care; 1) who should counsel? 2) where should this be done? 3) what should be done under the broad heading of counselling? There is of course another key question which underpins everything that follows and that is, how will counselling services be funded?

Virtually every part of our National Health Service is experiencing hardship and cutbacks following at least a decade of chronic underfunding. Apart from the clear humanitarian need to provide more resources for counselling, there is a good economic argument. In Chapter 18 we saw how improved communication generally resulted in more accurate diagnoses, better patient compliance, enhanced recovery periods and shorter hospital stays. However, we probably need more basic research demonstrating the true cost/benefits and cost/effectiveness of counselling before the more cynical holders of the purse strings divert appropriate financial resources the way of counselling services. Currently such data are scarce although there are some showing the cost-effectiveness of liaison psychiatry in the US (Levitan and Kornfeld, 1981) and also the cost-effectiveness of employing breast nurse specialist counsellors in the UK (Maguire *et al.*, 1982). For a detailed description of how costs can be calculated see also Pentol (1981). We will return to this topic again later in the chapter.

Who should counsel?

The most obvious and shortest answer to the question 'who should counsel?' is the person best able to do so. We have already rehearsed the argument that effective communication in general requires that the communicator possesses basic counselling skills and therefore all health care personnel should in theory be able to counsel. However this is patently not the case at the moment and very few of the people currently working within the health service have received sufficient training and support to counsel, despite their willingness, and others have neither the skills, time nor the desire to do so.

There is no fundamental reason why any health professional given appropriate training and support should not incorporate a counselling role as part of their work: but it is important to ensure that someone in the health care team assumes responsibility for counselling those patients most in need of help. A key worker such as a specialist nurse, psychologist or social worker with counselling training can be invaluable, not only in counselling patients and their families who require help, but also in acting as a resource for the health care team. Such counsellors could help facilitate effective communication between the professional and patients by discussing barriers and pinpointing confusing clinic practices. They could facilitate and improve interpersonal relationships between health care professionals themselves by uncovering and resolving boundary and hierarchical difficulties. Finally they could provide counselling support to other members of the team through such things as stress management techniques, thus helping to prevent the problem of emotional burn-out. However, such a vital and demanding role cannot be taken by someone who lacks training and experience, or they themselves are at risk of developing the very problems which they may be attempting to prevent or alleviate in others. The organization of effective counselling within any medical specialty requires careful thought; time must be provided for the key worker to obtain supervision and to attend workshops and courses in order to maintain and develop both the skills and the personal growth which such an important job demands.

In the following section we look at those areas of medical care where different members of the health care team have been actively involved in counselling, together with the implications that this has for the organization of health care delivery and training.

Doctors as counsellors

Some medical specialties attract doctors who do take on and see counselling as a fundamental part of their work, although there are very few clinicians working outside a primary care setting who do much counselling routinely.

Primary care

Much of general practice demands that doctors become more proficient at counselling and in the detection of the many psychosocial problems with which their patients present (see Weinman & Goulston, Chapter 3). Some writers have suggested that as counselling is such an essential and integral part of general practice, allocating it to a professional counsellor is wrong (Milne, 1983). Unfortunately it is difficult to see how even the most motivated GPs will be able to counsel patients themselves given the pressure to achieve their quotas of smears and immunisations under the new contracts which form part of the government's reform of the NHS. As general practices now have to run their own budgets, it will be sad if the encouraging recent trend of appointing practice counsellors is halted. Furthermore the new contracts will increase the number of patients whom GPs are expected to see and potentially this might limit the amount of information that the GP has time to provide. It has been shown in an American study of internists that there is an inverse relationship between the income of the doctor and the amount of information given to patients (Waitzkin, 1984). In other words those doctors who spent time providing patients with information and explanations and checked their patients understanding saw fewer patients and consequently earned less money.

Until quite recently very few practice counsellors were recognised by the DHSS as ancillary staff, thus preventing Family Practitioner Committees from reimbursing the doctor for the counsellor's employment costs. With no formal salary scales or conditions of employment, counsellor attachments were somewhat ad hoc and standards and codes of practice were variable. The British Association for Counselling (BAC) set up a standing committee for the advancement of counselling in general practice and this group has been busy formulating policy for standards of pay, conditions, training, accreditation and evaluation of general practice (Rowland, 1989). Hopefully such moves will enhance the likelihood of good counselling practice becoming an integral part of primary care.

Psychiatry

Some doctors within specialties such as psychiatry have a very obvious counselling role. However, they tend to work only with those patients who are mentally ill, although recently there has been an encouraging growth in the creation of more liaison psychiatry posts. This is especially welcome in areas of great emotional need such as oncology or terminal care (see for example Ramirez, 1989). Not only do liaison psychiatrists offer psychotherapy to patients, but they also form a vital support and supervisory role for the specialist nurses who can refer on patients with severe psychological problems which need psychiatric intervention. The liaison psychiatrist with experience in running support groups can also play an important part in helping all members of the health care team. The carers often need counselling as well as their patients and this important issue will be discussed more fully later in the chapter.

As far as medical education is concerned, the teaching of communication skills to students is often provided by psychiatrists or behavioural scientists. A potential problem is that students may then assume that good counselling is only appropriate within a psychiatry setting and fail to apply learned skills to other medical areas. Assumptions that communication is the preserve of psychiatry have been challenged on other worrying grounds; for example, Janek, Burra and Leichner (1979) have commented that psychiatrists themselves are often deficient in some of the basic skills underlying good communication.

Surgery

Perhaps it is not unreasonable for highly skilled surgeons to feel on balance that their talents are best employed in performing surgery. They might argue that although there is a necessity to communicate more effectively about management with a patient, counselling as such should be provided by someone else who has not received an expensive training in surgery. However, as noted in the previous chapter, Burton and Parker (1990) have shown how it is possible for a motivated surgeon to adopt a Rogerian type of counselling and consulting style which benefited both the surgeon himself and his patients with breast cancer.

The stereotypic surgeon is caricatured as tough and insensitive to his or her patients' needs and whilst there are plenty of people working in surgery to reinforce such myths, there are many others who have made big efforts to promote counselling within their specialty. For example, the establishment of specialist stoma therapists as more than just 'bag ladies' might not have occurred without the support of motivated surgeons who recognise both the nurses' desire for more professionalism and patients' needs. This produced an expansion of the stoma therapist's role to include not just practical assistance but also counselling. It could be argued that the presence of so many breast care nurse specialists who now counsel women in most of our hospitals is due in part to the pioneering advocacy of such posts by certain surgeons (Baum and Jones, 1979).

Most of the specialist chapters in this book have charted the psychosocial traumas experienced by patients and their families. We feel that there is sufficient evidence to demonstrate that those doctors who employ more effective patient-centred consulting styles can do a great deal to ameliorate problems. This means providing good, understandable information tailored to individual needs and developing skills in the assessment of psychosocial complaints. Adoption of a biopsychosocial model makes good scientific sense as well as being an ethical and moral necessity. However, not all doctors would want to embark on lengthy counselling sessions routinely, thus clinicians who lack the time or talents to fulfil a counselling role adequately need to argue more persuasively for the financial resources to employ a professionally trained counsellor in their clinics.

Nursing

Nurses in the course of their work often carry out a counselling type role and some are explicitly appointed as specialist nurses with counselling as a major part of their job descriptions. Unfortunately few of these highly motivated and caring individuals are given anything like the kind of training, supervision or support necessary to enable them to perform their tasks most effectively. A recent survey of the working conditions and responsibilities of oncology counsellors in the UK sponsored by the Cancer Research Campaign revealed that less than a quarter had any recognised formal counselling qualifications (this was especially true if the counsellors were nurses). The survey results presented an alarming picture of counsellors who were overworked, undertrained, under-resourced, insufficiently supervised and whose roles appeared to be better understood by their patients than by their fellow professionals (Roberts and Fallowfield, 1990).

Far too often nurses are appointed as counsellors on the grounds that they are kindly, well-motivated and have lots of 'experience' with patients.

Whilst these qualities are important, they do not guarantee that the nurse counsellor will also possess the other necessary professional skills for him or her to perform a counselling role adequately (Fallowfield, 1988). Although specialist nurses require much more training then they get at present, as with the doctors, nurse education in general should also include considerably more basic training in communication skills. Faulkner's study (1979) showed how limited nurses' communication with their patients was; by and large nurses set the agenda focusing predominantly on procedural, treatment related topics. If nurses feel incompetent or lack confidence in communicating with patients, then they specifically avoid talking to the very patients who need it most, such as those who are very distressed or dying (Conboy-Hills, 1986).

One major barrier to the promotion of better communication between nurses and their patients is evident in the mismatch that exists between the expressed desire for improvements in communication skills made by nurses and the actual priorities which staff place on various nursing tasks. Hockey (1976) interviewed senior nurses about the satisfying areas of their work and aspects of their job which they felt should be changed. Many stated that they would like to see more emphasis placed on talking and listening to patients and providing adequate information and explanations. Unfortunately these same nurses said that they did not attempt to communicate more with patients themselves because of administrative tasks which had a higher priority. So despite lip service being paid to better communication with patients, other tasks appear to be valued more highly by senior nurses. The staff who have most exposure to patients, and thus most communication with them, are likely to be juniors with even less experience and fewer formal communication skills.

Fielding and Llewelyn (1987) in a thought-provoking article about improving the communication skills of nurses, point out that not only does talking with patients have a low priority within the NHS, but there are other more troubling difficulties with which to contend. The absence of skills and need for an effective training programme to remedy this is merely a technical problem; of more concern is the fact that not everyone within the health service sees better communications as desirable. Fielding and Llewelyn state, 'Whilst neither publicly nor explicitly admitted, there may be many people, who within the specific circumstances that they find themselves in, will not cooperate with, or who will actively resist, initiatives to improve communications'. There is evidence from management in other organizations (Graham, 1981) that some managers feel that it is advantageous to leave communications rather vague as '. . . making things perfectly clear can result in a loss of power and/or mystique'. This philosophy can be seen in many areas of health care delivery; for example, in the reluctance of many clinicians and nurses to inform patients properly about what is wrong with them or to check their understanding of diagnostic tests, surgical procedures and drug regimens. The use of medical jargon is either an example of deliberately being unclear so as to retain 'power and mystique' or it represents a lack of concern for patients' needs, fears, anxieties and rights.

Volunteers

Volunteers and self-help groups have provided considerable support to both patients and their families in the absence of routine provision from within the health service. From an organizational point of view this may pose a variety of problems. Although many health care professionals welcome the assistance of volunteers or may actively support and encourage the setting up of self-help groups, this is by no means a universal reaction. Furthermore many self-help groups themselves are not enthusiastic about intervention from professionals and some are characterized by their anti-professional stance. This can produce conflicts especially if the group contains a dominant leader with a personal antipathy towards doctors.

Some professional supervision seems a reasonable requirement, if both patients and the volunteers are going to be protected from misinformation or psychological harm. Riessman (1965) has argued that the primary benefit of amateur counselling may be the therapeutic impact upon the volunteer rather than any tangible benefit to the counselled patient, the so-called 'helper-therapy principle'. Brager (1965) argues that the volunteer helper receives satisfaction from an improved self-image that is promoted by the sense of doing something worthwhile for a person in need of help. While there may well be something mutually therapeutic about counselling for both the victim and the victim/counsellor, this is not necessarily the case and concerns have been expressed about the potential psychological harm which could occur.

Riessman (1965) has pointed out that for the victim/counsellor there are at least three tangible benefits: 1) importance and status, 2) support from the implicit-thesis 'I must be well if I help others', and 3) as a major (distracting) source of involvement, diverting them from their problem and general self-concern. The worry from a health professional's point of view is that unsupervised, untrained volunteers, especially those with personal experience of the medical problem or area, may, unless they have worked through all their own problems, project difficulties onto the person needing help. Other health professionals worry about possible 'psychological contagion' from unstable, unadjusted volunteers working with newly diagnosed patients.

Mantell (1983) has highlighted lack of accountability as a further organizational problem and reason for the apparent opposition to direct counselling involvement of volunteers with patients. She also points out that apart from anecdotal observations 'there is no definitive evidence that the role model process helps recipients'.

All these concerns may be warranted, but there is no doubt that the lack of substantive counselling provision within the NHS means that volunteers and self-help agencies will be used to fill the many unmet needs of the patients and their families. These health professionals who are automatically antagonistic to such groups would do well to channel their energies into arguing more persuasively for resources to establish a professional service and look at areas of their own practice which might help patients more. This means of course better communication.

Where should counselling take place?

Primary obstacles facing people in a health care setting wishing to offer counselling are the lack of suitable facilities permitting privacy and the lack of thought given to making sure that interruptions by other members of staff are kept to a minimum. Often more respect for an individual's privacy is given to them by their bank manager, accountant or solicitor than by their health carers, who are forced to work in inadequate clinics, and yet the need for confidentiality, given the intimate topics being discussed, is just as urgent.

A private room with good sound proofing, no telephone, and a 'do not disturb' notice on the door (which others respect) seem fundamental requirements for an effective therapeutic encounter. They are nearly always lacking in the National Health Service setting in marked contrast to the private sector.

Those of us working within a hospital environment can become immune to the noise, the lack of privacy and the interruptions. In a study reported by Hogbin and Fallowfield (1989) in which patients with cancer were given audio-tape recordings of their 'bad news' consultation with their surgeon, the doctor commented that he had been completely unaware of how often his telephone rang during clinics until he heard them all on tape. The experience made him place a much higher priority on getting his out-patient sessions and rooms organized more appropriately for breaking bad news.

What should be done under the name of counselling?

Definitions of what constitutes counselling have already been discussed fully in Chapter 2. Some people define counselling rather loosely to include any helping activity and furthermore they fail to see professional training as a pre-requisite for employment as a counsellor. Whilst it is evidently true that many unqualified, untrained or minimally trained people can offer extremely effective counselling support because of their good basic communication skills, genuineness, and commitment to others, it is not universally true that anyone motivated enough can counsel without training. Counselling of the 'tea and sympathy' variety may well produce some short-term comfort for patients, but it rarely produces the sort of self-understanding and goal-setting which can assist patients to change and adapt to disease and its treatment. We will return to this issue in the section on training, but one of the problems with untrained counsellors is that they often have rather strange ideas about what counselling is, how to do it and what the goals and objectives of counselling should be. For example Roberts and Fallowfield (1990) found that some respondents to their survey felt that 'normalising' the patient was their primary goal. Too much of the counselling which occurs in medicine is of the directive, advice-giving variety and little emphasis is placed on one of the most crucial aspects of good counselling—that of listening to patients' worries and fears.

Many patients have a hidden agenda that rarely gets aired. Beckman and Frankel (1984) showed that the average patient is interrupted within 18 seconds of starting to tell his or her story. In the light of this evidence it is hardly surprising that psychosocial areas of concern may remain undisclosed. An excellent pragmatic discusion on such important issues as learning how to listen to patients more effectively when interviewing is provided by Lipkin (1987).

Organizational barriers to counselling

Time

The primary excuse given by doctors and nurses for not addressing the psychosocial concerns of their patients is lack of time. We suspect that this is not always the real reason. A more likely explanation is that lack of confidence and lack of skill in dealing with psychosocial issues through inadequate training causes emotional discomfort. Hence clinicians utilise what time is available during a consultation to discuss the more practical, physical and technological aspects of care. Some doctors suggest that teaching students psychological skills means that other more important parts of the consultation will be left out.

By now the reader should have little doubt that an adherence to a strict mind/body dichotomy is unlikely to be maximally helpful in either understanding the patient's problem or in determining what is the most appropriate management policy to pursue. Eliciting psychosocial parameters is as important as taking the blood pressure or pulse rate of a patient, especially if he or she is presenting with diffuse symptoms or is unknown to the doctor. The organizational structure has to change so that time can be found to incorporate these fundamentally important aspects of care. The automatic assumption that including such areas routinely as part of the medical consultation takes too much extra time is not necessarily correct. William Branch (1987) has pointed out that 'once these skills are practised—and become truly integrated into the doctor's repertoire—enhanced interest in and ability to deal with patients' feelings saves time in the long run, because

patients talk to their doctors more freely and co-operatively, their expectations are more fully met, compliance improves, and misunderstandings and
disagreements lessen'. Likewise Faulkner and Maguire (1984) found that
ward nurses taught relevant interviewing techniques to enable them to identify and monitor problems in their cancer patients were initially reluctant
because of the time that it took. As their skills and confidence in asking
about psychosocial matters increased, however, they found that it took less
time and could be integrated into their normal routine. These nurses also
reported greater job satisfaction through using their new skills.

Costs

Not only do we have little information about how cost-effective the implementation of a sensible counselling service within the health service would
be, we know little about the cost-benefits either. Industry has been able to
provide figures from cost-benefit analyses, showing the advantages of offering counselling. For example, United Airlines found a 16:1 ratio of benefit
for every dollar spent and General Motors 2:1. In another area economists
such as Millot (1981) have devised mathematical models showing the benefit
of student counselling services in universities (Ross, 1989). Some estimates
have been made of the costs of employing a specialist breast nurse counsellor (Maguire *et al.*, 1982), liaison psychiatrist (Levitan *et al.*, 1981) or psychologist in a group practice (Robson *et al.*, 1984) but these reports do not
provide sufficient data for analysis of cost-benefits in general.

The BAC research committee has been working hard to encourage effective research into the development and evaluation of counselling practice,
supervision and training, but difficulties remain (BAC Research Committee,
1989). Until the problems of evaluating counselling reliably have been overcome, in particular determining what the most appropriate outcome measures should be, it will be difficult to arrive at valid costing. This has led
some writers such as Martin (1988) to suggest that promoting the widespread adoption of counselling in the health service 'is unwise'. Martin
quotes Hampton (1983) as saying 'if we do not have the resources to do all
that is technically possible then medical care must be limited to what is of
proven value and the medical profession will have to set opinion aside . . .
when resources are scarce a greater proportion of them must be channelled
into evaluation'. Few counsellors would engage in their work without firm
convictions that they could help their patients. We all have many testi-
monials from patients who feel that they have benefited from counselling.
However, money for a properly resourced service will never be provided on
such a basis and counsellors do have to be prepared to co-operate in evaluation of their work (just as in any other therapeutic endeavour) if we are to
secure adequate funding and acceptance of counselling as a routine part of
the health care system rather than a luxury.

Hierarchical boundaries

The whole system of health care delivery in this country has been structured around a rigid hierarchical model which mitigates against effective communication. This is true not only for communications between health care professionals and patients but also between different professional groups. Nowhere can this be seen better than in the old hospital based schools of nursing where students were socialised into accepting a somewhat subservient role to clinicians. The more academic nature of nursing courses today has changed some of this, but the transition from a subservient hierarchically based relationship to one that is collegial is long and painful. Many nurses complain that doctors refuse to allow them to talk openly to patients about cancer, for example, and yet these same clinicians then ignore important feedback from patients. Maguire and Faulkner (1988) have described joint workshops designed to improve the counselling skills of doctors and nurses who work with patients who have cancer. Opportunities for participants to air opposing views have proved to be an important feature at the workshops.

Until hierarchical boundaries have been successfully breached within our institutions it is unlikely that efforts to counsel patients effectively will succeed. Stein, Watts and Howell (1990) have commented that this is particularly true if clinicians continue to be viewed by nursing colleagues 'as narrowly focussed technicians who treat illnesses and are uninterested in the humanistic aspects of health care, such as providing health education, preventing disease, and helping patients and families cope with chronic illness'. Many nurses see these areas of care as their domain and some are reluctant to share these functions with medical colleagues. There is evidence that schemes where a joint or collaborative model of nurse/doctor interactions are encouraged result in increased work satisfaction to participants and benefits to the patients receiving care (Corless, 1982). As patient safety is so dependent on good relationships between their health carers, institutions should give serious consideration to any initiatives aimed at improving the interpersonal skills of staff members. There is empirical evidence showing that the recovery of patients in an intensive care unit correlated with the level and quality of interactions between their physicians and nurses (Knaus *et al.*, 1986).

Technological advances and counselling

We live in an increasingly sophisticated technological age. Alongside the advances made in treating disease or correcting abnormalities, a wide variety of diagnostic procedures have been developed. The future in medicine appears to be with early detection of disease or defects together with prophylaxsis. A neglected aspect of these medical advances is recognition and acknowledgement of their accompanying psychosocial impact and consequently the appropriate counselling needs. Treatments that demand sophisticated, high technology equipment such as radiotherapy or diagnostic procedures such as CAT scans or NMR imaging, can be extremely anxiety provoking. Some patients also experience a profound sense of distress at losing control over their bodies and what is happening to them. Good communication, especially clear information about what the procedure involves together with explanations about the putative benefits and/or side effects of these procedures, be they diagnostic or therapeutic, is vital if psychologically damaging consequences are to be avoided. The impact of screening provides a good example.

Screening

In the past decade there has been increasing interest in screening people for various diseases or conditions. Preventive medicine, which aims to identify those patients at risk of developing such things as coronary heart disease and then offers advice about lifestyle changes (see Bennett and Hobbs, Chapter 17) to decrease the likelihood of disease, is increasing in many different medical specialties. Screening has major counselling implications which need to be considered before health authorities embark upon such projects.

People who go along for mammography screening for breast cancer, faecal occult blood testing for bowel cancer or those presenting for measurement of their blood pressure or cholesterol levels provide good examples of what needs to be thought about now at the planning stage. Women presenting for a mammogram or people being checked for hypertension are usually asymptomatic; they attend in general to have their perceptions of themselves as healthy confirmed by the screening centre. The discovery of a breast lump, which the woman herself had failed to detect, following a mammogram, or the knowledge that one has hypertension, can produce.a variety of psychological threats to an individual's sense of well-being. Skilled counselling is obviously an important requisite at such times, if the affected individual is to: a) cope with the unexpected bad news; b) develop appropriate coping strategies for the sudden changed status from healthy person to person with a disease; and c) ameliorate anxiety and/or distress at the necessity for treatment. Even the process of being screened and found *healthy* may provoke unpredicted difficulties; Marteau (1989) has described the importance of counselling before screening but points out that there are very few data available on how best 'to minimize adverse emotional and behavioural consequences of participation'. She cites Bloom and Monterossa (1981) who found that patients recalled for further tests for hypertension, who were subsequently told that nothing was wrong, nevertheless evidenced considerable psychiatric morbidity later.

Summary

No one can deny the physical benefits to patients that accrue from technological developments in medical care, but as we enter a new decade the future in terms of psychological care still looks rather bleak. A significant contribution to this reduction in concern for the psychosocial needs of patients is due to the organization of modern medicine rather than insensitivity on the part of health care professionals. This problem is summarised succinctly by Rice (1990): '. . . drives to increase efficiency and cut costs within hospitals mean that patients are now processed like goods on a conveyor belt. Out-patients endure long waits in clinics for the briefest of appointments; in-patient hospital stays are shorter to increase the through-put of patients; staff shortage amongst nurses and auxiliaries reduce the personal attention they can provide; and overworked hospital doctors have no time or energy to spend talking to patients.' It is frustrating for clinicians and others who recognise the importance of good communication and counselling to be forced to compromise their legitimate concerns for psychological care because of the organization of the system.

Alongside considerations of the impact that the organization of medical services has on patient care must come considerations of the training of health care professionals in communication.

EDUCATION AND TRAINING

Counselling/communication skills

In Chapter 2 we made a distinction between counselling skills and counselling. What we have to say here relates more to the former. The latter requires much more extensive training.

In 1980 the General Medical Council's recommendations on basic Medical Education stated that on graduation medical students should be able 'to communicate effectively and sensitively with patients and their relatives', and with 'medical colleagues and other professionals involved in the care of the patient'. The statement of such worthy aims did not provoke a rush of interest in formally teaching or assessing communication skills in our medical schools. By 1987 a Working Party Report concluded that 'this recommendation is not strong enough to encourage the proper development of teaching'. Although most medical colleges attempt some consultation skills training, few assess it other than for research purposes and few, if any, have teaching staff specifically employed to develop and co-ordinate the teaching of skills. Most medical schools still give communication skills very low priority in resource terms whilst paying lip service to its importance in medical education. Many of our doctors qualify without any formal training in this area at all, others may have had some during their psychiatry or general practice firm, or from behavioural scientists during their pre-clinical courses.

For the majority of doctors who have received an orthodox medical education, their training in communication and interpersonal skills is based on the notion that such things are naturally acquired over time with experience and can be learned through the odd lecture and the observation of senior colleagues. Engel (1982) in an entertaining but disturbing article feels that current training in interviewing techniques is analogous to teaching musicians how to play their instruments through 'presenting in lectures or maybe in a demonstration or two the theory and mechanisms of the music producing ability of the instrument, then handing the student an unfamiliar instrument and telling him to produce a melody. The instructor, of course would not be present to observe or listen to the students' efforts but would be satisfied with the student's subsequent verbal report of what came out of the instrument'. This analogy seems outrageous but it corresponds quite closely to the manner in which medical students are taught to take a history and how they are given little feedback on their performances. Whilst this apprenticeship model appears to have produced a few excellent doctors with very good consultation skills, it has dismally failed to help the majority. Surveys and studies of junior doctors (and for that matter of nurses and dentists) reveal that the health professional/patient relationship is the one area that they consistently feel least competent to deal with and the one which causes considerable stress and anxiety (Gerrard, Boniface and Love, 1980).

Ameliorating these deficiencies in the training of health care professionals is an important but complex task. Apart from the resource issues and organizational barriers already discussed, there is another fundamental problem in medicine caused by the historical separation of mind from body. Cartesian dualism had an indisputable logic in the 17th century. Indeed the freedom that this gave physicians to work in medical science would never have been achieved without it. However, it is (and always was) an artificial distinction; mind and body are inextricably linked. This statement is obvious to most but continues to be ignored by many of those involved in medical education.

Attitude change is another major prerequisite, if psychological care such as counselling is to be seen as a component part of healing rather than an optional add-on. Even some of those people who accept the biopsychosocial model of illness nevertheless express the worry that delving into psychosocial concerns may open up the proverbial Pandora's box, thus a time-limited and resource-limited service should concentrate on the better understood, and more easily delineated, physical problems. The longer this argument is pursued, the longer it will take to unravel and integrate the psychosocial dimension of illness. As Cassel (1982) has pointed out 'attempts to understand all the known dimensions of personhood and their relations to illness and suffering presents problems of staggering complexity. The problems are no greater, however, than those initially posed by the question of how the body works—a question that we have managed to answer in extraordinary detail'.

Many people working within the health care system remain extremely sceptical of the suggestion that communication can be taught, and espouse the view that students either have it or not, and that the latter will probably acquire the necessary skills with experience. There is little empirical evidence to support such a view in contrast to the large body of evidence suggesting quite the contrary. For example Matarazzo and Patterson (1986) reviewed the literature on the training of basic interviewing skills and concluded that there was considerable evidence that such skills can be trained. Nevertheless, they indicated the need for more detailed research into the teaching of more advanced skills. For example, a considerable amount is known about teaching basic skills to novices in the UK, but less about teaching the more experienced professionals (see also Kerr, 1986).

In the United States the pioneering work of the Task Force on the Medical Interview has already exerted considerable influence on the senior medical staff who have attended their faculty development workshops and these workshops have started to make an impact on the way communication and interpersonal skills are taught in US Medical Schools (Gordon and Rost, 1990). It is important to ensure that experienced clinicians are given the opportunity to develop and enhance their own skills when initiatives to provide students with more effective communication skills teaching begins. The senior doctors, who have not received any of this form of training may otherwise feel hostile and threatened by curriculum change. As it is they who will continue to provide the primary role-models for junior doctors and students, it is important to harness their co-operation and enthusiasm for any new teaching programmes.

Teaching basic interviewing skills

There are several studies showing that the basic interviewing techniques of students can be improved by the provision of handouts which clearly specify the areas to be covered together with helpful suggestions about techniques. The effect of such handouts can be enhanced by the use of video-tape to show skills in action (Maguire, Clarke and Jolley, 1977). The value of different forms of feedback has been assessed by Maguire *et al.* (1978) in a study in which 48 medical students received traditional training from their clinical firms. Thirty six students received additional training using handouts and one of three feedback methods: audio or video recordings with feedback from an experienced trainer, or discussion of direct ratings of the student's performance without the benefit of recordings. The students given feedback from video recording and to a lesser extent audio recording, improved most in terms of their ability to elicit relevant information and their general interviewing techniques. All the feedback groups showed improvements in contrast to the students who received only the usual apprenticeship training via their clinical firms.

In a follow-up study five years later Maguire *et al.* (1986) showed that in general the skills acquired as a result of the training were maintained. Nevertheless, there were still deficiencies, for example, in beginning and ending the interview appropriately and in covering relevant psychosocial aspects of a patient's problems. It is interesting to note that although interviewing skills had benefited from training, the doctors were still rather poor in providing information appropriately, an aspect of communication that had not been included in their original training.

The timing of appropriate training may be important as Engler *et al.* (1981) reported no improvements in the skills of doctors given only limited teaching during their pre-clinical years. One must also consider the amount of training as well as the timing and method. Ware, Strassman and Naftulin (1971) found a negative relationship between merely understanding the principles of good interviewing via lectures and classroom discussion and the actual interviewing performance of junior medical students.

In view of Byrne and Long's (1976) findings that doctors become fixed in their style of interviewing soon after qualifying, it seems worthwhile to provide teaching both for medical students currently in training and for doctors who qualified some time ago. Helfer (1970) has pointed out that medical students often start their courses with some innate skills and show warmth and an evident interest in people. As time goes by, however, many senior medical students adopt a cold, directive approach to patients and display a dispassionate mode of quick-fire questioning about physical symptoms with little concern for the psychosocial aspects of illness.

Maguire (1984) has agreed that although the evidence from studies presents a 'gloomy picture', students do appear to be aware of their deficiencies. In particular they report feeling uncomfortable about asking personal and emotionally loaded questions, they are uncertain about how honest they should be with patients and they have great difficulty tolerating silence. Armstrong *et al.* (1979) in a descriptive report of a communication skills course for pre-clinical students also highlighted the manner in which students rushed through their interviews using predominantly closed questions about physical symptoms. This often led to them rapidly running out of questions and facing what they felt were embarrassing silences. Students lacked the skills to use '. . . appropriate silences as a means of giving the patient time to think and time to provide further information'.

Learning how to listen is probably the key area in which counselling and effective communication overlap. Listening is a core skill in good counselling and should be equally important during exchanges between doctors, nurses, and all other health care workers and their patients. Unskilled communicators within the health care professions spend so much time worrying about what they should say to patients that they frequently forget that the patient has an important story to tell. An excellent demonstration of the failure to allow patients to collaborate in the medical consultation as experts of their own illnesses can be found in the book by Tuckett *et al.* (1986).

Most doctors are well-trained to elicit key physical symptoms, to perform a clinical examination and on the basis of these to determine differential diagnoses. Further laboratory investigations may then be requested to establish which diagnosis is correct. During consultations with patients about the diagnosis, investigations and proposed treatment, doctors traditionally take a very directive role when providing information or instructions. When these transcripts of doctor/patient dialogues are analysed it is clear that few patients are able to complete a sentence without interruption. Fletcher (1980) has described this as 'an "inquisitorial" technique that tends to inhibit listening.'

There is currently very limited emphasis placed upon the development of good listening skills in medical education. Active listening is very hard work initially and demands considerable attention and practice but the advantages in terms of eliciting important information and developing a good therapeutic relationship with a patient are worth the investment of time. Lipkin (1987) provides an excellent pragmatic description of active listening and its benefits during the medical interview.

Unless the skills of active listening and responding to the psychosocial areas of concern expressed by patients are inculcated into health care professionals' repertoire of communication techniques, there is little evidence that such skills will develop at all. Maguire (1984) also points out that the lack of direct methods of assessing students' skills fosters the myth that there is no problem. 'Deficiencies in essential communication skills will, therefore, go unnoticed and allow teachers to preserve their belief that medical training succeeds in equipping students with these skills.' An interesting paper by Janek, Burra and Leichner (1979) has revealed that the deficiencies in core skills of listening properly, handling emotionally laden consultations and establishing a good doctor/patient relationship are apparent in all specialties. Even psychiatrists in training have difficulty in all these areas.

We obviously need to provide our doctors with a great deal more training in communication and counselling if things are to change for the better. Fortunately there is plenty of evidence to show that appropriate training which includes traditional didactic teaching methods in the form of lectures and explicit handout in combination with more experiential, learner-centred teaching involving role-play, simulated patients and the use of model interviews can be effective in promoting positive change (See the review by Carroll & Munroe, 1979). Of paramount importance, however, is the need for structured, positive feedback from skilled trainers. Improvements are occurring in that the designers of the new medical curricula now take seriously the need for more time in teaching communication skills. However, we do have a dearth of people capable of helping the doctors who must teach students in this country and there is some resistance by clinicians towards behavioural scientists running such training programmes.

Training other professionals

Although the work outlined supports the view that training is beneficial, there is still the problem, identified by Matarazzo and Patterson (1986), of showing that people so trained are then more effective in relation to the patients they treat. This may be inferred from the studies, but it is important to show it directly. Evaluation ideally should be multivariate and occur on a number of levels, including changes in the trainee, as well as changes in the people with whom the trainee subsequently works.

One study in this area that has evaluated both trainee and patient changes was conducted by Davis and Rushton (1989 and 1991). This research is also somewhat unusual in that it was concerned to train professionals with considerable previous experience in their chosen profession. Twenty-six people, mainly health visitors and physiotherapists, were trained on a 60-hour course concerned to develop the basic skills of counselling families of children with severe disabilities. They were assessed on a battery of measures, exposed to a waiting period of six months on average, reassessed just before training, and then assessed again on the same measures immediately after their course. They were finally allocated to work with up to two families for an average period of 15 months. The families were also assessed on a range of measures before seeing the counsellor and then again at the end of the intervention. This design therefore enabled investigation of both changes in the trainees as a result of counselling training and changes in the families as a result of the work of the counsellors. The effects upon the families were evaluated against families randomly allocated to a no treatment control group.

The results indicated significant changes in the predicted directions in both the professionals and the families. The professionals gained appropriate knowledge of the frameworks of counselling, and changed significantly in their constructions of the aims and processes of counselling, as well as in their constructions of themselves as counsellors. Their constructions were assessed by means of a variant of repertory grid technique. The changes included them coming to see counselling as a more essential part of their job, as facilitating the ability of the person to understand parents, and as enabling parents to help themselves. They came to construe themselves as more able in counselling, as more respectful, as more honest, tactful, and more able to help parents to change. Videotape analysis of the trainees in counselling before and after training showed significant improvements in their ability. They became, for example, more empathic, respectful, and genuine and showed more effective behaviour on a checklist of items related to the skills and processes of counselling as outlined by Egan (1982). Not only did they, therefore, show improvements in counselling behaviour, their interactions with families were associated with significant improvements in the mothers' perceptions of themselves, their husbands and their children with disabilities, but also in the developmental progress and behaviour of the children. These changes are elaborated more fully in the chapter on the evaluation of counselling.

Much of this chapter has concentrated on the training of doctors, but the education of other health care professionals also needs close scrutiny. Appropriate communication and training in counselling has not been given sufficient time or attention in many other areas besides medicine. A prevalent view held by many is that nurses, social workers and psychologists must already possess good communication and counselling skills by virtue of their vocation, their experience and presumably their training. It is, however, not axiomatic that someone experienced in a job where such skills are imperative necessarily has them.

A large number of studies have shown how limited are many nurses' interpersonal skills (Hockney, 1976, Stockwell, 1972, Faulkner, 1979) and how much stress nurses experience as a result of their inadequate training in these areas (Llewelyn, 1984, Parkes, 1985). General nurses obviously require considerably more training in communication and counselling skills to enable them to help their patients and to help protect themselves from the potentially damaging emotional aspects of their job. Probably of more concern is the lack of any formal counselling qualification amongst nurses employed specifically as counsellors. Roberts and Fallowfield (1990) conducted a survey of nurses working as counsellors in the demanding field of oncology. They reported the disturbing finding that less than 18% of the 124 nurses who responded to the survey had any recognisable counselling qualification at all and that many of these were rather limited. The majority of nurses (78%) had attended a course at some time, but we have already cited the work of Fielding and Llewelyn (1987) who have outlined the dangers of providing a short communications course, devoid of any theoretical framework and then expecting the nurses to apply anything learned in the workshop. They express caution about courses that have no explicit conceptual framework or which concentrate entirely on the experiential aspects of communication and self-awareness. 'Although such experiences can be interesting and enjoyable, they are not very easily transferred to the ward situation, and as such are often deeply mistrusted by nurses or seen as a waste of time and effort.' This statement was reinforced by comments from nurses in Roberts and Fallowfield's survey who generally criticised NHS inservice training courses for being too short and superficial.

Probably as a result of their lack of formal training, only a third of nurses claimed to use any particular counselling model in their work and few made any formal assessments of their patients' psychological status before and after counselling. Almost half the nurses said that they worked in isolation, supervised by no one. This was especially disturbing as trained counsellors see supervision as a crucial aspect of monitoring and developing their competence. The BAC Code of Ethics and Practice for Counsellors states that 'Counsellors monitor their counselling work through regular supervision by professionally competent supervisors and are able to account to clients and colleagues for what they do and why'.

There is evidence from several sources that counselling is still misunderstood by many professionals working within the health service. In a recent survey of district health authorities (DHAs) reported by Breakwell and Alexander-Dann (1989) over half felt that none of their staff were engaged in counselling activities and only five of 39 DHAs felt that doctors had any counselling role to play. The DHAs required none of their professional groups to have qualifications in counselling prior to employment, with the exception of clinical psychologists. As this is the one group of people who are likely to have had some communication skills and counselling teaching during their training, it seems strange that it is the only group for whom an extra qualification is expected. Perhaps this is due to a misunderstanding about how broad counselling needs are within the health care area, with even DHAs assuming that only patients who are referred to clinical psychologists require help.

The Breakwell and Alexander-Dann study also revealed the paucity of in-service training provided. Most comprised of short two-day workshops and participation in training was entirely voluntary. Thus people employed as counsellors within the health service are not required to have any formal qualifications, neither are they required to accept any training. This is extremely disturbing as it is vital that the well-motivated, hard-working people who counsel patients are provided with the right kind of training to enable them to offer the most appropriate help to their patients. Furthermore, the professional skills that counselling demands and that protect patients from poor counselling, and protect counsellors from potential pitfalls such as emotional burn-out, cannot be acquired from a course lasting only a few days.

Conclusions

There is a clear need for many improvements in the training currently given to health care professionals in interpersonal skills. At present much of this receives very little attention in the medical and nursing curriculum despite lip-service being paid to its importance. Even people appointed to posts with counselling as a specific requirement of their job descriptions do not have to show any competence of their ability to counsel via an accredited counselling qualification. Furthermore, there are often major organizational barriers to the establishment of better communications in clinical and nursing practice which could obviate the need for more extensive counselling provision. None of this makes much sense from either a humanitarian or financial point of view and radical reforms are necessary if patients are to be helped and their carers are to gain more satisfaction from their jobs.

REFERENCES

Armstrong, D., Hicks, B.H., Higgins, P.M., et al. (1979). Communication skills to preclinical medical students: A general practice based approach. Medical Education, 13, 82–85.

BAC Research Committee (1989). Evaluating the effectiveness of counselling. A discussion document. Counselling, 69, 27–29.

Banks, M. (1989). Staff counselling in the National Health Service. Counselling in Medical Settings Newsletter, 19, 11–13.

Baum, M.J. and Jones, E.M. (1979). Counselling removes patients fear. Nursing Mirror, 148, 38–40.

Beckman, H.B. and Frankel, R.M. (1984). The effect of physician behaviour on the collection of data. Annals of Internal Medicine, 101, 692–696.

Bloom, J.R. and Monterossa (1981). Hypertension labelling and sense of well-being. American Journal of Public Health, 71, 1228–1232.

Brager, G. (1965). The indigenous worker: A new approach to the social work technician. Social Work, 10, 33–40.

Branch, W.T. (1987). Doctors as 'healers': Striving to reach our potential. Journal of General Internal Medicine, 2, 356–359.

Breakwell, G.M. and Alexander-Dann, C. (1989). Counselling in the non-primary sector of the NHS: A study of DHAs. Counselling, 70, 17–25.

Burton, M.V. and Parker, R.W. (1990). A randomised controlled trial of preoperative psychological preparation for mastectomy. Paper presented at the International Conference on Communication in Health Care. St Catherine's College, Oxford.

Byrne, P.S. and Long, B.E.L. (1976). Doctors talking to patients. London: HMSO.

Carroll, J.G. and Munroe, J. (1979). Teaching medical interviewing: A critique of educational research and practice. Journal of Medical Education, 54, 498–500.

Cassel, E.J. (1982). The nature of suffering and the goals of medicine. New England Journal of Medicine, 306, 11: 639–645.

Conboy-Hills, S.P. (1986). Psychosocial aspects of terminal care. International Nursing Review, 33, 1–6.

Corless, I.B. (1982). Physicians and nurses: Roles and responsibilities in caring for the critically ill patient. Law, Medicine and Health Care, 10, 2: 72–76.

Davis, H. and Rushton, R. (1989). An evaluation of basic counselling training. Counselling, 68, 1–8.

Davis, H. and Rushton, R. (1991). Counselling and supporting parents of children with developmental delay: A research evaluation. Journal of Mental Deficiency Research, 35, in press.

Egan, G. (1982). The skilled helper. Monterey, CA: Brooks/Cole.

Engel, G.L. (1982). What if music students were taught to play their instruments as medical students are taught to interview? The Pharos, Fall 12–13.

Engler, C.M., Saltzman, G.A., Walker, M.L. et al. (1981). Medical student acquisition and retention of communication and interviewing skills. Journal of Medical Education, 56, 572.

Fallowfield, L.J. (1988). Counselling for patients with cancer. British Medical Journal, 297, 727–728.

Faulkner, A. (1979). Monitoring nurse-patient conversations in a ward. *Nursing Times*, **75**, 95–96.

Faulkner, A. and Maguire, P. (1984). Teaching ward nurses to monitor cancer patients. *Clinical Oncology*, **10**, 383–389.

Fielding, R.G. and Llewelyn, B.A. (1987). Communication training in nursing may damage your health and enthusiasm: Some warnings. *Journal of Advanced Nursing*, **12**, 281–290.

Fletcher, C. (1980). Listening and talking to patients. *British Medical Journal*, **281**, 845.

General Medical Council (1980). Recommendations promulgated by the General Medical Council's Education Committee (Feb). London: GMC.

General Medical Council (1987). *The teaching of behavioural sciences, community medicine and general practice in basic medical education*. Report of the education committee working party (March). London: GMC.

Gerrard, B.A., Boniface, W.J., and Love, B.H. (1980). *Interpersonal skills for health professionals*. Virginia: Reston Publishing Company.

Gordon, G. and Rost, K. (1990). Evaluation of the faculty development workshops of the US Task Force on the medical interview and related skills. In M. Lipkin, S.M. Putnan, and A. Lazare (Eds), *The medical interview*. New York: Springer-Verlag.

Gorlin, R. and Zucker, H.D. (1983). Physicians reactions to patients. A key to teaching humanistic medicine. *New England Journal of Medicine*, **308**, 18: 1059–1063.

Graham, R.J. (1981). Understanding the benefits of poor communication. *Interface*, **11**, 80–82.

Hampton, J.R. (1983). The end of clinical freedom. *British Medical Journal*, **287**, 1237–1238.

Helfer, R.E. (1970). Observations of paediatric interviewing skills. *American Journal of Diseases of Childhood*, **123**, 556–560.

Hockey, L. (1976). *Women in nursing*. London: Hodder & Stoughton.

Hogbin, B. and Fallowfield, L.J. (1989). Getting it taped: The bad news consultation with cancer patients. *British Journal of Hospital Medicine*, **41**, 330–333.

Janek, W., Burra, P., and Leichner, P. (1979). Teaching interviewing skills by encountering patients. *Journal of Medical Education*, **54**, 401–407.

Kerr, D.N.S. (1986). Teaching communication skills in postgraduate medical education. *Journal of the Royal Society of Medicine*, **79**, 575–581.

Knaus, W.A., Draper, E.A., Wager, D.P. *et al.* (1986). An evaluation of outcome from intensive care in major medical centres. *Annals of Internal Medicine*, **104**, 410–418.

Levitan, S.J. and Kornfeld, D.S. (1981). Clinical and cost benefits of liaison psychiatry. *American Journal of Psychiatry*, **138**, 790–793.

Lipkin, M. Jr., Quill, T.E., and Napodano, R.J. (1984). The Medical Interview: A core curriculum for residencies in internal medicine. *Annals of Internal Medicine*, **100**; 2: 277–284.

Lipkin, M. (1987). The medical interview and related skills. In W.T. Branch, (Ed.), *The office practice of medicine*. Philadelphia. W.B. Saunders.

Llewelyn, S.P. (1984). The cost of giving: Emotional growth and emotional stress. In S. Skevington, (Ed.), *Understanding Nurses*. Chichester: Wiley.

Maguire, P., Pentol, A., Allen, D. *et al.* (1982). Cost of counselling women who undergo mastectomy. *British Medical Journal*, **284**: 1922–1935.

Maguire, G.P., Clarke, D., and Jolley, B. (1977). An experimental comparison of 3 courses in history-taking skills for medical students. *Medical Education*, **11**, 175–182.

Maguire, P., Roe, P., Goldberg, D., *et al.* (1978). The value of feedback in teaching interviewing skills to medical students. *Psychological Medicine*, **8**, 695–704.

Maguire, P. (1984). Communication skills and patient care. In A. Steptoe and A. Matthews (Eds), *Health care and human behaviour*. London: Academic Press.

Maguire, P., Fairbairn, S. and Fletcher, C. (1986). Consultation skills of young doctors: Benefits of feedback training in interviewing as students persist. *British Medical Journal*, **292**, 1573–1578.

Maguire, P. and Faulkner, A. (1988). How to do it. Improve the counselling skills of doctors and nurses in cancer care. *British Medical Journal*, **297**, 847–849.

Martin, E. (1988). Counsellors in general practice. *British Medical Journal*, **297**, 637–638.

Mantell, J.E. (1983). Cancer patient visitor programs: A case for accountability. *Journal of Psychosocial Oncology*, **1**; 1: 45–58.

Marteau, T. (1989). Psychological costs of screening. *British Medical Journal*, **299**, 527.

Matarazzo, R. and Patterson, D. (1986). Methods of teaching therapeutic skills. In S. Garfield and A. Bergin (Eds), *Handbook of Psychotherapy and Behaviour Change*. Chichester: Wiley.

Milot, B. (1981). *Student services: Rational, costs & utilisation*. Institute for research on educational finance and governance. California: Stanford University.

Milne, D. (1985). An observational evaluation of the effects of nurse training in behaviour modification on unstructured ward activities and behaviour. *British Journal of Clinical Psychology*, **24**, 149–158.

Milne, R.M. (1983). Counselling and the doctor. *Journal of the Royal College of General Practitioners*, **33**, 604.

Parkes, K.R. (1985). Stressful episodes reported by 1st year student nurses: A descriptive account. *Social Sciences and Medicine*, **20**, 945–953.

Pentol, A. (1981). Cost benefit analysis: Theory and practice in the health field. 2. A case study. Manchester: Dept. Social Administration, University of Manchester. (Working paper No. 51).

Ramirez, A. (1989). Liaison psychiatry in a breast cancer unit. *Journal of the Royal Society of Medicine*, **82**, 15–17.

Rice, G. (1990). *Understanding doctors: Getting the best health care*. London: Michael Joseph.

Riessman, F. (1965). The 'Helper' Therapy Principle. *Social Work*, **10**, 27–32.

Roberts, R. and Fallowfield, L.J. (1990a). The goals of cancer counsellors. *Counselling*, **2**, 88–91.

Roberts, R. and Fallowfield, L.J. (1990b). Who supports the cancer counsellors? *Nursing Times*, **86**; 36: 32–34.

Robson, M.H., France, R., and Bland, M. (1984). Clinical psychologist in primary care: Controlled clinical and economic evaluation. *British Medical Journal*, **288**, 1805–1808.

Ross, P. (1989). Counselling and accountability. *Counselling*, **69**, 11–18.

Rowland, N. (1989). Annual review of the CMS sub-committee on counselling in general practice. *Counselling in Medical Settings Newsletter*, **19**, 14–16.

Stein, L.I., Watts, D.T., and Howell, T. (1990). The doctor-nurse game revisited. *New England Journal of Medicine*, **322**, 8: 546–549.

Stockwell, F. (1972). *The unpopular patient*. R.C.N. London.

Tuckett, D., Boulton, M., Olson, C., and Williams, A. (1986). *Meetings between experts*. London: Tavistock Publications.

Waitzkin, H. (1984). Doctor-patient communication. Clinical implications of social scientific research. *Journal of the American Medical Association*, **2**: 252: 2441–2446.

Ware, J.E., Strassman, H.D., and Naftulin, D.H. (1971). A negative relationship between understanding interviewing principles and interview performance. *Journal of Medical Education*, **54**, 401–407.

Concluding Remarks

It is too simplistic to place all responsibility for the deficiencies of health care delivery on the shoulders of health professionals, especially doctors. Health professionals often have to work in physically unpleasant environments within a bureaucratic, hierarchical organization that is increasingly poorly funded. We compound the problems by inadequate teaching and training and paltry provision of staff support services. Nevertheless, we still have extraordinary expectations of these professionals: they must be experts in many fields at once, scientifically sound, technically competent and empathic and caring. Unfortunately, there has been a trend over the past half century to prioritize the skills relating to this triad of competencies with less emphasis being placed upon caring and communicating well.

Sometimes this has resulted in a quest for cure at any cost and a consequent diminution in the quality of patients' lives (Fallowfield, 1990). Failure to acknowledge that suffering has psychosocial as well as physical components means that methods of alleviating distress through better communication and counselling are given less importance than they deserve. As Cassel (1982) points out, 'the relief of suffering and the cure of disease must be seen as twin obligations of a medical profession that is truly dedicated to the care of the sick. Physicians' failure to understand the nature of suffering can result in medical intervention that (though technically adequate) not only fails to relieve suffering but becomes a source of suffering itself'.

We need a shift in attention from cure to caring, or as Berrington (1988) has suggested, 'doctors often need to be released from the perceived obligation to cure and . . . to show instead competence, care and concern'.

We hope that this book has demonstrated that good communication can and should be taught to all health care professionals, because of the benefits to be gained both by the professionals and their patients. The beneficial effects that would accrue to the people and their families who require health care might obviate the need for further counselling. However, there will always be some patients who require more specialist psychosocial help, and this must be provided by people who are well equipped through better training and support.

Encouraging more humanistic values in medicine can only succeed in helping sick people, if organizational barriers are breached and adequate support and training in personal growth is provided for our health

Counselling and Communication in Health Care. Edited by H. Davis and L. Fallowfield
© 1991 John Wiley & Sons Ltd

professionals. Asking them to get closer to the emotional needs of their patients without paying due concern to potential problems that this may pose for the doctor or nurse is both unrealistic and unwise. Either the health professionals will collapse under the psychological strain or they will retreat and communicate with the kinds of emotional detachment which so damages patients.

We have the evidence that good communication and counselling are effective means of preventing and alleviating psychosocial distress. We know a great deal about these endeavours both theoretically and empirically. We have also developed appropriate methods for teaching these frameworks and skills to professionals. However, we lack people with foresight, concern and courage to divert resources which would allow us to implement the changes that patients and many of their carers wish to see.

As we have seen in previous chapters, there are carers implementing counselling in the health setting, but they tend to work in isolation, fighting for meagre resources and frequently against the status quo. There are also those who are successfully developing teaching programmes to help others acquire appropriate communication skills. All the contributors to the book have shown the innovation that is possible and that is occurring in many areas. What is significant is that although the authors work in vastly different settings, they nevertheless have much more that is common than different, both in their approaches and their conclusions. What they have to offer is valuable and should be implemented on a much broader scale.

The task ahead is therefore one of dissemination of ideas and methods. It is important to convince more and more people of the value of counselling and counselling skills. To effect change requires *power*, and it is therefore important to convince the people who have the power to make changes occur. These include the professionals who run medical schools, and the equivalent training programmes of all the other groups within the health services. This should certainly include the student body, who are becoming more and more aware of the importance of counselling, and are, if well organized, in a strong position to persuade their trainers to change. There is also the option of harnessing the power of patients themselves via their various organizations. Many of the changes that have occurred in health care have been because of patient groups making concerted efforts, which eventually overcome the inertia of the system. This is particularly true in the area of disability.

There are examples of very good practice and these can be used as models from which to learn, not only about the curriculum, but also about the ways in which changes were brought about. Unfortunately, these examples tend to be outside the UK; they are in the USA, Canada and the Netherlands. It is interesting to speculate why this should be so. In part it is perhaps because like-minded people have got together to make more powerful groupings, but also to provide support for themselves in the face of constant opposition.

One very effective group, for example, is the Task Force on the Medical Interview in North America, part of whose function is to teach clinicians how to teach communication skills effectively. There are similar organizations developing in the UK in the form of the Medical Interview Teachers Association (MITA) and a network of people interested in communication set up about two years ago under the name of Comnet.

Therefore, there is a need for *power*, which should include effective teamwork, not only in the clinical setting, but also in the endeavour of creating change. Autocratic decision making by one profession is no longer an acceptable option, when there are many professions that can contribute to the understanding and implementation of effective psychosocial care and communication. There is also a need for *understanding* of the processes by which both individual and institutional change may be achieved. The more one understands the processes involved, the more able one might be to create the desired changes, by setting appropriate goals and developing relevant strategies. Certainly, there is a need for good *planning*. Change will be more likely under conditions where there is detailed consideration (and careful documentation) of the aims of change and the methods by which it is intended to meet them. This permits discussion, dissemination, planning, organization, evaluation and development of ideas.

Change cannot occur without *resources*, both to facilitate initiation of changes and to sustain the new system. We have discussed the latter, in that good communication practices and counselling require training and personnel. Creating change, however, also requires people, energy and commitment to plan, research and push in all ways for the desired outcomes. An important part of this is to provide *demonstration* of effectiveness. Every effort should be made in all schools to set up teaching or counselling projects that are visible and properly evaluated. This may serve the purpose of persuasion more than anything, in that benefits can be made evident to all the important groups mentioned earlier, the Deans, students and patients.

We would be pleased if our book in some small way contributes to changes in medicine. We sincerely hope that it will be useful in altering the present situation by providing models and demonstrations for the non-committed and stimulation and encouragement for those who are already contributing to the processes of change.

REFERENCES

Berrington, B. (1988). Patient teachers. *Journal of the Royal College of General Practitioners*, **38**, 290.

Cassel, E. (1982). The nature of suffering and the goals of medicine. *New England Journal of Medicine*, **306**, 639–645.

Fallowfield, L. (1990). *The quality of life: The missing measurement in health care*. London: Souvenir Press.

Index

Index complied by A. C. Purton